The Moro Morality Play

Robin Erica Wagner-Pacifici

The MORO MORALITY PLAY

Terrorism as Social Drama

The University of Chicago Press/Chicago and London

Robin Erica Wagner-Pacifici is assistant
professor of sociology and anthropology at
Swarthmore College.

The University of Chicago Press, Chicago 60637
The University of Chicago Press, Ltd., London
© 1986 by The University of Chicago
All rights reserved. Published 1986
Printed in the United States of America

95 94 93 92 91 90 89 88 87 86   5 4 3 2 1

Library of Congress Cataloging-in-Publication Data

Wagner-Pacifici, Robin Erica.
  The Moro morality play.

    Bibliography: p.
    Includes index.
    1. Terrorism in mass media—Italy. 2. Terrorism—
  Italy. 3. Moro, Aldo, 1916–1978—Kidnapping, 1978.
  4. Mass media—Social aspects—Italy. 5. Mass media—
  Political aspects—Italy. 6. Italy—Politics and
  government—1976–   . I. Title.
  P96.T472I89   1986   303.6′25′0945   86-11317
  ISBN 0-226-86983-0
  ISBN 0-226-86984-9 (pbk.)

Chapter 4, "Crisis: Recognition and Negotiation," appeared in
Politics and Society 12, no. 4 (1983): 487–517.

To Maurizio

Contents

Preface

This is a book about many things. It is about the ways in which a society "constructs" a social and political crisis and the roles that individuals and institutions play (or try to play) in this construction. It is about Italy in the turbulent year of 1978, and it is about terrorism. But it is not a book aiming to expose the international ramified community of terrorists (if such a unified entity exists); it is not about the causes of terrorism nor about its cures. While these are, no doubt, worthy projects, they do not take us far toward understanding the discourse of terrorism—the ways in which some actions are defined as terrorist, and the ways in which terrorism is publicly represented.

We will look here at one terrorist event in one country, the 1978 Red Brigades kidnapping and assassination of Italian politician Aldo Moro. The focus will be on the ways in which this event was presented to the Italian public during the fifty-five days of his captivity. Thus the primary datum of this study is that which was spoken, written, photographed, and filmed during this period. The claim here is that any attempt to understand contemporary terrorism must confront the highly structured way in which news of terrorist acts, hostage reactions, government positions and rationales for positions, and public response reaches us—the audience of a ubiquitous mass mediation. The examination of this structured representation must, I will argue, take into account not only political, police/security, economic, and moral imperatives but also, and importantly, aesthetic imperatives as well. Here we must recognize the significance of the mass mediated surround, a surround in which characters come and go on the nightly news, their stories being told in serials of varying length. We must also hypothesize, as will be explained in detail, the influence of historical antecedents and established aesthetic paradigms on the actions of public figures (terrorists as well as government officials), in fact, on the actions of us all. This may be as simple as the awareness that some gestures and phrases will be read as "serious" and others will be read as "frivolous" or "comic." But our individual definitions of what passes for serious (absolutist identification of and distancing from the "evil enemy" or a conflict-ridden dialogue with one whose methods and goals we cannot support), and for comic and for weak and for strong, must ultimately derive, in large part, from those generic aesthetic and historical models that we have absorbed. The discursive surround of a given event will reveal and shape just such definitions.

We, in the United States, have recently passed through two major encounters with terrorism—the Iranian hostage situation of 1980–1981, and the TWA flight hijacking of 1985. Both of these events monopolized screen and page for their durations. The lessons of the examination of the discourse of the Aldo Moro affair are most relevant for our own experiences with terrorism. One example might suffice.

In the Moro affair, as in many cases of political kidnapping, the role of the hostage was represented as ambiguous at best. In the broader field of "terrorism studies," a syndrome of hostage affective sympathy with the captors, the "Stockholm Syndrome," has been "discovered" and labeled. Thus, when the captors of the TWA jet passengers held a news conference at the Beirut airport, several news commentators spoke of the hostages, who spoke for several minutes, as "being on display." What does this simple phrase do? Primarily, it objectifies the hostages. Only will-less objects can be on display, the controls being manipulated by those who put these objects on display. Thus, by desubjectifying them, such phrases indicate to the audience that perhaps the words that the hostages speak are both "not their own" and "not to be taken seriously." Serious attention to the content of the hostages' speeches has been called into question.

Such are the issues that emerge in *The Moro Morality Play: Terrorism as Social Drama.* How are we to "think about" the protagonists? How are we to process their respective statements? What can be our goals? All of these are shaped through what I have called the aesthetics of discourse. The point here is, finally, not to collapse the Moro affair, or, by implication, any moment of political crisis, into a case of pure aesthetics. It is rather to show the way the public, aesthetic structuring of an event interacts with other felt imperatives to orient in a certain direction rather than in another.

The point is to reveal the multidimensionality of events and to make us conscious of the assumptions about reality that the representation of these events contain.

Acknowledgments

I would like to thank those who both guided and freed my thinking during the process of conceptualizing and writing this book. My teachers, Harold Bershady, Fred Block, and Charles Bosk provided encouragement, criticism, and intellectual expansiveness. Their willingness to support an unusual project and to bring their respective expertises to bear on it sustained me during the entire period of preparation and writing. I owe them a great deal. Thanks as well go to the following people for interest and critical commentary during various moments of the project: Erminia Artese, Bruce Bellingham, Franco Ferrarotti, Joseph Gusfield, Margaret Levi, Victor Lidz, Magali Sarfatti-Larson, and Barry Schwartz. Doug Mitchell of the University of Chicago Press provided enthusiastic and expert editorial advice.

Finally, my husband Maurizio Pacifici deserves thanks for many things. He supported this project with enthusiasm, provided endless translations of un-translatable Italian idioms, and he was my best Italian "informant." Not only would this study never have been written without his aid, it would never even have been conceived.

Swarthmore College generously provided funds for the typing of this manuscript.

1 Introduction

On March 16, 1978, the Red Brigades kidnapped the Italian politician Aldo Moro as he was on his way to Parliament to begin debates toward ratifying a new government. Moro's five bodyguards were killed in the ambush.

Thus we start, as did Italy on March 16, 1978, with the event itself—the kidnapping of Aldo Moro. Anything further that we say will constitute an interpretation of this event. But of course everything that was spoken or written during the fifty-five days of the Moro kidnapping constituted an interpretation of the event. So much was this the case, given the densely mediated and "explained" nature of the facts and significance of the Moro affair,[1] that this study turns its analytic beam directly on the interpretations. This book thus confronts and takes a stand on important epistemological and practical questions (the two, it is here claimed, being intricately intertwined): (1) How do citizens of a mass (mediated) society come to know, conceptualize, and know how to respond to social and political events? (2) How do alternative presentations of political events effect political participation?

These concerns about the knowledge we have of our societies regard not solely nor primarily a posteriori questions about which interpretations were the better or the more successful (in the sense of gaining their desired end). They regard questions about interpretations pronounced *during* an event that turn back on the event to actually shape it as it unfolds. The successful crediting or discrediting of interpretations moves an event in certain directions. In the case of a discredited interpretation, it may no longer have the epistemological, political, moral and/or aesthetic (this concept will be elaborated) strength to proceed in the direction the protagonists of the failed interpretation want it to go. As will be seen, this was precisely the fate of Aldo Moro's own interpretations of the Moro affair. Moro's mediations of his own dilemma were systematically discredited. The *mechanics* of the process of vanquishing interpretations is as much the subject of this study as is the *socioepiste-mological theory* of it. The Moro affair opens itself up to this interpretation of interpretations for many reasons. It stopped the Italian sociopolitical clock long enough to suspend the apparent inevitability of crisis-ridden "normal" time. Its time (fifty-five days) and its spaces (newspaper pages, television screens, radio amplifiers, courtrooms, piazzas, walls) contained and encouraged competing interpretations and forms of discourse. And its location in the, at least up to then, badly understood world of "terrorism" provided the impetus for explanations that expanded outward to encompass the whole terrorist phenomenon.

But, of course, the Moro affair is not only an occasion for testing or, better yet, for developing a theory of the epistemological status of political reality. It was an event that interrupted the course of the Italian government; it altered the lives of hundreds of Italians directly and thousands of Italians indirectly. It was an event that, from a purely police-work military/logistical standpoint, was handled badly, and to this day (Summer 1985) many lacunae vis-à-vis the investigation remain.[2] But one thing must be made clear at the outset. It is not the purpose of this study to uncover what forces or who was "really" behind Moro's kidnapping. Such a focus would be not only irrelevant to a study of the public presentation of this event, it would be, given the continuing parliamentary debates that have now even suggested a linkage between the Moro affair and the P2 secret masonic lodge affair,[3] necessarily speculative.

Event and Epistemology

> We must suppose historical narrations to have appeared contemporaneously with historical deeds and events. Family memorials, patriarchal traditions, have an interest confined to the family and the clan. The uniform course of events which such a condition implies is no subject of serious remembrance . . . It is the state which first presents a subject-matter that is not only adapted to the prose of History but involves the production of such History in the very progress of its own being.[4]

It is indeed the production of History that is at the heart of this study, although it is not only the protagonists of the state who figure in this production. Further, drawing out an implication in the last line of this quote, we are concerned primarily here with the self-conscious production of history on the part of those involved in the Moro affair.

The attitude of this study toward its subject is one derived from (and ultimately pushing beyond) the coinciding efforts of a number of schools of scholarship in several disciplines. From the domains of philosophy and literary theory, the tools of hermeneutics[5] and genre criticism[6] allow systematic intervention into various kinds of texts and raise important questions about the relationship between text and author and text and audience.

The projects of Northrop Frye and Hayden White figure prominently here. Frye's concern is with the worldviews contained in different literary genres and with the relationships of these genres to each other. Hayden White, examining historical works by such scholars as Marx, Tocqueville, and Michelet, posits a poetics of historical conception. Thus he, as in the case with Frye and literature, is led to a reading of histories that discerns certain generic orientations—Comedy, Romance, Tragedy, and Satire. Of particular importance here are the normative implications contained within the different generic emplotments of historical writings. To choose a Tragic rendering of a given historical period rather than a Romantic rendering implies a specific judgment of that period. White writes: "I consider the ethical moment of a historical work to be reflected in the mode of ideological implication by which an aesthetic perception (the emplotment) and a cognitive operation (the argument) can be combined so as to derive prescriptive statements from what may appear to be purely descriptive or analytical ones."[7] We are concerned here, as will be clear below, with the emplotment not of a literary work, nor of a historical work, but rather of a dynamic process of lived history. We are making the claim, however, that the same mechanism of generic choice and a combining of aesthetic perceptions and cognitive operations are salient in such a case.

From sociology and anthropology comes the epistemological discovery that the social world may fruitfully be viewed as a text accessible to hermeneutical analysis.[8] An important example of this mode of analysis is sociologist Joseph Gusfield's *The Culture of Public Problems: Drinking, Driving and the Symbolic Order*. In this book, Gusfield explores how the official (and fluctuating) rhetoric about "drunk driving" shapes the public perception of the relationship between restraint and release (as these concepts relate to alcohol distribution and consumption and to individual transportation) in American society. Gusfield's direct analytic focus on the rhetorical surround of a public issue and his exploration of the implications of such rhetoric for public policy is of much significance for the subject of this book.

Another important work coming, this time, from anthropology is Clifford Geertz's *Negara: The Theater State in Nineteenth Century Bali*. The Negara was, according to Geertz, the spectacle-state par excellence. In the Negara, the king's ability to dramatize his power was what gave him power (more so than the strength of an army or the size of a territory). This dramatization took place through the actual stagings of ceremonies and spectacles. Masses of participants, colorful objects, long processions all gave proof of and accomplished a king's preeminence. The relevance of *Negara* for this study concerns the variability of the *content* of state strength and the importance of the symbology of power. Italy is not a theater-state, but an analogous preoccupation with strength expressed and made real by amassing large numbers of demonstrators during the Moro affair makes *Negara's* focus on the spectacle of power particularly illuminating.

From the literary and anthropological disciplines come the structuralist and semiotic projects viewing narrative (literary *and* social) as one form of symbolic code among many.[9] This will be discussed at length below.

Political science, sociology, and history provide analyses of politics as fundamentally symbolic action. One recent study of the political culture and symbols of the French Revolution, Lynn Hunt's *Politics, Culture, and Class in the French Revolution*, deals with the rhetorical, persuasive significance of revolutionary political discourse. Here political discourse is approached as an object of the creative struggle to embody a new politics and a new society. Thus discourse is, in her study, privileged as an object of analysis. Hunt even begins to suggest generic distinctions between different phases of the revolution. This is an important step, but she never shows hows these different narrative genres intermittently gain dominance over others nor does she detail the implications of the genre changes for such things as political constraints and opportunities. The Moro study concentrates much of its analysis on doing both and, different from Hunt's work, for a contemporary society in whose discourse we are so immersed as to often accept it as natural. Here we also find studies in which contemporary politics is viewed as spectacle and contemporary political participation as "alienated."[10] Todd Gitlin's study (*The Whole World Is Watching*) of the mass media–student movement interactions during the rise and fall of the American Students for a Democratic Society organization is particularly enlightening here for its examination of the "packaging" and intermittent lauding and debunking of specific student leaders. Among other things, it shows how central the mass media are and how radically the perception of this has changed ideas of social movements and strategies toward participation.

And, finally, from an interdisciplinary nexus of all of the above, this study derives from a concern to elaborate the ideological relationships between text and context and between text and audience.[11]

Accordingly, this study proposes to view the Moro kidnapping and assassination as a social drama. In other words, we are saying not only that this event was presented to protagonists and audience alike as a series of competing interpretations. We are also saying that these interpretations were rhetorically structured in specific, namely narrative, ways. Before we can examine the Moro affair's dramatic/narrative structuration, the categorical parameters of two concepts already introduced must be described. These are the interrelated concepts of "event" and "narrative structuration."

Theoreticians and practitioners of history are currently engaged in a debate involving the structure and division(s) of historical time itself.[12] Without engaging the entire discussion,[13] it is possible to cite positions taken within the debate that are relevant to our concern to elaborate the concept of the "event." On one side, historians of the Braudelian school of the "longue durée" have explicitly turned away from the study of the "event" as traditionally conceived. In this schema, the traditional political history of the discrete event, with its assertion (implicit or explicit) of the primary significance of events (such as battles and inaugurations) already enshrined in archives, is rejected. Such event analysis, they claim, has neglected the longer, less explosive historical time spans of social and political institutions, demographic and geographical changes, and "mentalities."[14] Focus on such singular events, they say, ought to present these events as historical conjunctures of these longue durée, thus giving precedence to the context. On the other side, that of such "covering law model" theorists as Hempel, the discrete event is retained as an object of historical analysis but only on the condition that it be "explained" as a case of a general law.

Paul Ricoeur responds to both of these schools of historical analysis with his view of the essentially hermeneutic enterprise of the event-interpretor. Here he introduces his key concept of plot. According to Ricoeur and historian Paul Veyne, it is the emplotment of the facts of an event (by the interpretor) that qualifies that event as historical. Addressing himself to the Braudelians, following Paul Veyne, Ricoeur claims: "The long time-span is just as much about an event as is the short time-span, if plot is the only measure of an event. The nonevent marks the gap between the determined field of events and the already plowed region of plots."[15] Here we might similarly draw attention to the logical symmetry of the operations of "symbolic interactionists" in sociology. In the case of their investigations of what we might call the "micro-durée" of human interactions, each encounter is viewed as having the status of an emplotted "event," with a beginning, a middle, and an end. Here, framing devices, formulaic words, or gestures often put the seal on the "event" and, simultaneously, define what kind of an event it was. Against the covering law theorists, Ricoeur asserts the interpretive moment of historical analysis as: "when historians appraise something, that is, when they attribute meaning and value to it. This moment must be distinguished from the moment of explanation, which establishes causal connections between events."[16] Thus the meaning of an event cannot be deduced simply by explaining the event as one case of a general law.

While we will expand upon Ricoeur's notions of the "who" and "when" of the emplotment enterprise, here it is important to note the centrality in his philosophy of history of the concepts of emplotted event and interpretation.

While both the long and the short time spans can be emplotted events, we are concerned here with an event whose emplotments and staging were preeminent features of its evolution. It was framed by the kidnapping and the finding of the body. It also was an event that was of a society-wide scale, being of interest to a national (indeed international) audience. Given the predominance of rhetoric, interpretation, drama, and plot in the Moro affair, it will be useful to examine a theory of event analysis that posits the very centrality of such modes of structuration, the "social drama" theory of anthropologist Victor Turner.

The Social Drama

> . . . the heroes, as well as the parties and the masses of the old French Revolution, performed the task of their time in Roman costume and with Roman phrases, the task of releasing and setting up modern bourgeois society . . . The awakening of the dead in those revolutions therefore served the purpose of glorifying the new struggles, not of parodying the old; of magnifying the given tasks in imagination, not of taking flight from their solution in reality; of finding once more the spirit of revolution, not of making its ghost walk again.[17]

Turner's "social drama" schema derives from his attention to "experiential structures in the actual processes of social life." Turner, while fundamentally interested in an event's context, is interested in analyzing the internal structure of the social text of the event itself. The event that Turner has attended to most systematically is one that he claims is "cross-culturally isolable and which exhibits, if it is allowed to come to full term, a characteristic processual structure . . . which I consider to be the social ground of many types of 'narrative' and which I call 'social drama.' "[18]

The great advance of Turner's schema of the social drama is that not only does it, as does Ricoeur's schema, assert and employ a posteriori the narrative analysis of events but it also regards the social actors *themselves* as proceeding through and attempting to direct certain events with, among other kinds of consciousness and motives (e.g., political, moral, economic), a theatrical self-consciousness. The protagonists of the "social drama" respond[19] to and clothe themselves in their culture's stock of sedimented symbols, archetypal characters, and rhetorical appeals. In certain social contexts, such as that of the French Revolution referenced by Marx in the passage from the "Eighteenth Brumaire of Louis Bonaparte," quoted above, this enclothing can be a positive and invigorating strategy. In the case of the Moro social drama, we will argue that there was indeed an extraordinarily high level of theatrical self-conciousness animating the protagonist's procedure, but we must call into question the idea that the net result was socially or politically invigorating.

Structurally, the "social drama" is composed of a specific diachronic sequence of dramatic phases (which allow, however, for synchronic variation within each phase; this is where the particularity of each event is expressed). The phases are: Breach, Crisis, Redress, and Reconciliation or Schism. Turner writes: "At its simplest, the drama consists of a four stage model, proceeding from breach of some relationship regarded as crucial in the relevant social group, which provides not only its setting but many of its goals, through a phase of rapidly mounting crisis in the direction of the group's major dichotomous cleavage, to the application of legal or ritual means of redress or reconciliation between the conflicting parties which compose the action set. The final stage is either the public and symbolic expression of reconciliation or else of irremediable schism."[20] Here we see Turner presenting certain rather specific criteria by which we can identify cases of "social dramas": a socially crucial relationship must be threatened, the ensuing crisis draws in more protagonists and draws its strength from cleavages already extant in the society, redressive actions must be attempted, an end (either reunifying or dispersive) is anticipated and pursued. Certainly, not all of life's occurrences are experienced in this manner. However, those events which do draw in and concern a society-wide audience and which do threaten some relationship perceived as central in that society can certainly be understood as "social dramas." Indeed this is the case being made for the Moro affair.

Returning for a moment to the synchronic variations within Turner's "social drama" phases, we find an analogy with Ricoeur's elaboration of the relationship between events and narrative emplotment. Ricoeur highlights the oscillations between expectation and contingency, between rule-governed behavior and deviation. In the case under analysis here, we will be concerned to chart the "rule-governed deformations" pursued by the plot-carrying protagonists of the Moro social drama. We will ask, What symbolic-aesthetic expectations jumped into place, what expectations were not met, and which protagonists were successful in claiming victory for their plot over others? Obviously this will be revealed as having had powerful implications for the configuration of Italian politics.

It is useful to detail the evolution of the meaning of the "social drama" schema in Turner's work. Turner, progressively, thought of social dramas in four (not necessarily exclusive) ways: (1) social dramas as revelatory of the ongoing but normally indistinct social structures and relations, (2) social dramas as functional (attempted) remedies for societies in crisis, (3) social dramas as self-reflective moments for societies in crisis, and (4) social dramas as potentially "liminal" moments of social transformation.[21] Now the contingent (remembering Ricoeur on emplotment) aspect of social dramas is that each of the four "functions" can be more or less successful. Thus social dramas can be more or less effective in revealing the indistinct structures and relations, in curing social crisis, more or less consciously self-reflective and more or less existentially available to social transformation. And such contingencies can, it is the claim here, be calibrated in a given case by attending to the self-referential discourse (both verbal and gestural) of the protagonists of a social drama as it engages the mechanisms of the four phases (Breach, Crisis, Redress, Reconciliation or Schism). This is what we shall do in the case under examination here.

Most of Turner's empirical studies of social dramas have focused on those occurring within small-scale simple societies. Italy of 1978 was clearly a large-scale, industrialized, mass-mediated, and complex society. How does this change affect the social drama model? Does it require a change of idiom? Does it change the transformative potential of the "liminal" moments of the social drama?

As to the change of idiom, this study will uncover a shift that indeed takes place between the staging of a social drama in simple societies and that in complex societies. This transposition of idiom is best understood as being that from ritual to theater. This will be discussed below and in the Conclusion. In terms of the transformative potential of social dramas, it is useful to recall Turner's own discussion, in his essay, "Liminal to Liminoid in Play, Flow and Ritual," of this very issue. Turner makes two points that are particularly relevant here. First, he draws the distinction between the literal sense of the concept "liminality" when it is used to describe certain intervals of antistructure in simple societies and the *metaphorical* sense of the concept when it is used to gesture to presumed analogous moments in complex societies. Then, he reiterates his claim that the antistructural moments of simple societies are ultimately in the service of structure and communitas, but that many antistructural moments in modern societies are ultimately *destructive* of the normative order and are often the work of and in the service of individuals (although they may have mass effects). These phenomena he terms "liminoid." They are found in the margins and interstices of modern societies (unlike liminal phenomena in simple societies that are found in the ritual centers). Certainly the Red Brigades occupied the margins of Italian society. Turner concludes that, though the ratio has shifted from liminal to liminoid, both liminal and liminoid phenomena can be found in contemporary societies. On this point, however, Turner is very clear: even those remaining liminal phenomena in contemporary society are no longer society-wide. They are particularistic in their relevant constituencies (Turner gives initiation rites of clubs and the activities of churches as examples of the liminal in complex societies). Here, the obligatory power of the liminal ultimately reasserts the meaningfulness of the particular collectivity (which may be *metaphorically* projected onto the whole society that, because of its plurality and complexity, it cannot literally encompass). If liminoid experiences are more chosen than required, more like commodities than like ritual objects, and if the liminal can, given the determined pluralism of the modern society, never be society-wide, does not that indicate a transposition of idiom along the lines suggested by Turner's own assessment of the *metaphorical* quality of the liminal phenomena in modern societies?

The commodification of the liminoid suggests that the relevant unit of analysis is the individual, who is "free" to buy any number of competing "items"—sports events, television channels, political parties. It cannot be accidental that the liminoid appears in societies in which the individual qua individual has gained ever greater legitimacy and sanctity (perhaps even greater in some cases, though not, as we shall see, in the Moro affair, than the Reason of State).

With the structure and (variable) functioning of the event of the "social drama" outlined, we may turn to that which shapes the social drama's narrative path, the plot.

PLOT

Claiming that social and political events are experienced and retrospectively interpreted according to theatrical criteria (in conjunction with other criteria) is the first step. Prior to engaging this perspective in the analysis of the "text" of an actual social drama, it is necessary to further the claim with a considered understanding of the way in which literary theorists have approached these issues in their analysis of literary texts. We have a twofold reason for doing so. First, the hermeneutic tools are felt to be appropriate to the analysis of social texts for the reasons elaborated above. Second, we follow Karen Hermassi *(Polity and Theatre in Historical Perspective)* in asserting a dialectical relationship between a given society's theatrical heritage and its political heritage. Modes of theatrical presentation will absorb, reflect, and contour modes of political presentation for a given society. Such a dialectic can be a generative and regenerative thing for a society. This is the case Hermassi makes for the tragic theater of ancient Greece: "It is not merely that in its Greek beginnings, theatre brought men, women, children, slaves and prisoners into a single forum at the same moment, but that each aspect of the city's existence—historical, economic, social, political, religious, scientific—was brought to mind."[22] In another sociopolitical context, however, one frozen into an insecure, reified vision of itself (the claim here is that Italy in 1978 characterized this state), the demands of *good* (note the distinction) theater will prove too threatening, too revealing. Hermassi has some powerful and particularly relevant things to say about the provocations of good theater: "The intimidations of memory, as provoked in dramatic art, are, I believe, the main reason for the decline of theatre, for the obligations of recollection and participation on this level become too burdensome. The theatre's powers of education cut through too many defenses; they threaten the one-dimensionality of any polity or community by dramatizing its contemporary reality as merely one alternative in the future of its political life. This renders theatre intolerable for many societies."[23]

While remaining implicit in Hermassi's discussion, what gradually becomes clear to the analyst of the dialectical relationship between theater and politics is the crucial difference between good theater and bad theater and the inextricable connection between good theater and good politics and bad theater and bad politics. This distinction is suggested in the works of Christopher Lasch *(The Culture of Narcissism)*, Richard Sennett *(The Fall of Public Man)*, and John MacAloon ("Olympic Games and the Theory of Spectacle in Modern Societies"). Lasch is concerned to distinguish between convention-sustaining public performance and commercially motivated spectacularism. Sennett's book traces the modern victory of private (psychologically "authentic") self-absorption over the enactment of public roles. For Sennett, such a change implies that daily life is "inartistic." MacAloon responds to the sweeping indictments of Guy Debord's claim that society has become a spectacle itself with an analytic prescription to study particular cases of social spectacles to determine the levels of true involvement or clear alienation that they variably reach.[24] This study, perhaps most in line with Lasch's and MacAloon's formulations, claims that public roles have been *impoverished* rather than eliminated. We have not suffered a loss of roles, merely a loss of *good* roles. The distinction between good and bad theater will be a theme running through this work and, by ultimately arriving at a discussion of genre, will prove to be a key to understanding the Moro social drama. Here we will merely assert the theoretical position that good theater encourages good politics (what is meant by good will be elaborated in the Conclusion), that bad theater encourages bad politics, and that the theatrical aspects of politics can similarly be good or bad depending on the theatrical paradigms (going back to Turner and Marx) called forth.

Accordingly, it is useful to turn to the universally acknowledged paradigm of "good" theater, Aristotle's discussion of tragedy in his *Poetics,* in order to explicate the notion of plot.

A plot, according to Aristotle, must be a complete whole having a beginning, a middle, and an end. Thus the unity of the plot is a logical and visible one. Further, a plot must be "of certain length"; it must be long enough to be seen as a whole, yet not too vast "as if it were a creature a thousand miles long." The definition of the ideal typical plot is similarly provided by Aristotle, again in his discussion of tragedy: "Tragedy is a representation of an action, which is serious, complete in itself, and of a certain length; it is expressed in speech made beautiful in different ways in different parts of the play; it is acted, not narrated; and by exciting pity and fear it gives a healthy relief to such emotions."[25] While classifying both simple and complex plots, Aristotle prefers the complex variety. The elements of this complex variety are several: it should include peripeteia, that is, when action meant to produce result x produces the opposite of x; discovery, recognition of persons, things, or facts; and catastrophe. Picking up on this last point, the ending of the ideal tragic plot has been a controversial issue among many interpretors of Aristotle's *Poetics.*[26] This issue is an important one for interpretors of "social dramas" as well for it describes the contours of "acceptable" endings toward which protagonists aim. We will ask: What could a "happy ending" to the Moro social drama have looked and felt like?[27] The controversy revolves around a seeming contradiction in the *Poetics* itself. In chapter 13, Aristotle selects, as the ideal plot, that in which a rather (but not superbly) good man comes to a bad end. In other words, the reversal of fortune is from good to bad. However, in chapter 14, Aristotle then identifies as best those plays containing a plot in which a tragic action is intended but prevented by the truth being discovered in time. Here we clearly have Aristotle choosing a happy ending. The primary relationship affected by such a choice is that between the drama and the audience: What ideas about the possibility of reconciliation or transcendence of conflict might the audience take home? How does this change with the variations in plot? The subject of the social-dramatic audience and its possible responses and roles is ultimately the reason for pursuing an analysis of the theatrical implications of plot variation. For in political theater the audience not only considers the messages and ideals of the plot, it also ultimately determines its success. The public/audience can decide either to applaud the production of political reality, to passively and indifferently (or resentfully) withdraw attention by, for example, turning off the television or abstaining from voting. Or, it may decide to deny the particular dramatic resolution and thus deny that protagonist's legitimacy. The audience reaction therefore is directly linked to the political legitimacy of the protagonists of the social drama. This relationship will be discussed fully in the Conclusion when we consider Alan Wolfe's concept of "alienated politics" and Christopher Lasch's ideas about political spectacle.

The Significance of Social Hermeneutics

To put it in few words, the theatre persists so long as the city is caught in a tension between its spiritual vision, its need for recollection, and the maintenance of its political order. Once the city moves to eliminate the contradictions between these objectives instead of living with them, its public life shrinks into passivity and empty ceremony. A theatre that is an *audience* can possess no more life than what is revealed in the memory of its spectators.[28]

The kidnapping of Moro is the greatest spectacle of
modern history, superior to Cape Canaveral, to Disney-
land and to the [Soccer] World Cups. It is more involving and more pacifying. It is bloodier, as we have come
to like. It lasts longer and then, there will be the second
part.[29]

It is the aim of this study to examine the Moro affair as it
"stopped the clock" in Italy just long enough to provide a freeze-
frame view of the long-term social and political malaise (ironically
"normal time" for Italy) out of which this event erupted. The act of
viewing the Moro affair as theater includes but, as should be clear
from the theoretical discussion above, goes beyond proposing that
the event was a product of the Italian mass media. It is the larger
intention here to reveal the way in which all of the event's protagonists (identified and described in Chapter 2), in their attempts to
claim "ownership" (in Gusfield's terms), and to control the outcome of this extraordinary occurrence, were preoccupied by questions and issues of a theatrical nature. All of the protagonists had
distinct ways of conceptualizing the drama, distinct "ideal" plots,
and each wanted that plot to dominate the stage. However, it is
important to state at the outset that this work is not claiming that the
dramatic protagonists proceeded through this public crisis with the
sole intention of making good theater. Each had a distinct political
agenda and political self-conciousness. Each had, potentially, much
to politically gain or lose by the way this crisis was resolved. Rather,
the claim here is that the dramaturgic agendas with their variable
aesthetic imperatives, dialectically interacted with the political and
moral imperatives arising during the development of the event.
Certain plots moved the crisis along certain political directions,
other plots implied alternative orientations. There were, in fact,
several plots being enacted simultaneously, reflecting the state of
political and cultural fragmentation in Italy. All of the plots were,
however, mediated, interpreted by the mass communications
"stages" in ways which did not allow all protagonists an equal
opportunity to have their drama play. We will examine the moments of plot emergence in detail as we move through the event
with the protagonists.

The theoretical approach developed here, as well as those similar
approaches referenced above, owe much to the ground-breaking
work of Kenneth Burke. Burke developed a "dramatistic" method

of analysis that proposed that "the most direct route to the study of human relations and human motives" was via an inquiry into the terms that people used to speak about themselves and their world. As opposed to seeing these terms as mere symbolic expressions of political or psychological processes, Burke, and those who followed him, focused attention on the symbols themselves as they moved into and out of *systems* of symbols. This study will analytically approach the symbolic terms that scripted the Moro social drama, terms such as political legitimacy, terrorism, negotiation, sacrifice, family, and the State, among others, from the essentially Burkean perspective. And, like Burke and Hermassi, I am not interested in terms that avoid ambiguity but rather in those "terms that clearly reveal the strategic spots at which ambiguities necessarily arise."[30] Such strategic points of ambiguity may be illuminating as they necessarily offer up for consideration alternative readings and plot moves that may have been wittingly or unwittingly suppressed. (This will be particularly evident when we examine the issue of negotiation in the Moro social drama.)

Aldo Moro's kidnapping is striking in its accessibility to dramaturgic analysis. It is, for reasons we have begun to explore, a good case, following Levi-Strauss's formulation, "with which to think." It erupted as a discrete event in the midst of a long-term crisis in the economic, social, and political spheres in Italy. It endured over two gruelingly tense months, thus giving the drama time to unfold,[31] and directly involved, as the major protagonists, the most visible and influential political individuals and forces in Italy at that time. It was also a media "event," one that would monopolize screen and page for fifty-five days.

METHODOLOGY: THE ETHNOGRAPHY OF THE SOCIAL TEXT

The dramaturgic methodology builds upon a congruent set of theoretical positions and methodological tools that derive from diverse disciplines of the humanities and social sciences. They are congruent in that their approach is qualitative and their object of analysis is best described as the intertextuality of the written, spoken, and gestured world. In the case of this study, the social world is listened to: the many competing voices are distinguished, and their relationship to each other and to those who are silent is analyzed. That these voices already encapsulate interpretations of social and political events means that we interpret history mediately. Here language is our primary guide and datum.

Building up to the highest level of protagonist/interpretor conception, that being the event emplotment, we start with the basics. These might differ from case to case. For example, Italian is a language that includes both a formal and an informal voice. It also contains an even more formal third person singular pronominal form—*voi* (which also means "you" plural). Mussolini mandated the use of this form in 1938 as part of his attempt to show himself to be, in Denis Mack Smith's phrase, "a man of culture." Thus we start with modes of address (Aldo Moro would use the familiar form of address in his letters to Italian heads of state and government and the formal form of address to his secretary; the pope addressed the Red Brigades with love and the second-person plural form; members of Moro's party would simply not address Moro at all), with stylistic variations (the extremist rhetoric of the Red Brigades against the SIM—the multinational villains; the equally extremist rhetoric of the governing coalition against the Red Brigades "beasts" and for the Resistance; the complicated and often contradictory styles of both Moro and many ultraleftists), and with (in Dell Hymes's terminology) various codes and channels (the variable access to the media of the government, the Red Brigades, Moro, and the public; the private radio stations and press organs of counterinformation; the underground communication network allowing Moro to send and receive letters). We delineate then, the many "texts" that constituted, in their totality, the Moro social drama: political speeches, newspapers, radio and television news articles, editorials and photographs, Moro's letters, communiques of the Red Brigades, public appeals (and then, in the case of Kurt Waldheim, explications of these appeals), journalists' diaries, party flags, reappearing getaway cars, and symbolic points of departure (Via Fani) and arrival (Via Caetani).

As to texts analyzed, the following figure centrally: (1) Radio news program transcripts for the day of March 16, 1978, including the first and second national RAI (Radio audizioni Italia) stations; several independent, ultraleft stations (Radio Onda Rossa [Red Wave Radio] and Radio Città Futura [Radio of the Future City]). (2) Television news program transcripts for March 16, 1978, including the first and second national RAI channels. (3) Newspaper news articles, editorials, letters to the editor, and photographs for the entire fifty-five-day period of sequestration (March 16–May 9). Newspapers for which every day's editions were read in their entirety include: *L'Unità,* the Communist Party daily; *Il Popolo,* the Christian Democrat Party daily; *Il Messaggero,* an independent Rome daily; and *Corriere della Sera,* a centrist, independent, Milan-based daily with wide international circulation. As well, *La Repubblica,* an independent, left-leaning, intellectual daily; *Lotta Continua,* the ultraleftist daily organ of the Lotta Continua Party; *il manifesto,* another ultraleftist daily (attached to the PDUP Party); the rightist *Il Giornale* (newspaper under the direction of the extreme conservative Indro Montanelli); and the conservative *Il Tempo* were surveyed for their positions on the Moro affair during the fifty-five days of Moro's sequestration. (4) All publicly available letters of Aldo Moro (forty-nine are known to date). (5) All of the nine communiques of the Red Brigades (plus the false seventh communique). (6) Texts of speeches delivered during this period by Prime Minister Andreotti, Pope Paul, and Kurt Waldheim. (7) The two "shrines" established as the spatial frames of the event (both in Rome): that on Via Fani, location of the abduction, and that on Via Caetani, location of the recovery of the body.

The selection of texts to analyze was, to a large degree, because of general availability, a matter of applying rational criteria. For example, the newspapers selected for daily scrutiny—*L'Unità, Il Popolo, Il Messaggero,* and *Corriere della Sera*—represent, respectively, the two major political party protagonists (PCI and DC), the press of the popular, liberal Rome community and that of an internationally oriented community. *L'Unità* and *Corriere della Sera* have a circulation of over 500,000 copies each; *Il Popolo,* over 50,000; *Il Messaggero,* a circulation over 200,000. Italy is not a big newspaper-buying country and thus, with the exception of the still important (for other reasons) *Il Popolo,* these are high Italian circulation figures.[32] There were, however, certain decisions that were constrained by availability criteria. Sometimes these constraints coincided with the logic of the study. For example, complete transcripts of radio and television programs were only available for the twenty-four-hour period after Moro's kidnapping. On this first day no letters, photos, or communiques had yet been produced. When they finally began to pour out of the "People's Prison," they were sent straight to the newspapers rather than to the media of the airwaves. Thus they, and the responses to them, seemed to all protagonists and audience to work better in the printed media than in the spoken and filmed media. Perhaps this indicates something about the need of interpretors to slowly work with and work over the texts of a social drama, something the speed and ephemerality of the airwave media do not allow. In fact, the number of television viewers actually declined during the Moro affair. We will have cause to speculate on the possible reasons for television audience decline at greater length in the Conclusion.

Clearly, in the dramaturgical method lies the presupposition that language is symbolic action and that, as such, it leads both inward to the world of individual meanings and outward to the world of social action. The Moro social drama protagonists were acting with and through their largely linguistic rhetoric. They were constructing their own stories, projecting an end that would satisfy their political needs, and deconstructing the stories of others. The dramaturgic methodology is sensitive to moments of self-conscious reflection upon the aesthetic progress of social dramas. (We shall see Prime Minister Giulio Andreotti express a desire for drama rather than farce, see the mass media become hyperbolically patriotic, see Moro's playing upon the metaphor of "family.") It identifies the points at which an event crystallizes for the public; when definitions of "what is happening," "what is at stake," "who is the victim," "who is the winner," and "who is the loser" lock into place. The dramaturgic methodology can thus analyze the epistemology of social crises.

Organization of the Book

The heart of the book tells the story or, better, the stories of the Moro social drama. And it tells these stories by calibrating their plots against the sequence of phases outlined by Turner. First, however, in Chapter 2, the sociopolitical context of Italy in 1978 and the protagonists of the Moro social drama are described. Following is a brief precis of the central chapters.

PHASES OF THE SOCIAL DRAMA

Breach. In this first substantive analytic chapter, the way in which the kidnapping of Moro and the killing of his bodyguards constituted the social drama's initial breach will be explored. The social and political density of the one day, March 16, was extraordinary: the leading Italian politician is kidnapped, a new government is installed, a general strike and mass demonstration take place throughout the country, and, on the part of the Communist Party, a specific attitude toward expected requests of negotiation by the Red Brigades is hardened. In addition, the other dramatic protagonists (the Christian Democrats, the Socialists, the Mass Media, the Ultraleft) will hasten to develop and go public with their initial responses to the breach. These responses will take the form of defining the villains and the victim(s) for the audience (the Italian public). Demonstrations of national solidarity are held, and tentative eulogies to Moro are published in the national press. The Breach chapter charts the responding protagonists' "discovery" of the renewal of Italy via an analysis of the pageantry of this one critical day.

Crisis. The most explicit point of cleavage was that which opened around the issue of negotiation with the Red Brigades for Moro's release (once it was made known that he was still alive). In the discord and debate this issue elicited, we can locate the Crisis phase of this social drama. This chapter examines the way in which the practical business of negotiating with the Red Brigades is fundamentally constrained by the framework of cultural definitions imposed on the terrorists by those protagonists declaring "ownership" of the crisis. The Red Brigades alternately will be afforded and denied rcognition as (1) human beings, (2) political insurgents, (3) legitimate political foes. The victorious "no negotiation" protagonists (the Christian Democrats, the Communists, the Mass Media, the Catholic church hierarchy, etc.) continued the process, begun during the Breach, of defamiliarization of the Red Brigades in their rhetorical campaign of decrying negotiation, and they presented the idea of negotiating as doing symbolic damage to specific ideas and institutions sacred to Italy (e.g., the Resistance, the Constitution).

Redress. Redressive action in the Moro social drama came in several forms. Most salient was the continuous resorting to appeals to "root metaphors." These root metaphors (the concept of root metaphor refers to those sedimented symbols and archetypal characters discussed above; it will be explicated in this chapter and distinguished from what I shall call "root metonymies") were called up to provide moral sustenance and grounding for the various political positions held by the protagonists. An examination of them, and of the selective use of them by the various protagonists, will reveal the *means* by which alternative options were suppressed. The struggle to find and flourish the ultimate, unsurpassable root metaphor would parallel and condition the struggle to make negotiation policy.

Reconciliation/Schism—"Theory and Practice." The ultimate decision not to negotiate for Moro left Moro as, paradoxically, a kind of dramatic residue. The redressive mechanisms invoked in this social drama had to play a double function. On the one hand, they were called forth as a response to the original breach, in which the Red Brigades were the central characters of provocation. On the other hand, they were needed as a response to Moro's (unwelcome) protestations, lodged in his letters, against the no-negotiation position. In his protestations he reasoned on many fronts—negotiating precedents, the needs and claims of his family, his party, and his country, the sanctity of human life. By carrying out this campaign, he attempted to draw the spotlight back to himself. Against Moro's campaign, the no-negotiation protagonists denied Moro the autonomy and authority he asserted by claiming that he had been either drugged, tortured, or otherwise forced to write the letters. Thus in the place of the single, animated Moro of a straightforward reading of the letters, two other "Moro's" were proposed: a Bad (contaminated) Moro and a Good (stoic despite the coerced display of negotiation readiness) Moro. In this way, his letters were discounted. The claim of this study will be that the no-negotiation protagonists attempted a reconciliation by way of the "sacrifice" of the Good Moro but that the resulting reconciliation only superficially covered a deeper and more enduring schism.

Conclusion. The final chapter of this book addresses the question of the particularity of Italy and Italian politics vis-à-vis a theatrical self-conciousness. In so doing, the generalized change of idiom from ritual to theater will be given a historical context. Finally, this chapter concludes that the failure of the dramatic protagonists to create harmony from discord in the Moro social drama can, in large part, be explained not by the fact that a theatrical idiom dominated their presentation of the event, but rather by the fact that they made a certain *kind* of theater. In this regard, the key issue of political genre will be explored. For just as generic choices in theater effect the internal complexity of the characters, their range of relationships with other characters, and their possible relationships with the audience, so do generic choices in the theater of politics condition the amount and quality of public participation and character richness and psychological complexity. Here, the two ends of the generic continuum will be represented by Tragedy and Melodrama—Tragedy allowing for and encouraging audience identification with the tragic victim and his or her decisions, dilemmas, weaknesses, and fate; Melodrama excluding the audience both from such identification and from any engaged participation beyond that of the prescripted booing of the villain and cheering of the hero. Ambiguity is a key term, and the discussion of the presence or absence of a recognition of ambiguity and complexity will provide the link between dramatic idiom and political action. This will make it possible to explore the relationship between generic options and official views of terrorism, political authority, legitimacy, and public participation. This analytic approach will be enriched by a consideration of political scientist Alan Wolfe's suggestive theory of "alienated politics" (particularly that aspect of it dealing with the relationship between depersonalization and depoliticization in the "schizophrenic citizen") as well as a consideration of Christopher Lasch's concept of "politics as spectacle." Such a discussion of the possibilities for true political participation on the part of the public is the ultimate reason for exploring the internal structuration of the theater of politics.

2 Italy 1978

The word "crisis" is commonly used to describe the state of Italian politics and Italian society in general.[1] The frequency with which this word is analytically and emotionally employed is a fact that itself is significant for this study. The Italian crisis-consciousness, a consciousness that spans the political spectrum, reveals a dramatic sense of "always being on the verge of collapse and fragmentation." Despite such characterizations as that evinced by the title of Italian philosopher Norberto Bobbio's article, "Italy's Permanent Crisis,"[2] it is possible to identify particular moments in Italy's history during which the word "crisis" takes on a greater than normal descriptive accuracy. Early spring of 1978 was one of those moments.

In the early months of 1978, Italy was traversing a period of genuine crisis. In January of that year, Christian Democrat Prime Minister Giulio Andreotti's third government, formed in the summer of 1976, had collapsed. Andreotti's government had been based on a political attitude epitomized by a linguistic formulation that immediately betrayed its political weakness, the principle of "non-sfiducia" (not no-confidence). This goverment, in which the Communist party (representing approximately one-third of the electorate) agreed a priori to abstain from a vote of no-confidence, was destined to be, at best, politically ephemeral.[3] And in fact, by mid-December of 1977, a "government of emergency" was being called for by several parties in parliament—including the Communists, whose sense of exclusion from most of the important moments of decision making had intensified.

Along with this political crisis, Italy was experiencing an ongoing economic crisis that, by late 1977, was most evident in continued high inflation (hovering around 17 percent) and high unemployment. Andreotti's government had aimed all efforts at balancing Italy's payments and, in so doing, had sacrificed these economic younger siblings. The already high unemployment was further inflated by the ever-growing numbers of new university graduates searching for nonexistent jobs.[4]

Simultaneously, the Lockheed scandal was coming to the surface. This international scandal, it will be recalled, involved representatives of various nations' governments and armed forces accepting bribes from representatives of Lockheed to insure the sales of Lockheed's C-130 Transport Planes to these countries. In Italy, the Italian branch of the scandal was just beginning to break in February and March of 1978 with the indictments of eleven individuals, including a DC parliamentary representative. Ultimately, the Lockheed scandal would force the Christian Democrat president of the republic, Giovanni Leone, to resign. Implicated along with Leone were many other top Italian politicians (with substantial representation of the Christian Democrat party), businessmen, and military leaders. By way of foreshadowing here, we note that on March 15, 1978, the Lockheed story received major press attention in Italy. Three front page columns in the *Corriere della Sera* were devoted to the scandal, as was a second page *L'Unità* story linking businessman Antonio Lefebvre and Vittoria Leone (the president's wife) to the case.[5] *Il Popolo's* morning edition of March 16 (they were to put out a special edition later that day after Moro's kidnapping) included a page 2 article: "The Lockheed Trial to Begin April 10." Unfortunately, this was the last real major attention the establishment press (both party organs and independent papers) would give to Lockheed for the duration of the Moro affair. The next mention of it in *L'Unità* would occur on March 20 on page 4; in the *Corriere della Sera* it would occur on March 16, but on page 6 in the section called "Internal News"; and in *Il Popolo*, official organ of the Christian Democrat party, it would all but disappear. There the next mention of it would come on March 30, in a small page 6 article that merely noted the condition of Lefebvre's health. This absence in *Il Popolo* may indeed indicate a convenient (if temporary) forgetting of a scandal that would wreak particular havoc on this party.

Finally, in this already strained national context, systematic violence was occurring with almost daily regularity. Terrorist groups, the nature of which will be discussed below, were engaging in kneecappings, kidnappings, and outright assassinations. An estimated 342 acts of political violence had occurred in January of 1978 alone.[6] In addition, what must be termed *the* news story of the month, the trial of the "Red Brigades historic leaders" in Torino, was finally, after two years of delays, getting off to a start. We will have cause to discuss this trial at length.

The tense atmosphere of this period might best be summarized by this example of black humor circulating in Italy at this time: "A businessman describes his daily trip to work in the following way—Every morning I get up and turn on the radio. I wait until I hear the report of the daily kneecapping. Then I leave the house and go to work." This vignette captures well the sense of fragility and fatalism of this Italian "normal time."

This was the moral and political atmosphere in Italy in March of 1978. And it was in the midst of this already shell-shocked period that Aldo Moro, then president of the Christian Democrat party, five-time prime minister, was ambushed and kidnapped on his way to Parliament the morning of March 16. Despite the familiarity most Italians already had with the force and ubiquitousness of the Red Brigades, this action still had the power to startle the whole country. No one had believed that the Red Brigades were capable of targeting and achieving so high an official, one of the highest in Italy, in fact. The breach this event opened up, wide as it threatened to become, was, however, quickly jumped into by several social and political groups declaring themselves to be directly effected and interested. These various groups would assume specific roles in the Moro social drama, and thus it is important to introduce them at the outset. The cast then included parliamentary political parties (the Christian Democrats, the Italian Communist party, the Socialist party, the Republican party, and the outlying ultraright parliamentary party, the Italian Social Movement), the major political movements outside of Parliament (the ultraleft—composed of distinct parties and areas such as Lotta Continua, Autonomia Operaia, Movimento, Manifesto, and, in what will prove the power of post hoc reconstitution, Potere Operaio),[7] the Red Brigades, the Catholic church hierarchy, Moro's family, the establishment and anti-establishment mass media, and Aldo Moro himself.

The Protagonists

THE ITALIAN COMMUNIST PARTY (PCI)
Giorgio Galli, one of Italy's most respected political scientists, has

christened the Italian mode of making politics a "bipartitismo imperfetto" (imperfect bipartism). This phrase refers to the asymmetrical relationship between Italy's two largest political parties, the Communists and the Christian Democrats. These parties have each sustained, with some not insignificant recent fluctuations,[8] approximately one-third of the national vote for nearly a decade.

Ever since January 21, 1921, when Amedeo Bordiga, together with fifteen other ex-Socialist party members (including Antonio Gramsci) founded the PCI, the Communists have been a significant political presence in Italy. Despite their enforced exile during the twenty years of Mussolini's Fascist regime, the PCI was able to attract members (19 percent of the electoral vote in the first [1946] postwar elections), make alliances (with the Socialists and a few Christian Democrats during the Popular Front days of the Resistance), and cultivate leaders who, in their person (Togliatti) or their writings (Gramsci), would become internationally known for their efforts to develop a specifically Italian form of communism. This form, which came to be known as "la terza via" (the third way), asserts a commitment to democracy and a gradually increasing refusal (short of total disassociation) of the Soviet model and of Soviet imperialism (see the increasing crescendo of the critiques of the Soviet invasions of Hungary, Czechoslovakia, and Afghanistan).

After the war, however, the PCI's legitimacy and effectiveness was nearly decimated by the results of the 1948 national elections. These elections, distinguished from the 1946 elections by the serious anti-Communist campaign of the DC, overtly and adamantly guided by Washington,[9] effectively denied the PCI any formal participation in any national government, at least for the forseeable future. This electoral defeat and government exclusion led, as Donald Blackmer has written, to a temporary reversion to "classical themes of class struggle and confrontation with Capitalists, Christian Democrats and the Church."[10] These rhetorical moves were, to some degree, given life in the form of peasant mobilizations for land reform, industrial strikes and mass demonstrations against NATO and the Marshall Plan: "The response of the government to such attempts at mass mobilization was in most cases immediate and brutal. It has been estimated that the years 1948–1954 saw 75 dead and 5,104 wounded as a result of police intervention against such protest; there could no longer be any question that a climate of confrontation and repression had definitively replaced the constructive collaboration of a few years before."[11]

The introduction of the related themes of violence and illegitimacy is important for an understanding of the way that the PCI's historic responses to these issues ultimately shaped its role in the Moro social drama. Several historical positions need to be cited. During the fascist era, Togliatti labored long to convince his fellow communists that contrary to their fiercely held belief that fascism was essentially an elite and declassed-based regime, it was really a reactionary regime with *mass* characteristics. Second, given the ability of reactionary parties to attract a heterogenous (in terms of class) mass constituency, the PCI had to aim *its* appeal beyond its traditional working class constituency, to the middle classes in order to "deny any nascent reactionary movement a mass base."[12] What did this mean then in terms of the classic revolutionary, Bolshevik rhetoric? Prior to anything else it meant a conscious toning down, if not altogether elimination, of the idea of a *violent* revolution. Violence became, after the experiences of fascism and the cold war, synonymous with the forces of reaction in party rhetoric. If the PCI wanted to be a legitimate party in Italy, which it did, it had to constantly remember both the violence and the mass character of the fascist epoch. This it did by dispossessing itself of any identity that linked the party with violence and by building alliances with sections of the middle classes. (There were, and continue to be, of course, members of the party who still feel a primary identity with the USSR. Sometimes referred to as "Stalinist" in their orientation, these members, represented in the leadership by Armando Cossutta, do not have much internal power.) However, given this turning away from violence, the fact of the Resistance, a necessarily violent epoch and movement, remained to be rhetorically integrated. Historians of the Resistance have indicated that, while violent, the Resistance was not a revolutionary movement and that it was Togliatti himself who constantly put constraints on those who wanted to move it in a revolutionary direction. The violence of the Resistance, in other words, was defensive and legitimate. After World War II, as Massari writes, "Violence—the leadership of the Communists would come repeatedly to say, by now more and more frequently—is always reactionary."[13]

Donald Blackmer has suggested that the postwar PCI history can be analytically divided into three phases: (1) participation (1943–1948) during which the ultramodern Italian Constitution was written with Communist participation, (2) confrontation (1948–1956), (3) opposition within the system (1956–present). And, in this third phase, the alliance strategy seemed to be successful in bringing the PCI close to actual legitimate membership in Italian government. This success was highlighted in 1976 when the PCI reaped an all-time high of 34.4 percent of the vote. The previous high of 39.6 percent obtained in 1946 was actually a tally of the combined Communist and Socialist vote. Thus it was largely on the basis of the PCI's 1976 parliamentary strength (obtained through its alliance strategy) that that party could realistically comtemplate inclusion in the governmental majority in 1978.

That government-to-be of March 1978 was the legislative capstone of the famous "Historic Compromise" between, as Enrico Berlinguer (PCI party secretary) wrote in October 1973 in *Rinascita,* the PCI weekly magazine, "forces that collect and represent the great majority of the Italian people."[14] What is significant about the speech of Berlinguer's transcribed in that article is that its basic themes were defensive in nature.[15] The title of the speech was "Reflections on the facts of Chile," and in it Berlinguer referred explicitly to the "ever-impending menaces of reactionary adventures." Thus even in this moment of growing electoral strength and potential governmental inclusion, the PCI was still thinking and acting defensively, seeking alliances with conservatives (the DC), decrying violence by characterizing it as fascist-inspired and accepting NATO. This defensiveness was not, however, the result of paranoia: a survey conducted in 1972 by Giacomo Sani revealed that most voters *still* viewed the PCI as illegitimate.[16] Further, the period of the late sixties and early seventies in Italy was one characterized as the years of the right-wing "Strategy of Tension." This strategy, which included bombing of public places and attempted coup d'états by factions of the military, will be discussed below in the section describing the terrorist protagonists of the Moro social drama. Here, we need to note the particular vulnerability of the PCI to this highly ramified movement of right-wing forces in Italy. Indeed, Berlinguer specifically alluded to this phenomenon in his discussion of the necessity for the Historic Compromise: "At present, there is an urgency to prevent, with far-sightedness and tactical skill, the stable coalescing of the center and the right, the broad front of a clerico-fascist nature, and to, instead, succeed in moving the centrist social and political forces toward consistently democratic positions."[17]

Finally, it is necessary to ask why, on the basis of their remarkable electoral vitality in the 1976 elections, was the PCI leadership so anxious to solidify an unequal governing relationship with their traditional enemies? Why did they not rather seek to join forces with the Socialist party or, alternatively, on the heels of yet one more Christian Democrat government failure (Andreotti's third in January 1978), demand either full participation (the Historic Compromise government would acknowledge the PCI as bona fide participants in the majority but would grant them no ministerial portfolios) or a return to bona fide opposition in Parliament? Here again we need to refer to the PCI postwar history of exclusion and delegitimation, particularly in force during electoral campaigns (many believed that the PCI decision not to cooperate with the DC in 1978 would indeed have led to another round of elections), to the "Strategy of Tension" of the early seventies, and to the leftist terrorism steadily increasing in the late seventies. The emergency of 1978, it was the opinion of the PCI leadership, left no choice but cooperation. This decision, and similar decisions throughout the Moro social drama, we will see, had a direct impact on both the ability of the PCI to assert its political legitimacy and the possibility of the "Historic Compromise" to be effective and endure.[18]

One last contradiction in the identity of the PCI needs to be outlined. One of Antonio Gramsci's most important theoretical contributions was his idea that the PCI had to build its presence in Italian society from the bottom up; that an elite, top-down way of making politics would neither truly change the way in which people viewed their world and their role in it nor would it provide a firm and steady base for the party. This base-up, top-down distinction corresponds, perhaps, to that between what it has come to mean, in Italy, to be a "Partito di Lotta" (Party of Struggle) or a "Partito di Governo" (Party of Government). In the early months of 1978, the PCI was, in fact, about to attempt the transition from the former to the latter. This transformation was not, however, a clear-cut or untroubled one. Much discussion was carried out in the party organ *L'Unità* about precisely what it meant to be both in and against the government of a capitalist state at the same time. This discussion focused as much on the complex and apparently contradictory identities of individual PCI members and supporters as it did on the party actually joining in a government with the Christian Democrats. An example of the former comes from the February 2 edition of *L'Unità*. A page 1 story, "The Victims of Violence," refers to the two communist managers of a company who have been attacked by leftist terrorists. The title of the article defending the two victims poses, but does not go far in answering, the question: "What does it mean to be both a communist and a manager of an agency?"[19]

Many scholars have questioned whether the PCI has ever actually succeeded in creating that Gramscian organic presence in Italian society or whether it was, beginning with the postwar reestablishment of the party, already on its way to becoming an elite Partito di Governo. While it is not our task here to answer this historical question, the Moro affair offers an excellent test case in which this contradiction was plainly exposed.

THE CHRISTIAN DEMOCRAT PARTY (DC)

Approximately fifteen years after the proclamation of the Kingdom of Italy, in 1860, Italian politics became dominated by the "blocco storico," the coalition of northern industrial, commercial, and financial elites and southern gentry. This coalition was reinforced with new members primarily by way of an overt policy of patronage. It endured over forty years until the onset of fascism. Some factors in Italian society had changed, however, in the early decades of the twentieth century, factors which, according to several interpretors of Italian history, including Denis Mack Smith in his recent biography of Mussolini, aroused a fear among the elite that ultimately allowed for fascism's rise. The critical changes were the universal suffrage in 1913 and the removal by the Catholic church of its ban on Catholic participation in Italian politics. Addressing these changes, Martin Shefter has written that "two new actors have moved onto the political stage. The working classes, organized chiefly through the Socialist and then the Communist parties and then the Christian Democrats."[20]

The Christian Democrat party was founded as a new party in 1943. Many of its members, however, had originally been associated with the Italian Popular party (1919–1926) which, in one of the last pre-Fascist elections in 1919, had received 20.5 percent of the vote. After the war, the DC, with major U.S. backing, gained political ascendancy in Italy, adopting basically the same approach to fears of socialist/communist-inspired revolutions as that adopted by the "blocco storico" in the late nineteenth century, and attracting (partly as a result of the weakened position of the Liberal party, former mobilizer of the "blocco storico") many of its traditional clients. This was an attraction, however, with a new twist. The DC, unlike the older "blocco storico," was a mass party with a heterogeneous (if still predominantly bourgeoisie) mass base. Its mass appeal was based squarely on one multidimensional concept: security. On an international level, the centrist DC party has the support of the United States and NATO and thus Italy, home of the largest Communist party in Western Europe, has military "security." (Recently this "security" has included the installation of United States cruise missiles. These missiles were installed in Comiso, Sicily, despite Communist party and popular protest.) On a microlevel of the personal career security of loyal DC supporters, the tradition of "clientelism" (patronage) has continued. This tradition gained, with the emergence and dominance of the DC, new classes of beneficiaries: "The DC has taken advantage of its control over the bureaucracy to place hordes of well-paid ushers and janitors on the public payroll. It provides subsidies to marginal businesses, firms that could not survive in the absence of state support and whose owners and employees become dependent upon the party for their continued prosperity and employment."[21]

Thus the electoral base of support for the DC has indeed been heterogeneous. And, it has been so in several ways: it is heterogeneous in terms of class, geography, and, Douglas Wertman notes, gender. (Women were granted the right to vote in Italy only in 1946. The DC electorate has been, since 1947, at least 60 percent female.)[22] Wertman has identified four factors that are significant in explaining the DC electorate: (1) the religious factor, (2) strong female support, (3) appeals based on anticommunism in particular and antiextremism in general as well as on the role of the DC as the main protector of Italy's democratic institutions and liberties, and (4) clientelism.[23]

One of the effects of this wide net the DC has cast and of the many different species of fish they have farmed within it has been the proliferation of numerous intraparty factions. This extreme factionalization (twelve currents identified in 1980) has led Giuseppe Di Palma to write: "How can insistence by DC respondents on partisanship and party duty be reconciled with the fact that their party is essentially a federation of allied factions whose attitudes toward each other are, at best, those of friendly enemies? And what to make of their asserted ideological attachments in a party that is more know for its attachment to power than to principles of action?"[24]

If, as much of the extent analysis of the DC party reveals, the party does not, itself, emphasize its particular program as much as its ability to protect Italy (mainly from the Communists) and its own various fiefdoms, then we are forced to understand the DC's way of doing politics as being essentially a-political. Alan Stern, in fact, in his analysis of the DC northeastern (Veneto) stronghold, has called the DC mode of political domination one "composed of a stable social organization that deemphasizes the place of politics in community life."[25]

In 1976, however, the DC was forced to confront a changing political map. The PCI had gained a significant two percentage points in the elections. The DC was in danger of a slow but steady erosion of its hegemony from the left, but also, as Paolo Franchi notes, from the right as well. Three factors can be identified as having "saved" the DC from a real and sudden loss of its dominance: the continued support of a United States none too sympathetic to the burgeoning PCI, the continuing support of the electorate[26] (in the 1976 elections, the DC gained three points), and the tentative nature of the Communist claims of inclusion: "The DC of the early seventies, no longer representative of the whole Catholic world, exposed on its left to the flight of social, political, and cultural sectors long held by their hegemony, to the right was the antidemocratic reaction of groups and classes struck or scared by the workers' advance; and even more influenced by a growing consensus of disaffection on the parts of the most advanced sectors of Italian capitalism (the interview with Gianni Agnelli in *L'Espresso* on the necessity of a social contract that had the function of being antiparasitic and, in the final analysis, antidemocratic is from 1972), should have appeared to be on the brink of madness or dissolution. And only the ancient and persistent communist pessimism about the fragility of the bases of Italian democracy could explain why, in front of such a situation, the choice was that of proposing to such a diminished DC an agreement instead of pressing on the accelerator of an open and, perhaps frontal, attack."[27]

Two final aspects of the DC party history need to be introduced.

The first aspect concerns what seems to be the perpetual scandal involvement of the Christian Democrat party and members. The DC has been involved in every one of Italy's major scandals since the end of the war. Here we simply list a few of these: the Fiumicino Airport scandal (paybacks to politicians by real estate speculators that induced these politicians to approve the building of the airport on a swamp), the Lockheed scandal, the Petrolio scandal (the selling of incorrectly identified oil for higher prices than the government allowed), the P2 secret masonic lodge scandal (an organization of leading political, military, and business leaders designed, in some obscure and secretive way, to control the Italian government). Some of these scandals merely involved illicit finances. But some, still unresolved years later, probably involved attempted right-wing coup d'états. As one young DC deputy put it: "Not even the DC militants and officials . . . can deny that the corruption of the Palace constitutes not so much an alibi for terrorism as it does for the detachment of a section of the public opinion. The 'golden barges' do more harm to the party than the terrorist bullets."[28] This history and self-consciousness provoked, it is not surprising to learn, a defensive attitude on the part of the DC. In *Il Popolo,* the party news organ, the cry went out that the DC was unequally singled out for blame by the media-conscious and agile left: "The left uses the press, the cinema, the television, story-telling, the essay, the theater, the magazine, the cabaret, and popular music to persuade everyone that the Catholics [DC] are corrupters, corrupt and corruptable. We, on the contrary, are engaged in the creating of institutional conditions that maximally eliminate the motives of scandal, that do not reduce space, that enlarges the efficiency of the controls in the various passages of the administrative life."[29] Contrast the rhythmic cadence of the alleged accusation in the first part of this quotation (it reveals what seems almost a longing for the apparent theatrical/aesthetic ability of the left to present their case against the corruption of the DC) with the ponderous and opaque bureaucratic language in the second sentence (in which the DC is theoretically making its own best case for itself). This attention to language is at the heart of the dramaturgical analysis, and it is crucial to begin to draw attention to the use of language and other media of communication by the protagonists. The Moro social drama will, it will be shown, provide an occasion for the DC legitimately (Moro was, after all, their president) engage in the multifaceted theater of politics and political theater.

Finally, a salient feature of DC parliamentary behavior is that which is best captured by the word "logoramento" (dragging-out). The DC is notorious for its ability to prolong debate and hold off legislative action. It is not that *no* legislation successfully makes its way through the Italian Parliament, it is rather the case that very few *significant* laws get passed. Those laws that do make it are most often of the "leggine" (little laws) variety. This term, used by Giuseppe Di Palma to refer to the swiftly executed minor parliamentary matters, can be placed in the context of Italian Parliament as follows: "Any institution unable to form agreement around decisions does not stop making them; it rather adapts its processes and products to the circumstances. It disaggregates decisions, it falters and slows down on more divisive issues, it responds rather than initiates, it postpones government programs, etc."[30]

This trivialization of the legislative product was, in fact, mentioned by a PCI trade-union delegate, interviewed outside the gates of Fiat's Mirafiori plant during the weeks of Moro's sequestration: "In 35 years, what have we had? Laws made by Mussolini and that's all. Other laws have not appeared. And instead of passing laws against criminals, they've passed laws for putting mirrors on cars."[31]

The reference to "laws made by Mussolini" points to the common knowledge in Italy that many of the laws on the books (particularly the Penal Code) were codified during the fascist regime. There have been, of course, modifications since the fall of the fascists. But even these innovations, according to a sociologist of law, Vincenzo Ferrari, have been more the result of the work of the Constitutional Court (the Italian Supreme Court) than the legislature.[32]

While the structural reasons for the "logoramento" propensity are many and complex, having to do with, among other things, the different interpretations that the two major parties, PCI and DC, have of the Constitution, it is important to simply note it here as a salient characteristic of the DC and of its leaders—one of whom was Aldo Moro.

One of the most powerful and enduring of DC leaders, Aldo Moro had been literally at the center of DC politics, with few interruptions, for thirty years. He was a member of the Doroteo faction ("the heart of the heart of the DC"), five times prime minister of Italy, a frequent president of the DC, and, in author and Radical party deputy Leonardo Sciascia's terms, "il meno implicato di tutto" (the least implicated of them all). Here Sciascia refers to Moro's general, if not total, diffidence toward corruption.[33] Moro's usual role in DC-involving scandals was that of symbolic defender. In fact, in the days before his kidnapping, Moro had delivered a speech defending a fellow DC deputy, Gui, who had been indicted in the Lockheed scandal.[34]

Where Moro *was* an archetypal Christain Democrat though was in his natural proclivity toward logoramento. Moro's mode of logoramento was linguistic. He spoke and wrote a dense, logically circular Italian. We shall have occasion to analyze this Moro language in depth in later chapters. Sociologist Franco Ferrarotti has written of the existential logoramento of Italy's "powerful men" (of whom Moro was one) who "aim at lasting rather than leading. To lead, after all, means to choose, to take decisions and apply them in practice, thus provding specific opportunities for evaluation. And every evaluation is seen as a danger by the Italian man of power. To be eternal, one must do nothing. One must wait for problems to wear themselves out sufficiently in order that they may solve themselves."[35]

Aldo Moro was born on September 23, 1916, in the small southern town of Maglie in the region of Lecce. His parents were both educators; his mother a teacher, his father a school principal. At the age of twenty-one, Moro took a degree in law at the University of Bari and subsequently obtained a post of assistant professor in the philosophy of law, history, and politics. But it was his involvement with the Catholic church that consumed most of Moro's time and energy as a university student. In fact, in 1939, in an Italy still dominated by Mussolini's fascists, Moro was elected president of FUCI (Federation of Italian Catholic University Students) and held this post until he was called to do military service in 1942. Aniello Coppola, Moro's political biographer, writes that Moro encountered significant resistance from the Barese Christian Democrats when he first attempted to join the party in January of 1944. Coppola attributes this resistance to a general diffidence toward Moro (that would continue until June 1946 when Moro was finally placed and elected on the DC list of candidates for the Constitutional Assembly) who had lived "an a-political cultural and moral experience in the space that the church had succeeded in preserving for itself thanks to the Concordat (Lateran Pacts) with Mussolini's regime."[36] While serving on the Constitutional Assembly, Moro supervised the section on the "Rights of the Individual and the Citizen," an interesting linguistic breakdown of identities that would reveal itself to be highly relevant to Moro's own plight more than thirty years later. Once elected as a DC parliamentary deputy in April of 1946, Moro was continuously present in the DC leadership ranks for the next thirty years. He held, among others, the posts of minister of justice (called, in Italy, Grazia [Grace] and Giustizia [Justice] (1955), minister of education (1957), secretary of the DC, (1959) and prime minister (1963, 1964, 1966, 1974, 1976).

We can best understand Moro's political positions and placement via a discussion of his political and intellectual style. Above all things, Moro believed in the superiority of the intellect. Moro's FUCI days and his university career had nourished this belief by providing him with the time and the structures for meditating on such questions as the problem of error and sin and the historical forms of law, politics, and humanism. With such a background, it should not surprise us to learn that Moro reached decisions slowly, after long and persistent ratiocination. Nor is it surprising that his mode of political discourse was complex, sometimes to the point of becoming arcane: "It is up to political initiative to make an appropriate synthesis and to organize consensus not around particularities, however important, but around a comprehensive design and, in its complexity, complete and stable. To reach unity means to bring a great understanding of things, a total vision."[37] In parliamentary debate, he could be and often was exhausting.

With the above in mind, we can now approach Moro's politics as a natural extension of his intellectual disposition and his personal, religious, and academic history. In his politics (particularly with his creation of the centro-sinistra [center-left] governments in which Socialists were included), Moro attempted to combine his Christian faith and traditionalism with his Enlightenment vision. He tried to do this from the center of what was an extremely fragmented party and in a period of great turbulence in Italian history.

The centro-sinistra governments of the mid-sixties were a partial attempt to stave off what some, Moro among them, knew would be the inevitable explosions caused by the economic boom of the late fifties and the early sixties. Few, however, could predict how very explosive the situation was. Moro, it could be claimed, ultimately paid the price for his and others' incomplete analysis of the explosive nature of the period. The boom had happened largely because the wages of Italian workers had been kept so very low during the years of growth. In the late sixties, however, the workers started to become more adamant in their demands for higher pay. As well, larger numbers of students were attending the newly opened-up (to all economic classes, with free tuition and open enrollment) universities, with the result that a new generation of Italians was posing new questions. The force of these combined movements finally erupted during the now-famous student/worker explosion of 1968 and the worker/student Hot Autumn of 1969. The centro-sinistra government had not been able to contain this force. Aniello Coppola writes: "But finally, the center-left was revealed to be too small a cage to contain the civil, social and cultural growth of the country, the explosion of the student, worker, and feminist movement, the diffusion of democratic anarchy, the affirmation of a generalized need of live participation of a libertarian inspiration."[38]

Was Moro, who identified so personally with his centrist and generally conservative party, merely reacting, as some critics have it, in a pragmatic post hoc fashion to these new and disturbing phenomena? Or did he, in fact, hope to bring about and direct the flow of some of the changes? Certainly his position was, from the mid-sixties on, consistent with (qualified) openings first to the Socialist party and later, in the years of the Historic Compromise formula, to the Communists. Yet Moro was, if nothing else, unequivocally an anti-Communist.

Moro's was not an easy role to play in the early months of 1978. He had to convince an internally fragmented and ideologically variegated party that the Historic Compromise, that "programmatic accord" as he put it, was both necessary and essentially nonthreatening to his party's identity. There were those in the right wing of the DC who publicly denounced Moro for his overtures to the PCI and went so far as to call him a "Marxist." This nomenclature was, of course, picked up and reported by *L'Unità* in an article called "Get Rid of That Marxist Moro" that described an assembly in Genova of the new DC right: "The communists—De Carolis [a rightest DC member] affirms—have constructed a political and even aesthetic [n.b.] masterpiece. Step after step, concession after concession, we have put ourselves in the hands of the PCI, swallowing insults."[39] The guilty party in this yielding up was, of course, Moro. Another role Moro was simultaneously playing was that mentioned above, of defending fellow DC members implicated in Lockheed.

Both Aldo Moro and Enrico Berlinguer strongly believed that the Historic Compromise government was timely. They had, however, different reasons for doing so and differing visions of what such a government would look like. For the PCI, the Historic Compromise represented, first, their political legitimacy in a period of great insecurity for even legally constituted socialist governments (Chile was ever present in their minds), and, second, an important step toward achieving a democratic socialist state. For Moro, the inclusion of the PCI in the majority signified a way to "eliminate the 'anomaly' of the Italian democracy, with respect to the other European democracies, which was the lack of alternation between different blocs in the government (laborites and conservatives, Social Democrats, and so on)."[40]

Thus Moro was not willing to risk, and certainly was not auguring a real structural change in Italian politics. He was, after all, a Christian Democrat. He had even, as late as the end of 1977 when the PCI refused to continue their abstention policy and asked to enter the government, attempted to put off the whole decision (logoramento) until the end of 1978 when he might, as was being discussed, have been elected as president of the Republic—a role which could have significantly muted his primary identification with the Christian Democrats. The Communists did not want to wait for this eventuality though, feeling that the force of history could not suffer too many more delays. Moro had a very different vision of the motor of history, one which he had sustained since 1944 when he wrote the following: "The center is thus not an immovable point, but a process, a tiring, committed process rich with unknowns. It is not a matter of stopping the course of history, against the perennial exigence of the motor, of stopping it at the center . . . it's a matter, instead, of insuring the continuity of the process and therefore of accelerating the motor, increasing its vigor, but controlling it at the same time because nothing that is human and was tiringly conquered should be lost."[41]

Thus it was Moro, alone in this rich but potentially threatening processual center, who was kidnapped by the Red Brigades. Enrico Pozzi, a professor of literature, considers the Red Brigades choice in the light of the paradoxical isolation of Moro inside the "heart of the heart of the DC": "But would the Red Brigades have kidnapped a Fanfani, a Forlani, or a Zaccagnini had these men occupied the same position [as Moro] and brought to a conclusion the same political operation [the historic compromise]? Above all, would they have submitted them to the same prolonged ritual of public destruction? We cannot justify our sensation, but we believe the answer is no. Because Moro represented, in the social fable of the powerful figure in Italy, a case by himself. His power was latent, incarnated in a weak body, a body—according to years-old rumors—that was dying. An invisible power, not supported by a strong organization, not linked to powerful economic or financial groups, not accompanied by showy symbols of power . . . Thus a power simultaneously inexplicable and crucial: otherwise put, power in its highest and most numinous form . . . self-legitimating charisma. And it is this abstract power, this, we would say—*concept* of power that the Red Brigades kidnapped on March 16."[42] Critically, the vision that the Red Brigades held of Moro when they decided to kidnap him was almost identical to that of this scholar. In an interview with Giorgio Bocca, Mario Moretti, whom Bocca calls the "real leader of the operation," had this to say about "why Moro?": "It isn't the position that the Christian Democrat holds, but the power . . . Why Moro? Because his was, for almost twenty years, the supreme direction of power in Italy, because he was the demiurge of the bourgeois power . . . I don't recall that anyone thought about any other person for the big campaign of spring of '78."[43]

THE ITALIAN SOCIALIST PARTY (PSI)

The Italian Socialist party, founded by Filippo Turati in 1892, has had a strategic importance in postwar governments that is disproportionate with its actual numerical following. In fact, with approximately 12 percent of the vote (in the 1983 elections), the PSI remains the smallest Southern European Socialist party.[44] Yet since Moro's first centro-sinistra governments, the Socialists have often been normally included (with portfolios) in the ruling majorities and now (1985), of course, Socialist party secretary, Bettino Craxi, is prime minister.

In the sixties and seventies, the ideological position of the Socialists could best be characterized as humanitarian—one focused on
the panoply of human-rights issues that became salient in Italy in
those years. These issues included divorce, birth control, and abor-
tion. The PSI were consistent supporters of liberalization in these
areas.

Recently Craxi, representing the coalition government with the
Christian Democrats and small lay parties, has developed a hard
"austerity" line. One example of this stance was Craxi's admonition
to the Italian people *not* to vote on a referendum forwarded by the
PCI this summer (1985). That referendum would have restored the
"cost of living adjustment" (the Scala mobile) payed to workers to
its past scale (this had been diminished in recent years). Craxi's
political maneuverings and his recent overt appeals for more cooperation with the DC at the local level are indicative of the kinds of
moves that have led many to accuse the Socialists of "trasfor-
mismo"; a Protean ability to be anything at all in the search for
power.

Thus despite their direct governmental participation, the Socialists have often been referred to as a party in search of an identity.
Clearly, with the substantially larger PCI claiming for itself the role
of (sometime) opposition, the Socialists are caught in a kind of
no-man's land between the DC and the PCI. Their strategic vitality
is due to their role as the "acceptable" left party that can make or
break coalitions by switching allies; siding now with the Communists, now with the Christian Democrats. The early months of 1978
were confusing and frustrating ones for the PSI. For the Communists were sidestepping the Socialists in order to deal directly with
the DC, largely in the person of Moro. In the eyes of the Socialists,
the Historic Compromise stood essentially for the negation of the
strategic role the PSI had played, for so many years. And they were,
frankly, opposed to the PCI preempting their role. Franchi writes:
"The Socialists speak openly of more advanced equilibria, they
maintain their position of being able to represent, in the decisional
realm of government, the totality of the social and political left,
communists and trade-unionists in the first place. They are convinced they can overcome the crisis that succeeded the historic
center-left coalitions and, against the failure of the social-
democratic unification, they propose themselves as a kind of moving societal frontier . . . more than all others able to take advantage

of an uncertain transitional situation. It's a role they have neither the head nor the legs to play and the Communists don't intend at all to delegate to them."[45]

Legitimation Crisis

In order to place our next two sets of protagonists, the ultraleft groups and the Red Brigades, in their political, historical contexts, it is necessary to bear in mind a related issue. For the purpose of simplicity, this issue may be termed the "crisis of legitimation."

The reference to the "legitimation crisis" in Italian politics indicates a general sense of political immobility and impotence. Here, we are not primarily concerned with the related issue of the perceived legitimacy or illegitimacy of particular parties, a complex and central question for the Moro affair which this study will develop at length. Rather, it is the perceived illegitimacy of the entire political sphere that is of immediate concern.

After World War II, the newly formed or reformed Italian political parties staked out and colonized substantial blocs of Italian voters. We have seen how one party, the DC, managed to occupy the government almost single-handedly for thirty postwar years, thus creating a situation in which there is no political alternation (either within one system, as Moro claimed to auger with the Historic Compromise, or from one system to another). The result of this straightforward DC domination has, then, been the paradoxical situation of political turbulence and political stalement at the same time. (Italian government coalitions rise and fall with what has become by now a cliched regularity. There have been forty-four governments since World War II. Socialist Bettino Craxi became prime minister after DC Amintore Fanfani's government fell in April 1983 and new elections were held in June of 1983.) Several political theorists have addressed this situation and have developed a series of explanations for it. Jean Blondel proposes that the multiparty systems dominated by one party, as is the case in Italy, give rise to the least stable conditions. Giuseppe Di Palma attributes Italy's general political instability to a lack of clearly shared decisional rules among the various parties. In fact, he finds that the acceptability or unacceptability of a decision is not tied to the actual substance of the decision but rather to who is backing it: "The test of the acceptability of a decision becomes more and more not its content but who sustains it and who opposes it. Similarly the test of the legitimacy of a coalition does not revolve around its programs but around which parties and factions it includes and which it leaves out."[46]

Giorgio Galli has highlighted the disproportionate amount of time and energy spent on vague rhetoric in Italian parliamentary debates, a tendency that indicates the threatrical self-consciousness of the parliamentarians.

To these elements we must, of course, add scandal, corruption, factionalism, and, according to Norberto Bobbio, the fact of the "criptogoverno": "Weak government, however, is only part of the story. As far as Italy is concerned . . . it is true that the government is weak, but it is also true that the 'sub-government' (sottogoverno) is strong . . . one cannot understand our political system if one fails to acknowledge that under the visible government there is a government that acts in the shadows, and a still lower one that works in absolute darkness. The first of these already has a name, used only by journalists, which should take its rightful place in the technical discourse of political scientists: sub-government. The second does not as yet bear a name, but one might call it cripto government (criptogoverno). I will not say much about the latter term because we do not as yet know much about it. Yet from the time of the Piazza Fontana massacre [1969] to the discovery of a secret masonic lodge [P2] whose leader was indicted and who is politically suspect, we know that an occult power exists although, because it is occult, no one is as yet in a position to state exactly what might be the nature, the goals and the effects of its machinations."[47]

Finally, at the more visible level of ideological hegemony, we must bear in mind the original reliance of the DC on the traditional authority of the Italian Catholic church. In some areas, particularly the Northeast DC (Veneto) stronghold, the DC would often meet in the parish house, not bothering to keep a separate party headquarters.[48] Here it is useful to refer to Jurgen Habermas's analysis of capitalist ideological dependence in his book *Legitimation Crisis:* "Capitalist societies were always dependent on cultural boundary conditions that they could not themselves reproduce: they fed parasitically on the remains of tradition."[49] However, over time, this reliance on the sacred aura of religious tradition in Italy has been displaced and supplemented by the development of clientelism—different factions of the DC (and, to some extent, the

PSI) colonizing specific geographical locales. As Alan Stern, referring to the Veneto area has written, ". . . the DC elite seems to be
supplanting sources of traditional legitimation with the fruits of
government patronage."[50] Despite this gradual abandonment of
reliance on religious legitimation, however, the weight of the past
and of tradition is still felt. One PCI deputy described the stalemate
in the following way to Robert Putnam: "Parliament has stopped in
midstream. Why? There is strong pressure from the past, from past
laws, past conceptions and there is strong pressure from the groups
with economic power who influence various parties and, in particular the DC, who accept verbally the idea of the implementation of
the Constitution but in fact always put on the brakes . . . We have a
crisis of the Parliament, yes, and of the state, but it is a crisis of
immobility."[51]

While it is not possible to trace the origins of the Italian political
legitimation crisis in these introductory pages, we can note that the
crisis precedes, by many years, the recent social and economic
(inflation was still approximately 14 percent in 1984 but has come
down to about 10 percent in 1985) crisis. And we must ask what the
effects of this legitimation crisis on the political parties and their
constituencies have been. What has been its effect on public life?
What has been its effect on the younger generation's involvement in
politics?

A tentative answer to these questions, one which will be helpful
in understanding the "politics" of the parliamentarians as well as
the "politics" of the ultraleftists and of the Red Brigades, may be
posed. This answer derives from Alan Wolfe's theory of "alienated" politics, to which we will have occasion to refer at length in
the conclusion of this study. Simply defined, alienated politics is
that form of politics in which "parties and interest groups become
responsible for absorbing the common power that people possess
and for using this power over the people from whom it came in the
first place."[52] There are many ways in which alienated politics can
evolve. The dramaturgic analysis of the Moro affair highlights a
moment of alienated politics at its most overt. On a very gross level,
the ramifications of alienated politics can be calibrated in a simple
decline of voters. In fact, Carrieri and Lombardo Radice refer to
precisely this manifestation when they discuss the "wearing out of
the political conscience of the Italian citizens" in the early eighties:
"We are referring to a danger that has its first manifestations in an

incipient, measurable decline in the percentage of voters, which still remains among the highest, if it is not in fact the highest, in Europe, and in an incalculable fall of passion and basic participation in the public cause."[53] Others have shown how, through a series of transformations and regressions of social movements coming up against both the repression of the state and the institutionalization of the traditional Left (that might be another way of explicating alienated politics), terrorism is born. Alberto Melucci, for example, has written,."The systematic practice of violence, up to the final desperate end of terrorism, is the result of the process of decomposition of social movements."[54] Unlike Giorgio Bocca's analysis, in which terrorism becomes the only way to feel alive in this world where the young no longer have faith in the established political parties, Melucci's schema places terrorism in the context of the structural development of *other* social movements. We may now trace the outlines of two distinct moments in this development/regression process of social movements by looking at, respectively, the ultraleft and the Red Brigades.

THE ULTRALEFT

A catch-all phrase for the numerous movements, parties, and "areas" that developed to the left of the PCI in Italy, the ultraleft traces its origin to the student movement of 1968 and the workers movement ("Hot Autumn") of 1969. It was during this period that the most militant of these groups, Potere Operaio, was formed and commenced, in September 1969, publication of its own homonymous newspaper. In the early 1970s several other ultraleft groups, each with its own news and ideological organ, including Lotta Continua, Manifesto (a group of ex-PCI members) and Avanguardia Operaia (which grew out of a combination of 1968 student experiences and 1969 factory "unitary committees of the base" [CUB] experiences) had formed. These groups grew up largely in the northern industrial cities of Torino, Milano, and Genova. Their attitude toward the PCI was one of hostility; they claimed that the PCI had evolved into, at best, a reformist, social democrat party and, at worst, an apologist for the DC and the capitalist interests that party represented. The early activities of these various groups consisted of school occupations, the promotion of political strikes, the occupation of vacant houses, and the purveyance of "controinformazione" (counterinformation). The latter took many forms and, according to Patrizia Violi, originated in the creativity of communication forms developed during the French May 1968.[55] The basic idea behind all forms of counterinformation was to provide alternative versions of the life of factories, schools, the police, the fascists (this was, after all, the period of the "strategy of tension"), and the ultraleft movement than that provided by the establishment mass media. Later in this chapter we will describe one instance of particularly significant counterinformation. Here it is important to note that this attempt to open up both the flow and the content of the information included another crucial element. The *form* of the communication of information was to be opened up as well. Here, particularly, language was a key. Groups such as Lotta Continua sought to rennovate political discourse by rejecting the bureaucratic jargon of the establishment media presentation of politics. The aim of this move was to make the discussion of politics relevant to the actual experience of the workers and the students.[56] Violi, in her analysis of the language of the ultraleft mass media claims that, while there was some initial success in re-creating political discourse, most of the groups, with the possible (and significant) exception of some of Lotta Continua's discourse, failed in this attempt and fell into a discourse that mirrored the establishment media. We will return to this important discovery in the Conclusion.

Potere Operaio, one of the most militant of the ultraleft groups, could trace its roots back to the critical analysis of those sociologists who studied the workers movement and factory conditions in the early sixties. In 1961, Raniero Panzieri founded the magazine *Red Notebooks* in which these studies could be published. The *Red Notebooks* group dissolved in 1965 but it had, in the meantime, spun off Potere Operaio. Potere Operaio itself disbanded in May of 1973 (this is an important fact for the Moro affair; the leaders of this group would, years later, be accused of meeting with and actually controlling the Red Brigades in 1978), and its members were, reflecting the amorphousness of the new host movement, absorbed into the militant area of Autonomia and into Lotta Continua. Toni Negri, one of Potere Operaio's original founders, looked back on this period in a 1979 interview with Italian journalist Giorgio Bocca: "One proof of the very rudimentary state of the organization, of the tendency of the comrades never to close the door on the [more nebulous] 'movement' is that we came to 1973 and to the dissolution without even having [written] a statute [of member's rights and responsibilities]."[57]

The mid-seventies saw a change of venue for the groups of the ultraleft. Violent actions escalated as demonstrations ultimately developed into armed combat with the police. The moment of greatest intensity of violence came in 1977 with the eruption of what has generally come to be known as "The Movement." This was a period marked by the occupation of many universities—Rome, Palermo, Naples, Florence, Torino, and, finally, the most violent of all, Bologna. One movement exponent described the general goals of these occupations: "University communities became general quarters for a wave of social struggle that had as a fundamental theme the refusal of the capitalist organization of work, the rejection of that system which generates exploitation and unemployment as the two poles of socialized work."[58]

One of the themes that wended its way through all of the writings (books, magazines, scholarly journals, pamphlets, newspapers) of these various groups was this question of violence. The epoch of the violent "strategy of tension" seemed to be diminishing. The ultraleft exposed the instrumental utilization of a part of the state by the fascist terrorists. The police, secret service, and the governments of the years 1969–1974 tolerated and, at times, even promoted right-wing attacks in order to create a climate of tension in Italy that was, in its turn, supposed to promote public demand for law and order. The net result of this chain of causes and anticipated effects was that the state security forces would be able to crack down on the leftist activists (many of whom were also being blamed for the paradigmatically right-wing attacks—no chances were being taken by these security forces). Thus violence was not, in the mid-seventies, a new element in Italian political life. Whatever else one might say of their methods, the ultraleft cannot be blamed for having *introduced* violence into the Italian society. However, for several reasons, the issue of violence was one of great preoccupation for the ultraleft activists. Perhaps the single greatest cause for this preoccupation was the expressed need of these groups to distinguish themselves from terrorists such as the Red Brigades. Even before this particular issue was the focus, an elaborate debate had evolved. Basically the discussion of violence followed two distinct and opposed lines of reasoning. The first eschewed all violence and (somewhat along the same lines of the PCI) declared that all violence was fascist. For example, Lidia Menapace, in a preface to a collection titled *On Violence: Politics and Terrorism: A Debate within the Left,* wrote: "It is difficult if not impossible, not to be infected by this destructive crisis. But it is important not to forget what is its source, its contaminating source. In this sense, violence, that which is individual, physical and exhalts and justifies the 'exemplary act' as an end in itself, is always fascism, that is, is always the oppressive face of bourgeois power that finds its way inside each one of us."[59] Menapace does go on to distinguish this form of violence from a legitimate self-defense (which she, herself, had practiced during the Resistance). However, the overriding message from her essay is a multilateral refutation of the violent activities of Autonomy, the state, and the terrorists.

The other major strand of this debate developed a qualified approval of violence: violence was an approprate method of struggle if and only if it was an expression of the will of the mass. Discussing the antiviolence front of the PCI-DC "coalition," one Lotta Continua group from Torino wrote in late 1977: "It is necessary to specify that this 'anti-violence front' has, as its primary goal, the political expropriation of the masses and is, from this perspective, allied to the class enemy who proposes the same object. We, instead, must be ready to develop the capacity of the movement to strike the enemy even with avant garde actions when these actions have a real mass reference. And it is on the mass representativeness, on the capacity and opportunity to develop politically and to develop the revolutionary process that we judge violence and the determined use of offensive weapons."[60]

While these tentative positions taken in the debate on violence were, in truth, satisfying to no one (demonstrators were, it must be recalled, being killed and wounded on a weekly basis), the real dilemma was that of evaluating the violence of the Red Brigades, particularly in the light of the Moro kidnapping. We will see, in this study, the way in which the ultralefts' alleged and/or real kinship with the BR was used to discredit the various ultraleft movements. Thus, this debate would, in the spring of 1978, take on a singular importance. The emblematic form in which the accusations of co-involvement would, in 1978, appear was the following, written by terrorist-scholar Vittorfranco Pisano: "Elements of the *Autonomy* or even of the broader 'movement' often wittingly or unwittingly abet the work of the terrorists through their own violence and agitation. Such elements are often seen as being auxiliaries of terrorism."[61]

Now, it would be wrong simply to say that this issue was ever definitively and unequivocably addressed and resolved by the ultraleft. (In fact, two ex-Potere Operaio exponents, Lanfranco Pace and Franco Piperno, would insist that ambiguity was the proper stance in view of the more than ambiguous situation.)[62] However, many attempts were made to distinguish the ultraleft from the Red Brigades, and these attempts centered, as usual, on the discussion of violence—not always though, as Bocca points out, on violence per se: "The 'autonomists' or at least their theoreticians do not discuss armed violence in itself: some of them come right out and affirm that to discuss violence is a pure waste of time given that violence is implicit in the class struggles: rather, they discuss and harshly criticize the BR's attempt to 'institutionalize this violence, to legitimate it, to newly stamp it in special [BR] courts which condemn to death in the name of an abstract proletariat.' "[63]

All of the internal debates were defensive in tone, and, in this the ultraleftists had little choice. Perhaps the most significant recognition of this entire period was that of ultraleftist Franco Berardi's when he noted that the strength of the Red Brigades was directly proportional to the weakness of the Movement. Thus, in March of 1978, after a year of actions and demonstrations that both proposed and elicited (on the part of the state) violence, the ultraleft was in a particularly vulnerable position. A Movement convention held in September of 1977 had failed to develop a positive program, leaving the Movement in a state of dispersive crisis. The Movement's ambiguity and, at times, arcane intellectualism was felt to be too threatening, ironically, by both the BR and the state. The ultraleft would thus become, during and after the Moro affair, a target shot at from both sides.

THE RED BRIGADES

Contemporary terrorism wounds that which seems to us to be one of the few judgments of value we all find ourselves in accord with—that the democratic regime is the best and that it has fewer defects than any other mode [of government] yet tried.[64]

1878, like 1978, was a peak year for terrorist actions. 1878 was the year in which the highest number of attempts were made on the lives of European monarchs in the nineteenth century, and 1978 was the year in which the late twentieth-century terrorist era would reach a peak in Italy with approximately 3000 incidents,[65] including assassinations and kidnappings. But numbers do little to give a sense of terrorism in context, and it is important for our purposes here to locate 1978's terroristic episodes in the general historical context of armed combat in Italy.

Various forms of terrorism have been extant in Italy throughout its history. Sardinian bandits, the Carbonari brothers, the late nineteenth-century anarchists have all carried on their diversely motivated, separate wars. We are most interested here in that early brand of terrorism which aimed at being overtly political, the anarchist terrorists. These early anarchist groups, whose actions could be said to have culminated with the assassination of King Umberto I at the start of this century, viewed their actions as constituting a "propaganda of the fact." In other words, they considered their various attempts to be exemplary rather than directly constitutive of a revolutionary uprising. Marletti claims that the period of time during which this ideology of exemplary actions prevailed was fairly circumscribed, lasting from around 1880–1910. The next major wave of terrorism can be located during the immediate post–World War I period and was pretty much the exclusive work of the fascists. We will later explore the structural distinctions between leftist and rightist terrorism as these distinctions, it will be seen, may be manipulated in order to present or misrepresent particular incidents as being either Left or Right. Here we need only state that the "squadristi" of Mussolini created a "reign of terror" sufficient to overwhelm a parliamentary government. It is important to note also that the aim of fascist terrorism has always differed sharply from anarchist or other leftist terrorism. Fascist terrorism "does not aim at teaching anything, it has no pedagogical element, except perhaps in the worst punitive sense—that of 'giving a lesson.' Its second priority is to provoke a reaction of uncontrolled fear."[66]

The concern here is with the most modern manifestations of terrorism in Italy, both red and black. We have already noted the most recent period of fascist (or neo-nazi) terrorism in Italy. This period began in December 1969 with the bombing massacre of Piazza Fontana in Milan. This incident set off a series of similar bombings. Blame was slow in coming and, when it did, it was initially placed on anarchists rather than fascists. One such case of what later came to be generally recognized as misattribution of blame was that of the anarchists Valpreda and Pinelli. Originally blamed for the Piazza Fontana bombing, these anarchists were both indicted and jailed. Pinelli died while in jail in an incident that was, at first, presented as suicide. It was actually in the investigation of this case that the Lotta Continua counterinformation campaign scored its first victory. The newspaper of the group published the results of its own investigation of the bombing and subsequent death of Pinelli. The true fascist culprits were identified, their links with the powerful men of Italy were detailed, and the cover-up of Pinelli's assassination was exposed. Many commentators have admitted that without this counterinformation campaign of Lotta Continua, many of the facts of the case would have remained submerged. But despite their efforts, Valpreda spent ten years in jail before the two neo-fascists, Freda and Ventura, were finally investigated and charged and convicted (though under rather casual surveillance in house arrest, from which they ultimately escaped). In fact, it was during the early months of 1978 (months coinciding with the Moro affair) that a new phase in the Piazza Fontana trial, aimed at exploring right-wing infiltration of anarchist circles at the time of the bombing, was in session (nine years after the incident). This trial would be covered by the press intermittently and half-heartedly. For example, it would never make *Corriere della Sera's* front page (which was dominated by the formation of the government, France's elections, the Red Brigades trial in Torino, and, after March 16, the Moro case) but could rather be found inside, in that section called "Internal News." We will have further occasion to reflect upon the differential attention payed to the various ongoing trials in this period. Further, perhaps reflecting the "riflusso" of the early eighties, Valpreda is again under investigation.

While some political commentators were, in the first year of this decade, shown to have been premature in their pronouncements of the end of the "strategy of tension" (i.e., before the Bologna train station bombing of August 1980 and the 1984 Christmas season bombing of the Florence-Milan train), it is unclear to what extent the right-wing activities will continue.[67]

While antifascist rhetoric continued to play a dominant legislative role in the early and mid-seventies (see, for instance, the official Parliamentary reports accompanying that piece of "exceptional" legislation, the "Legge Reale," passed in 1975, for its antifascist rhetoric of justification), the major focus of Italian criminological, military intelligence, governmental and media attention since the beginning of the seventies has been on leftist terrorism, of which the Red Brigades was one wing. We will now briefly trace the origins and history of the BR (Red Brigades) from several years before its inception in 1971 up to the year of its most elaborate operation, the kidnapping of Moro, 1978.[68]

There have been approximately three generations of Red Brigades. We are interested here in the first two generations, the second of which was responsible for the kidnapping of Moro. The first generation of Red Brigades itself had many different roots, the main sources of which can be reduced to three: (1) the atmosphere of the northern Italian city of Trento which, in 1962, was the home of both the most progressive wing of the DC and the first, fully accredited, university department of sociology in Italy; (2) the general political climate of the region around Reggio Emilia, the PCI stronghold and the region where the PCI and its youth organization FGCI were the most open and progressive; (3) the Europewide student/worker movement of the late sixties.

Renato Curcio, one of the BR's founders, came out of the Trento Catholic/Sociologist matrix. One of Curcio's early political involvements was in the 1967–1968 "Movement for a Negative University" in Trento. This movement proposed the teaching of anticourses that had overtly revolutionary readings and agendas. Such a proposal was not uncommon at Trento nor was it immediately squelched by the university authorities. Francesco Alberoni, a left-wing sociologist, had been brought to teach at Trento specifically in order to promote, but channel, academically progressive enthusiasm. One emblematic and prophetic student document, published in November 1966, claimed that "the intent of sociology to study society inevitably has social consequences, as the sociologist operates on a reality that cannot help being political, the sociologist is necessarily a 'political being.' "[69] No one was entitled to be neutral.

Curcio was, along with his companion and future wife, Maria Cagol, also a practicing Catholic. Although it is not clear to what extent they were religiously involved, it is interesting to note that, even as they were about to leave Trento for a life of political activism in Milano in 1969, they were married in church.

Meanwhile, other future BR members were experiencing their primary political involvements in Emilia Romagna, the region in which Bologna stands as a symbol of long-term PCI dominance in city adminstration. Youth such as Roberto Ognibene, Prospero Gallinari, and Alberto Franceschini, all of whom would be defendants in the 1978 Torino trial, were, in the late sixties and early seventies, moving leftward from the FGCI starting points. The class backgrounds of these activists varied—some were children of (PCI-leaning) workers, some children of "contadini" (farmers), and some, like Curcio, children of middle-class parents—while the level of education of the future brigatisti was fairly high, with several university graduates among their ranks.[70]

The BR historian, Alessandro Silj, has noted the many common elements shared by the Reggiano future-brigatisti: ". . . a categorically negative judgment regarding the political, economic and social conditions of the country, the incompatabilty (theoretically perceived and personally suffered) between a certain type of revolutionary communist militancy and the strategy of the PCI; a dogmatism and, let us say it, a 'moral' rigor that leads to, among other things, a refusal of every compromise; an impatience that goes beyond a strictly generational thing—one that also passes judgment on the vain wait of 30 years of reformism; and finally the valuing of the results that armed struggle can bring."[71]

By 1970, Curcio was in Milano and having frequent correspondence with the radical group Sinistra Proletaria. This group belonged to the Marxist-Leninist sector of the new ultraleft social and political movements and published such newspapers as *To Serve the People*. Of this sector and its papers, Violi writes the following: "Their press, in general minimally informative, is often full of self-exhaltation and is extremely sectarian as regards other [ultra-left] groups."[72]

Self-exhaltation and sectarianism, it is not surprising to find, characterized the Red Brigades publications as well (ample examples of this style will be presented in this study). Further, if style means anything, and a dramaturgic approach claims it means quite a lot, Violi is indicating a radical difference between two groups, Potere Operaio and Sinistra Proletaria (which eventually flowed into the Red Brigades), that Italian officials would, in 1979, consider to have been one and the same.

Late in 1970, Curcio's group, known at that time as simply "the group of the apartment" (where they met), fused with Sinistra Proletaria. The clandestine group, Red Brigades, was composed of those members of Sinistra Proletaria who believed that the moment of armed struggle had arrived. We are now in 1971. The rest of the group will flow into the general area of Autonomia Operaia.

This first generation of the Red Brigades would become known as the "Historic Nucleus," and it would be this group that would be on trial in Torino in March of 1978. The first year of BR actions consisted of setting automobiles on fire and clandestine distribution of pamphlets within Milan industrial plants. Their first major action was carried out in 1972 when, on March 3, a personnel manager at Sit-Siemens, Idalgo Macchiarini, was kidnapped. This kidnapping, short in duration and without injury in its result, was followed by five others in the period before Curcio's capture in 1974. One analyst of this early period, Pisano, unwittingly reveals the relative innocence of it by indignantly referring to one victim, Vincenzo Casabona, who, according to Pisano, had been "subjected to a haircut." Things changed, however, after the Curcio capture and Mara's (Maria Cagol, wife of Renato Curcio) death in a skirmish with the police in June 1975. The level of violence increased. This also marked the moment of the dissolution of the first BR generation and the formation of the second.

It is important to note some of the operational differences between the first and second generations. While the first generation had begun with pamphleting, burning cars, kneecappings that resulted in the eventual return of the hostage and only toward the end became involved in violent police skirmishes that resulted in deaths, the second wave of Red Brigades members often shot to kill. Thus one of the first noted differences was an increased level of violence and a miltary efficiency to go with it. Under the leadership of Mario Moretti, himself a member of the first generation (but one of the few not imprisoned), the Red Brigades defined their actions as constituting a "war against the state." From the perspective of the incarcerated historic BR group, these new cadres were qualitatively different. In the words of Alberto Franceschini, there were "the 'hot' brigatisti in jail and the 'cold' ones seeking shelter in a bureaucratic logic, outside and in power. The automatic victor was the party executive, the bureaucratic machine with its prudent but totalizing militarism."[73]

Thus both an increasing bureaucratization and militarization may be cited as characterizing this second wave of BR activists. This would be the generation responsible for *carrying out* the Moro kidnapping. Two things need to be clarified here. First, though a differing orientation to the organization marked those who were in and those who were outside of jail, we will see how these differences were blurred, both by the BR members and the other Moro social drama protagonists during the fifty-five day period of Moro's sequestration and the ongoing Turin trial of the BR historic group. Second, while the actual individuals participating in Moro's kidnapping have been identified as belonging to this second generation, it is necessary to repeat that it is not the concern of this study to reveal who "really" was behind Moro's kidnapping. As noted above, many lacunae in this "story" still remain.

The period of second-generation activity, 1976–1978, was one in which kneecappings and assassinations came to dominate BR activities. This was truly a transition moment for the BR, one in which as noted they moved from a belief in and practice of exemplary actions to that of "class war." Historians of political violence have, in fact, presented this moment and this transition as being the crucial difference between the nineteenth-century anarchists and modern leftist terrorists: "The former [anarchists] constituted themselves around the exemplary gesture and presented themselves rather as pedagogues of violence. Today, while the first BR actions, for example the kidnappings of Macchiarini, Labate and Amerio, still had many elements of the exemplary action of classical terrorism about them . . . the successive operations aspire more and more to present themselves as guerrilla actions, true and proper, as an expression of an 'armed party' at the head of a proletariat that is about to inaugurate a civil war."[74]

Actually, the only thing that the modern terrorists would allow that they shared with their historical antecedents were their principle organizational schemes. While the stated theoretical grounding of the BR was Marxism-Leninism, the actual organization of the BR cells was based on a combination Carbonari "secret society"/ Tupamaros guerrilla structural model (the early BR often referred to themselves as "Italian Tupamaros"). The BR cells were composed of members who, theoretically, only knew one or two other members, took all orders from one cell leader, and thus would be largely uninformative informants if ever captured or turned "pentito" (stool pigeon).[75]

Before Moro was kidnapped, the targets of the BR attacks had been individuals at the middle levels of many spheres. Businessmen, journalists, government representatives had all been the victims of kneecappings and, in the later period, assassinations. Moro constituted a "salto qualitativo" (a qualitative leap) for the BR, and his abduction required a technical efficiency of the highest order. The Italian public was, or course, familiar with the Red Brigades from their previous exploits, but the media coverage had never before approached the levels it would reach during the fifty-five days of Moro's sequestration. And it is with the introduction of the mass media as our final major protagonist that we may reapproach the particular theory and methodology of this study.

THE MASS MEDIA

> One of the frequent reproaches lodged against the Italian press, particularly by American journalists, is that of almost never separating the news from the comment [about the news]. This is explained historically . . . the Italian daily paper was born as an expression of power more than as a public service, as an instrument of a political belief more than as a means or participation in a local reality . . . the journalist . . . in his hurry to make a comment, doesn't even give you the news.[76]

While the national mass media in Italy exerts a considerable social and political influence, they have attained only a mediocre level of public consumption. This paradoxical presence in Italy can be attributed partly to the fascist epoch's repression of any press but that published by the Fascist party, partly to the predominance (still noteworthy) of regional identities over a national identity, and partly to the monopoly of the RAI (Radio audizione italiana) television and radio national public corporation that until 1976 (when Law no. 202 was passed allowing for privately owned channels and stations to operate at local levels) was absolute.

As far as the press is concerned, media analyst Giovanni Bechelloni has described a situation in which "there has never existed a true daily paper of the 'popular' variety; the Italian newspaper is a typical mixed product, one which was directed toward the ruling political class and to the politically active part of the middle classes. There has never existed a 'national' paper, present in all of the country, with the exception—beginning with the second world war—of the Communist party paper, *L'Unità.*"[77] Thus that which is

published privileges both political discourse and politically sophisticated, powerful, and active readers. Bechelloni argues that all of
the mass media in Italy, and not only the press, have been viewed as
instruments to be used by the political and economic powers-that-
be. (One salient indicator of the restricted audience of newspapers
is the fact that only one out of every ten Italians buys a daily
newspaper, making Italy's national "readership" lower than most
other European countries.)[78] Thus large private companies, such as
Fiat *(La Stampa)*, Montedison *(Il Messaggero)*, and Rizzoli *(Corriere della Sera)*, own controlling interest in many major newspapers. From the state side, the Christian Democrat–dominated government controls ANSA, the main national news agency, and ENI,
the nationalized hydrocarbon conglomerate, owns the paper *Il
Giorno*.

In the period immediately following World War II, newspapers
published in Italy were exclusively those attached to political parties (this was the initial decision of the CLN [National Liberation
Committee]). This media partisanship resulted, according to
Bechelloni, from the general loss of memory, after thirty years of
the Fascist party press monopoly, of any other model of "informa-
tional" press. One effect of this initial restriction of the field was
that the concept of "journalist" was collapsed into the concept of
"militant." The idea of a journalist aiming toward the objectivity of
a "professional" and not necessarily supported by a specific party is
only now, in the early eighties, taking hold.[79]

The fifties and the sixties were years during which those papers
not directly connected with a specific party tended to support,
rather than criticize, the establishment economic, social, and political institutions—in other words, the DC. This conformity was
coupled, especially in weekly periodicals, with a tendency to highlight "escapist" articles featuring movie stars and exiled monarchs.

The radio and television in Italy has had its own history of
dependence on the state. Television came to Italy on January 3,
1954. At that time, and until the 1976 law declaring the monopoly
constitutionally illegal (RAI still holds the monopoly over *national*
transmission), the RAI corporation controlled not only both
national channels (channel 1 under the aegis of the DC, and channel
2 largely dominated by the Socialists) but forbade any private
stations from developing. Further, it was not until 1975 that a law
(no. 103) was passed that transferred actual control over the RAI

from the DC-monopolized government to the more heterogeneous parliament. As a result of law 103, an administrative council for the RAI was established that was to be specifically representative in its make-up (though it did not turn out to be proportionally so: in 1980, e.g., it was composed of seven DC, four PCI, three PSI, one Social Democrat, and one Republican). One significant trend is cited by Bechelloni. It seems that in the realm of radio the private stations have managed to outstrip the public stations in afternoon and evening listeners. Private television is also gaining ground, with the public channels still obtaining 80–85 percent of viewers and private channels obtaining the remaining 15–20 percent. One reason for this popularity of the private channels is that many of them respond to and represent the interests and perspectives of those, such as the Radical and other extremist parties, who are not structurally included in the RAI council and who do not recognize the public networks as representing them.

Despite their establishment origins however, the Italian mass media were as provoked as were their backers by the movements of 1968–1969. Giorgio Galli writes that in this period weekly magazines, such as *L'Espresso, Panorama* (both left leaning), and *Tempo* (right leaning), and many newspapers were, in 1969–1970, already developing critical interpretations of contemporary Italian society. "[They] were not accepting as a given the 'truths' that the government presented regarding the cause of the strong social tension and of the episodes of terrorism that constituted the first wave of the strategy of tension."[80]

In the seventies, this incipient criticism against what Bechelloni has termed "the optimism pill of mass culture of the 60's" would explode into the phenomenon of "counterinformation." Outside of and against the monopoly of the RAI, the independent presses and radio and television stations arose to critique the dominant political class. John Downing, in his book, *Radical Media,* notes that in 1978–1979 there were nearly 100 self-managed, (self-declared) revolutionary radio stations throughout Italy. While each had its own character, format, and use of language, these radio stations, such as Radio Popolare in Milan, Radio Alice in Bologna, and Radio Città Futura in Rome (the last being one of the stations whose March 17 transcripts we shall be examining) were similar in expressing a desire for an engaged interaction with the listening public, a focus on the major issues of students and workers as *experienced* through local actions, and for an internal structure that was markedly democratic. At the same time, such independent presses as *Lotta Continua* and *il manifesto* had each emerged out of new movements to the left of the PCI. Ultimately, the papers would assert their "independence" from their own ultraleftist party lines. As with the radio stations, these newspapers stressed the issues that affected and concerned (in the case of *Lotta Continua*) the "emarginati"—those individuals pushed to the margins of society and (in the case of *il manifesto*) the leftist intellectuals disaffected with the PCI (*il manifesto* was originally linked to Pdup—Party of Proletarian Unity).

Together, these radio stations and newspapers provided Italy, during the period in which we are interested (*Lotta Continua* was forced to close in 1981 after an unsuccessful campaign to find financial backers), with "counterinformation." They picked up stories the establishment media had dropped or deemphasized, they focused on local experiences, they criticized the establishment parties (each from a slightly different angle), and they sought to include the voices of their reader and listenership in their discourse. One of our purposes here in closely studying the mass media's role in the Moro affair is to gauge how well this trend toward counterinformation and criticism withstood the pressures of the extraordinary event.

Our more immediate concern has to do with another reason for analyzing the response of the mass media. This concern is best expressed by posing the question: "In what way(s) were the mass media 'protagonists' of the Moro social drama?" To answer this question we must reintroduce the idea of "spectacle" and specify our claim that the Moro affair developed as the Moro social drama largely, although not entirely, through the services that the mass media offered to the other protagonists.

Thus, one purpose of mass media was that of offering itself as a stage on which the various duels were fought, the most obvious (although not necessarily the most important) one being that between the Red Brigades and the Italian state.

The idea of the mass media acting as a stage for the presentation of deviance is not a new one. In fact, the *idea* has become commonplace. But the exploration of this idea via a case study of an actual moment of it has, with the exception of Joseph Gusfield's work on drunken driving, and Todd Gitlin's work on the sixties radicals in the United States, been largely neglected.[81]

In conjunction with the above media/stage insight, several scholars, notably Kai Erikson and Elias Canetti, have noted that the mass media became a stage for the presentation (and punishment) of deviance at the precise moment in history when public execution ceased. It is useful to quote Erikson in full here: "Today of course, we no longer parade deviants in the town square or expose them to the carnival atmosphere of a Tyburn, but it is interesting that the 'reform' which brought about this change in penal practice coincides almost exactly with the development of newspapers as a medium of mass information. Perhaps this is no more than an accident of history, but it is nonetheless true that newspapers (and now radio and television) offer much the same kind of entertainment as public hangings or a Sunday visit to the local gaol. A considerable portion of what we call 'news' is devoted to reports about deviant behavior and its consequences, and it is no simple matter to explain why these items should be considered newsworthy or why they should command the extraordinary attention they do . . . they constitute one of our main sources of information about the normative outlines of society. In a figurative sense at least, morality and immorality meet at the public scaffold, and it is during this meeting that the line between them is drawn."[82]

Although the deviant is normally presented on the pages and screens of the mass media *as* a deviant whose actions ought to be execrated and punished, many media analysts as well as politicians have publicly expressed their concern that media attention paradoxically legitimizes and/or makes celebrities of these deviants.[83] Jim Karyan, former public television director in the United States, was quoted in the DC weekly magazine, *La Discussióne*, as declaring that not only did television and terrorists share a "community of interest" but that television offered the terrorists the opportunity to become "stars."[84] On the other hand, such theorists of political terrorism as Barbano have remarked upon the way in which the random mixing of "stories" in the mass media, sports, politics, advertisements, all appearing in rapid succession, has diminished if not vanquished the symbolic significance of the "propaganda of the act." Thus, regarded from this perspective, everything broadcast or published becomes undifferentiated "news."

Both points of view, that declaring that media attention naturally elevates the terrorist's status and that holding that media attention diminishes the particularity of the terrorist action, agree that media attention and availability to terrorists serve to create dramatic performance. Bechelloni has attributed this performance creation to a general "cultura di massa" (mass culture) which prepares both the journalists and the audience to experience public events as spectacles: "By now whoever writes and reads the newspapers, whoever produces and tunes into the radio and the television, are all immersed in a universe of messages strongly marked by the 'cultura di massa' and its most popular genres: the western, the police drama, the war movie, the adventure film, etc . . . ours is a society of spectacle and politicians and journalists cannot escape the realization that its messages and words are read and de-ciphered in a context of messages dominated by the 'cultura di massa.'"[85]

Thus we have finally arrived at Guy Debord's "society of the spectacle" (the preface of the fourth Italian edition of his book is devoted to the Moro affair), in which all protagonists are predisposed, in a Gombrichian way, to both experience an event as a dramatic performance and, to the best of their abilities, attempt to manipulate the performative mechanisms (including the genre). In the Moro social drama this includes political parties, media organs, Red Brigades, and Moro among others.

One final mass media–related issue must be introduced. If the mass media can be a protagonist by providing a stage for duels fought between other protagonists, it can be a protagonist, also paradoxically, by *removing* itself from the fray and denying the combatants a stage. In other words, it can institute a news blackout. In fact, such a news blackout was imposed on the West German mass media during the Schleyer kidnapping when, as Werner Sonne, the radio representative to the government at the time, has indicated, not only would the media not report terrorist-related news but it would also broadcast government-fabricated news that was simply false.[86] During the Moro affair, Marshall McLuhan's recommendation that the Italian mass media agree to a self-imposed news blackout would provoke much commentary (pro and con), but ultimately such a self-censorship did not come about. As well, the Italian government would choose not to impose a blackout on the Italian mass media as the West German government had done during the Schleyer affair. However, even though the general decision was to keep the channels open, there were many strategic decisions that would still have to be made vis-à-vis *what* would be published and broadcast and what, if any, editorial lines were to be taken toward what was thus displayed. As it turned out, these decisions about selective presentation would be, as we shall see, particularly thorny ones for the Italian mass media. There would be a plethora of documents that would arrive, often directly, to the studios and editorial rooms of various media organs; nine BR communiques, two photographs of Moro, numerous letters from Moro, texts of speeches from Italian politicians, the pope and the U.N. secretary general, to name some of the more outstanding. Finally, some communications scholars have claimed that the entire putative "blackout dilemma" is gratuitous, that in a country such as Italy, with a rich underground network of "counterinformation," a blackout simply could not be achieved. Umberto Eco has noted: "A piece of news squelched by one newspaper would be transmitted by an independent radio station, squelched by the radio, it would be carried by pamphlets, manifestos, messages written on walls, the verbal drum-beat. This has been a great democratic conquest—the information channels control each other. But then, to invoke silence and censorship regarding certain news items becomes beyond immoral, technically impossible."[87]

I do not wish here, in this introductory section, to present a flattened-out discussion of the reality creating, sustaining, or denying qualities of the mass media. Obviously the issue of deciding what, if anything, to publish is full of subtleties. For example, the decision to publish a Red Brigades statement leads to many further decisions: How do we publish the statement—in its entirety, or only fragments? Do we publish it alone or with a comment and rebuttal? Do we put it on the front page or bury it inside? The mass media have the power, according to the ways that they resolve these questions, to change the valences (positive or negative, strong or weak) of the other protagonists. We will see if that power maintained its independence or, in the heat of the crisis, actively remembered its party or state or capital benefactors. We will also be concerned to discover the way in which other news was handled during the weeks of the Moro affair: Did the media organs neglect these other events, or did they sustain the public discourse on them? Such attention or neglect, media analysts claim, does effect the trajectory of the news itself. Here we will ask, If terrorism holds center stage for months, what happens to such issues as inflation, unemployment, or, as in Italy, a scandal such as Lockheed? Similarly, as we have asked already, if trials of leftist terrorists dominate, what happens to the reporting of concurrent right-wing terrorist trials? This study is concerned with such issues and will, in the course of analysis, directly address them.

While several other protagonists of the Moro social drama, including Pope Paul and the then secretary general of the United Nations, Kurt Waldheim, will be introduced at the point of the story where they enter the stage, one protagonist must be acknowledged at the outset. This protagonist, we will see, had a very peculiar role, the variations of which were hypothesized in the Introduction and in the "Legitimation Crisis" section earlier in this chapter. We are, of course, referring here to the audience of the Moro social drama, the Italian public. Granting that "in no other society preceding the advent of the mass media was it theoretically possible for all of the citizens to become conscious of public affairs and even to know who were the principle protagonists,"[88] consciousness of public events and of protagonists does not insure full, democratic disclosure of and participation in those events. The audience can simply be expected and conditioned to passively absorb and applaud the predetermined production. The performance, with its frantic rhythms, flash interviews with the powerful, and scenes of violence, is magically brought into the intimate sphere of the living room or even bedroom. It can be made to feel both familar and alien at the same time, both a reality you can touch and one that is light years away from daily life. It can also make you feel alone and powerless, not so much as a member of the masses as a member of nothing at all.

This contradiction, to be addressed more fully in the Conclusion, is at the heart of the discussions of "politics as spectacle," and the jolting intermittence of the calls for activity (voting and demonstrating in support of the extant state) and passivity (important policy decisions should be left to those in charge) results in what Alan Wolfe has termed the "schizophrenic citizen" of contemporary alienated politics. The mass media brought the Moro social drama into the homes of the Italian public. They brought it as news and as entertainment, a piece of theater, a consumable commodity. We will see that the protagonists also *lived* the Moro social drama as theater as we now begin our story.

3 Breach: The Country in the Streets

The Critical Event

A man of rigorous habit, Aldo Moro departed from his home in the Monte Mario section of Rome every morning at nine o'clock. On the morning of March 16, 1978, he had two stops, likewise habitual, planned; the nearby church of Santa Chiara, where he prayed every morning, and then Montecitorio, the site of the Parliament where the ratification debate on the Moro-fashioned government was due to begin. In this daily personal voyage between the institutions of the Church and the State, Moro, representing well his own personal and public history of institutional involvement, embodied the combination that his party claimed to represent on a grander scale.

Moro was escorted each day by five men, all from the south, all from poor backgrounds. The party rode in two cars, two men with Moro, three in the other car. Neither car was bullet proof. (A debate would subsequently arise as to why Moro had had no bulletproof car despite the repeated request of his chief bodyguard, Oreste Leonardi.) Midway between Moro's house and Santa Chiara lies Via Fani. It was on this street, now the site of one of the two Moro affair "shrines," that the abduction took place. Approximately ten people, male and female, carried out the ambush. Some wore disguises designed to make them appear to be Alitalia airline pilots waiting at a bus stop. Others waited in parked cars, another on a motorbike. At the corner of Via Fani and Via della Camiluccia, the Red Brigades closed in. One of their cars backed up from ahead, feigning a confused driver unsure about the road, one approached from behind. They opened up machine-gun fire, and in a minute it was over. All of the bodyguards were dead (four killed immediately, one later at the hospital). Moro was pushed into one of the commando cars which sped off. He was then transferred to a waiting, ambulance-styled van which, siren blaring, raced through the city to an unknown destination.

At approximately 10:15 A.M., newsrooms in Rome, Milan, and

Turin received phone calls in which the Red Brigades claimed responsibility for the attack and the kidnapping. They claimed nothing more. The unqualified nature of this acknowledgment on the part of the BR was both politically and dramaturgically significant, as we shall soon see. For the moment, it suffices to state that nothing was included in the Red Brigades' March 16 statement about Moro's possible release.

Thus Italy was left without a government, without a credible and effective political class, without even a legitimate opposition to step into the breach, and, now, without Aldo Moro. In the weeks before March 16, Moro had methodically pushed for passage of the government of his construction. This government, headed of course by a Christian Democrat, Guilio Andreotti, was to include the Socialist, Republican, Social-Democrat, Christian Democrat, and Liberal parties. And, in a precedent-breaking move, the Communist party was to be included in the parliamentary majority. This uneasy coalition was already straining to break apart. Some of the more right-wing factions of the Christian Democrat party were still resistant to the very notion of Communist inclusion. Moro had been painstakingly bringing these factions around to acceptance. Of this effort, Gianfranco Pozzesi, a journalist for the *Corriere della Sera,* wrote on March 2: "The current Christian Democrat leadership has been accused, not only suspected, of doing anything possible to make an agreement with the Communists, and of avoiding, at all costs, early elections. Those sustaining this thesis affirm that the Christian Democrat left-wing fears early elections because they know that a bitter electoral confrontation would alter the internal balance of the [DC] party in favor of its most intransigent members." And later in the same article: "When he wants to, Moro even succeeds in speaking clearly. But only a clarity close to brutality could recall the more emotional and confused [DC] parliamentarians to their responsibilities and to set right a situation that Tuesday morning seemed virtually compromised. Thanks to Moro, instead of that, Andreotti has received the [DC] leaders' mandate to conclude negotiations with the other parties."[1]

Thus, in spite of the factional strains, the last-minute departure of the Liberals from the coalition, the Socialist and Communist objections to the inclusion of the Social Democrats, and the anticipated long series of ratification debates before the Easter holiday deadline, the prospects had actually looked bright. Moro's work was largely done: he himself had no designated role in the new government of his creation. This could have made him a fairly liminal political actor if he was not, as he most definitely was, being spoken of as Italy's next president, the highly symbolic post scheduled to become vacant in December when then President Leone's term finished. There was no question, however, that the combination of the Lockheed scandal on one side and the residual intransigence toward accepting the Communists on the other could ultimately destroy the new coalition's chance of passing. Even Moro's persuasion might be ineffectual in overcoming this resistance. One might even argue that Moro's own role in the proceedings had reached its logical and political limits (particularly as his name was being tentatively linked to the emergent Lockheed scandal, though he was soon cleared of involvement). Moro's current structural location may indeed have been critical but it was, given the projection of success for his governmental construction, to be incipiently, if temporarily, liminal.

In fact, newspaper articles on Moro were beginning to appear that were literary biographical in nature—a kind of summing up. One such article claimed that Aldo Moro's portrait could be found in the famous nineteenth-century novel by Manzoni, *The Marriage Vows.* We will find other such examples of media attempts to categorize or "fix" Moro by connecting his persona to historical or literary archetypes.

Whatever symbolic role Moro had been meted out, he had constituted the linchpin of the complex mechanism of the Historic Compromise. With Moro gone, the mechanism could have flown instantly apart. This, at least on the surface, did not happen. Instead, the coalition, bereft of Moro as a reference point, had to find some other grounds for staying together. These grounds had, in the midst of the crisis, to be discovered and publicly accomplished. And its accomplishment constituted the first phase of the Moro social drama: the Breach.

The Structure of a Breach

The initial phase of the social drama, the Breach, may appear to be both too precipitous and too brief in duration to augur a significant social crisis. And, in fact, our Breach consisted of one twenty-four hour period from the morning of March 16, 1978, to the morning of March 17, 1978. According to Victor Turner, however, the breach only seems to be precipitous and is rather "the expression of a deeper division of interests and loyalties than appears on the surface."[2] Such divisions have usually been some time in the making. In this chapter, the Breach phase of the Moro social drama will be analyzed. Turner's notion of breach will be utilized in this analysis for its ability to follow the protagonists' initial responses to a serious threat to social stability. As was emphasized in the Introduction, however, each social and political event has a unique procedural logic and unique generic tendencies, and it is one of the primary aims of this study to discover the specific procedure and genre of the Moro social drama and to account for the ways in which such patterns evolved. Only then may we attempt to theoretically connect the aesthetic outcomes with the political outcomes. Thus the dramaturgic concepts cannot be—nor would Turner propose that they be—applied formulaicly or imposed upon the events. Rather, they can provide a guide for listening to the protagonists at various moments in social dramas and for interpreting the transitional phases.

The key characteristics of a social drama's Breach phase are the following: (1) the Breach must disrupt what Turner calls a "key relationship" within the social order, (2) must be timed and positioned (the setting) so that this disruption will be marked by the relevant public(s), (3) must be significantly rich in its symbolic presentation.

While the above definition differs somewhat from Turner's in that it emphasizes both the initial symbolic presentation and the specific (thus variable) participation of the audience, it is fundamental to begin with Turner's explication. (Turner includes the structural criterion of a rich symbolic presentation only in the Reconciliation/Schism phase, though of course he is sensitive to its presence all through the social drama.) According to Turner, the Breach stage of the social drama provides both the setting and many of the goals for the entire drama ahead. The particular form in which the Breach occurs determines the contours of the social drama. But what is the nature of a Breach? Turner writes: "The first stage [of a social drama] is often signalized by the overt, public breach of some norm or rule governing the key relationship which has been transformed from amity to opposition."[3] The rules involved can be rules of morality, law, custom, or etiquette.

Two key terms stand out in Turner's definition: *public* and *key relationship*. Our task is to explore the way in which Moro's kidnapping was indeed a public breach of a rule or norm governing a key relationship in the society. Further, we will gauge the richness and meanings of the symbolism of presentation. But first, by way of counterpoint, the Lockheed scandal will be analyzed as an affair that did *not* eventuate in a social drama, one in which a Breach was not declared.

COUNTERPOINT: THE LOCKHEED SCANDAL

Breaches are recognized and legitimated in much the same ways that other social phenomena, movements, and problems are.[4] They have their "moral entrepreneurs" and their public arenas of action. They are contoured and, according to many analysts, rearranged by the mass media.[5] Their ability to be recognized as a bonafide Breach is always *contingent*. And some situations which may appear to meet the criteria of constituting a Breach will, for reasons we will now explore, never be recognized as such.

The Lockheed scandal and others like it involved moral discrepancies and infractions of what political scientist Murray Edelman calls "unchallenged rules implicitly permitting evasions and explicitly fixing penalities."[6] On the other hand, political plots and, it will be shown, terrorist actions involve attempts to subvert "rules asserting the exclusive validity of a belief-disbelief system which is challenged by a heresy . . . Symbolically, the two kinds of law enforcement amount to the difference between mutual threat (the command) and mutual role-taking (the game)."[7]

Thus what is essentially different about these two types of infractions is not the extent of damage inflicted on a society but rather the *kind* of damage inflicted and the differential natures of the responses with which they are met. Terrorists burning the car of a Fiat director in the name of the proletariat are made to appear "naturally" more frightening and are met with greater repressive measures than are top-level administrators of the state or military who are involved in the disappearance of millions in funds destined, to give a true-life example, to reconstruct an earthquake-destroyed region. For those whose sense of justice is more disturbed by the plight of people without homes than by the destruction of an automobile, the former act *appears* to do less social damage than the latter.[8]

Despite the hegemony of the Christian Democrats in Italy, the

Lockheed scandal, in the weeks prior to Moro's kidnapping, was beginning to be recognized as a major delegitimating event by both the ruling class and the public even though it was a "game"-like infraction. While the extant persuasive "command" campaign was aimed primarily at the ultraleft groups, spanning from the generally nonviolent Movimento to the more violent Autonomia to the Red Brigades themselves, the Lockheed "game" was slowly evolving into the "command" category itself. A further development of the implications of Edelman's schema here would propose that crises falling in the mutual threat (command) category reach a relatively quick and intense climax (usually involving the purgation of the finally identified contaminating enemy) and crises of the mutual role-taking kind (game) develop as wave after wave of scandals exhaust, over the long run, the possibilities of the participants' moral and/or political legitimacy.

Both types of public exposure and accusation can, then, be equally discrediting because both ultimately turn on moral issues. It is hard to say at what point the "game" violators lose all their credibility—how many times they must break the rules, or how many different rules (accepting bribes, nepotism, political favors) they must break before their claims to legitimacy are revoked. There is a fine line between being greeted by a public tolerant of the fact that "all politicians do X" and a public that withdraws its votes from a party composed of such politicians. It is at that point, perhaps, that the "game" infractions are suddenly revealed as "command" infractions, indicating that the two categories lie at different points on a single continuum of behavior labeled illicit. As Joseph Gusfield (1981) and Victor Lidz (personal communication) have pointed out, Nixon's role in the Watergate affair had this quality of transforming "dirty tricks" into heresy: "As public drama Watergate has many meanings, but one of those is its dramatizing of the rule of law—the doctrine that no person, even the president, ought to be beyond responsibility for illegal acts. At stake, then, is the legitimacy of the political order."[9] Nixon's heresy was to have pushed too hard and too often against the American belief in the sacred quality of the presidency.

Why then did the Lockheed scandal, one in a long series of scandals, not constitute a "Breach" in the same way that Moro's kidnapping did? Part of the answer lies with the issue of the *key relationship* which will be discussed below. Part, however, lies with the way in which the Christian Democrats, thanks largely to their capacity to successfully claim the role of definers of the legitimate contours of the Italian social/political map, prevented the Lockheed affair (which was swiftly becoming an Italian Watergate) from provoking a rupturing social drama by shifting the spotlight to Moro's kidnapping and inaugurating the Moro social drama. The Moro kidnapping permitted the Christian Democrats to postpone (they hoped permanently) the further development of the long-term corrosive "question of morality" initiated by the Lockheed revelations. No small-time caper, the Lockheed scandal eventuated in judicial proceeding in which, for the first time, the defendants included ex-ministers and, for the first time in postwar Italy, a president of the republic was forced to resign. Analogous occurrences were sufficient to keep millions of Americans glued to their televisions and radios for the summer of 1973 and to strain the foundations of the American political system almost to the breaking point. In Italy, Lockheed, despite its profound roots and results, all but disappeared.

THE SPECTACULARITY AND SETTING OF THE KIDNAPPING

In every way, Moro's kidnapping was a "natural" for public attention and concern. It was abrupt, unexpected, violent, and jarring. It took place in the capital of Italy, the city of Parliament and political party headquarters, the site of the Vatican and of the RAI headquarters. And it was, as are all kidnappings at the point of inception, an unfinished event. There was more to come.

Where exactly did the attack take place? According to the authors of a RAI study of the Moro kidnapping and of the media coverage of the day of abduction: "The attack takes place in the capital which is, at the same time, the seat of political power and of most of the communication and information services; even more, as some newscasts have hastened to underline, the zone of the kidnapping is extremely close to the main offices of the RAI."[10] We must underline the way in which this passage locates the kidnapping in a politically strategic context and, further, the way in which it personalizes the attack by emphasizing the nearness of the ambush to the RAI headquarters, almost as if the Red Brigades did it for the benefit of the RAI or, alternatively, as if the Red Brigades were actually targeting the RAI along with Moro. This was not an unusual assessment for the Moro social drama protagonists. Each participant, as we shall see, would view the kidnapping as a direct hit aimed at them.

Setting is indeed, however, an issue of much significance in an analysis of the Breach phase of a social drama. The setting can provide or deprive the protagonists of a necessary symbolic arsenal. In Moro's case, the lack of sufficient symbols of authority at the scene of attack would affect Moro's later bargaining power. Edelman observes: "Setting, one notices, fades in and out of attention in intriguing correspondence with . . . the need to establish or reinforce a particular definition of the self in a public official."[11] Here we recall that Moro was neither in his church of daily prayer (Santa Chiara) nor in the Parliament building (Montecitorio). He was *merely* on his way to Parliament to ratify a government of which, as we have noted, he would not even be a member. Thus at the precise moment of the assault, Moro was not the *physical* responsibility of any institution, despite his legitimate membership in both the Christian Democrat party and the Catholic church. The claim made here is that his physical absence from the official grounds of these institutions would make it easier for these institutions to disclaim Moro as one of their own further on in the Moro affair's development. Moro, at the scene of the attack, was liminal. An alternative initiating setting might have helped the Moro who would seek release right from the beginning. This particular public official's definition of self was not helped by being yanked out of a car on a shaded residential street rather than being yanked out of his senatorial seat, or church pew, for example.

In fact, in an interview with Giorgio Bocca, Red Brigades member Lauro Azzolini, indicted for participation in Moro's kidnapping, reflected on the exact choice of setting in a way that gives credence to our theoretical reflections: "We could have sequestered Moro either in Via Fani or in the church of Santa Chiara where he went to mass every morning. The sequester in the church was excluded because it was too risky, [it was] particularly politically risky."[12]

This statement certainly reveals a heightened sensitivity to the symbolic ramifications of setting on the part of the protagonists.

It is useful to compare this abduction scene, spectacular as it was from the point of view of military efficiency, with the more official and symbolically sedimented contexts of the American embassy hostages in Iran and the Spanish parliamentarians during the 1981 attempted coup d'état by the Guardia Civile. Both of these sets of hostages were attacked and sequestered in their respective official chambers of authority. These locations backed up their claims of legitimacy while also bolstering the legitimacy of the very institutions of embassy and parliament themselves. Thus, the abduction contexts in these two cases significantly lowered the possibility that either the United States government or the Spanish king would disclaim and/or virtually abandon the captives for any reason (including the adoption of a "never negotiate with a terrorist" stance, a unique form of abandonment). A strong case could be made for the contribution of the context (the parliamentary chamber setting in the Spanish incident) to the failure of the military coup. The deputies were in their rightful place and the Guardia Civile were *visually* the usurpers (made more so by the presence of the television cameras). Rather than force all of the deputies out of the Parliament, the conspirators invaded. This was tantamount to an admission that the notion "Parliament" had some significance, even for them. As well, one might ask if the same fiercely proprietary rhetoric and sustained, if largely ineffectual, initiative would have been mounted by the United States government in the United States—the Iran incident had, for example, a U.S. chargé d'affaires kidnapped in the marketplace and delivered to an unknown place, out of sight rather than in his embassy and sequestered right there.

Finally we come to the issue of the key relationship which will, in a sense, occupy the rest of this chapter and much of the entire book. For, bound up in the question, What was the key relationship that the breach disrupted? is the issue of identifying, defining who the parties of the relationship were. On a superficial level, we can easily identify the Red Brigades and Aldo Moro as the key parties of the breach. But it is only when we begin to look at whom or what these represented or stood for that we may really answer the key relationship question. We will, in fact, find many "Red Brigades" and many "Moros" in the Moro social drama. Thus the next section of this Breach chapter will present an analysis of the definition work performed by the identified participants in the Moro social drama at this stage of the event. This work constituted attempts to answer such questions as: Who are the Red Brigades? Who/what is the true "target"? In what condition (war, seige, etc.) does the attack leave

Italy? (The question, Who is Moro now? would most directly be confronted later in the social drama.)

Definition

All that has occurred up to an hour ago belongs, by now, to prehistory.[13]

One of the meanings of the word "rhetorical" is "persuasive." The definition work of the major participants in the Moro social drama was designed to be persuasive but was inevitably defensive in task and in tone. The aim of these protagonists (particularly the DC and PCI) was, we are claiming, to re-solder the legitimating link between themselves and their selected constituencies. They would attempt to accomplish this by persuading those audiences of the truth of one dominant message: the enemies come from without and Italy is united against them. Thus for the DC and the PCI as well as for other protagonists, as we shall see, there was apparently no *internal* long-term rift fragmenting Italy along many fault lines, the existence of which this Breach was merely exacerbating. Rather, these protagonists were the quickest to jump into the breach in order to declare that there *was* no breach: there was only the serious fact of an alien invasion (alien, of course, being defined differently by each protagonist).

But who were the Red Brigades? As discussed in Chapter 2, the Red Brigades had a known history, with origins in both the student movements of Emilia-Romagna and Trento and the Workers Autonomy area of Milano and other Northern industrial cities. But no history is innocent, and interpretors will emphasize now one aspect of a group or movement, now another aspect. Some particulars of orientation or action may disappear altogether. Allessandro Silj discusses this process in the chapter "The 'Catholic Matrix'" in his book *Never Again without a Rifle (Mai più senza fucile).* Silj refers to the process of highlighting the Catholic backgrounds and messianic tenor of the beliefs of some of the historic leaders of the Red Brigades. This highlighting process was cultivated in a debate within certain sectors of the left in Italy during the first years of the Red Brigade's appearance: "In reality, it is hardly possible to speak of a debate, but rather only of oblique references with which certain sectors of the left would like to liquidate the problem of violence, which they associate not with precise social and political conditions but rather with a sort of vice or original sin defined, exactly, as the 'Catholic matrix.'"[14]

This was written in 1977. In 1978, the left would shift its analysis to suit the needs of the moment. As will be evident, the Catholic aspects of the Red Brigades would be forgotten by the PCI in particular and replaced with the imputation (unsubstantiated) of a "fascist matrix" infusing the Red Brigades.

The symbolic valences of the differentially configured (by the Moro affair protagonists) Red Brigades can be calibrated along three separate, but interacting, oppositional pairs: indigenous versus foreign, common criminal versus political criminal, left versus right. These sets of markers are useful in discerning which actors were involved in the threatened key relationship. They also have significance for issues that concern the Italian self-image and the desire, on the part of some protagonists, to deny that a true Breach had occurred.

FROM WITHIN OR FROM WITHOUT

The first questions confronting the stunned protagonists (political parties, mass media, trade unions, the public) on the morning of March 16 were: Who are the Red Brigades? What is the nature of this aggression and, for some (selecting out and framing, as do all protagonists, the questions deemed important), against whom do we assert our strength as a collectivity? Oreste Scalzone, ultraleftist of the Potere Operaio group, wrote the following in the immediate aftermath of the Moro affair: "The only constant [in a mass of contradictory accusations linking the Red Brigades to secret services of various countries] is this obstinate will to find some explanation that proves that the Red Brigades are exogenous to this society, to the Italian situation of class contradictions. The very power that terrorism reveals in this type of society—one thinks of its use of information channels—becomes the very source of the argument used to negate its independent, *endogenous* character."[15] (Scalzone is now in hiding from the police after having been, in June of 1984, found guilty of three counts of attempted homicide in the course of a robbery as well as guilty of subversive association and membership in a clandestine armed band. These are extremely controversial judgements based largely on the testimony of the similarly missing "repentant" terrorist Carlo Fioroni. Scalzone was condemned to twenty years imprisonment.)

The Christian Democrats and the Communists were among the most vociferous in proclaiming the exogenous origins of the Red Brigades. On the front page of the March 17, 1978, edition of *L'Unità,* the PCI asks the tantalizing question (of which more below): "One of the killers was speaking German?" (p. 1, "Extraordinary Democratic Tremor—the Italians Come Together in Defense of the Republic"), and the next day reiterates this theme with an article about the German antiterrorist experts' predictions of mixed (nationalities) squads carrying out terrorist attacks. *Il Popolo,* in an interesting front-page article on March 19, "Symbol without Alternative," refers to the "remote origins and the current complicities" of the Red Brigades. It does manage to loosely link terrorism to the more general crisis in Italy, but only insofar as terrorism is one of the most "acute and terrible revealers" (not a result) of the crisis. We may also want to note here the subtle way in which the DC newspaper delegitimates the Communists in the title of the article. Moro is the symbol without "alternative," and it was precisely in order to present an alternative government to the Italian people that the PCI pushed for the Historic Compromise. Of course, remembering the debate around the alternative/alternating issue, we might also view this phrase as even more subtly delegitimating Moro himself who, after all, was the very artificer of the Historic Compromise and now, in this configuring, has been confined to the ranks of symbols. We will return to this confinement below.

Factions of the ultraleft, including the Movimento group, also reverted to exogenous attributions. In the newspaper *Lotta Continua,* on March 17, 1978, a front-page article declared: "The suspicions of a violent destabilization plot in Europe and the Mediterranean on the parts of the great powers are increasingly being confirmed." Page 1 of the March 16 special edition of *il manifesto* was headlined "Aldo Moro Kidnapped . . . The Red Brigades Claim [Responsibility] and the Secret Services Take Over in Italy; Frontier Country . . ." and the main story immediately launches into an assessment of the action that locates its international origins: "The bloody kidnapping of Aldo Moro . . . reveals a force and a complexity of international connections at the state and secret service levels never before exposed so clearly: everyone is convinced that this morning's coup goes well beyond the capacity of the Red Brigades . . ." Finally, a March 16 editorial broadcast of the radio station operated by the Movimento, Radio Città Futura (Radio of the Future City), declared that "Italy has become the country in which maneuvers are being conducted by American and Soviet secret services above all, and then those secret services of dependent countries, Czechoslovakia, Poland, Hungary and then, naturally, the Germans and Israelis and Arabs. That is, Italy has become essentially a battlefield in which the secret services are all operating with their different interests."[16]

The motivation for this exogenous attribution of the Red Brigades on the part of the ultraleft groups were largely those of decontamination. The ultraleft, we will see, had a most difficult role in the Moro social drama. They sought to escape the repression associated with the imputation of being "terrorist" at the same time as they sought to assert a distance from the state and the newly formed government. It will be particularly significant to interpret the ultraleft positions in terms of dramatic generic choices. For example, the single-mindedness and perfect bifurcation of the moral universe of melodrama cannot accept the ambiguity of a phrase such as "neither with the state nor with the Red Brigades," a phrase adopted by many ultraleftists. In initially attributing foreign derivation to the Red Brigades, the ultraleft sought to simultaneously remove the taint of contamination through identification and to establish a terrain on which to build a double-barreled critique.

As for the motivations of the Christian Democrats, they aimed at disowning the Red Brigades who were certainly "not their children" (although, as the case of the son of Carlo Donat Cattin [a Christian Democrat deputy] soon made clear, some were indeed their literal children). The Communist party, to its own discomfort, had a share of both problems. It had to assert both that the Red Brigades were not *its* children in particular, dutifully carrying the "revolutionary" party perspective into armed practice (thus the burden of decontamination), and it had to assert that alien powers were operating behind these non-Italian invaders; to deny that the Red Brigades members were Italy's children in general (disownership). The threat, in both cases, was a form of contamination. With the fear of contamination came the need to assert that the "Party" or the "Country" was still pure, the boundaries constituting a magic circle. The distinction between the two imperatives, decontamination and disowning, are relevant to the already introduced notion of legitimacy, an issue at the heart of this study. That the Communists were burdened with both of the above symbolic purifying tasks shows very clearly the tenuous nature of their legitimacy at the time of Moro's kidnapping. With one foot in the legitimacy sphere, they had to assert Italy's internal purity. With the other foot still dangling outside the legitimacy sphere, they had to assert the party's internal purity. All of the choices and positions taken by the PCI in the Moro social drama had this double-edged quality to them.

Of course, accusations of international agents swarming into Italy had to be publicly explained. Why was everyone from the Germans to the Arabs taking such a particular and disruptive interest in Italian affairs? A newscaster for the second (center-left) channel of the RAI, I. Moretti, reported the DC and PCI theories for such occurrences. Referring to statements made by both Berlinguer and Zaccagnini (a DC leader) in mid-1977, he noted that "both Berlinguer and Zaccagnini referred explicitly to the possibility of the presence of foreign organizations with general headquarters beyond our borders . . . the two prevalent theories are the following: one proposes that the Eastern European secret services consider the Communist party to be involved in embracing a heresy, namely, Eurocommunism, and they thus wish to embarrass the Italian party. The other, opposite, thesis refers to the Western secret services, American above all and then the German, the Israeli and others. In this case, the project could be that of preventing a political shift in Italy that could have consequences for the NATO military zone and other mediterranean countries . . . It is certain that Italy occupies a strategic and extremely delicate political position. It is also certain that any interventions, by foreign powers, find an arena of action that must be favorable to terrorism in Italy."[17] Here we must note that this explication of both Berlinguer's and Zaccagnini's 1977 statements about foreign intervention is reviewed in the media on the day of Moro's kidnapping, thus linking these foreign agencies with the Red Brigades.

Thus, whether the accusations came from the far left, the PCI, or the center (DC), they concurred in locating the roots of terrorism outside of the country's boundaries and in presenting a wide selection of possible culprits. As reviewed in Chapter 2 and as noted above, the Red Brigades had a known or discoverable history. Each member evolved by way of participation in Italian student organizations and political groups. These groups published their perspectives and platforms in newspapers, journals, and pamphlets. Why then, in the face of such evidence, was there a need to pretend ignorance, to adamantly locate the origins of the Red Brigades "beyond our borders?"

The answer lies in the issue of the "key relationship." Turner's definition is specific on this point. The Breach must occur between members or groups of the same society. The attempt to *disown* the Red Brigades constituted precisely an attempt to deny that any serious *internal* rift had taken place. The claim here, however, is that a most threatening rift had, indeed, occurred. This rift was that between the generations, and the key relationship threatened by the Breach was that between "parents" and "children." The worst thing about the existence of the Red Brigades and the Movimento and Autonomia in Italy was that it revealed a younger generation that could not and would not be absorbed into the established political arena of parties and trade unions. Such a refusal menaced the very continuity of rule and power of these institutions and the current political class entrenched within.

The parent-child breach was picked up and used by the media and other involved protagonists in a metaphorical way. But it was not, in these instances, being constructed to signify the political withdrawal and opposition of the younger generation—the claim about the breach we are making here. The difference in usage can be made clear by sampling some newspaper headlines. From *La Repubblica* of March 16: "It Is as if They Had Kidnapped Our Father—in the Milan Christian Democrat Headquarters, Anger Explodes." Here the implication is that the Christian Democrat "family" is being torn apart by outsiders, the DC children deprived of their father. The use of the metaphor to delegitimate the PCI was also prevalent. The right-wing *Secolo d'Italia,* more than happy to believe that the Red Brigades were indigenous and the offspring of the PCI, headlined an article decrying Communist participation in the government, "Children of the System."

The appearance of the metaphor of family and the use of the family motif was not solely metaphoric, however. The DC, in particular, appealed directly to the literal familial social unit. Newly reinaugurated Prime Minister Guilio Andreotti delivered a speech to the Italian television audience on the night of March 16, the night of the kidnapping and the first night of his new government. In this speech, reproduced in its entirety in the notes at the end of this chapter,[18] Andreotti addressed the "families" of Italy. In fact, he refers to "family" five times in the course of the brief speech. So well aware of the power of the family in Italy, the social unit demanding and receiving the strongest of loyalties from its members, Andreotti actually belied his party's claim that the terrorists were foreign to Italy by appealing to the families' power in the following passage: "But there must be mothers, families who can, before it is too late, speak to them [their children] and make them rethink their unhappy associations."[19]

Thus families were to do their all to convince their children not to get involved in extraparliamentary politics and/or terrorism. Only the families, according to Andreotti, and not the society at large nor the schools, nor the political parties, have this natural authority. The tendency in Italy to remand all social problems to the private sphere is at the heart of Edward Banfield's analysis of "amoral familism" in Southern Italian towns. Joseph Gusfield describes Banfield's thesis succinctly: "Banfield observed the absence of sentiments of public welfare among the population and found instead a ruthless amorality and self-interested character in the individual villager's response to public affairs. At the same time, the villagers displayed strong concerns for the welfare of their family and towards its continuing solidarity. Banfield called this duality a pattern of amoral familism. Towards one's kin there is a deep sentiment, affection and loyalty; toward those outside of it, there is only naked self-interest."[20]

The other tradition, equally strong, in Italy is of course that of the piazza-minded PCI. The Communists have traditionally taken social issues to the public, the DC have dealt (or have tried to deal) with them in private. In a later section of this chapter, we will see that the DC experimented with a seemingly more public mode of responding to crises on March 16, 1978, as it actively competed with the PCI for dominance over the public spaces.

The breach was conclusive despite the expense of so much effort to deny its occurrence. It had touched a sensitive nerve in the Italian political class; their ability to depend upon the continuity of their exclusive, legitimate control of political institutions via absorption of each new generation. This preoccupation must not be confused with an apparent fear that the Red Brigades would actually contend for control with the establishment institutions by rousing the populace. Such a prospectus, regardless of the incident-to-incident military efficiency of the Red Brigades, was never seriously considered by any of the protagonists. The worst-case scenario foresaw disintegration from the inside out, the Red Brigades expressing, in however exaggerated a form, the disaffection of the future political leaders, trade union delegates, and workers.

The rhetorical counterpoint, that no serious breach had actually occurred, begged for empirical "evidence." On this tumultuous day, the only attempt at such evidence of the exogenous origins of the terrorists was an eyewitness account that claimed to have heard one of the Via Fani ambushers shout orders in a foreign accent (the German speaker of the *L'Unità* article). The mass media reiterated this report many times during the day. However, any sense of the linguistic geography of Italy must suggest that in a country of hundreds of dialects (some, especially in the North, sounding remarkably like German or French) such an assessment cannot stand on its own as evidence of foreign involvement.[21] The sole other piece of evidence brought forward was the very efficiency of the commandoes themselves. The Red Brigades not only got clear away from the ambush site with their hostage but had also cut many telephones lines in the area preventing a hasty arrival of the police. For the Communists, this efficiency could only mean that the Red Brigades were foreign or they were fascist or, best of all, they were both foreign and fascist. A *L'Unità* article stressed the relationship between the efficiency of the Red Brigades and their alleged fascist essence: "And whoever has eyes to see has realized how the same "military" perfectionism attained by the Red Brigades is nothing other than the consequence of their belonging to the reactionary logic, of drinking in the same polluted streams as the black eversion" (March 21, 1978, p. 2). The construction put on the events by the PCI was largely that of the "fascist matrix" noted above. They spent the full thrust of their polemic in the immediate aftermath of the kidnapping on precisely this accusation. The final dyad, left versus right, will focus on the significance of this distinction, particularly for the political legitimacy of the PCI during the Moro social drama.

The Red Brigades had also slashed the tires of a flower vendor's cart the night before—a vendor who stationed himself daily on Via

Fani. He never got to work that day, a day spent getting new tires. Thus the only certain witness was eliminated and the media zeroed in on this fact, building whole stories around it, as revealing how the Red Brigades had thought of everything. The reporting of this absence in *Il Popolo* (already the day before having pointed its readers to the incredible efficiency of the attackers, pulling off "an action of a true military commando . . . among other things prepared in the most minute particulars," and inviting its readers to "relive together those tragic moments" [March 16, page 2]) on the front page of the March 17 edition also reveals how the dramatic self-consciousness of the Moro social drama protagonists automatically locked into place. The article about the flower vendor was titled "The Bothersome Character of the Drama," and it describes this character in the following way: "And thus it was. The flower vendor, a minor character in this ferocious story, unconsciously passed through the plot and remains, at least for now, the only one who, if he had been interrogated, would have been able to give even a very weak sign of alarm" (*Il Popolo,* March 17, 1978, p. 1). Granting the confused construction of the last part of this passage, what comes through quite clearly is the way in which the media, in this case a party organ, was quite obviously constructing a dramatic plot out of the events, designating major and minor parts, and imagining roles for those who were present as well as for those who were, in fact, only involved through their absence. This use of a dramatic paradigm for intercepting and constructing the event is, of course, at the heart of this study, and a representative presentation of such moments of appearance of this self-consciousness constitutes our own plotting of the various plots.

Why was the efficiency of the attackers evidence of foreign intervention and control? Clearly some notion of Italian "inefficiency" was at work here. Leonardo Sciascia, Italian author and European parliamentarian from the Italian Radical party, has written of the Italian tendency toward self-denigration in questions of efficiency: "Of an institute that doesn't function, of a hospital in which patients are mistreated or in which there is no room, of a late train, of an airplane that doesn't take off, of a letter never arriving . . . the motto is always the exclamation, "Cose nostre!" (our things). Yet, there is at least one thing that functions, and it is exactly that which by now is par excellence, "cosa nostra" . . . The Red Brigades function perfectly; but (and it's the but that is important) they are Italian. They are our thing [cosa nostra] whatever pretexts may be given that they are linked to revolutionary sects or secret services of other countries."[22]

The logic informing the typical reactions outlined by Sciascia is the following: because the Red Brigades are efficient, and we Italians are inefficient, the Red Brigades cannot be Italian. But, as Sciascia, born and raised in Sicily, knows, at least one Italian thing is efficient and homegrown. It is the Mafia. No politician has ever claimed that the Mafia is manipulated by the KGB or the CIA or the PLO for that matter. And the critical difference here is that while both the Mafia and the Red Brigades are illicit organizations engaged in illegal and violent activities, the Mafia coexists with and counts on the continuing survival of the extant Italian state. The Red Brigades were claiming that they were out to destroy the state.

Media critic Giovanni Bechelloni presented another perspective on the efficiency question, one which interpreted the Red Brigades efficiency as efficiency by default: "It is immediately discovered that the absence of an armoured car and the lack of certain elementary safety observances [such as varying Moro's route every day] have rendered the operation much easier. Instead, [the mass media] has underlined the ferociousness of the crime and the extraordinary ability and efficiency of those committing it, implying that we are perhaps on the brink of a coup d'état manipulated by mysterious and powerful foreign organizations."[23]

Common Criminals or Political Combatants

Our second pair of oppositions is that of common criminal versus political criminal. This salient opposition will be thoroughly analyzed in Chapter 4 in connection with the recognition/negotiation question. Here we will look at the willingness/unwillingness of the protagonists to grant any political designation to the Red Brigades on the day of their attack.

A political designation brings a specific status to a group, both in terms of a general reception by the public and in terms of an official recognition by the established authority. For example, if a group is granted political recognition, that group can legitimately appeal to the Geneva Convention Accords in the event of the capture of its members. Such an eventuality was sharply preempted on the day of Moro's capture. Prime Minister Andreotti, in his televised speech, spoke of the victims of other kidnappings and, at a crucial moment, "caught himself" in a dangerous recognition of the Red Brigades. Alluding, at the end of his speech, to the restoration of Moro and the other kidnapping victims to liberty, Andreotti refers to the kidnappers as "political" and immediately followed and finished his speech with: "I refuse to use this adjective. I would say pseudo-political or common criminals, whichever. Criminality has no adjectives and criminality is against the soul of our people."[24]

The Red Brigades perceived themselves to be quintessentially political, and those members who had already been captured by the police had declared themselves to be political prisoners. But a glance at some of the newspaper headlines of March 16 reveals the mass media's reluctance to accept such a self-identification: *Il Giornale Nuovo,* "Delinquents"; *La Stampa,* "Desperate Criminals"; *Il Messaggero,* "Criminals"; *La Repubblica,* "Not revolutionaries, not romantic executioners, bloody as they are, not lunatics made barbarous by solitude and clandestinity, but an efficient organization of killers." The Communists, who were among the most vociferous (as we will see in the next chapter) in decrying the political presumptions of the Red Brigades self-identification, had, it should be pointed out, seemed to accept such a distinction earlier in the year. On February 4, a front-page *L'Unità* article had calculated that 342 criminal episodes had occurred in the month of January and then went on to identify them precisely as "342 politically derived criminal acts ['fatti criminosi di origine politica']" (February 4, 1978, "Impressive Rise in Assaults and Violence").

Alessandro Silj analyzed the way in which the Italian mass media (party-linked and independent) and coalition-belonging political parties depoliticized the Red Brigades. (The right-wing parties did stress the political nature of the Red Brigades, intent as they were on drawing the direct connection between the PCI and the BR.) He wrote: "For years the problem of the Red Brigades was set aside, relegating it to the class of common criminality, of madness or, in the best of hypotheses, of plots essentially extraneous because maneuvered by occult foreign centers. Now Aldo Moro was kidnapped. In referring to the victim, one could not speak only of a political leader, because that would be the same as recognizing the action of the Red Brigades as a political action, carried out by a political organization."[25] The importance of Silj's interpretation of the depoliticization of the BR lies in his recognition that any public assessment of the Red Brigades was dialectically bound up with an assessment of the identity of Moro. In other words, both victim and assailant found themselves tied together via a process of reciprocity of identity. To begin with Moro, and identify him as political and as *only* political, one risked falling into an identification of the Red Brigades as political (due to their choice of a quintessentially political target). This is simply a preview of the full-blown shape this problem would take for the Moro social drama protagonists. But it should give us some clue as to how refusing a political identity to the Red Brigades on the day of Moro's kidnapping made it logically (and, of course, politically) impossible to grant an untroubled political status to Moro later on.

RED OR BLACK

> And on the basis of this "decontextualization" all of the official power and the bourgeois publicity maintain that the extremism of the left and that of the right are interchangeable. This unhooking of "terrorism" from theory and this neutralization of the political differences make possible a purely anticriminal reaction against "terrorism," such as is indirectly reflected in the global refusal of asylum for "terrorists."[26]

The third set of oppositions, left versus right, of necessity brings the political back into consideration. For, in attempting to locate the Red Brigades along the left/right spectrum, the major participants in the Moro affair tacitly admitted to the premise of a political cast to the group and its activities. It is once again useful to refer back to the explicit history of the Red Brigades in particular and terrorism in general up to the point of Moro's kidnapping.

To reiterate briefly, in the last hundred years, a structural paradigm has emerged with which it is impossible to distinguish in Italy, with a fair degree of certainty, between leftist terrorism and rightist terrorism. Rightists tend to set bombs in public places and to attack in an indiscriminate fashion in squads (this was the particular modality of Mussolini's "squadristi"). Leftists tend to select specific targets and use firearms, rather than bombs, to either wound, kidnap (for purposes of carrying out a trial), or kill that target. The key to the differentiation is the matter of indiscriminacy versus discriminacy, whether the target be property or persons. (Of course, fascist terrorists do, on occasion, select and attack specific targets. We will note an ongoing trial in Florence during the Moro affair, the trial of those ultrarightists accused of killing the judge Occorsio, which lies outside this "military" and strategical paradigm. But, in general, the model holds.)

Despite the general reliability of this paradigm, accusations of a counterlogical nature have been a hallmark of Italian politics for the past twenty years. The sixties and the early seventies were years, it has been shown in Chapter 2, overwhelmed with attempted coup d'états from the right and the military, with police complicity in rightist bombings and with the involvement of the Christian Democrats (even Moro, as noted, associated with one particular case of covering up an attempted conspiracy). These were the years of the "strategy of tension." Thus it (only) seems paradoxical that it was on the anarchist groups and, to some extent, on elements of the PCI, that the state often placed blame. As Roberto Massari has written, in his book *Marxism and Critique of Terrorism,* "It should not be forgotten, in fact, that often the fiercest 'illegalisti' were none other than police agents, infiltrated and disposed to execute any type of crime in order to throw the discredit onto the anarchists or, as in the more recent case of Valpreda, on the workers movement more in general."[27]

In fact, as we have seen, only in 1978 was the Piazza Fontana trial, in session in Catanzaro, finally investigating the neo-fascist infiltration of the anarchist circles. As well, a concurrent trial in Rome was exploring a (disbanded in 1976) secret service (SID) section's involvement in the cover-up of the attempted coup d'état in 1970 by Prince Valerio Borghese.

It is important to keep in mind that the PCI, during this wave of rightist attacks, was still shrugging off the label of complete illegitimacy imposed upon it during the 1948 election campaign. The center and right parties would continue to play off that illegitimacy for as long as possible, using every opportunity to accuse the PCI of insurrection against the state.

If this period was dominated by accusations that apparently right-wing terrorism was, actually, left-wing terrorism, the mid and late seventies saw the defensive backlash of this on the parts of the PCI and some areas of the ultra-left. This took the form of accusations by these parties of the left that what seemed to be left-wing terrorism was actually fascist, right-wing terrorism. The PCI and Movimento claimed that the leftist, international, pro-proletarian

positions taken by the Red Brigades was mere rhetoric. The accusation of "catholic messianism" that had been at the center of the
PCI's former critique of the Red Brigades now receded as the
"fascism" of the Red Brigades was "discovered" in the mid and late
seventies. A. Bolaffi, a PCI exponent, wrote in the February 9,
1979, issue of *Rinascita* (the PCI magazine): "One can speak of a
'social-fascist turn' of terrorism and of the attempt to liquidate the
new developments that emerged from the struggles of the decade
between 1968 and 1978."[28] Michelini, another PCI exponent, carried this idea to its furthest consequences. In another *Rinascita*
article (February 2, 1979), he discussed the series of rightist-type
attacks in the late sixties and early seventies and the inexplicable,
sudden disappearance of such attacks in the mid-seventies: ". . .
then the openly black [fascist] design no longer revealed itself, at
least not outwardly, and all of a sudden, the bloody flower of the
Red Brigades bloomed. Is this only a coincidence, a casual
accident?"[29]

This notion of a secret fascist campaign to discredit the whole left
by engaging in apparently leftist terrorism was not only found in the
writings of the political elite. Some of the rank-and-file workers in
Italy shared this conviction. An interviewer at the Fiat Mirafiori
plant was told by one worker on March 16, 1978, that the Red
Brigades were part of the "strategy of tension," a phrase used to
designate the general neo-fascist design.[30]

L'Unità, the PCI daily, published an article during the period of
Moro's sequestration with the headline: "The Language of Freda [a
known fascist terrorist] Is the Same as the Language of the Red
Brigades." In this article, extracts of Freda's writings are presented
and the reader is guided in drawing the comparison with the Red
Brigades. Both texts do militate for a "revolution," but the real key
in the texts, disproving their identity or identity of interests, is, as
Silj perceptively observes, the difference in professed techniques.
As noted in the paradigm elaborated above, militants of right and of
left in Italy usually give themselves away when it comes to tactics.
Silj writes of the *L'Unità* article: "In fact, Freda writes that 'to the
wooden clubs and machine guns of the police one can (or better:
one must) respond with iron bars and bombs.' Iron bars and bombs
are typically fascist arms not Brigade arms."[31]

With their explicit references to foreign secret services and their
further assertion that the Red Brigades' actions are aimed at a

reenforcement of the state, *Movimento's* radio commentators imply that these Red Brigades may be fascist as well. A *Lotta Continua* editorial of March 17 specifically linked the new Andreotti government to a rightward turn to authoritarianism: "In Europe and in the Mediterranean there is now a vast destabilizing maneuver taking place. This is the rich terrain of the cultures of state authoritarianism . . . the new Andreotti government, the institutions and all of the parties . . . work to channel the rejection of terrorism toward an accelerated authoritarianism" (p. 1).

On their side, however, the Communists were making their assertions of a Red Brigades "fascist matrix" do double duty. Two weeks before Moro's kidnapping, *L'Unità* published an editorial condemning the Red Brigades and condemning those sectors of the ultraleft who persisted in calling the Red Brigades "comrades in error": "The 'comrades in error' are in reality . . . primarily enemies of the working class. They differ from the fascists in nothing but words, and not always even these. To collaborate with them signifies to collaborate in the undoing of society and the preparations of the days of oppression. For everyone, not just as communists" (February 23, 1978, p. 1). Thus, by association and by implication, those ultraleftists who, even linguistically, maintained some connection with the Red Brigades were probably fascists as well.

From the right of the political spectrum, however, came a different line. As far as the ultraconservative parties were concerned, the Red Brigades were nothing but the children (legitimate if not recognized) of the Communist party. These parties explicitly referred to the Red Brigades as "communist terrorists" and announced their dismay at the entrance of the PCI into the government: "[The National Right] denounces, in the presence of all Italians, the emblematic simultaneity with which, in the same day almost at the same hour, Andreotti has presented to the parliamentary chambers the new government with communists in the majority and the communist terrorists have kidnapped Aldo Moro, massacring his bodyguards. In the two facts flow together decades of the gradual communistization of the state."[32]

One last aspect of the left-right paradigm differentiation process must be addressed. By 1978, many terrorism experts and establishment political figures had already decided that no matter how destructive the bombs and attempted coup d'états of the neo-fascists had been, the threat from the right was basically defeated, and whatever residue there was need not be taken anywhere near as seriously as the threat from the left. One indication of this general lapsed concern with fascism can be discerned in the change of rhetoric accompanying two pieces of "law and order" legislation. The first, the already noted Legge Reale, passed in 1975, was presented with almost exclusive preoccupation with neo-rightists. As sociologist Vincenzo Ferrari notes: "The majority speakers Boldrin and Mazzola had recognized that 'behind fascist violence there exists a detailed, organic and complex project, extremely dangerous for the survival of the Democratic Republic born from the Resistance.' "[33] Yet two years later, in 1977, another series of "exceptional" measures (the Leggi Bonifacio) was passed without any reference to fascist violence at all.

Similarly, a scholar of Italian terrorism would write, in 1979, that despite bomb attacks in the seventies (and, although the writer could not know it, more were to come in the eighties) that killed scores of people and injured hundreds, "right-wing terrorists in Italy appear more vulnerable than those of the left to changes in the political direction of the country as a whole, and it was this vulnerability as well as their more haphazard organization and spectacular propensities that weakened their position."[34]

Thus we see how in the space of a few years, the public image of the fascists has been transformed. In 1975, they have a "detailed, organic and complex project." In 1979 they are vulnerable and haphazard. While numbers prove nothing in themselves and are open to interpretation, it is, finally, interesting to note that, as of 1979, 259 left-wing terrorists were in jail, convicted or awaiting trial, and 1812 right-wing "extremists" had been arrested. Our argument here really consists in revealing the power of rhetoric to place and displace concern. Again, this will be evident when we appraise the differential emphasis on the Torino Red Brigades trial and the several rightist trials simultaneously taking place in various Italian cities.

Thus the ritual denunciations of the Red Brigades appeared in diverse forms. The right asserted that the Red Brigades were communists, the PCI claimed that they were fascist. Each party chose its line of attack on the basis of its own particular sense of the best strategy to use to assert *its own* legitimacy. Here, as at so many points in this analysis of the Moro affair, we find the participants

less concerned to understand the conditions allowing for the growth
of the Red Brigades, in fact, even less concerned with discussing the
content and contexts of the claims made by the Red Brigades than
they are interested in reinforcing their own legitimacy. Such an
approach need not have been the only one. What else might they
have done to discredit the Red Brigades while increasing their own
legitimacy? For one, they might have supplemented their denunciation with explicit references to the real past of the BR and to the
specific positions taken by the Red Brigades in their writings. In this
process, they might have revealed many of the logical contradictions in these positions. They might have stressed the disjunction
between the Red Brigades' stated ends and their actual means. In
other words, they might have made a case for their own legitimacy
by indirection, by submitting evidence to the public that the Red
Brigades had none at all. This process would still have fallen in the
domain of the rhetorical. But, the pitch might have been less
frenzied and the content of the accusations would have been based
on a known history and revealed texts rather than on, as it was with
the imaged-up specter of the secret services of all the world's
countries invading Italy, a large measure of fantasy. Of course, the
Moro affair participants did not do this. An approach to the known
history and positions of the Red Brigades would bring many of the
participants to some rather ambiguous and uncomfortable conclusions about themselves. Not the least of those likely to be so
affected was the Communist Party. Oreste Scalzone wrote in this
regard "The 'demonization' of the SIM [Multi-National Imperalist
State, the selected generic target of the Red Brigades], the idea of
an Italian capitalism 'subordinate to world capitalism,' aren't these
[phrases] the children of the anti-monopolism, of the third-
worldism, of the old ideas about ragamuffin capitalism, . . . about
popular unity . . . [all old mottos and targets of the PCI]? And you
lament if someone—as opposed to yourselves—followed the consequences of this? If someone seized the practical consequences of
this type of discourse?"[35]

The implications of the above statement are important for this
study. The key is the notion that discourse has other than purely
discursive consequences, that to revile monopolies means that if
opportunities arise to destroy monopolies they will be taken. Words
build bridges to actions, and some people will choose to walk over
those bridges. How indeed could the PCI refuse all responsibility

for actions that *appeared* to be consistent with its own stated policy? It could be so only if one or all of the following criteria could be met: (1) it could prove that these appearances were illusory, (2) its policies had changed due to changes in the social and economic context, or (3) it had now become itself *institutionalized* and thus had the authority to simply deny the question of patrimony with no other justifications than its own situation. Not incidentally, Scalzone addressed those close to the PCI as "dear friends of the new, *neo-institutional* left." This study is exploring and will continue to explore which of the above alternatives best fit the situation of the various left parties and groups in Italy during the Moro affair. This will include an analysis of the process of delegitimization imposed on the ultraleft group of which Scalzone was a member, Potere Operaio (Workers Power). This process proceeded on the basis of precisely this issue of the nature of the relationship (necessary, accidental, probable?) between engaged stated theory and engaging practice.

Attention must now be turned to the participant's work to define the "target" of the Red Brigades attack. The issue may appear to be gratuitous. The concrete, immediate targets were Moro's bodyguards and, more to the point, Moro himself. This study, however, is concerned with the rhetoric and the drama of such things as defining social events. Before the protagonists of the Moro affair could draw up their defense they had first to identify, for the public and themselves, exactly what it was that was being attacked.

Identifying the Target

In a certain sense, Aldo Moro was a collective figure. He was the "Symbol without Alternative," a character out of Manzoni, as we have seen. Most explicitly, he stood for the Christian Democrat Party, for the relative harmony between the Catholic church and the state and for the proposed Historic Compromise. He, more than any other single individual, represented these particularly Italian phenomena. It is, though, necessary to distinguish between Moro as the embodiment of the collectivity and Moro as a collective figure. This distinction is difficult but important. In the former, Moro *is* the collectivity, the two are identical and one cannot be thought without thinking the other simultaneously. (This indeed was Moro's reading of his own status. In later chapters, the conflict between his reading and that of his party will be revealed as the cause of a great rift.) Here it is useful to evoke the image of a charismatic leader, such as the Ayatollah Khomeini, for comparison. Khomeini is, or at least was at the time of the Iranian revolution, the sacred embodiment of both the church and the (sacralized) state of Iran. To harm his person would be tantamount to harming Iran. Khomeini is the embodiment of the collectivity. For millions of his countrypeople, he is Iran. (While this comparison has important heuristic qualities, it obviously brackets the reality of dissenting views in Iran.) In the latter configuration, a person viewed as a collective figure, the implication is that he or she may represent one or some aspects of the collectivity, may serve in one or many collective positions but that he or she is not the embodiment of the collectivity. In other words, it was possible to think about Aldo Moro as *simply* a Christian Democrat, a father, or a man. He was not Italy. Significantly, the way an individual is ultimately appraised determines, in advance, the available means that will be adopted to deal with him. (The relevance of this to the issue of negotiation will be seen in Chapter 4.)

At this point in the social drama, all of the participants except the still silent Moro, the Red Brigades, and Moro's family were in accord in subscribing to the latter characterization above. Moro was viewed as *a* man of the collectivity. Better still, we might say that he was the door through which the collectivity could be approached. Thus for many participants, *Moro* was not really the "target" of the attack. The "target" was something larger than Moro, somewhere behind Moro. He was, perhaps, the guard who had unwittingly allowed the Red Brigades to enter the door leading to that "target."

As one of the theoretical claims of his study is that "*the* collectivity" of Italy does not exist and that, in its place, are to be found several different collectivities, it follows that the collective "target" would have been configured differently by each participant, each appealing to its respective public. A survey of "targets" acknowledged by the various participants reveals their numerousness and diversity. The "target" was alternately identified as the heart of the State, the Historic Compromise, Democracy, the Christian Democrat Party, the Communist Party, the Republic, the Institutions of the State, and, as noted, the Mass Media.

The Communists privately understood the primary target of the Red Brigades to be themselves, more precisely, their delegitimization. Evidence of this position can be found in the Communists' characterization of the Red Brigades as foreign agents and neo-fascists. This view, however, had only particularistic value and reference. Thus, publicly, the Communists opted for an assessment of the terrorists' target as being Democracy and the Democratic State. It should be recalled here how supremely important it was for the Communists, on the morning of March 16, 1978, to present as universalistic a self-image as possible. This was the day the PCI planned to move from opposition to majority status. The community(ies) to which it now appealed had to be as broad as possible within the generic limits of actually being designated a *communist* political party.

An article in *L'Unità's* March 17 edition neatly assessed the "target" and portrayed the universalistic nature of the appeal: "It's not only a question of human solidarity, but of the full understanding that whoever, regardless of his political and social placement, becomes the target of terrorism—in him one strikes that which is the first condition of renewal—that is democracy."[36]

The Christian Democrats, as will be further evident from the discussions of the demonstrations below, expressed their opinion that the real target was the Christian Democrat Party. Moro was *its* president after all. But the Christian Democrats had historically (after 1948) identified itself with the whole of Italy. They felt no qualms about asserting that this attack was aimed at the Heart of the State. After all, they considered themselves to constitute the Heart of the State.

This Heart of the State target-identification appeared in most of the national independent newspapers on March 16. Rome's *Il Messaggero* headlined its front page editorial; "War against the State." *La Repubblica* similarly headlined its lead editorial; "They Have Struck the Heart of the State," and the conservative *Il Tempo* framed its editorial concern by identifying the attack as "The Highest Point in the Attack on the State." Giovanni Bechelloni discussed this characterization: "The Brigades hold the floor in the sense that immediately the image [of Italy] transmitted by the mass media is identical . . . to that held by the Red Brigades: a society that has a central core which on being hit, the entire society enters into crisis. Today, however, it has been noted that the modern society does not possess a central heart."[37] This absence is explained, in another context, by Giorgio Bocca who wrote that in the place of the central core of the state there are "centers of power, associations, some of them parasites like the Mafia, some productive like Fiat . . ."[38]

Those Red Brigades who were communicating with the public through the mass media, the Historic Leaders on trial in Torino, were also designating the State as the ultimate target. *L'Unità* published an article on March 19 in which Renato Curcio is quoted as claiming, from behind the bars of his "cage' inside the Torino courtroom, that "Moro is in the hands of the proletariat and with him will be tried the whole State." This article highlighting the imprisoned "brigatisti" statements is further significant in that, while reporting these statements, it simultaneously condemns their heretical *and* their aesthetic form: "The claiming of responsibility [for the attack] has arrived, punctually and predictably. This act [the claiming of responsibility] was a given and not even the excited squabble between defendants and public minister succeeded in conferring the anticipated theatricality to it" (p. 2). Thus the reporter's reaction is an explicit mixture of condemnation and disappointment. The Red Brigades are to be reviled, certainly, but they are also expected to produce "theater," and there is almost an aesthetic disappointment voiced when they do not.

Closely associated with the Heart of the State target-characterization was the characterization of the target that identified Democracy at the center of the terrorist aim. The Redress chapter will highlight the rhetorical work done with the concept of Democracy. Here, we will note that many of the major protagonists immediately linked the symbolic significance of Moro to the attack on Democracy. The March 16 Special Edition of *L'Unità* contained the headline: "The Enemies of Democracy Will Not Succeed." Berlinguer wrote, in a *L'Unità* editorial discussing the significance of the attack, "It has been asserted that Aldo Moro was kidnapped precisely in order to attack a symbol, among the most significant of symbols of the forces intent on preventing the political and institutional dissolution. But beyond the person of Moro (with whom we renew, in this terrible moment, our esteem and solidarity) they wanted to strike the integrity of Italian democracy . . . The democratic regime and the Italian Constitution are decisive and nonrenounceable conquests of the popular movement . . ." (March 19, p. 1). Moro is presented here by Berlinguer as being *a* representative of Democracy, not Democracy incarnate, nor even the main force (which was rather the popular movement) responsible for the augmentation of democracy in Italy. As for the Christian Democrats, they combined the two "victims," the Heart of the State and Democracy, in their party paper, *Il Popolo's* March 16 headline, "Ferocious Challenge to the Democratic State."

We have noted the importance of the *setting* of the abduction above. Here, in our analysis of the "target" of the assault, we must also be concerned with the *timing* of the attack. The two events scheduled to occur on March 16 that were most relevant to the Red Brigades were the parliamentary ratification debates and the trials in Torino of the Red Brigades' historic leaders. As regards the debates, the March 17 edition of *La Stampa* noted: "It is impossible not to link the kidnapping of Moro, principle artificer of the difficult alliance between parties that gives such a large majority to the new government, with this particular political moment: the coincidence between the abduction and the debate is certainly not casual."[39] The logic behind this "target" identification was the following: because Moro had brought the PCI and DC this close together, Moro's presence was needed to complete the connection. Kidnap Moro and you would leave the country without a government. However, another line of causality is being proposed in this study. Moro's *absence,* even more than his presence, would insure the passage of the government, for Moro's absence would provide the government with precisely that very short-run crisis needed to justify its coming into existence.

The idea that the Torino trials were the real "target" of the abduction made a certain amount of sense. Most of the historic leaders of the Red Brigades were on trial for armed insurrection against the state. However, concluding that the aim of the Red Brigades in kidnapping Moro was solely to retaliate against the Torino trials meant imposing a limited scope to the Red Brigades' sense of the meaning of its own activities. In this regard, it suffices to read any Red Brigades document (several of which will be approached later in this study in terms of their relevance to the Moro affair) to realize that the Red Brigades saw much more at stake than stopping or postponing the trials of the historical leaders; at stake, in their eyes, was the proletarian revolution. And Aldo Moro was, for them, the archetypal representative of bourgeois power.

The various interpretations proposed, during these first hours after the attack, of who the terrorists were (foreigners, fascists, communists, criminals?) and what their true target was, led to a generalized feeling of victimization. For example, if the PCI felt that the Red Brigades were fascists, they would inevitably be led to believe that they were themselves, on this dawn of their new legitimacy, the real targets of the attacks. But the PCI was not, as we have begun to see with the mass media and will explore further vis-à-vis the protagonists in this next section, alone in their personalization of the attack. This general reaction was captured by a Radio Onda Rossa commentator on the evening of March 16: ". . . who is the victim of the action, 'victim' between quotation marks, because the direct victim is Moro, the direct victims are the five agents and carabinieri killed. But victim as well, or better, *making* victims of themselves as well are the DC, the PCI, the trade unions, in short the whole lot of institutions have made themselves the 'victim.' "[40]

Defense

Once the various protagonists had satisfied themselves in their definitions of what had happened, they set about immediately to defend themselves, victims as they all were, from the attack. Thus we may now turn to the defensive work of the participants. This includes both the symbolic work of rhetoric, strikes and demonstrations and the instrumental work of passing a government and setting up roadblocks. As already mentioned, the defensive work proceeds side-by-side with the definition work. In fact, the process of defining a problematic and threatening situation, grasping the situation cognitively, is the first concrete step of defense. The interpretations have already begun as a very part of the cognition itself.

There were several arenas of defense on March 16. Each arena had its own logic of procedure, but their respective processes were cross-referencing. The significant arenas were the legislative arena of Parliament, the criminal justice arena (split in the case of Italy into Polizia, Carabinieri, the Military and the Secret Services), the urban, public arena of the piazza, and the trade union arena of the factory.

It has already been established that the coalition government proposed by Aldo Moro was being given a good chance of passing. Yet two weeks remained until the Easter break of Parliament and there were no signs that the traditionally long ratification debates would be foregone. Now the breach had occurred. Crisis was in the air and Italy had no government with which to respond. The only proper response, according to all political parties except the Radicals and the ultraright "Missini" (Italian Social Movement) was to pass this new government as quickly as possible.

Interestingly, the first reaction of many of the deputies, on hearing the news of Moro's kidnapping, was one of comic disbelief. Guiseppi Di Palma has alluded to the theatrical nature of Italian politics and has suggested that its favorite genre is farce. A newsman covering Parliament reported that the deputies believed the news to be a joke: "It was such a horrifying thing, made more so because many deputies thought it to be a joke, something, even if malicious, circulated in order to liven things up a bit. It seemed so impossible that the terrorists could reach so high. And then, instead, they became conscious of the reality and, naturally, from this attitude of disbelief there was a turn to a phase of disgust and discussion."[41]

The above statement strikes one on two accounts. First, it reveals the total absence of a realistic assessment of the ability of the Red Brigades on the part of the parliamentary deputies. This is surprising as the Red Brigades, by 1978, had already been operating successfully for four years with ever more difficult targets. It also reveals a readiness to joke, even about rather "sacred" subjects, a tendency to seek the mask of farce rather than that of tragedy, even in the face of weekly acts of terrorism.

The news proved true however and the mass media reporters ran to get the "hot" statements of the spokesmen for the various parties and institutions. There were appeals made by Cossiga, minister of internal affairs, De Martino, a Socialist; Biasini, a Republican; Di Giulio, a Communist; Leone, a Christian Democrat holding the office of president of Italy; Zaccagnini, Christian Democrat and close friend of Moro; Rossi, president of the Corte Costituzionale (Italy's Supreme Court), and Father Panciroli of the Vatican. What could all these individuals actually have to say? Concretely they deplored the act, reiterated faith in democracy, and bade the public to remain calm. However, as our concern here is primarily on the theatrical pitch of the Moro social drama protagonist responses, we need attend to what these individuals represented in terms of symbolism and aesthetics. By their status and their number they say that indeed something terrible has occurred, there is good reason to worry. But by the same token, they also say that there are still many institutions left standing, that they can represent those institutions adequately to the public, that Moro was after all not the whole of Italy. Instrumentally, they can speak on the most efficacious and appropriate defense to adopt. But their task was only minimally instrumental. It was maximally symbolic. This can be further seen in the attention paid by the mass media to these spokesmens' *emotional exhibitions*. The media's interpretation of these exhibitions is most important for getting at the rhetoric of unity and strength that would become the leitmotives of the day ". . . the emotionally moved reactions of the parliamentarians have expressed the real cohesion of a political society that for 30 years between alliances and polemics, has represented the legitimacy of the power of the republic."[42]

This bit of patriotic fervor on the part of *La Stampa* nicely turns the crisis on its head. The logic runs as follows: yes these institutional representatives have *said* that there is a severe crisis, but their grief reveals the fact that there really has been no breach, that we are not entering a crisis stage, because their grief spells unity and where there is unity there is strength. The public is being instructed not to listen to the *words* of these people but to attend to their *emotions* as evidence of a unified Italy led by responsible and responsive leaders who have things under control. There will appear other moments of the semiotic power of gestured emotions. For example, the tears of the crying Zaccagnini will be used to gauge the profundity of DC involvement in seeking Moro's return.

We shall now turn to the various defense positions suggested by the participants on March 16. The variations of defense were the proposals of passing extraordinary measures allowing the police greater arrest and perquisition powers, declaring a state of national emergency, reintroducing the death penalty, limiting the parliamentary session on March 16 to a discussion of the kidnapping, immediately passing the new government, and obtaining Cossiga's resignation (Cossiga was minister of the interior, responsible for terrorist surveillance). Each of these suggestions was dramatic, in the sense that each proposes unexpected and extraordinary action. However, it is also true that these suggestions override a national emergency plan codified some years before. This plan was drawn up specifically for situations of this type, a nationally relevant social

crisis. It is hard to see how some of the motions, notably reintroducing the death penalty and immediately passing the government
without discussion of any kind, would actually aid in what seems
should have been the logical goals of the legislature; these being
obtaining Moro's release and eliminating the Red Brigades. To the
contrary, the actual goal the legislature set for itself was another,
that being the discrediting of the Red Brigades and the reaccrediting of the Italian state institutions. Almost all of the defense work of
March 16 revolved around this one idea. The mass demonstrations
represented the most important moment of this strategy of discrediting and reaccrediting. Essential to this strategy were the
melodramatic characterizations of the central actors as heroes and
villains. This approach allowed the major participants to present
the situation of Moro's kidnapping to the public as one about which
the public need have no doubts. The public must be clear about the
protagonists in the breach *and* about itself (the public in its essentially "supporting" role). Northrop Frye has written: "In melodrama, two themes are important: the triumph of the moral virtue
over villainy and the consequent idealizing of the moral virtue
assumed to be held by the audience."[43]

Meanwhile, at Montecitorio, site of the Parliament, the Radicals
were demanding Cossiga's resignation, the Republicans were demanding the reintroduction of the death penalty, and nearly all the
parties in Parliament were concordant on the need to pass the new
government sans debate. The Breach was already widening into
Crisis. In fact, for some, the kidnapping was seen as the final blow in
a general, system-wide crisis already too long endured. The political forces, according to a newsman of the second radio station,
agreed that "the Government must immediately present itself . . .
and the parties must concentrate on reducing the debate to a
minimum, to focus solely on the sense of emergency and on the
sense of cohesion expressed by a country hit so hard in this moment,
precisely in this instant in which it was beginning to officially resolve
the crisis which has already endured two months."[44]

The new government was passed, with practically no discussion,
by the evening of March 16. In this day, composed of so many
exhortations to defend "democracy," it is interesting to note, as did
this writer for the leftist *Quotidiano dei Lavoratori (Worker's
Daily):* ". . . the immediate consequences of the abduction of Moro
are such that they violate even the most elementary rules of the

formal democracy of parlementarianism. Andreotti . . . presented himself yesterday in the Chambers for the vote of confidence having already reached an accord with the parties on the uselessness of the debate: thus the sanction of the new government occurred in a form that would be euphemistic to define as democratic."[45]

The few residually intransigent Christian Democrats had had their hands forced. They had to accept the coalition. However, they did not all do so gracefully. Massimo De Carolis, one of the intransigent DC group, exploited the day's development in order to cast suspicion on the left in general and the PCI in particular. His effort consisted in following the familiar tactic of imputing a specific (incriminating) symbolic goal to the Red Brigades. De Carolis's claim was that the "real" goal of the Red Bridgades was to bring Italy to a national state of emergency and thus, inevitably, to a government of national solidarity which would include the PCI. Thus De Carolis said, it was very much in the interest of the PCI that Moro had been kidnapped.

In the establishment mass media, dissenting opinions such as that of De Carolis were absent or mentioned only briefly. The appeals for extraordinary police measures, for the death penalty, for force beyond the traditional democratic means were neither realized on March 16 (although the first would ultimately be made law in May of 1978) nor given much airspace by the establishment media organs. However, the ultraleft mass media focused almost exclusively on the Republican's death penalty nomination. The unique preoccupation of the ultraleft was their forced inclusion into the ranks of those viewed as dangerous to the state. They saw themselves as unwilling victims of a witch hunt. The focus on the death penalty and extraordinary measures appeals, by the ultraleft, served another function. It provided some issues for the ultraleft on which they could take a clear and adamant position. This was in contrast to the general issue of the Red Brigades phenomenon which, it will be shown later, elicited tortured and confused assessments on the part of the ultraleft.

The first two acts of the new government on March 16 were symbolic appeals to the Italian public. The first was Andreotti's speech, noted above, on television at 8 P.M., and the second was Cossiga's invitation to all citizens to collaborate with the government by reporting any terrorists recognized from the twenty photographs of "known" terrorists flashed on television.

Andreotti's speech was largely self-congratulatory, paying homage to the Christian Democrats. He began by noting how proud the DC had been in being responsible for bettering the lives of the Italian people and for making those lives tranquil, that is, tranquil before the outbreak of violence a few years ago. Once again the dramatic appeals to democracy were voiced: " . . . we find ourselves having to confront, with the instruments of a democratic state—precious instruments, you ought never stray in believing the false conceptions that the democratic state is weak—a hostility exploding in diverse forms."[46]

This panegyric was none other than what Turner calls, in connection with another threatrical event, Watergate, "stage business," especially that aspect he terms "high-minded principle and low-minded political opportunism." It suffices to cast our memories back only one day before, to March 15, when many of the DC leadership were in court in the Lockheed trial for undermining that very democracy being praised on March 16. It also seems in somewhat poor taste to commence a speech about an event as dolorous as Moro's kidnapping on such a self-congratulatory note, basking in the light of so much asserted past DC benevolence. But the claim of this study, that the symbolic mechanisms of defense had to be set into action immediately after the breach, can help make sense of this apparent paradox. Again, the melodramatic division of protagonists into morally righteous (here the Christian Democrats) and the villainous (Red Brigades) had to be made the symbolic property of the public. And it was the task of the political class to pronounce on these categorical assignments. Indeed, this was the purpose of Andreotti's speech.

Here we see how useful it was to deny the Red Brigades indigenous status. Andreotti had no need to develop any discussion of internal contamination and of the reasons such violent groups could evolve in Italy. He could start right off in a triumphant key by declaring a war, albeit a democratic war, on the invaders.

As for Cossiga's twenty photographs shown nationally on television, two of the individuals were soon discovered to be already in jail, and another suspect appeared twice in the photographs, once with a mustache, once without. That these were, almost all, photographs of people who had Italian names, that they looked quintessentially Italian, confirmed, for *instrumental* purposes, that the country was facing a problem "between Italians." The opposing *symbolic* assessment of exogenous contamination was rhetorical and thus not subject to *evidence* presented in the instrumental arena, or only selectively so.

At this point, we will take a close look at the police and military intelligence work on March 16. When approached analytically, the apparently instrumental nature of these investigatory operations reveals itself to be flushed through with rhetoric and the symbolic imagery of drama. Symbols of power, efficiency, and appropriate inclusion in the event accompanied these police forces. For example, some minutes after the Red Brigades' bogus ambulance van went careening off to its clandestine location, the police received the first calls reporting the attack and the escape of the Red Brigades. Bocca wrote: "Immediately after the ambush of Via Fani, there occurred that which is repeated in all Italian cities on the occasions of Red Bridgades' attacks: all of the police cars, rather than spreading themselves to control and block the widest possible zone, converge where the terrorists are certain not to be, the place of attack."[47]

Logic might decree otherwise, but the hypnotic pull of the instantly photographed and crowded place of the event was somehow overwhelming. There was only one instrumental reason for proceeding to that location, that being to seek clues and witnesses. This could easily be accomplished by a few investigators. Yet the traditional fascination in Italy with sites of accidents, crimes, and violent demonstrations meant that dozens of police and carabinieri cars instinctively flocked to the site of the abduction. This fascination has a more than profane curiosity about it. Many of these sites eventually become shrines where photographs are mounted and flowers continually supplied. The legitimate sanctioning of such a shrine occurs when a permanent, that is, metal, plaque is installed. Some time usually passes before this permanent feature is installed; time, it is here argued, in which to gainsay the lasting power of the event and the site on the relevant public. Via Fani was the first of two shrines produced by this social drama. It symbolized the first breach (as the second, on Via Caetani, will be shown to symbolize the second breach). The police were as enticed as the rest of the public by the power of a shrine in the making. And, the police had the benefit of asserting a definite "instrumental" need for their presence. Thus even those who should operate most convincingly in the instrumental arena, the state's law enforcement personnel, are lured by the symbolic potency of being "where it happened."

During the sixties and early seventies, the police in Italy were extraordinarily violent in their responses to any leftist agitations or demonstrations. As noted, military complicity in right-wing conspiracies was the rule rather than the exception. The combination of these factors led, in the mid-seventies, to investigations exposing the illegitimate nature of the security forces. As a result, these forces were largely dismantled. Thus it was that an extremely disorganized and discredited security force was dealt Moro's kidnapping.[48] Despite this, the strength of the state had to be asserted, and thus the investigations were presented to the public as doing everything and doing it quickly. Public astonishment at the extraordinary efficiency of the Red Brigades had to be countered by public acclaim of the investigators' efficiency. Silj wrote of the establishment media's approach to the "forces of order": "Considering the fact that even the independent [nonparty] newspapers emphasized the timeliness of the intervention of the forces of order, only *La Repubblica* advanced the hypothesis that the timely arrival of the police might have been prevented by the black-out of the telephones."[49] (This last was the result of the cutting of most of the telephone lines in the Monte Mario section of Rome by the Red Brigades.) In fact, the police were delayed by enough time to give the kidnappers a good thirty-minute head start before the roadblocks were set up.

If we were to appraise the performance of the police on purely instrumental terms of efficiency and effectiveness, the judgment would be quite critical. Too many police huddled for too long a time at the scene of the attack. Even *Il Popolo* felt compelled to remark on the bungling of the first day that "the false alarms and the simply untrue reports [such as the bomb that supposedly exploded in the Palazzo di Giustizia, in Piazza Cavour that, having gone off was supposed to have killed another four people; such as the chase on the road to Fumicino of a helicopter of the Carabineri that claimed to have identified the automobile of the brigatisti that held Moro] . . . " (March 17, p. 1). Add to such false starts the twenty misidentified photographs flashed to the Italian public on television and one gets the sense of frustration that began the first day and continued until the end.

For, the joint police and military investigations would prove to have few instrumental results during the entire Moro affair and none that were substantial. But the establishment mass media and the parties of the government would continue to present these investigations under the profile of constant diligence and thoroughness. *Il Messaggero*, Rome's popular daily, had front-page photographs of the "forces of order" on nine days during the fifty-five day sequestration of Moro. These photos featured the military servicemen and police engaged in road checks and house-to-house searches. Machineguns were often prominently featured. In the month of April alone, *L'Unità* featured front-page photos of similarly engaged security forces on six separate days. For the PCI to approvingly present and even highlight the coercive state apparatus indicated that (1) they now considered themselves to be fully integrated and legitimated within that state, and (2) that as a member of the govermental majority they were actually in a position to oversee the military arm of the state. It was both a projective and a preemptive assertion and, unlike the more comfortably established DC, the assertion could not, at least not until late in the Moro affair, contain a ridiculing critique of the failure of these forces. In fact, on the contrary, as the March 21 headline, "The Scientific Inspection of the Blue "128" Fiat Found on Via Mario Fani," indicates (we shall see *how* this car was found below), *L'Unità* strongly pressed the image of an efficient, "scientific" security force doing its duty.

The results of the security operations would be minimal. Here we merely note that neither Moro nor his captors were found during the fifty-five days of captivity. The closest anyone got was the discovery of an apartment containing Red Brigades literature. And, this cache was found only because the tenant of the downstairs apartment had called the firemen to report a water leak.

One more aspect of these investigations is crucial for the issue of the interaction of intrumental and symbolic modes of defense. In a break from all precedent, the military had joined forces with the Polizia, the Carabinieri, and the Guardia della Finanza in these investigations. They had done so in "assetto di guerra," literally translated as "in war trim" or "in fighting trim." Was Italy then indeed in a "state of war?" And what were the ramifications for such things as civil liberties if Italy was indeed in a war? It is interesting to note here the casual use of war terminology that had been used earlier in March to describe the confrontation between the state and the BR defendants in Torino. A *Corriere della Sera* commentator wrote, on March 9, that "this trial, already dirtied by so much spilled blood so that it might not proceed, is more and more headed for the path of fear and of the most creeping and insidious civil war fed by terrorism" (p. 5).

There were, in fact, many warlike references on this first day of the attack. *L'Unità* interestingly noted the comments of the Christian Democrat deputy Bartolomei in a March 17 article: "The head of the DC group, Bartolomei, had asserted that the fact of the coinciding of the beginning of this government and the transformation of the guerrilla movement into a sort of military war—in the frontal attack against the State—cannot be an accident" (p. 2). This quote constitutes not only an example of legitimation via choice of representative source, it also reveals the PCI reluctance to claim that there is a war going on themselves but their willingness to let other do it for them. Their own reluctance will be explained in our discussion of the mass demonstrations that (to a large extent) the Communists organized on March 16.

Ugo La Malfa, leader of the small but influential Republican party, pushed for a definition of the situation as a war, one in which even those "confines which every democratic person considers to be sacred and inviolate . . . could be surpassed for this exceptional moment."[50] His definition of the situation is significant in that it reveals the limits against which the various participants struck in their attempts to fit the incident into a traditional armament of bellicose rituals. They could not, in fact, officially declare war. This was a breach, despite all overt protestations to the contrary, that had come from within. No foreign invaders were visibly landing on Italy's shores, nor were there any threatening to do so. Nor was Italy in a civil war. No section of Italy had attempted secession. The structure of terrorism was qualitatively different from the structure of a war. We are now in a position to understand the following ambiguous, evasive but still bellicose statement of La Malfa on March 16: "I don't proclaim a state of war but I certainly consider this a state of war."[51]

La Malfa's sentiment was shared by the conservative areas in Italian politics as well. The ultraleft presses and radio stations fixed on this conservative sentiment and perceived in it the most dangerous aspect of the just accomplished breach. As such, the ultraleft spent much of its time on March 16 defining itself in contradistinction to the Red Brigades. Radio Onda Rossa opened and closed all their editorials with the phrase, "Onda Rossa is not the radio of the Red Brigades. Onda Rossa is a radio of the Movement." If war was in the offing, it was better not to be taken for someone else. The ultraleft's definition of the situation and the defense they adopted were arrived at in a tortured manner. Since their most dangerous moment, the moment of most contradictions, is still to come during the debate over negotiation, I will postpone further discussion of their participation until then.

Thus far, this most concentrated of days has seen the abduction of an extremely important political figure, the killing of his five bodyguards, the passing of a new government, and massive police and military involvement in the search for Moro. But in terms of dramatic accomplishments, the half-day national strike and the mass of demonstrations were most clearly, according to the establishment mass media and the participants organizing the strike and demonstrations, *the* events of the day. They represented the most spectacular moment of the symbolic defense work of March 16.

The news of Moro's kidnapping spread through Italy by way of ANSA (Associated Press) dispatch at 9:28 A.M. The ANSA employees had been on strike but broke the strike to spread the news. The allure of being in on what was judged to be "big news" was too great. Normal time had been ruptured by "news time" and to block the news was unthinkable—but wasn't the power to block news exactly the power of a strike?

Immediately upon receiving word of the assault, the combined leadership of the CGIL (Confederazione Generale Italiana del Lavoro), CISL (Confederazione Italiana Sindacati Lavoratori), and UIL (Unione Italiana del Lavoro), Italy's three major trade unions, met with Andreotti and other political leaders and decided to proclaim a general strike. The strike would begin immediately and end at midnight—a long strike by Italy's standards. This, the trade union leadership declared, would be "the first act of mobilization of all workers for the defense of liberty and the democratic institutions."[52]

Reading the newspaper reports of the strike and the demonstrations (with the exceptions of the reports in *Lotta Continua* and *il manifesto,* two ultraleft papers and *Il Giornale Nuovo,* a conservative paper) one can discern a generalized picture of the public face the media gave to them. The picture of these events of the day contained three aspects: the strike and demonstrations were (1) spontaneous; (2) unanimous; (3) revealed readiness for further and more elaborate action, all on the part of the striking workers, specifically, and the Italian citizens, generally. In order to be able to declare these activities a *success*, all three requirements needed to be met. And, more than any other task at hand (with the exception of disowning the contaminating Red Brigades), declaring the strike and demonstrations a success was the most important task of the day for the coalition parties and the establishment mass media. The demonstrations were the most spectacular act of defense against the breach performed on March 16. As an act of defense, it attempted to counter the breach point by point. First, the demonstrations and the national strike affirmed the solidarity between youth and elders (the identified key relationship). Next, these spectacles received as much publicity as did the breach itself. Finally, the demonstrations were as (if not more) symbolically rich in their presentation as was the kidnapping itself. Each of these criteria will be illustrated in the course of the analysis of these demonstrations below.

It is useful to begin some days earlier in Torino, the Italian city of industry (particularly the auto industry) par excellence and the city in which the trials against the historic leaders of the Red Brigades were proceeding.

Lietta Tornabuoni, a reporter for the *Corriere della Sera*, visited Torino during the early days of March 1978 and wrote her findings up in an article appearing in the March 10 edition. She described the joint campaign of the DC and the PCI to collect workers' signatures on a petition against terrorism and quoted, in her article, the PCI regional secretary Ferrero: "It hasn't gone well. Of 43,800 workers, only 11,000 have signed. But Mirafiori (the site of the Fiat factory) is a city, a factory so big as not to be grasped, only thirty percent unionized . . . [Ferrero] explains that people are afraid to put their first and last names on paper and that a sense of extraneousness from the state endures here, that many workers retort, when asked to sign, "What about Sindona [the banker involved in a financial scandal of huge proportions recently found dead in his Italian prison cell], what about the trial of Catanzaro? The many cracks in the whole big 'Italian Affair' are very deep."[53]

Of course, not surprisingly, *L'Unità* felt quite differently about the success of this petition. On March 6, an article titled "Tens of Thousands of Signatures against Eversion" claimed: "The mobilization will continue, even in the weeks ahead, in the widespread knowledge that the struggle against terrorism and eversion must become a permanent duty of the masses" (p. 6). This differential assessment of the participation and involvement of the mass public would continue throughout the Moro social drama. However, as will be clear, audience participation would be reduced to the assertion of audience participation.

Meanwhile, Tornabuoni continued her analysis of the Torino scene in her article by commenting on the vigor with which the PCI had worked to realize the trials: "The Communists have worked without rest in order to arrive, at the very minimum, at a commencing of the trial against the Red Brigades. And if something should happen, twelve factories are organized to 'give a massive response in Piazza Statuto.'"[54] Two points are salient here; the first, that there was no unanimity among the workers on the terrorism issue and the workers participation in it (for a variety of reasons, including alienation from the state), the second, that there was already a provision, at least in Torino (and, given the plethora of attacks already occurring in the early months of 1978 throughout Italy, it would be safe to assume in other large Italian cities as well), for a mass response should *something* occur. This something could be precisely an event like the Moro kidnapping. These revelations certainly call into question the alleged spontaneity of the demonstrations, the idea that they were evidence of some intuitive sense of the state on the part of the workers. However, before further evidence is brought to bear on this issue, it will be useful to look first at the public responses of the DC, the PCI, and the establishment mass media to the strikes and demonstrations, to attend to the rhetoric and symbolism of solidarity and success.

The Italian Communist party has a long tradition of the "piazza." The Communists are agile organizers of demonstrations and are capable of attracting hundreds of thousands of people to participate in them. March 16 was no exception. Demonstrations were held in the larger squares of Rome, Milan, Turin, and Bologna. *Paese Sera,* a newspaper associated with the PCI and read predominantly by young people, claimed, in its March 17 edition: "It is necessary to go back to July 14, 1948, to the attack on Palmiro Togliatti, to find another such spontaneous strike, put into effect even before the unions proclaimed them, the piazzas swarming with citizens in immediate response to the popular political forces."[55]

The article goes on to draw the comparison between an Italy divided at the time of Togliatti's wounding, into the "sea of popular anger" and the "conservative fear" and the Italy of today, unified in its strength against the terrorist attack.

L'Unità printed an article in its March 17 edition that was similarly panegyrical: "The image that Italy, the working class, the grand mass of women workers, the youth, the students and all the nation offered yesterday is—we say it without rhetoric—an image that can be compared only to other grave hours of our recent history, hours in which the popular conscience knew spontaneously how to respond to the reactionary challenge instinctively, even before the trade unions and political parties' appeals had reached them. There was something today that was reminiscent of July 14, 1948, the assault of Togliatti."[56]

There was never so much rhetorical pride as that which was said "without rhetoric." But in both of these statements the rhetoric can be clearly assayed. Both emphasize the spontaneity and the solidarity of the people of Italy, the instinctive, organic knowledge of the "correct" way to respond. The PCI knew these assertions to be, at least partly, rhetorical as it had been they who had formulated the contingency plan should an emergency event occur. Both statements then refer back to Togliatti, the Communists' own Moro, as it were. Togliatti and his link to the Constitution and the Resistance (important symbols in themselves, as will be shown in Chapter 5) was a symbol of PCI political and social legitimacy. The appeal was one of an unambiguous antifascist tradition. But in comparing Moro to Togliatti, the PCI was placed in the paradoxical position of granting heroic status to a member of the Christian Democrats, the long-time political nemesis of the PCI. Commenting on these strange bedfellows, Giorgio Bocca wrote: "The Communist Youth Federation even proposed, without arousing the slightest scandal, the construction of a single youth organization of all constitutional factions, catholics and marxists; the old flags of the Resistance cover a convenient unanimity. Suddenly we have discovered that DeGasperi's party (DC) was the protagonist of the Resistance and the cornerstone of progress and not, as it seemed to us to be, almost totally absent from the partisan battles and most occupied with restoring the old state."[57]

As one worker at the Mirafiori plant succinctly put it: "We were always against the DC and now they have us strike for the DC."[58]

For the Christian Democrats who, unlike the Communists, had no tradition of the "piazza," these demonstrations were a real coup. After all, Moro was thoroughly a Christian Democrat. Andreotti referred, in his speech, to the fact that the impressive demonstrations of the day had witnessed the participation of men of all classes (read: not just the working classes, easily mobilized by the PCI) in a "response of solidarity."

The PCI and the DC and the establishment mass media worked laboriously yet enthusiastically with the rich symbols of the demonstration spectacles. They all concentrated on three recurring images: the flags of the political parties (red-PCI, white-DC), the heterogeneity of the crowds in terms of age, most of all, and occupation and sex (this has already been seen in the statements of Andreotti and the comments in the PCI newspaper articles), and, finally, the Resistance. (The Resistance was everybody's favorite root metaphor. But it had to be used very carefully. Further discussion of the various uses of the Resistance legacy must be postponed until later.)

Those flags were particularly fertile symbols. They were visual, dramatic in their movements, and could be described in terms of the proximity of one color (flag) to another: the closer together they were, the more solidarity could be claimed for the Italian people. The demonstrations were, of course, televised so that the proof was there "for anybody to see." A reporter for the *Corriere della Sera* wrote: "In Napoli . . . students and teachers began to leave the schools around 11:00 in order to unite with the workers . . . in the procession of flags of the DC beside that of the flags of the PCI. Songs of the Resistance were intoned."[59]

The PCI, through its various media organs, praised the intermingling of the red and the white flags above all other things. The DC, however, was quite a bit more diffident. Their presentation of the "success" of the demonstrations was more muted than the PCI's and less inclined to stress the heterogeneity of the demonstrations than was the PCI. In the March 17 *Il Popolo,* the demonstrations are dealt with in depth only on page 5. There, the photographs of the crowded Piazza San Giovanni in Rome reveal only Christian Democrat white flags. The headline—"The Civil Protest of the People with the DC"—does not highlight the worker participation, as does the PCI presentation and the discussion of the visual presence of the flags notes only the DC cross and shield symbols and the trade union banners that have, in an unprecented move according to *Il Popolo*, accompanying the "usual writings of the factory council and the union, hard words of condemnation against terrorism." There is no mention of the mixing of DC and PCI flags in *Il Popolo*.

But as far as the establishment mass media and the coalition party leadership were concerned (particularly the PCI), the unified visual field magically banished the specter of total political delegitimation that had, just yesterday, loomed so large with Lockheed and the two months without a government. The PCI was more than satisfied to use this opportunity to discard any residual tinge of illegitimacy. In this regard, the following analysis of two RAI scholars of mass media is pertinent: "The necessity, in terms of indications for responding to an emergency, of turning to a major authority of the state, goes hand in hand with the other requirement . . . of calling forth a unification of the political forces, without discrimination. And it is by way of these modalities of representation of the political system . . . that the relegitimization of the political forces springs forth."[60]

For the PCI, the spring of 1978 was to be a period of relegitimation. The joint participation of the Communist flags and the Christian Democrat flags in the demonstration symbolized, for the PCI, their own transformation. *L'Unità* stories of February and March of that year had frequently focused on the demonstrations taking place in the cities of Italy—demonstrations against terrorism, against the Autonomia movement, of women against violence. The demonstration-consciousness of the PCI was formidable.

This consciousness and orientation matched the historical emphasis on public ceremony and ritual in Italy more generally. The energetic embracing of public demonstrations in Italy has been amply documented. One recounting, Richard Trexler's study of Renaissance Florence public life, uncovers the rich ceremonial context for civic decisions and transformations. Trexler notes the way in which crises were resolved through the transformative powers of public ceremony. In these moments, the key to resolving the crisis (Trexler stresses this point time and again) was the successful reshuffling of the socially stratified extant public roles. Specifically, socially and politically liminal categories of constituents had to be incorporated (as was the case with the Florentine youth in the period 1528–1530) into the civic sphere. These groups possessed a latent energy that was, because of their marginal location, potentially both dangerous and beneficial. Anthropologist Mary Douglas has identified this power of the incumbents of the social margins as being basically the power of category maintenance—the insiders are buffered from the outsiders. Trexler focuses on the ceremonial aspects of the incorporation of these groups in Renaissance Florence during moments in which their power and invigorating energy could redignify and revive a flagging civic sphere. He writes: "These processions [1529 and 1530] were the first in Florentine history in which the giovani marched as a unit in order to propitiate God and, just as amazing, they were the first in which the women of Florence had achieved their own distinct ritual character . . . With these processions of grief and repentance, in which the liminal populations were incorporated into the processional community with distinct identities, the ritual revolution had reached its logical conclusion. At the center of this total ritual population stood the virile saviors of the militia. In their charismatic persons, the republic had made its ultimate attempt to infuse honor into a base political order."[61]

By contrast, the "piazza-consciousness" of Mussolini, choreographer of public demonstrations par excellence some four-hundred years after the Renaissance Florentine processions, understood the power of public participation differently. While still cultivating the presence of citizens in the piazza (particularly Piazza Venezia which was right outside his office in Rome), Mussolini viewed them as crowds to be managed and manipulated. As his biographer, Denis Mack Smith writes: "[Mussolini] used to refer to the balcony outside his office as his 'stage': standing on this stage, he would invite the crowd to answer his rhetorical questions in chorus so as to involve them in active participation. He confessed this gave him the pleasure of feeling like a sculptor wrestling with his material, 'violating' it, molding it into shape."[62]

Thus while the piazza remained an arena of social activity and political participation, the *content* of this participation varied widely throughout Italy's history. March 16, 1978, brought the crowds into the piazza once again.

The historical precedent of Florentine processions is particularly interesting to note in the light of *L'Unità*'s daily references to the antiviolence demonstrations of students in their schools and women in the piazzas throughout the early months of 1978 and continuing on into the months of Moro's sequestration. It revealed *L'Unità's* attempt to highlight the active participation of these marginal groups in combating the corrosive problem of violence.

However, the attempt to project the image of the fervent loyalty of the liminal groups in contemporary Italy, radically opposed, as they were presented as being, to the Red Brigades, broke against another rhetorical campaign that was contemporaneously decrying the disaffection, alienation, and violence of the youthful students of the Movimento and, even worse, Autonomia. This latter group had (10,000 strong), in 1977, demonstrated against the state in the major cities of Italy and actually clashed with the police in such places as Bologna. But here too, historical precedent was not lacking for, as Trexler acknowledges, it had taken years and a civic life-threatening situation before the elders of Florence would grant the "giovani" civic legitimacy. They were simply not trusted: "From the death of Lorenzo the Magnificent until the return of the Medici in 1512, the youth of Florence bore the brunt of blame for almost every disaster that befell the commune."[63]

But the Breach opened up by Moro's kidnapping actually provided, or so thought the major political parties, an occasion for asserting (and thus making true) the transcendance of the youth/elder confrontation. And the March 16 demonstrations were viewed as having accomplished this. The March 17 *L'Unità* edition was literally dominated by a discussion of, or more appropriately, the homage to, the demonstrations of the day before. A large banner-filled photograph on page 1 pictured Piazza San Giovanni and was captioned (getting all of the characters their acknowledgment in the playbill) "Rome—an immense crowd of workers, youth and women filled Piazza San Giovanni where the secretaries of the CGIL, and UIL [the trade unions] spoke." Inside the paper, the entire page 14 was given over to more photos, all of which, similar to the one on the front page, featured the mixed DC and PCI flags. One caption on page 14 was particularly interesting in its message: "The participation, moved and responsible, of women and workers in Piazza San Giovanni." This vaguely condescending description begins to reveal the PCI idea of what was appropriate public participation in the Moro affair. It was both necessary and sufficient to be emotionally moved and to act responsibly, but beyond that it was anybody's guess what else the public could or should do. Note also that women and workers are being presented here as two separate roles, as if they were naturally separate categories. This is the key, as it is, indeed, the one-dimensional presentation of the audience and the protagonists that is the theoretical problematic of this study. An acknowledgment on the part of the PCI that not all workers are men could have led, once the issue of identity was thus opened up, to a questioning of the concrete significance of the presence and activity of the demonstrators more generally. Might these women actually have played some role as a social group capable of healing the Breach? Might this have been an occasion for truly incorporating them, for elevating their ritual status. The tentative reason presented here for the absence of such a true transformation is one that will need to be developed as the study proceeds. The preliminary appraisal is that the predominant framing of the demonstrations was theatrical and not ritual. The significance of this framing distinction has been touched on in the Introduction and will be developed as more of the social drama is revealed. The analysis hinges on the discussion of the difference between small-scale societies and modern, pluralistic societies. The varieties of (often conflicting) social identities and interests that coexist in a society such as contemporary Italy would make logically suspect any appeal to complete social solidarity. Yet it was just such an appeal that the official organizers and interpreters of the mass demonstrations were making for them and for Italy on March 16. The competition among several groups during the Moro social drama to successfully define and channel the events/plot makes the triumphalistic framing of the day's demonstrations problematic. While the change of idiom (from ritual to theater) that has been marked as relevant here does imply much about possibilities of public commitment and participation, the purpose here is to explore specifically the various *interpretations* of the demonstrations, not to impute affection or disaffection on the parts of the demonstrators. We *will* want to use the theory being developed here to speculate, in the Conclusion, about the parameters of possible experiences in such a setting. However, sensitive to the already noted critique John MacAloon has developed of Guy Debord's sweeping and overly general indictment of the "society of the spectacle," we will confine ourselves here to a discussion of the framing of the demonstrations. We will, though, now turn to the voices of some of the participants themselves insofar as they can reveal an *other* framing of the demonstrations from that which the exulting official interpretors were claiming. It is necessary to keep in mind here that no voice comes to the reader uninterpreted. Interviewers and journalists edit and shape. The point is to explore whatever framing actually makes it to the printed page or gets a public hearing. That discourse is our data.

We begin with the discovery that many official interpreters, from Andreotti to Berlinguer, were inserting the phrase, "we say this without rhetoric," in their speeches. So our first question is: Why did there seem to be such trepidation about being associated with rhetoric?

Rhetoric is a word allowing diverse connotations. It can mean showy or eloquent language and it can mean persuasion. The first meaning would indeed seem unsavory in this context as it would imply empty words, sheer theatricality. The second sense of the word might seem less unappealing. Surely leaders have always sought to persuade their constituencies to share their convictions. But the stress, in this situation, was on the *instinctive* persuasions (in the sense of beliefs) of the constituencies, their innate sense of what was right, their spontaneous (unpersuaded) movement to enact what was right. The last impression that Italian political leaders wanted to create was that the people of Italy needed any persuasion at all. It is important to keep in mind the statement of Hugh Duncan, quoted by Murray Edelman: "Identity is compensatory to division: for if men were not separate from one another, there would be no need for the rhetorician to stress their unity."[64]

The recurrent disclaimers of rhetoric suggest the existence of the possibility of diffidence, a sense of extraneousness and outright hostility on the part of segments of the audience that the drama was being perceived as a melodrama. The convoluted reasoning of the following statement in *Paese Sera* affords a view of the absurdity of the PCI perspective on what Moro's kidnapping actually did to the relationship between the PCI and its usual political opponent, the DC: "It is the very fact that our ideas, our way of understanding politics are so different from those that Moro embodies with such subtle talent that makes us feel that he and his world are on our side of the Constitution that we believe is being put on trial, as if we had been attacked ourselves."[65] Historical memory of the explicit opposition between the PCI and the DC has fallen away in the exclusive service of rhetorically drawing new lines of legitimacy. How else would it be possible to understand how the difference in perspectives between the two parties is what makes them the same?

ALTERNATIVE PERSPECTIVES ON THE DEMONSTRATIONS
It is now time to expose the darker, dissenting side of the March 16 national spectacle of solidarity. The questions such an exploration asks are: How are we to understand the "participation" of the demonstrating masses on this day? How are we to make sense of the trade union leaders' statement that the strike was the "first act of mobilization of all workers for the defense of liberty and the democratic institutions?" If the strikes were to be the first step, what would constitute the successive steps?

On March 16, two political scientists, working for a leftist political journal, went to interview the Fiat workers at the Mirafiori plant. They would continue interviewing for the entire fifty-five days of Moro's sequester. The following comments came out of the March 16 interviews. They represent the opinions of the workers on the following issues: Was the strike really spontaneous? Were all the workers in accord with calling the strike (question of unanimity)? For or against what or whom did they consider themselves to be striking?

While the following are in no way statistical indicators of the opinions of all Italian workers on March 16, 1978, they do express a point of view widespread among the workers. The Mirafiori plant outside of Torino attracts workers from all sections of Italy, south as well as north. It is thus a more than appropriate site from which the perspectives of the working class in Italy may be discerned.

The first theme that emerges from a reading of the interviews is that rather than being a strike, March 16 resembled more a lockout. One Southern Italian worker made the following comment about the Communist party leadership: "I think that they all talk so much about democracy, but this is not democracy. They close the gates and force workers to line up. But they really haven't ever accomplished anything. If they knew how to rule and make just laws, they wouldn't need strikes or anything."[66]

And on the same issue another worker stated: "For the workers to be personally involved, they had to do the following: proclaim the strike and wait to see who was striking. In this way one could be deciding personally. But like this we are obliged to strike . . . Here there are thousands of people and all have struck, but why? Because they closed the factory."[67]

In fact, this undercurrent of resistance to the strike on the part of some of the workers would be echoed in *L'Unità* some weeks later. On March 31, a page 2 article unwitting revealed the coercion that apeared to have characterized certain aspects of the PCI's "encouragement" of the workers to strike on March 16. This article, titled "Defend the Strike for Moro—Fiat Sacks on the Spot," disapprovingly describes the firing by the Fiat management at a Milan factory of a worker/PCI union delegate on March 17: "The day after [the strike], March 17, the management of the turbo gas production fired a delegate with extraordinary [summary] procedures. The accusation: verbal unruliness toward three workers who were reluctant to strike." *L'Unità* defends the sacked delegate in this article, primarily on the grounds of the summary firing, this being the less ambiguous aspect of the event. The reader of the article is nonetheless forced to reconsider the "spontaneity" of the mass strike and demonstrations of March 16 in the light of this evidence of explicit pressure applied by the representatives of the PCI on those workers who may indeed have felt extraneous to the organized protest.

While thousands clearly did feel engaged in the antiterrorist demonstrations of March 16, the claim of complete "spontaneity" is problematic. In fact, in several cases the factory gates had been closed even before the workers had been informed of the strike. Called during the middle of the first shift, the strike confronted the workers of the second shift on March 16 as a fait accompli—the gates were locked. The dramatic appeal of a "spontaneously mounted strike of the workers" was indeed great, but much of the spontaneity appears to have been imposed from above. Further, the timing of the announcing of the strike revealed a negligent attitude toward the schedules of the workers on the part of the trade union leadership and of the factory management. Interviewer: Do you endorse this strike? Worker: Well, to do it in such a rush like this . . . They could strike tomorrow no? "Tomorrow morning . . . At least we would know about it first . . . We who come from as far away as outside of Torino. We have to travel forty kilometers to get here. Tomorrow morning, if I knew of the strike, I would stay home, no?"[68]

The worker quoted above may indeed have identified a concern of those protagonists who organized the day's strike (PCI, DC trade union leadership, and factory management); if we don't do this immediately, we may not be able to collect a massive public showing, and thus we might not be able to "prove" to ourselves that Italy is fervently united. Once it had been determined that Moro's kidnapping constituted an event that was an "emergency," it was the "spontaneous" and mutual decision of the traditional opponents (labor and management, PCI and DC) to put into effect the already codified plan of a striking defense.

We will now take up the second issue, that of the alleged unanimity of all the workers. It is interesting to begin here with a comment of a trade union delegate who was extremely confident in his assessment of perceived unanimity among the workers in support of the strike: "Delegate: When a strike proclaimed by CGIL, CISL and UIL succeeds one-hundred percent it seems to me that there is no confusion on the part of the workers."[69] This confounding of the notion of success with that of unanimity can be problematic. In contrast to the delegates' satisfied assurance is the following report of a worker regarding the response inside the factory to the news of the attack: "The news was given while we were in the cafeteria, while the workers were eating. A trade union delegate arrives, 'Permit me two words—he says—Moro has been kidnapped and his bodyguards killed.' In that moment there was wild applause! 'Ah good, good!' many said. Crash, crash, as the bottles were thrown on the ground. That was the first reaction. Then the second reaction was that of opposition to the union, to the decision to strike."[70]

And, in a similar vein, another worker commented: "They imposed this strike . . . here they repeat that we are in a democracy, but then they go ahead and impose a strike on us . . . The first shift which was free to do what it wanted to do, didn't strike, here in the body-work shop of Fiat."[71]

While much vehement opposition to the strike was expressed by the interviewed workers, there was also a large measure of sympathy for the strike, often coupled with a resigned approach to the idea of the relative importance of certain events: "If they kidnapped the three of us [a worker and the two interviewers] what would they do? Nothing. They kidnap Moro because he represents the party. They hit the party and thus automatically they hit the nation. We are nothing as citizens, but he represents Someone. Unfortunately, for better or worse, we have to adapt ourselves."[72]

We have seen so far that we would be hard-pressed to define the strike as either spontaneous or unanimous. It is now important to note the ways in which the striking workers *defined* the strike: Against or for whom or what did they perceive themselves to be striking? Three possible targets have emerged from a reading of the interviews. The strike was seen as, alternately: (1) for Moro, (2) for the five bodyguards, (3) for the democratic state and liberty and against violence. These alternative visions of the point of the strike could be held separately or in various combinations.

In terms of the first option—for Moro—it is important to distinguish between sympathy expressed for Moro "another human being" and Moro "the politician." Many of those interviewed wished Moro well as one human being to another, but they stressed that the only reason the *strike* had been called was because Moro was a political "pezzo grosso," a big shot. And the sympathy of the workers did not extent to Moro as a "pezzo grosso." The resistance to support for this vision of Moro can be read in the many comments complaining about the lack of supportive strikes for other victims of similar attacks. *"Worker Number One:* For that marshal they killed last week [Berardi], for all those heads of families like us, they kill them and no one ever does anything. They take Moro and all of Italy is in a turmoil. *Interviewer:* Do you see this strike as solidarity for Moro? *Worker Number Two:* Solidarity with Moro up to a certain point. As a human being, O.K., but more than anything else, if I strike, I do it for those five that they killed . . . *Worker Number Three:* No one speaks of striking for the five dead ones, the important one is Moro. And who is this 'mangiapane a tradimento' [exploiter], who is this owner of Piedmont having fun with his cronies on our money . . . Bastards!"[73]

The overwhelmingly asserted reason for the strike, however, as far as the workers were concerned, was sympathy for the five bodyguards. A few defined the strike as a protest against violence, but even on this point there was often an engagement of an ironic perspective: "Unfortunately this is the way it goes. If a worker dies, nobody moves . . . In the factory, the workers *never* die! In the factory, nobody dies . . . Outside the gates, yes, but inside never! You never read about *these* kinds of death in the newspapers!"[74] We must address the issue of why so much rhetorical time was made with the grand success of the half-day strike. And why were the workers presented by *L'Unità* in particular (though not by *IlPopolo*) as the most strategically important audience?

There were several reasons for the centrality of the working class to the day's events. First, the working class was the Red Brigades' designated client and ally. Many of the members of the Red Brigades had themselves worked in Italy's factories, and there was no doubt that some Red Brigades or other terrorist group members still operated from within the factories, placing pamphlets in strategic places seeking to influence, in clandestine activities, their fellow workers. As well, the Italian working class had its own very definite history of violence. There was no guarantee that the workers could be counted on to condemn any violence that harmed the state. Indeed, the fear of worker complicity with the Red Brigades even managed to creep into the panygyrics of the trade union leaders' speeches at the demonstrations. These leaders incited their rank and file to "definitively expel all those manifesting weakness, kindness or solidarity with the terrorists from the working class." Finally, enforced solidarity against a defined common enemy facilitated the postponement or cancellation of problems specific to the working class. The Moro kidnapping provided the establishment political parties and the trade unions with an opportunity to assert that all other problems within the factory were secondary and essentially diversions from the *big* problem of terrorism. They even pushed this logic a step further and claimed that worker preoccupation with these other problems was tantamount to treason: "If we speak of our problems in the factory, they tell us, 'either you are with us or you are with the brigades.' There is no longer the opportunity to discuss things in the factory."[75] Just as it had done a great service to the DC by effectively getting rid of the Lockheed scandal (at least for a while), so the Moro affair temporarily took care of internal worker conflicts by delegitimating those very conflicts.

If, as indeed was the case, this one day was the only time in which this so very central audience was called upon to support the actors, almost to be actors themselves, what can be said about the significance of their response? Here it is worth quoting the interpretation of one of the interviewers of the workers: "That strike was, certainly, the one moment during the entire affair of Moro's kidnapping that directly involved the working class; the fact that

. . . penetrated most profoundly inside its social composition, calling upon all the components, provoking involvement, imposing the taking of sides. And it was precisely this inclusion that the working class refused; and this attempt at involvement was negated by the raising the barricade of extraneousness and entrenching oneself in the firm ground of the factory in order to affirm one's difference. And this was done . . . not only to escape from the attempt to create an image of the working class completely integrated in the State, but to affirm—drastically—its own separateness from the entire mechanism of the Moro kidnapping."[76]

We are now able to address the scene of those highly publicized red and white intermingling flags at the demonstrations. When looked at closely, those picturesque flags appear to have resisted a bona fide mingling. Alessandro Silj recounts an illustrative incident involving those flags and the political youth carrying them: "First the young Christian Democrats take off. Several thousand young Roman Communists are held to one side. Massimo D'Alema, secretary of the FGIC (PCI youth group) had proposed that they demonstrate together, with mixed flags. The Christian Democrats refused. The Christian Democrats begin to march . . . some meters ahead, the Communists follow. The DC quicken their step: 'Moro is ours and we want him,' 'DC, Liberty, DC, Liberty.' The Communists quicken their step as well, they attempt to stay attached to the tail of the DC corps and shout, 'Socialism, democracy, the working class has chosen this road.' At this point, the DC literally run away in an attempt to discourage these 'troublemaker Communists.' 'But who wants *them?* Who invited them? Let them demonstrate on their own.' Someone reaches D'Alema. Listen, at this point let's go do our own thing. We can hardly run after them!"[77]

The DC youth explain later that they felt the Communist presence to be taking away from their own first experience with The Piazza. And, after all, Moto did *belong* (at least this was temporarily a point of pride) to the DC. As to the demonstrations themselves, *Lotta Continua* wrote that, while most of the press viewed the demonstrations enthusiastically, its own perspective was different, more historical: "Whoever had seen many mobilizations, from sixty-nine to today, could not help perceive, today, the emotional extraneousness that characterized those in the piazza . . . little applause and consistent whistling . . . Only the banners of the PCI

were raised in the parade. When the [DC] Communion and Liberation group passed hisses were heard. These were the only moments
of life."[78]

In order to understand why it was that so much interest was being
taken in the location and configuration of the various party and
trade union banners in the piazzas on March 16, it is important to
understand both the pictoral nature of Italian culture, where gestures are read in the same way that words are read and the historical
importance of banners as public emblems of identity. Here again,
Trexler's discussion of Renaissance Florence is revealing. Discussing the Ciompi revolt of 1378, Trexler writes: Then in July they
seized the most important flag in the city, the Standard of Justice.
"And with that flag in hand," a horrified communal official wrote,
"they did the greatest damage." Observers wrote as if people were
mere adjuncts of banners throughout the summer. "All the flags
[were] in the Piazza, with the people under them."[79] So if the civic
flag could do irreparable damage in the wrong hands, maybe the
solidarity of political and union flags could perform a magical
healing in the right hands.

The institutions of the state had designated two audience–response criteria as necessary and sufficient for March 16: (1) the
public had to publicly demonstrate a supportive a-critical posture
vis-à-vis the state (given that it was fruitless to require a demonstration unilaterally *in support of* the state—a subtle and important
difference), (2) these demonstrations had to be "democratic"
(read: no curfew impositions or vigilante violence). Democratic did
not mean, for example, the possibility of the Fiat workers voting on
the strike issue or the parties of the proposed coalition elaborating,
refining, or changing their participation expectations in a debate of
any significant duration prior to ratification. But to what end were
these two conditions of response necessary and sufficient? They
were not necessary to find Moro and were only partially sufficient in
legitimating the PCI and in discrediting the Red Brigades. Rather,
they were, on and (exclusively) for March 16, 1978, necessary and
sufficient for giving a rebirth to Italy. This was the object of the
demonstration and of the panegyrics recited about them. By all
accounts, March 16 ought to have been a day of bitter realization:
realization that things had generally dissolved around the political
class, that a long crisis was ending only to give way to a paradoxical
union of opposites in government, that the Lockheed scandal was

using up all the remaining moral credit, that terrorists had achieved an unprecedented peak in efficiency and choice of target . . . How was it that, despite this bitter reality, such scholars as the PCI member Paolo Spriano could write in a *L'Unità* article titled "The Piazza and the State": "Is it not perhaps true that we have never in thirty years seen, as we saw the day before yesterday [March 16] the country and parliament so united, the former supporting the latter which, with its vote, interpreted the anxiety and the will of the former?" (March 18, p. 1) How was it that March 16 had been transformed into one of the most glorious and picturesque days in recent Italian history? It is the position of this study that a large measure of *cognitive* satisfaction was derived from the ability of this social (melo)drama to generate distinct heroes and villains. As well, a large measure of *affective* satisfaction was derived from the realization that "We" ourselves (the Italian citizens) are the heroes. Mary Douglas's notion about the need to define and keep separate distinct categories of phenomena (derived from Durkheim's ideas about the sacred and the profane) is most relevant. The sense of extreme diffuseness and indeterminacy that had permeated Italy in the months before Moro was kidnapped had left the political class and the public without many of the old certainties, certainties that included the understanding that the PCI was a clear opposition party or that somehow, despite all the corruption and clientelism, the Christian Democrats would still manage to sustain a government, if not to actually govern. The immediate effect of Moro's kidnapping was the realignment of all the familiar components of Italian social and political life. They were not exactly what they had been before, were in fact in brand new relationships to each other, but they were at least, once again, conceptually distinct. Melodrama, unlike other, more ambitious genres, facilitates the recognition of the characters and the identification of their normative valences.

As for emotional satisfaction, a case could be made here for a kind of artful attempt to craft a Durkheimian "collective effervescence." Thus while the spectacle of the demonstration was actually, it is here being claimed, a piece of theater, it was presented as a sacred and reinvigorating ritual. Of course, it is possible, bearing in mind MacAloon's analysis of the modern Olympics, to discover true rituals and feelings of belief nesting in the larger spectacularized events. Collective effervescence occurs during collective rituals in which not only are old traditions and values renewed but new ones are actually forged. This, it will be recalled from the Introduction, is akin to Marx's analysis of the borrowing of ancient traditions by the revolutionaries in France during the Revolution of 1789. Indeed, the borrowing in the Moro social drama was ample and politically variegated. Chapter 5 will present the terms and significance of these "sacralizing" references as they symbolically shored up the negotiation decisions. On March 16, the immediate task at hand was to convince the audience that such a renewal had indeed almost instantaneously occurred over the wreckage of the day's events. This idea permeated the media presentation of the public responses of the day. Enzo Forcella, director of GR3 (third national radio station), made the following claim during his program "First Page" on the evening of March 16: "Maybe yes, the only thing I would like to say, to note as a political observer, as a citizen of this country: this is an extremely torn, lacerated and divided country in which, it has always been said, there has never been a common base of co-habitation. Well, this has been a day, not only dramatic, not only tragic but, I would say, also historic. The reason for this is that we have had the sensation, maybe for the first time in years, in decades, of a country that responds, that rediscovers its communal base."[80] Such a claim, along with the constant phrases "renewed solidarity" and "democratic tremor" running through the media reports and both the DC and PCI statements, clearly aimed at denying the breach that other tremors had opened up.

The focus of this chapter has been on revealing this renewal as a renewal "discovered" only by the establishment media and the coalition political parties (particularly the DC and PCI). But even for the most vociferous, it would be a renewal enduring only a day, a kind of Brigadoon risen from the mist every hundred years. The ultraleft was already busy, on March 16, making theoretical time with both the large numbers of people who *had* demonstrated and the many who had *not,* who had exhibited a marked indifference toward the events of the day that even one Communist parliamentarian had had to acknowledge, although the indifference in that case was termed fear (a significant difference).[81] Scalzone again: "There were large masses of people who exhibited extraneousness to the demonstrations for Moro. There were also large numbers who went out to the piazza. Let us see what was the complex of motivations of those who demonstrated. Who can be certain that the enormous number of workers mobilized acted with the notion of sustaining the state? In reality, it was a question of diverse motivations. Thus, this is a *terrain* of work for revolutionaries, a rich terrain of contradictions and areas and *not* something bad to be exorcized."[82]

While not supporting the Red Brigades or only doing so in an extremely qualified way, the ultraleft resisted the call to unilaterally support the state. Hence the phrase: "Neither with the Red Brigades nor with the State." The Red Brigades action was viewed, in the March 17 edition of *Lotta Continua,* as another obstacle to any mass movement to bring about true change. More will be said of the ultraleft's positions in later chapters.

In the midst of all the self-congratulatory fanfare, one item that should have been prominent on the agenda seems to have slipped through the cracks. And, as it is always just as important to take note of what is missing as it is to note what is present, this particular absence is most meaningful. Of course, the absence to which I refer was Aldo Moro himself. Naturally, neither Moro nor the Red Brigades could publicly, openly, participate in the day's events. They could do so only by proxy, phone calls, or message drops. Only one communication had, in fact, been received in which the sole message was the claim of the Red Brigades of the attack and kidnapping of Moro. There was no message from Moro nor any reference to negotiation. What is of interest here are the ways in which the participants imaged the absent figure of Aldo Moro on March 16.

The analysis of this day's definition and defense work has exposed numerous moments of useful forgetfulness. The Red Brigades' known history had been ignored in the process of configuring it as an externally derived contamination threat. The Christian Democrat party's rather sideline showing during the Resistance was exchanged for the image of a party full of freedom fighters. Now, the natural instinct after any individual has been the victim of a violent attack (as long as that individual was not previously considered an unmitigated villain) is to upgrade his or her total image as well as the image of the organization with which the person is associated. Much the same happened to the image of Moro on March 16. His interminable, incomprehensible speeches were figuratively shelved in order to emphasize his enlightened legislative work. His strategy of exhausting opponents by dragging out legislative proceedings was transformed into humble patience. Even the Communists presented, as shown above, their differences with Moro as the reason they felt themselves on the same side of the barricades as he. Only the ultraleft "remembered" another less altruistic Moro, one whose membership in the Christian Democrats could only signify the taking and keeping of power. Radio Città Futura interviewed people in Piazza Vittorio in Rome and in a Roman bank. From the responses they received, they concluded the following: "The indifference, with respect to the dramatics [of the day], revealed in employees who did not want to strike for Moro nothing else than a refutation of the figure of Aldo Moro, of all the suspicious events, the plots."[83]

So far, we needn't be surprised by the image of Moro conjured up on March 16. What is a surprise, though, is the sensation derived from reading the newspapers and the radio and television transcripts of the day, that Moro was already being eulogized, was already being taken as "as good as dead." *Il Messaggero* had a four-page Moro life-history spread, replete with obituary-like youthful photographs and important personal and public dates in his life. Bechelloni wrote that "the most tragic hypothesis about Moro's destiny were being advanced, with the result that most were surprised and felt they had been mocked when it was discovered that Moro was alive and that no exchange had been requested."[84]

To what purpose was the notion that Moro was dead constructed? Would not the logical approach be one of expressed hope that Moro was still alive and refundable? To this hope, indeed, could be added the evidence of eyewitnesses who saw Moro being pushed alive, bent over into one of the Red Brigades' cars on Via Fani, and the lack of any blood stain of Moro's type at the scene of the attack. But testimony of this kind is not preferred by melodrama. Rather, the major participants in the drama were soliciting rightful indignation and mournful shocks, attitudes reaching their highest pitch only in cases of death. The hypothesis that death was imminent was only second best, but it would become the attitude that would be sustained until the second breach after the irrefutable evidence of a photograph of Moro reading a current newspaper arrived some days later. After the second breach, the imminent death hypothesis would be replaced by the fear that death was *not* imminent. But for the time being, the "imminent" position was bolstered by much press attention paid to the alleged fragile nature of Moro's health. An autopsy would reveal much later that Moro was in good health at the time of his kidnapping and for the duration of his sequester. But there was a reason for insisting that Moro was so extremely delicate, a sort of hidden agenda of suspicion. This was the fear that Moro might just be fragile enough to do something stupid. Silj refers to the sotto voce fear that Moro might "talk." There was also the idea that Moro might, as indeed he would, press for negotiations between the Red Brigades and the Italian government. The watching, institutional eyes of Italy were already set to judge Moro's performance. From the *Corriere della Sera:* "It is up to Aldo Moro, one of the great statesmen of our time, to undergo a tremendous test. But we are confident that he, with the force of his spirit and with the height of his civil and religious faith, even in the fragility of his health and for all that.he is human, will remain in every moment, himself."[85] A few days later, *Corriere della Sera*'s watchful eye would again raise the question of Moro's health with an article titled: "Moro's Doctors Are Certain That He Will Know How to Deal with Difficulties" (March 18, p. 6).

More a warning than a compliment, the sentiments of these articles were echoed by many political leaders. The autonomous person Moro, dead or alive, was already dissolving. In his place was being erected a sort of oracle cave to which various interpreting sibyls would give their ear: ". . . the second reflection [of this newscaster, Gustavo Selva] concerns Moro's life, which perhaps is in danger in this moment: yet with the great service that this discrete, intelligent and delicate man now asks of us is that no one yield, in any way, to the blackmail of the kidnappers."[86]

At the point of this broadcast on March 16, no word, on any subject, had actually been received from Moro. How Selva could intuit Moro's wishes will ever remain a mystery. In fact, events would prove Selva to have been a rather poor interpreter of the whispering voice he thought he heard. Indeed, taken apart, the meaning of Selva's statement is full of contradictions. It says that yes, Moro is discrete and intelligent but that he is also delicate. It says that we (journalists and politicians) have to make sure that we point Moro in the direction of his strength. We can't be soft with him. We will have none of this notorious "Stockholm Syndrome" captive complicity with terrorists. And Selva was a journalist sympathetic to the DC.

The position to be taken toward eventual real-life negotiation requests from Moro (as well as from the Red Brigades) was already being hardened on March 16. But March 16 was not really a day devoted to Moro. He was, perhaps, the least attended subject of the day despite the fact that his kidnapping actually occasioned the day's events. Far more important was the rebirth of Italian institutions, far more important the PCI attempt at auto-relegitimation, far more important the Christian Democrat "discovery" of the piazza. Moro was merely that (however frightening) off-stage "death" that provides the motor force of the play.

Of the protagonist's dramatic self-consciousness, we have seen ample evidence. The next weeks would see an amplification of this as regards the various narrative resolutions anticipated and/or desired. Here we will leave the breach with its relative unconcern with Moro by giving a taste of what was to come. A few days later, on March 19, the first Red Brigades communique is delivered into the hands of the press (via drop-offs in municipal trash cans) along with the first photograph of Aldo Moro and the first of many letters written by Moro, this one addressed to the minister of internal affairs, Francesco Cossiga. The communique announces, among other things, that Aldo Moro will be tried by his captors. Both *Il Popolo* and *L'Unità* use the same exact phrase in describing this trial. They both call it a "tragic farce" (*L'Unità,* March 19, pg. 1; "This is the image of a man whom his kidnappers aim to make a martyr out of in one of those tragic farces they call a trial"; *Il Popolo,* March 19, p. 1 headline; "A Tragic Farce is Announced against Moro"). This duplication of descriptive and analytic metaphor is striking. Surely other terms, such as "joke" or "travesty of justice" might have been used. But the theatrical idiom had already, we have just seen, locked into place and the protagonists were getting ready to watch, and, if possible, contour the dramatic series just beginning: "Other messages will arrive, along with the supposed "confessions" of a tragic farce of a trial" (*Il Popolo,* p. 2).

But preempting the plot in this way would prove less easy than the Christian Democrats and the other protagonists anticipated, as we will see. Farce was fine as long as it was the Red Brigades' farce and not that of the state. Selecting the right genre was as important as playing the correct role. A further difficulty would develop as that uncomfortable character, Moro, would attempt to actually appear on the stage. On March 16, however, his was the most conspicuous absence of the day.

4 Crisis: Recognition and Negotiation

As its power increases, a community ceases to take the individual's transgressions so seriously, because they can no longer be considered as dangerous and destructive to the whole as they were formerly. . . . As the power and self-confidence of the community increase, the penal law always becomes more moderate; every weakening or imperiling of the former brings with it a restoration of the harsher forms of the latter.

FRIEDRICH NIETZSCHE[1]

The a priori refusal to negotiate (nota bene, I am saying negotiate, not exchange "prisoners") is proof of weakness, not of strength. Only one who feels himself to be weak and insecure avoids confrontation with the enemy.

ALESSANDRO SILJ[2]

The Protagonists Claim Their Positions

By the evening of March 16, the very day of Moro's kidnapping, many of the social drama's protagonists had already hardened positions on the issue of negotiation with the Red Brigades. Given the absence of any mention of negotiation in the Red Brigades' statement claiming responsibility for the attack, the alacrity with which these positions were decided upon and publicly presented was notable. In fact, it is the claim here that the single most critical and problematic issue of the Crisis phase of the Moro social drama (if not the entire drama itself) was precisely this issue of negotiation. The period of time during which negotiation possibilities appeared and (swiftly) disappeared was the time during which the original breach was widened in the direction of the "dominant cleavage in the widest set of relevant social relations to which the parties in conflict belong."[3] In identifying the issue of negotiation as the goad to the Moro social drama's widening crisis, this chapter aims at revealing that which Giovanni Sartori claims traditional studies in the sociology of politics are likely to miss, that is, "the fact that 'objective cleavages' can be largely manipulated, that is, used as resources, and thereby over or underplayed according to alignment and coalition strategies."[4]

During this Crisis phase, all of the major and the minor protagonists developed precise positions on the question of negotiation with the Red Brigades. The positions and their political and dramatic significance (these two aspects, as always, interacting dialectically) comprise the data for this chapter's analysis. However, it is also important to attend to the respective protagonist's moral presentation of their positions. In other words, each protagonist presented its negotiation position as being motivated by adherence to specific principles and values. The ensemble of these principles comprised a set of themes I will identify, following a number of anthropologists and sociologists[5] who have located similar socially contextuated phenomena, as "root paradigms." The particular set of root paradigms salient to the Italy of the Moro social drama are presented, in detail, in the following chapter. There we will see the practical implementations of the theoretical decisions explored in this chapter. For the present, the task is to explore the range and depth of the interwoven issues of recognition of and negotiation with the Red Brigades.

In the last chapter, the one dealing with the Breach phase, we saw that after the Red Brigades kidnapped Moro Italian officialdom jumped immediately into the breach, paradoxically in order to deny that a breach had actually occurred. This they did by attempting to "defamiliarize" the Red Brigades, a process that will be analytically expanded below. Their strategy was, in some sense, on target as, it will be recalled, Turner is explicit that a breach occurs between individuals or groups *within* a social order. It is endogenous. The defamiliarization process of the Red Brigades reached its zenith during the breach phase (the immediate twenty-four-hour aftermath of Moro's abduction). It will be recalled that it consisted of avowals on the parts of representatives of the Christian Democrats, the Communists, the establishment mass media, and sections of the ultraleft (each for their own reasons) that the Red Brigades were foreign-born, foreign manipulated, and common criminals rather than political insurgents. This, despite a known and documented history of the Red Brigades in which their indigenous origins and political activism had been amply charted. Thus the efforts to defamiliarize or disown the Red Brigades constituted precisely an attempt to deny that any serious internal rift had occurred.

The defamiliarization process would continue during the Crisis phase. In this phase it would be used as part of the rhetoric of justification backing up the decisions regarding negotiation. For, the very discussion of the identity of the Red Brigades became, through a series of logological transformations, simultaneously a discussion of whether or not negotiations could be accepted. In order for this to occur, a number of separate, distinct issues had to be collapsed. Negotiations were presented, by those protagonists refusing it as an option, as being necessarily concomitant with a recognition of the Red Brigades, and recognition of them was presented, again by these same protagonists, as tantamount to their legitimation. And the legitimation of the Red Brigades, as we will now see, was something that had to be avoided at all costs. Before developing the discussion of the implications of this collapsing of categories, we first need simply chart the several protagonists and their negotiation positions.

Our calibration of the negotiation positions, though, must first pose a question: Why did so many of the drama's protagonists, particularly the major political parties, regard it is necessary to decide upon policy positions regarding the possibility of negotiations with the Red Brigades in the immediate aftermath of Moro's abduction? Why in fact did they go so far as to preempt the abductors themselves in bringing up this issue and in "going public" with it? To begin responding to these questions, it will be necessary to identify the various positions taken.[6]

On the night of March 17, Gustavo Selva, director of the news program of the Italian national radio's second station (GR2-Giornale Radio Due), was editorializing on the radio that "Carlo Donat Cattin [a leading Christian Democrat] who is first and foremost a friend [to Moro] and only after that a party colleague, has justly said that no blackmail could or would be accepted from the brigatisti."[7] On the following day, March 18, the Christian Democrat leadership held a meeting exclusively devoted to the development of a party line in the case of a negotiation request on the part of the Red Brigades. The nearly unanimous decision of the party was negative—no negotiations under any circumstances. The only dissenting voices within the party were so mild and ambiguous that one would, in fact, be hard pressed to call them bona fide dissenters. An example of a "dissenting" statement was the following, quoted in the *Corriere della Sera,* elaborated by a DC deputy named Cavina. He was being interviewed by a reporter immediately prior to the meeting of his party to discuss the negotiation issue: "I don't know—it's [the prospect of negotiation] a problem we hope will not be posed. In any case, Moro's family, before anyone else, must consider the possibility and then, the party, as Moro's second family."[8] Preliminary, tentative qualifications aside, the Christian Democrats resolved to adopt the no-negotiation stance without significant internal debate.

The Socialist party did not adopt an explicit position on the negotiation issue in the immediate aftermath of the kidnapping. They would, however, later arrive at a conditional favoring of the prospect of negotiation and, for the duration, identified themselves as the "Party of Negotiation." The Socialist's ability and willingness to take such a position requires some explanation. Here it is necessary to refer to the structural location of this party within Italian politics in 1978.

While representing approximately only one-tenth of the Italian electorate, the Socialists are, as noted in Chapter 2, strategically vital. As the "acceptable" left party, they can make or break coalitions by switching alliances, siding now with the Communists, now with the Christian Democrats. Not surprisingly, the Socialists have been called a party in search of an identity. Less forgivingly, some have called them opportunists.

As the Party of Negotiation in the Moro social drama, the Socialists claimed, albeit in a prevaricating way, that Moro's life was more sacred than any abstract idea that the hardliners might present as inviolable. We will see examples of this praxis in the following chapter on "root paradigms" in the Moro social drama. But the Socialists were indeed being consistent on this point. Together with the Radical party, the Socialists had, for years, defended and promoted human-rights issues in Italian politics. Thus, by conditionally favoring negotiations with the Red Brigades, the Socialists were trying to kill two birds with one stone. They were trying to remain true to their humanitarian stance and, under the overtly ambitious party secretary, now the prime minister, Bettino Craxi, they were attempting to stake out a personal territory in the forest of symbolic politics. In this event, the accusations of opportunism agaist the Socialists were plentiful. Giorgio Bocca's assessment of the Socialist strategy and its detractors is illuminating: "The Socialists sallying forth, according to many, was opportunistic. They claim that the Socialists were attempting to escape from the silence and the progressive electoral erosion to which they had been condemned by the Historic Compromise. But this is a moralistic accusation. In politics everything is in some way opportunistic and the fact that minor parties desire their own survival and look for some space to open up is natural."[9] The Historic Compromise having robbed the Socialist party of their accustomed roles of both intermediary and interference between the Communists and the Christian Democrats, the party had nothing to lose by charting its own unique negotiation course.[10]

The various groups and movements of the Italian ultraleft, including Lotta Continua (Continual Struggle) and the Democrazia Proletaria (Proletarian Democracy), developed a generally positive attitude toward negotiation. The decision-making process was, itself, fraught with tension and difficulty. A close analysis of the working out of this position will be developed in this chapter.

The independent (as opposed to party affiliated) mass media organs, including the several national radio stations and television channels, followed the line of the major political parties in immediately rejecting any type of negotiation.[11] Similarly, the Vatican adopted the no-negotiation stance and never altered it.

Both Moro (via his letters) and his family (in its capacity as proxy) adamantly pressed for negotiations. Indeed, Moro would be the party chosen to officially present the Red Brigades' actual negotiation request.[12] The Red Brigades did ultimately press for negotiations in their own right, although they did not explicitly mention negotiation until their seventh (of nine) communique, sent to several newspapers on April 19, more than one month after Moro's kidnappng. Up to that point, their position regarding the negotiation issue could indirectly be gauged via the repeated emphasis on negotiations in Moro's letters.

Finally, the position of the Communists (PCI) requires some immediate explication. The Communists were, from the very outset of the Moro social drama, the single most explicit protagonist in adopting a position on negotiation. They were adamantly opposed to any negotiation (which they termed "ricatto," blackmail), outdoing even the Christian Democrats in their unwavering firmness.

This "hard line" of the PCI presents us with one of the most glaring paradoxes of the entire social drama. Why, given the importance of Aldo Moro to the PCI, to its future political legitimacy, was this party so swift to close off the only concrete option available for obtaining Moro's release?[13] Why, in other words, did the PCI take a position that virtually assured Moro's death when having Moro back was clearly in their best interest? The answer to this question is, in many ways, critical to both the form and content of this dramaturgical study. It is so central first because it locates the central axiom behind the logic of all case studies, dramaturgic or otherwise, that is; that particular *events* and the particular responses they evoke can give us access to the more general *situations* of the protagonists and of the societies in which they occur. In the Moro affair, then, the PCI was faced with two simultaneous "events," the kidnapping of Moro, and the precipitous (though of course not altogether unanticipated) change in their own status as the government of Moro's construction was hurriedly passed on the very day of his kidnapping.[14] But the raison d'être of the case study must be slightly reformulated here into a question: How do particular protagonists deal with events when (and because) they cannot deal with the larger, enduring situation? And it is at this point that the symbolic, and the dramaturgic, must be foregrounded.

In the single decision of whether or not to favor negotiation, much can be read about the recent history of the PCI, a history that, in the words of Carl Boggs, has led the party to a state of "structural impasse."[15] In Chapter 2, it was shown that this state of impasse is the result of an inability to overcome the contradiction of being both a "partito di lotta" (party of struggle) and a "partito di governo" (party of government).[16] Several theories have been put forward in an attempt to explain the PCI's Moro affair nonnegotiation position. Three of these seem reasonable and are not mutually exclusive: (1) The PCI feared that negotiating with the Red Brigades would provoke an authoritarian, right-wing reaction.[17] (2) The PCI feared provoking the wrath of the U.S. government already disgruntled by Moro's opening the door to the Communists in the first place. Thus the PCI had to toe the antiterrorist hard line at all costs.[18] (3) The PCI feared that negotiating with the Red Brigades would provide further ammunition to its critics who were already accusing the party of being the progenitor of the Red Brigades.[19]

It is significant that all of the explanations above are framed in a defensive way. The response of the Communists was nearly universally interpreted as being defensive rather than offensive in nature. And, indeed, the response was a most telling one. It should be recalled that the PCI was, in 1978, a party that had labored for thirty years to cast off the mantle of illegitimacy imposed on it by the elections of 1948. The recent acquisition of legitimacy offered them, ironically by Moro, was felt by the PCI to be both precarious and incomplete. Given this insecurity, and given the party's recent strategy of avoiding risk and defending law and order,[20] the nonegotiation position can be said to have almost automatically locked into place. To have done otherwise would have meant breaking with a very deeply ingrained tradition.

These then were the central protagonists and their respective positions on negotiation. Other public individuals and organizations, such as Amnesty International, Caritas Internationalis, the International Red Cross, and the United Nations (as represented by Kurt Waldheim, U.N. secretary general), stated, at various points in the social drama, their willingness to operate as intermediaries in any negotiation arrangements.

All of the protagonists agreed on the centrality of the negotiation issue. They disagreed in terms of their responses to it. Each protagonist publicly dramatized its position on this question by way of statements released to the press, demonstrations organized around the theme of negotiation (either pro or con), and appeals published throughout the period of sequestration. These vehicles of public explanation developed moral cases for the position held by containing appeals to a discrete set of high-order principles. The position developed would, then, be linked to some principle(s) providing moral foundation.

With the above in mind, we are now in a position to develop a dramaturgic understanding of the PCI (as well, we shall see, as the other protagonists') positions. The taking of a position on the negotiation question constituted, in the Moro social drama, the single concrete action taken in the attempt to deal with the event. In other words, here the relevant question is: What do particular protagonists of social crises do when not only can they not deal with the general situation but, as well, cannot even deal with the discrete events? The answer is that they do the only thing left to them. They use the ammunition of rhetoric. And, thus, it is imperative that analysts of these events focus on the symbolic positions and quarrels as they become the most important processes for those who have no other weapons but symbols and rhetoric with which to fight.

Thus we may now analyze the central issue of negotiation in the Moro social drama in order to understand why it is played such a critical role. As well, we can begin to delineate the diverse ways in which this issue was defined and treated by the various protagonists for, as shall be seen, negotiation was not a univocal phenomenon.

The Significance of Negotiation as
an Exchange Activity

In order for negotiations of any sort to occur, the parties involved must address each other, either through direct dialogue or indirectly, with the aid of a mediator. This orientation to the other entails some specific kind of recognition of the other. As distinct from official indifference, willingness to negotiate means that the other now lies within one's own horizon (in this case, political horizon) and may thus be perceived as being composed of elements and possessing goals not altogether unfamiliar, strange, or untranslatable. In other words, the other is now recognized. (We will be concerned below to elaborate the significance of recognition.) This, as yet unspecified, recognition of the other is a prerequisite of negotiation as negotiations are, among other things cooperative endeavors. Those engaged in negotiations are negotiating toward something together. They must possess some common vocabulary, at least one common end, and be willing to engage in some kind of exchange. As Crelinston and Szabo have written: "Negotiation also implies a give and take on both sides. Negotiation should not be confused with mere dialogue, whereby the authorities try to keep the hostage-taker talking, either to wear him down or to distract him."[21]

In the case of a state negotiating with declared enemies, there must be some set of transcendent, codified rules that can provide a common arena and common reference points. Thus, in such cases, the contending parties usually appeal to the generally recognized laws of war, currently embodied in the combined declarations of the various Geneva Conventions.[22] The situation becomes more difficult, however, when the enemies come from within and the state does not want to declare a state of war.[23] In such a case, the struggle to find a common ground on which to negotiate (by those desiring negotiation) or the attempt to prove that no such common ground can exist (by those refusing negotiation) gets immediately mired in the discussion of the correct way to define this enemy.

Before we unravel the strands of this discussion, it is important to mention the issue of public knowledge of and involvement in negotiations. The standard relationship of the public to such negotiations has been described by Murray Edelman as essentially being one of exclusion from all but the rhetorical surround: "The significant function of the hortatory style is its reassurance of a mass public so that directly involved groups may function more freely in the later policy-making stages. In the case of bargaining, avoidance of a mass public response and of clear awareness that bargaining is even taking place is sought."[24] In contrast to this, in the Moro social drama, this standard practice was proscribed by the Red Brigades' insistence that there be full public exposure of all of their documents and of all of Moro's letters and by the mass media's willingness to publish these documents. Although those protagonists directly responsible for developing policy on the negotiation question in the Moro social drama did indeed automatically engage the mechanisms of rhetoric in demonstrations and editorials, their ability to privately reinterpret these publicly proclaimed positions, an ability theoretically due them during the policymaking stage, was thwarted by two factors; certain published statements of the Red Brigades and the already introduced factor of the structural precariousness of their own legitimacy.

In their fifth communique, published on April 11 by *La Repubblica, Il Messaggero, La Gazzetta del Popolo, La Stampa,* and *Il Secolo XIX* among other major newspapers, the Red Brigades made their first mention of negotiations (as noted above, this task had, up to this point, been designated to Moro or—alternately interpreted—up to this point, the Red Brigades had given tacit approval to Moro's requests for negotiations).[25] However, the first time they themselves actually mentioned the issue, the Red Brigades did so only in typical iconoclast fashion. They denied that any *secret* negotiations were taking place: "Despite everything that we have said, in the preceding communiques, the organs of the press of the regime continue their campaign of mystification, trying to spread the idea of the existence of 'secret negotiations' or of mysterious 'talks'; we feel we must reiterate that that is the kind of thing that the Regime wants while the position of our Organization has always been and will always be: NO SECRET NEGOTIATION. NOTHING MUST BE HIDDEN FROM THE PEOPLE."[26]

If we may believe, as Alessandro Silj tells us,[27] that the independence of the press substantially dissolved during the Moro social drama and that the press functioned essentially as a representative of the government, it is not unrealistic to suppose that the government purposely leaked the idea of secret negotiations to the newspapers in the hope that the Red Brigades might accept the idea and make private contacts with the government. This would have substantially followed Edelman's schema regarding the relationship between public assertions of hard-line positions (in whatever direction) and private flexibility in negotiations.

We begin to get a sense of the kind of enemies the Red Brigades were portrayed as being. During the Breach, it has already been shown, the major political parties and several other social drama protagonists represented the Red Brigades as foreign (manipulated, if not born) common criminals who deserved no political registration at all. To have done otherwise would have meant being placed in the position of recognizing this terrorist group as engaging in some form of politics.

Now the designation of a group as "political" has many implications. It axiomatically incorporates other fundamental, baseline recognitions that were not, in fact, granted to the Red Brigades. It will be useful to construct a stratified typology of modes of recognition relevant to terrorists in general and to the Red Brigades in particular. Once elaborated, this schema of types of recognition can provide some ideas about the precise elements of official acknowledgment necessary for the occurrence of negotiation between a recognized sovereign state and an oppositional (including outright belligerent) group.

Varieties of Recognition
HUMAN BEINGS

The most basic level of recognition consists in the acknowledgment that terrorists (here the form of belligerents with which we are concerned) are authentic human beings, possessing sentiments, ideas, and the capacity to render moral judgments. The decision to grant such status to terrorists indicates a willingness to recognize that they do not stand irrevocably and necessarily outside the boundaries of human civilization—that they may even, in the midst of their terroristic activities, share something in common with both their victims and their detractors.

We must ask now whether there was any protagonist in a position to grant even this minimal recognition (minimal not in the sense of unimportant but in that of being the primary level) to the Red Brigades during the Moro social drama. Who, in other words, could accomplish this without having to pay the consequences of being a party to an alleged legitimation of the Red Brigades (such consequences including the possibility of having to negotiate with them). It should be recalled that members of this group had just killed Moro's five bodyguards in a fierce ambush. The act of imputing human emotions and moral capacities to beings who were publicly castigated by most of the protagonists in the social drama for murdering "innocents" came perilously close to being interpreted as an act that accepted these actions as rational and motivated by human sentiments. Indeed, only one social institution in Italy would be able to acknowledge the humanness of the Red Brigades without incurring the wrath of the public moralists and the public mass. This institution was, of course, the Catholic church, caretaker of the moral order and of divine forgiveness. On the twenty-first of April, Pope Paul VI publicly presented his "Appeal to the Red Brigades."[28] There were, actually, a number of different modes of recognition incorporated in this one appeal. But, in their totality they amounted to what we are here terming a recognition of the first order. The Red Brigades were being addressed as human beings. The pope directed his appeal to the Red Brigades directly. He used the name that they had chosen for themselves. He addressed them with civility—the strongest adjective he applied to them was "implacable." He wrote that he was praying to them on his knees, thereby giving them a form of deference, admittedly calculated. He cited, and thus recognized, their conscience and finished his grand epistolary gesture with the sentence: "Men of the Red Brigades, give me, the interpretor of the wishes of many of your co-citizens, the hope that a victorious sentiment of humanity still resides in your souls." As a parting gesture, the pope stated that he loved these men of the Red Brigades. The very fact that this terrorist group had elicited the personal attention of the pope implied a status eleva-

tion. Such an action did not, however, place the pope in a com-
promising position for the church claimed a universal tutelage and
an infinitely forgiving benevolence.

What is most significant for this analysis about this appeal of the
pope's is that none of the other dramatic protagonists could even
come close to telling the Red Brigades that they loved them. Only
the pope could do so with impunity. This was so because only the
pope could love the Red Brigades and not have such public love
open the door to official recognition. The pope was opening no such
political doors to the Red Brigades. The only door he opened was
the spiritual door. In order to grasp the full significance of this
peculiar freedom of the pope's, it suffices to imagine the repercussions of the PCI writing that it loved the Red Brigades in an editorial
in the party newspaper, *L'Unità.*

The PCI daily was, on the contrary, steadily denying that the Red
Brigades could even be considered human beings. On March 19, a
page 1 article accompanied the reproduction of the photograph of
Moro sent to the media and characterized the Red Brigades as
follows: "These are beasts who are even difficult to compare with
the fascists." Fascists, it seems, were to be included in the human
species, the Red Brigades were not. This differential assessment is,
if the horrors of the fascist epoch are remembered, truly puzzling.
The level of indignation had risen to a new extreme. The protagonists of the new era of violence falling off the map in both directions,
the Red Brigades into the realm of beasts,[29] the PCI into the lap of
the constitution, Parliament, and the state—in other words, fully
legitimate. This going to extremes in the construction of identities
pushed the Moro social drama, as we have already had occasion to
note, clearly in the direction of melodrama.

Another aspect of the pope's appeal should be noted. He asked
that the Red Brigades release Moro "without conditions." In other
words, the pope, as representative of his church, would not consider the possibility of negotiation. Thus, in spite of the seeming
magnanimity of the recognition, it stopped short of going beyond
that basic level of acknowledgment of humanity. Indeed, this fell
far short of what the Red Brigades wanted. Despite the fact that, as
Robert Katz has written: "On his knees supplicating he had recognized in them all the things the men on the left side of the Tiber had
so jealously withheld,"[30] the sociological difference between recog-

nition by religious forces and recognition by political forces is most relevant for a group having the overriding goal of being recognized as *political.*

The phenomenological limits against which the pope's letter pushed were made explicit by several journalistic commentators. Eugenio Scalfari, the socialist-leaning editor-in-chief of the national daily newspaper, *La Repubblica,* was one of those who commented on the special privilege of the pope. At the same time, he subtly reminded the political parties and the pope himself of the limitations of such privilege. On April 23, Scalfari wrote the following piece: "But the Pope's letter has also functioned as a model . . . They [the members of the newly formed 'party of negotiation' including Socialists, ultraleftists and independent intellectuals] should compare their language to his, compare his respect for the Italian state with their subtle pietism and should learn that which their trembling layman's conscience ought to have known for some time: that Caesar must administer with the law and God knows how to command with prayer. Neither Caesar nor God negotiates with sinners because the former castigates them, the latter pardons them and—if possible—saves them."[31]

The idea that, as a result of the pope's appeal, the Red Brigades would release Moro "without conditions" strikes us as absurd. The terms of the conditions can shift, but the structure of a political kidnapping demands the presentation of certain conditions. (We will examine the nature of these conditions below.) The journalist Selva, along with many others, did, however, display a kind of willful ingenuousness in this regard when he wrote: "The Pope's appeal is the new fact that could represent the way out in these dramatic hours. How will the Red Brigades respond to the request to release the prisoner without conditions? Will they be satisfied to have succeeded in moving—a most exceptional event—the Pope?"[32]

Selva, politically astute journalist that he was, should have known (most likely did know—but appeared not to in the above-quoted entry in his journal/book) that the Red Brigades would not recognize the pope's recognition of them. This was not the recognition they wanted, and they would not share the point of view in which the symbolic meaning of a personalized papal letter constituted either sufficient enough deference (acceptance of the form) to indicate a Red Brigades victory or sufficient enough admonishment (acceptance of the content) to induce them to feel and display shame and consequently release Moro.

As insufficient as the Red Brigades believed such basic recognition to be, it nonetheless represented a qualitative break from the standard image of the terrorist. H. C. Griesman, in his article on the reification of terrorist imagery, distinguishes between terrorist acts performed by an individual against an organized state and terrorist acts performed by an "official" (state representative) terrorist. The former, he claims, are depicted as being carried out "as part of a violent syndrome in some deranged mind, while the terrorist himself is depicted as a psychotic murderer with clenched fists and a heaving breast who grinds his teeth as the veins stand out on his reddened face."[33] Such melodramatic imagery is, not surprisingly, typical of all social dramas which, as Turner says, "generate their symbolic types: traitors, renegades, villains, martyrs, heroes, faithfuls, infidels, deceivers, scapegoats."[34]

The point here, however, is that psychotics with bulging veins are located in some uncharted realm where humanity leaves off and the savage world begins. Greisman's claim is that the objective act of violence is not the crucial variable determining the public image of the violent actor. Rather, the determining variable is the assessed legitimacy of the organization supporting the violent actor. Greisman asserts that official terrorists have a public image that is the obverse of the public image of the independent, antistate terrorist. The official terrorist "is not unattractive in appearance to the 'studio audience': his body is under control, he moves with organized speed and with a calmness born of delegated authority."[35] Clearly such an individual possesses all those characteristics we associate with human beings. We will return to the distinction between official (legitimate) and unofficial (illegitimate) acts of violence below. For the present, it is sufficient to reiterate a basic tenet of this study relevant to the reification of images Greisman analyzes. In a social drama, nothing about the public image of any of the protagonists may be taken for granted. The potential for shifts in the images and statuses is, in fact, what gives a social drama its inherent tension, what allows the drama to proceed toward some resolution of the central conflict(s). Thus a shift of the Red Brigades' image from being subhumans to being humans (and, potentially, back again to subhuman) represents an attempt on the parts of the official crisis definers to move the drama along.

Before proceeding to the next structural level of recognition a terrorist group can, potentially, receive, it is important to note a subsidiary issue involved in the primary level of recognition. I refer here to the issue of whether or not the Red Brigades were identified as Italians. Simply being granted human status in no way insured that the Red Brigades also would be recognized as bona fide Italians. We have noted that many protagonists had, during the Breach phase of the social drama, made major efforts to prove that the Red Brigades were, in fact, not Italians. Such efforts continued, less successfully in the face of public knowledge that specific Italian suspects were being sought by the police, in the Crisis phase. The analytic distinction relevant here is that between insiders and outsiders. Every higher-order recognition granted to the Red Brigades by the other protagonists made the Red Brigades both more familiar and, in some sense, more legitimate. The negotiation issue was a particularly tricky one as it had the potential to undermine the defamiliarization of the terrorist being effected by so many of the no-negotiation camp protagonists.

POLITICAL BEINGS

The second structural level of recognition in our schema consists of identifying a group of terrorists as a bona fide political group with a distinct (though not necessarily admissible or legitimate) cause. Refusal to grant such recognition would signify that the group's members (in this case the Red Brigades) were violent, nihilistic criminals or, at best, anarchists with no recognizable political cause. Such types cannot be viewed as "legitimate enemies" and thus can neither merit nor be trusted with honorable treaties, negotiations, or exchanges. This second stage of recognition is a complex one. The inclusion-exclusion decision has wide-ranging implications. To view a violent group as politically organized around a political cause means that one must make the codified laws of war available to the group. It means that the members of the group are justified in claiming political prisoner status when they are captured. It means that negotiations and exchanges of prisoners are conceivable. And, in some ways most important, it means that such negotiations, once concluded, must be honored by all the participants. An illuminating and paradigmatic historical precedent is found in Cicero's *On Duties*. Cicero recites the story of Marcus Atilius Regulus, a Roman consul: "In Africa, while Marcus Atilius Regulus was consul for a second time, the enemy captured him by a trick; the Carthaginian commander was Xanthippus the Spartan, serving under Hannibal's father Hamilcar. The enemy authorities then dispatched Regulus to Rome. His instructions were to meet the Senate, and request the return of certain aristocratic Carthaginian prisoners. In case, however, he should fail in his mission, he placed himself under oath to return to Carthage . . . even warfare has its legal obligations; an oath you have sworn to an enemy very often has to be honoured. That is to say, if you swore with the clear intention of keeping your word, then you must do so . . . imagine, for example, that you have been captured by pirates, and you agree with them to pay a ransom for your life. Yet even if your agreement had been on oath, your failure to deliver the ransom would not count as fraudulent. For a pirate does not come under the category of regular enemies since he is the enemy of all the world—as far as he is concerned, good faith and oaths do not come into the picture at all . . . Regulus . . . was not entitled to perjure himself by renouncing the terms and conditions of warfare agreed with the enemy. For our operations against them originated from a regular formal declaration of war, and relations with enemies thus defined are governed by our whole code of warfare as well as by many international laws."[36]

Later chapters of this study will develop the discussion of the way in which Aldo Moro diverged from this paradigm of the correct behavior of a kidnapping victim. Here, however, we are immediately concerned to highlight the distinction Cicero is making between "regular enemies" and "pirates." Regular enemies—that is, legitimate and recognized enemies—merit inclusion in the honor-bound world of oaths, treaties, declarations of war, and negotiations. Toward "pirates"—that is, illegitimate, unrecognized enemies—one need not honor any oaths sworn. All such promises will be viewed as having been extorted.

It is clear that any decision to grant the Red Brigades "legitimate enemy" status would have entitled them to participate in "legal" war-based negotiations and agreements. In a previous kidnapping case, that of the Red Brigades' 1973 abduction of Mario Sossi, a Genovese magistrate, the Red Brigades had indeed been granted (and quickly had rescinded) provisional "legitimate enemy" status and were promised their demanded release of eight members of another "revolutionary" movement (The 22nd of October) on trial in Genova, in exchange for the release of Sossi. This promise was revoked at the last minute by the regional attorney general's appeal to the Supreme Court. Robert Katz writes of the Red Brigades' response to this betrayed negotiation: "The Red Brigades, believing that they had actually shown that the state does not respect its own laws, freed Sossi with an admonition to 'wise up.'"[37]

To the contrary, the actions of the representatives of the Italian state did not reveal a lapse in their respect for their own laws but rather revealed real confusion and conflict about identifying the appropriate and politically safe situations in which to activate its laws. Here we are led to reiterate a major thesis of this chapter. The continually shifting organizational status granted the Red Brigades was the result of the unresolved conflict between those political forces in Italy willing to recognize the Red Brigades as a political group possessed of a (not necessarily legitimate) cause and those forces unwilling to do so. In the case of the PCI, we have seen that much of their unwillingness derived from their sense that they were unable to do so.

When Mario Sossi, after his release, stated that *he* respected the Red Brigades as enemies, their public status momentarily was elevated to legitimate enemy level. Statements such as Sossi's and the more recently released American general James Dozier (released January 28, 1982) who remarked that he viewed the Red Brigades as very intelligent, dedicated to their cause and efficient, reveal that the ex-(note the emphasis on *ex*) victims of political kidnappings comprise one set of individuals licensed to grant this second level of recognition to their abductors. This license, while qualified, is considerable and often unique to the victims. By virtue of their victimization, they are, to a large extent, immune from normal sanctions against recognition of terrorists. They are the innocents who have suffered, and thus there is a general reluctance to further curtail their freedom after their release. Another reason for the victim's relative freedom of speech is the very proximity to and familiarity with the terrorists that the victims is assumed to have attained, thus making him or her something of a terrorist expert. However, the state to which the hostage belongs usually debriefs the released hostage to forestall and mitigate any unusually generous assessment of the terrorists the victim may harbor, a residual effect of the so-called Stockholm Syndrome in which the hostage forms an affective bond to the captor. Thus even the victims' relatively ample freedom to grant various types of recognition to their terrorist captors is subject to censorship when the protagonist state would present a different scenario of the terrorists' ability and status. Dozier's comments, for example, were *not* aired on Italian national television or radio.

We have not yet approached the highest level of recognition that an insurgent group may attain. This level is that of legitimacy whereby the relevant group is officially designated as having a legitimate, political cause. (In reality this recognition rarely occurs through peaceful means and thus is something of an ideal type.) However, here as well, we may cite instances of such recognition being provisionally (and/or unwittingly) granted by those with "special license."

Mario Sossi made a point of remarking on the risotto his captors had made him for his dinners, indicating that they had a human face. Both Sossi and Dozier referenced the Red Brigades' dedication to their cause. In other words, both viewed them as residing in the camp of respect-worthy enemies. But the third-level recognition becomes more perilous, even for the victims of terrorist abduction. Here we may cite the case of Pattty Hearst who actually joined the Symbionese Liberation Army (for whatever reasons and however provisionally). In the Hearst case, the limitations of the victim's license to grant ontological status to terrorists are revealed by the statement of Hearst's prosecutor, Attorney General William Saxbe, that "there are now two crimes. We've got the kidnapping, *if it was a kidnapping* and we have a bank robbery."[38] In other words, not even the victim is entitled to legitimate antistate terrorists. When such an acknowledgment is attempted, the victims themselves are socially reviled as contaminated by the terrorists' illegitimacy and thus become, themselves, suspect and illegitimate.[39]

The issue of the acknowledgment of the Red Brigades' political organizational status provided the basis for several cases of misunderstanding and ritual denunciation during the Moro social drama. The very words used to characterize and refer to the Red Brigades came under close scrutiny. No ambiguity was to be suffered by the most avid state-defending protagonists. Nor, in contradistinction to the above protagonists' insistence on unbudging clarity, could the protagonists favoring negotiation successfully resolve their ambiguity. Kurt Waldheim's televised appeal on April 25, 1978, and the internal debate of the "Lotta Continua" group are illuminating examples of points of slippage in the recognition/nonrecognition campaign.

Both of the following cases are emblematic of the general symbolic potency of language in a social drama. To call an armed revolutionary organization a gang of criminals is to dispossess them symbolically (if not instrumentally) of their political potency. When, as in the Moro case, the instrumental efficiency of the police forces to weaken or destroy the Red Brigades was at a minimum, these symbolic, linguistic skirmishes became all the more significant. Indeed, at the time, they represented, as previously noted, the state-defending protagonists' sole weapons. Here in the case of official recognition we find one extremely salient instance of the interrelationships of symbolic actions and instrumental actions that develop in the midst of social dramas and that move them along. The back and forth between instrumental and symbolic relies on the different kinds and amounts of capital each protagonist possesses. For example, forced total reliance on the symbolic arsenal brought with it, in the Moro social drama, a sense of desperation. We can read this out of the transcript of the Turin trial of the "historic" leaders of the Red Brigades taking place during the very weeks of Moro's kidnapping when the public prosecutor, brought to a high pitch of frustration, exclaimed, "You are nothing but a gang," and received Renato Curcio's complacent response, "A gang that in the meantime has Moro in its hands and will place the entire Italian political class on trial."[40]

The Kurt Waldheim minidrama occurred within the context of the larger Moro social drama. It revealed the limits beyond which no political organization, not even a neutral and international one as the United Nations, could go in terms of granting specific statuses to the Red Brigades. Waldheim's appeal (in Italian), like that of the pope's, was addressed directly to the Red Brigades and was, in fact, read over the national television channels. Waldheim also requested the immediate, unconditioned release of Moro, just as the pope had done. In these gestures, Waldheim was simply exercising his license as an uninterested, neutral party and was not liable to official sanctioning.[41] The real trouble began when Waldheim made the following statement: "Certainly you know that you have attracted the attention of the entire world with your requests. But you must certainly know that the continued detention of Mister Moro, with the terrible anguish that this provokes in his family and all those who are everywhere following the event, can only damage your cause, whatever that is."[42] The key word in Waldheim's statement was the word "cause." Waldheim had attributed the Red Brigades with having some identifiable cause. They were not, then, according to him, merely nihilists engaged in some mindless and directionless terror. It is interesting to note that at least one major newspaper that reproduced Waldheim's speech in its entirety, the *Corriere della Sera* (April 26), changed the word "cause" (causes) to "obiettivi" (objectives), clearly neutralizing what was quickly becoming a controversial issue. (Perhaps the paper was relying on a U.N.–provided English text that indeed substituted the word "purposes" for "causes.")

In fact, almost immediately after Waldheim had read his speech to the nation, the accusations against him began. Republican party deputies La Malfa and Biasini sent a joint telegram to Waldheim protesting against the "sense" of the appeal, suggesting that Waldheim was possessed of an "incomplete understanding of the reasons which lead the democratic forces to defend the authority of the State." Selva wrote in his diary that "I agree with the humanitarian significance of Waldheim's words, but behind the words isn't there perhaps hidden the risk of a recognition of the Red Brigades as a political organization?"[43] Silj cited *La Repubblica*'s editorial against the Waldheim appeal: "The Secretary General of the U.N.," we read, "has said one word too many." For example, he has said that a prolonged detention of Moro could damage "their cause." "What cause?" asks *La Repubblica*. "There is, then, some brigatista cause that is capable of being damaged? This is, to put it mildly, an odd phrase, if not, speaking frankly, one which is most imprudent."[44]

In his own defense, Waldheim was meanwhile claiming that the appearance of the word "cause" in his appeal was the result of a mistranslation of the word "purposes" that he had used in the original version of the speech he had written. We may ask, at this point, why Waldheim felt that "purposes" was a legitimate designation while "cause" was not? What Waldheim seemed to be implying was that all social actors, including common criminals, operate on the basis of some purpose, pose objectives, and are at least minimally organized in order to make plans. He was drawing a sharp distinction between what he had actually written and what he had been accused of having meant. Even this clarification of Waldheim's did not suffice to vanquish all doubts and preoccupations about his intent. Selva wrote: "Those who are accustomed to weighing the meaning of words and even the meaning of syllables, believe they have discerned in the expression "your cause" which refers to the Red Brigades' proposals, nearly a patent of nobility. If effectively—and what reason do we have for doubting it—this was all the result of an error, such a hypothesis makes no sense."[45]

By adding the phrase "and what reason do we have for doubting it?" Selva suggests that his listening and (eventual) reading audience may indeed ask themselves if there is some reason they can discover for doubting that the error was, in fact, an error. But then what was Waldheim doing in alluding to the Red Brigades' purposes?

It is only possible to place Waldheim's recognition of the Red Brigades in some category of public types of recognition if the nature of the United Nations as an international, mediating organization is stressed. In some sense, the United Nations is the archetypal stage on which the dramas of shifts in political legitimacy of various groups are played out. If, for example, the United Nations recognizes the Palestine Liberation Organization as a legitimate or a quasi-legitimate group representing a bona fide cause, the group's international standing will reflect this recognition. The Italian protagonists of the Moro social drama were then justifiably concerned by the phrasing of Waldheim's speech as, error or no, it did seem to grant a form of recognition to the Red Bridgades whereby they were viewed as, in some undefined way, political. For Waldheim to say that releasing Moro would further the Red Brigades' cause or purpose implied that public approval might, in such a case, be forthcoming. Further, any cause capable of eliciting general approval from the public had at least the possibility of being legitimate. This logic was indirect and based on supposition, but such reasoning is the very stuff that conditions the moves of social dramas of legitimacy.

This fear of somehow, even accidentally, legitimating the Red Brigades was clearly expressed by the DC-sympathizing Selva: ". . . the DC party reallying around its secretary Benigno Zaccagnini, has chosen the exploration of every humanitarian road for the liberation of Moro, and, in order to accomplish that which is politically necessary, has refused every recognition of the anti-state"[46]

The Communists were actively engaged in a campaign against granting political status to the Red Brigades. One way to get at the political hue that the Red Brigades sought to cast was through their actual writings, in other words, through their communiques. A leading member of the PCI, Paolo Bufalini, wrote the Communist response to the second Red Brigades communique, sent to *L'Unità* on March 25 and published the next day, Easter: "The readers will find, in another part of the paper [actually on the next page, p. 2] the ample reproduction of the second message of the Red Brigades. They will thus be able to develop an exact opinion of the 'ideology' that inspires this group of assassins. That which strikes one before anything else in the message . . . is the typically paranoid structure of the reasoning, the recurrence of fixed ideas, the arbitrary connecting of facts that don't, in fact, have an objective connection . . . One can't help seeing the threatening signs contained in the formula that speaks of 'judging' the president of the DC. They are preparing a tragic end to this farce called a trial" (*L'Unità*, March 26, 1978, p.1). Once again we see the PCI in the act of delegitimation. Here the Red Brigades are not merely not political, they are also not sane, not rational. Once again the end of the story preempts the actual working out of it—the trial of Moro (dealt with in Chapters 6 and 7) will of necessity have a tragic end. And here we also note a recurrent feature of the Moro social drama—the world in quotation marks. In this case, the quotation marks clearly call into question the political relevance, potency, and soundness of the ideology and practice, of the Red Brigades. So many things were trapped inside quotation marks in the Moro social drama. It often seemed, reading the media interpretations of the events, that nothing could be taken as what it claimed to be, not Moro's letters, not the Red Brigades communiques, not the U.N. secretary general's speech. In fact, as this study is demonstrating, nothing could be so taken, all interpretations were up for grabs and competing with each other. The quotation-mark syndrome was merely an explicit and public rendering of the suspension or the overturning of the obvious. Another particularly salient example of the quotation-mark configuring of reality came on March 31, the day after the first letter from Moro arrived. Here again, the campaign to deny political status to the Red Brigades is in full force. A front page *L'Unità* story titled simply "Firmness," again works backward from an assessment of the condition and identity of Moro to the identity of the Red Brigades: "What is the significance of having imposed the definition of 'political prisoner' [onto Moro] if not the attempt to give legitimacy to the armed struggle of a criminal gang, to impose on the democratic State the recognition of another 'power' of an 'anti-State.' But this would be the end of every civil cohabitation" (March 31, 1978, p. 1).

At the extreme end of the political map, the ultraleft was engaged in an intense internal debate as to the way it ought to recognize the Red Brigades. The issue here was to decide if the Red Brigades were to be declared comrades, comrades who were in error, political enemies, or even (an identification indicating extreme disaffection) criminals. Again, phrases and single words were scrutinized. Here personal anecdotes are emblematic. One ultraleftist I know was severely chastized by her comrades during the viewing of a television program on the Red Brigades in the weeks of Moro's sequestration for casually referring to them as a "banda" (gang) rather than as a "gruppo" or an "organizzazione" (group or organization). To call them a gang meant denying any moral or political legitimacy to their actions. It implied that they were mere criminals engaged in self-serving violence. Such sensitivity was not surprising among those who, it will be shown, were themselves imperiled by the Moro kidnapping.

The crisis within the ultraleft, in terms of its relationship to the Red Brigades before and (especially) during and after Moro, substantially grew out of the inability of the various ultraleft groups to reach a consensus on the correct way to conceptualize the Red Brigades. Two comrades of the "Lotta Continua" group wrote in March of 1978 in the homonymous newspaper: "We continue to use the term 'comrades' when referring to the comrades of the Red Brigades and this usage bothers quite a few of those among the 'Proletariat Democracy' group, the 'Manifesto' group and the PCI and those to their right. Perhaps we can discuss the appropriateness of the use of this term at length. But, the fact remains that this term connecting us refers to our past history, in many instances the same history as that of the comrades who have chosen the clandestine life. They are our comrades of our past and present errors. For this reason, the (ultraleft) formula, sensationally presented and denounced in L'Unità: 'The Red Brigades are comrades in error,' is perfectly acceptable to us. This does not mean that there are not actions and—if you wish—errors which are so mistaken and wrong that they become [our] antagonists."[47]

While the newspaper *Lotta Continua* took an editorial position repudiating the Red Brigades, featuring daily headlines condemning the action (March 17: "Moro Kidnapped: This Is the Dirtiest and Heaviest Joke Ever Pulled against the Italian Proletariat"), it is significant that it continued to publish letters to the editor expressing a variety of attitudes toward the negotiation/recognition issue. And we have seen how important reader involvement in this paper was considered to be. Even the March 17 editorial already points up the highly qualified and complicated way in which the group condemned the action: "General rejection of the action and the practice of the Red Brigades. Fear, sensations of impotence, will to react, are mixed in the strikes taking place throughout Italy already in the morning [of March 16]. In the afternoon, great demonstrations in Rome, Milan, Florence, Bologna, Torino, Genova, attempt to channel the protest toward consensus with the new regime that is requesting the 'death penalty'" (*Lotta Continua*, March 17, 1978, p. 1).

Ultimately, *Lotta Continua* would, during Moro's sequestration, come out to fully endorse negotiations with the Red Brigades for Moro's return. The symbolic basis for their doing so will be explored in the next chapter. But that endorsement, plus *Lotta Continua*'s embracing of what it felt was the genuine ambiguity and contradictoriness of the situation, made the group a target of attack. The protagonist taking up the cudgels of that attack most persistently was the PCI. On March 22, *L'Unità* published an article accusing *Lotta Continua* of "applauding" every crime of the Red Brigades and, picking up this refrain again four days later as they indicted the ultraleft for being one of the Red Brigades' chosen constituents, *L'Unità* asserted that the second Red Brigades communique contained "'Slogans' and 'Openings' toward the extremist [left] area" (*L'Unità*, March 26, 1978).

The section in the Red Brigades communique that *L'Unità* was referencing in the statement cited above was indeed troubling to *Lotta Continua*. The citation references the end of the communique no. 2 where the Red Brigades had written: "Honor to the comrades Lorenzo Jannucci and Fausto Tinelli assassinated by the killers of the regime." The reference here was to two ultraleft youths who had in fact been killed, most likely by Fascist youths in the week before the release of communique no. 2. Here was a real dilemma for the *Lotta Continua* and other ultraleftist groups. In the midst of the quite painful and careful discussion of how the ultraleft wanted to recognize the Red Brigades, if at all, came a straightforward recognition of an expression of solidarity for the ultraleft by the Red Brigades. Thus the Red Brigades were attempting to blur any distinctions between themselves and the ultraleft. They would not accept the assertion of distance and critique from these groups. Simultaneously, we have seen, the Communists were collapsing the groups together claiming that they, as well, could see no differences between the terrorists and such groups as *Lotta Continua*. Attempting to hold its own, *Lotta Continua* responded to this "salute" of the Red Brigades in their March 26 edition: "This is an hallucinatory and sordid recognition. As friends of Iaio and Fausto we send it back to them: 'not welcome.'"

Other ultraleft groups were struggling to formulate an adequate terminology to describe the distance they felt from the Red Brigades without exclaiming total alienation from them. Some, though, sought to resolve the problem by overtly repudiating the Red Brigades' left political location. And so the Red Brigades became the "so-called Red" Brigades. On March 17, one Radio Città Futura (ultraleft radio station) commentator was already insinuating that the Red Brigades' self-proclaimed revolutionary purposes were a mere facade: "Our task [is to] denounce this entire series of maneuvers, these absurd attempts, these absurd kidnappings, claimed by the Red Brigades, because a major political clarification of these things is necessary. The public must know what type of plot lies behind all of this. This is not mere incident, simply carried out by some terrorists but an action, in our opinion, that has a much greater significance and that is supported and backed up somewhere else . . . that is, there are secret services that have been and are now hard at work in our country."[48]

During the breach phase of the social drama, several protagonists had already attempted to deliberately blur the the accepted distinction between leftist violence and rightist violence in order to claim that the Red Brigades were really fascists. This distinction, to reiterate briefly, refers to the structural paradigm of both means and ends that has emerged in Italy by which it is possible to calibrate the general (left/right) orientation of a given terrorist attack.[49]

However, the history of official response in Italy to indigenous terrorism since the sixties has been dotted with examples of paradigmatic right-wing terrorist attacks being attributed to leftists (e.g., the Piazza Fontana bombing). Thus it ought not surprise us if, in the Moro social drama, apparently left-wing attacks are designated as fascist-inspired. The symmetry of counterlogical attribution on both sides belies, however, the very real concern of those in the ultraleft and even in the quasi-legitimate PCI that the so-called leftist terrorism is designed precisely to discredit the left and has, in this, as we shall see, been substantially successful.

For the ultraleft, the imputing of fascist origins to the Red Brigades represented an attempt to stave off its own crisis of identity. It denied that there existed a common heritage between the Red Brigades and themselves. And thus, it avoided a profound discussion of the implications of choosing clandestine violence. Some activists of the ultraleft did effect a more direct confrontation of such implications. Students at the University of Rome held an afternoon meeting in the Student House on the day of Moro's kidnapping. A Radio Città Futura commentator reporting on this meeting referred to its similarity to other ultraleft student assemblies in which "that [clandestine] kind of [political] placement, those phrases, if you will, without conclusion, without any political breath to them have always been rejected.[50] These students did not, then, grant second-level recognition to the Red Brigades. They found them to be, on the contrary, devoid of any political character. The rejection of clandestinity as the only revolutionary option reflected their general ideas about the stage the revolutionary struggle had reached in Italy. They did not share the Red Brigades' conclusion that the only effective politics now was that carried out clandestinely. Even Autonomia Operaia, the group perhaps closest to the Red Brigades in its assessment of the possible role of violence in the struggle against the state, was explicit in its rejection of clandestinity. The April 7 edition of *Lotta Continua* reported the statement of Autonomia Operaia made during a press conference the day before. *Lotta Continua* wrote that the group's representative asserted: "Ours is a mass movement . . . to enter into the clandestine life would cancel this characteristic of our group. It is an invitation that will not be accepted."

While the speaker in the studio of an ultraleft radio call-in program spoke of the Red Brigades' members as "comrades," he also "repeatedly invited the listeners to discuss the 'political' fact in general rather than the nature of those who had committed the act."[51] His appeal was making a tacit reference to the potential damage the Moro kidnapping (and eventual assassination) might do to the ultraleft in general, to the need to begin developing strategy to confront this potential danger. At the same time, it swiftly dealt with the Red Brigades' recognition problem, implying that it was an issue both clear-cut and minor at the same time. The Red Brigades were "comrades," but "let's hurry on to talk about what is really important here." This approach reveals the need felt by those in the ultraleft to deflect attention away from the kind of recognition their fellow travelers were granting the Red Brigades. By automatically and casually calling the Red Brigades "comrades," these ultraleft activists hoped to draw the attention of their radio audience to the more general theoretical and political discussion of the immediate political moment. They claimed a desire not to "waste time" debating the precise nomenclature they ought to apply to the Red Brigades. Nor would they want to open up that debate to the extent that it acquired a significance capable of backfiring in their faces. Here we see quite clearly the way in which these symbolic quarrels were recognized by the ultraleft as potentially leading to real and, given the volatile and desperate political context of 1978, necessarily grave consequences.

Of the crisis of the ultraleft's recognition of and relationship to the Red Brigades, one can conclude only that it was both serious and potentially rupturing and that it was recognized as such. The phrase "neither with the state nor with the Red Brigades" indicated the highly qualified way in which the ultraleft presented its own position on recognition.[52] In truth, there was no real consensus within the ultraleft as to the way in which the Red Brigades ought to be viewed.[53] Some activists saw them as a political group with a cause that had once been legitimate. Some viewed them as comrades possessing a legitimate, even common, cause. Others viewed them as hypocrites, masquerading as leftists. What is important here is to understand the ultraleft's struggle to hit upon the precise recognition formula that would prevent their own further delegitimation and that would, at the same time, be theoretically consistent with the ultraleft's revolutionary agenda and common history with the Red Brigades. The unresolved quality of that issue, the lack of *a* formula for recognition, reflected the extreme difficulty, if not impossibility, of this task. Ultraleftists' responses to their own slips of tongue, to the use of ambiguous words, to the reshuffling of phrases within the ultraleft were dramatic. The ultraleft would ultimately come out in favor of negotiations, adopting as their ultimate rationale the irrevocable sanctity of human life.[54] This appeal provided, however, only a brief respite from the continuous symbolic hand slapping of activist by activist as each tried to come up with the *right* way to recognize the Red Brigades. Furthermore, this ultimate formula could not, as we shall see, prevent the concrete repressive repercussions of the Moro social drama from ultimately besetting them.

How, though, did the Red Brigades themselves want to be recognized? The fact that they did want a particular kind of acknowledgment from the establishment mass media, the political parties (parliamentary as well as extraparliamentary), and from the general public (not only from their own chosen constituency, the working class) revealed their very dependency on those groups and institutions. At the same time, they could never openly abandon their unequivocal hostility toward and alienation from the Italian state and its political institutions. The paradoxical situation of the Red Brigades was precisely that they were depending upon those that they were rejecting as illegitimate to bring about their own legitimation. Their appeals continued to be ostensibly directed to the Proletariat but their more immediate and, in many ways, more realizable goal was to force the official Italian state to grant them recognition. Giorgio Bocca discussed this paradox: "Another contradiction, dramatically revealed in the days of Moro's kidnapping, is that between the ever increasing need of the Red Brigades to legitimate itself, to be recognized, to become an institution that is capable of carrying out anti-trials, anti-justice, the other state and, the whirlpool, the terrorist logic that demands that they eschew every compromise, every cohabitation, every agreement."[55]

LEGITIMATION

One thing was clear. The Red Brigades sought universal recognition as a political organization with a legitimate cause. They presented themselves as vanguard insurgents appealing to a potentially revolutionary mass. They were, however, obviously aware of the denial of this image by most of the other social drama protagonists. In one of the pre-Moro Red Brigades' published resolutions, it had been written: "There is a campaign on to go all out in criminalizing political struggle. This campaign defines as criminal not only the revolutionaries, the comrades who struggle, with or without weapons in their hands, against the multinational capital, but all those who deviate from the ever more rigid juridical regulations and the fixed behavior of the bourgeoisie."[56] When captured by the police, the Red Brigades members would declare themselves to be political prisoners, with the apparent expectation that the relevant Geneva Convention articles would then apply to their cases. All this, again, despite explicit denials of such status attribution by the major parliamentary political parties. One Italian political commentator, Gorrieri, wrote: "The Communist deputy Antonello Trombadori said it very well the other night: "Despite erroneous descriptions there are no political prisoners in Italian jails (as the "brigatisti" claim themselves to be) but only *delinquents* and these are in prison not for what they have thought but for what they have done.'"[57] We will take up a discussion of the assumptions of this statement later when we explore the forms and contents of the Moro social drama trials. First, however, I will refer briefly to the discussion, among legal scholars, of the possibility of applying Geneva Convention articles to insurgents in an attempt to unravel the logic of the kind of recognition necessary for Geneval Convention eligibility.

Insurgents are among those combatant groups not generally incorporated in the sovereign bodies eligible to appeal to the extant laws of war. Indeed, the original Geneva Conventions applied only, according to its Article Two, "to all cases of declared war or of any other armed conflict which may arise between two or more of the High Contracting Parties even if the state of war is not recognized by one of them."[58]

As Peter Trooboff has written: "This provision is particularly significant because it makes clear that the detailed obligations under the Conventions do not apply in so-called internal conflicts, i.e., those that do not involve at least two of the high contracting parties."[59] One special article of the 1949 Conventions, Article Three, did open the door to insurgent coverage. Despite the fact that, on most counts, the Red Brigades did not pass muster, one stipulation of Article Three would have made it possible for the Italian state to grant limited Geneva Convention coverage to the Red Brigades. Indeed, this one condition, if met, could have resolved the most pressing concern of many of the Moro social drama protagonists—that the Red Brigades not be legitimated—that, in other words, they not receive what we are here terming third-level recognition. This condition held that application of Article Three protections "shall not affect the legal status of the Parties to the conflict."[60] In other words, there was no *necessary* link between receiving, for example, political prisoner status and being accorded either temporary or permanent legitimacy.

The fears associated with such possibilities of transformation, however, were not unfounded. One can point to many precedents of illegitimacy transformed, by the course of history, to legitimacy. Among these, of course, the case of the Bolsheviks figures strongly. As well, the Resistance fighters of the Second World War ultimately became not only legitimate but heroes.

Despite most of the major protagonist's refusals to grant the Red Brigades "legitimate enemy" status, there were those who attempted to actually predict the Red Brigades' possible moves on the basis of an analysis of what Geneva Convention adherents would do and thus were, in a sense, tacitly granting such status to the Red Brigades. An example may be found in the following statement issued by Eduardo di Giovanni, a lawyer for the Red Brigades: "I do not believe that the policy of the Red Brigades allows for the cold-blooded killing of a man. There is still a thread of hope. An article of the Geneva Convention provides that in cases of armed conflicts within the territory of one of the signing nations, the parties to the conflict are reciprocally forbidden from condemning prisoners to death and are required to do everything possible to achieve the liberation of the respective hostages.[61]

As it was, the above was exactly the line of reasoning that Andreotti, now prime minister (after the hurried passage of Moro's government), and other coalition party leaders abjured. Their opportunity to do so publicly came when they were forced to refuse the stategy offered by Moro's son Giovanni, to apply the Article Three of the Geneva Convention's code to the Red Brigades and to call in the International Red Cross as arbiter. Andreotti replied to Giovanni Moro's scheme in a memorandum. There he wrote that applying Article Three to the Moro case "would acknowledge that a state of civil war existed in Italy, and while the killings, woundings and taking of hostages constitute serious fragmentary conflicts, that would not be true."[62] Acknowledgment, it seems, was all. Such a formulaic approach contradicted the very tone of the Geneva Convention Article Three. Article Three was specifically designed to be a flexible guide to ambiguous internal situations. Thus, Trooboff has written: "In order to encourage more protection for the victims of internal wars, Article Three of the 1949 Conventions states that the 'Parties to the conflict should further endeavor to bring into force, by means of special agreements, all or part of the other provisions of the Geneva Conventions.'"[63] In other words, there was substantial room for interpretative maneuvering with the various articles of the Geneva Conventions. What was lacking in the Moro affair was the administrative will to creatively use the Geneva Convention Articles for the purpose of having Moro released.

It is interesting to compare the Italian government's response to the claims of the Red Brigades that they were political combatants and political prisoners with the case of the similar claims of the members of the Irish Republican Army. As Denis Donoghue has written: "On June 13, 1972, leaders of the Provisional I.R.A. invited Whitelaw, secretary of state for Northern Ireland, to discuss the possibility of making peace. The invitation was publicly rejected, but a conversational line was held open, mainly because John Hume of the Social Democratic Labour Party acted as mediator. Within two weeks a truce was effected. The British government agreed to five demands: 1) the prisoners have the right to wear their own clothes; 2) they would not be required to do 'penal labour'; 3) they would have the right to associate freely with their colleagues within their own prison area; 4) they would receive certain educational and recreational facilities, and 5) prisoners who had lost remission of the sentence because of their protesting behavior in prison would have it fully restored. In return, the IRA agreed to stop the campaign of violence."[64]

The five demands revealed the very strong desire of the IRA members to be recognized by the British state as political prisoners, to obtain, ideally, third-level status or, at the minimum, second-level status. The victory won by achieving this distinction would be purely symbolic. Certainly Northern Ireland would not be instantaneously transformed into an independent state as a result of this status change. But the process of edging toward ultimate legitimacy that such a status elevation would involve could not be taken lightly. In fact, as Donoghue goes on to describe, the British government could not accept this state of affairs for long and later, in 1973, a new policy was enacted in which acts of violence committed by the IRA were to be considered ordinary crimes. In other words, the political status was rescinded. The ambivalence of the British government in these proceedings is noted by Donoghue: "Of course it is an embarrassment to the British government to be reminded that what they now regard as matters of principle were treated by their predecessors as negotiable."[65] The IRA had a strong desire to be acknowledged as an organized political group possessed of a cause. This desire was furthermore conditioned by the member's self-identification with past heroes in the cause of Irish liberation. These heroic referents provided the IRA with its major symbolic weapon. As Donoghue posed the question: "But why are the prisoners [both the IRA and the smaller but even more violent Irish National Liberation Army] so insistent upon special category status or political status . . . the IRA leaders are determined to take possession of the entire Republican tradition from the Rising of 1798 to the Fenians and the Men of Easter Week in 1916."[66] In this sense of owning the national problem, the IRA laid claim to being the rightful heirs.

Donoghue also introduces an important distinction associated with the several types of recognition. This is the distinction between the sacred and the profane. When a violent act is perceived to have been motivated by a political cause, it acquires the aura of sacrality. If, as may be seen in the next chapter, the Red Brigades adorned themselves with the sacred vestments of the Resistance fighters, their actions could then be viewed as partaking in that sacredness and legitimacy. In much the same way, the IRA members have presented themselves as missionaries following their own sacred traditions. The British government, however, denied the IRA this spirituality when it rescinded political recognition in 1973. IRA crimes would be regarded henceforth as profane acts. It is Donoghue's claim that the hunger strikes of 1981 constituted an attempt to repossess the lost aura of sacredness.

Thus far, I have shown how the recognition issue figured critically in the dramatic presentation and reception of the Red Brigades in the Moro social drama—the license to grant any or all of the three levels of recognition: (1) membership in humanity, (2) membership in an organized political group with a (not necessarily legitimate) cause, (3) membership in a political group with a legitimate cause is contingent upon the structural location within that society of the granting agent. The pope could say that he loved the Red Brigades, ex-victims could claim they were efficient and intelligent, anyone could issue the appeal that they unconditionally release Moro,[67] but nobody, not even Kurt Waldheim, could, in the Italy of the Moro social drama, declare them to be participants in a political cause—legitimate or illegitimate.

We have seen how, during the Crisis phase of this social drama, a series of issues and statuses were being collapsed, one onto the other. Negotiation was being presented as necessarily indicating recognition, and recognition was being presented as necessarily leading to the Red Brigades' legitimation. In other words, the major parliamentary political parties, the Catholic Church and the mass media, were all presenting the options of the Italian state in the following prescribed way. Their public presentations consisted in the proposition that, if the Italian state negotiated with the Red Brigades, then they would automatically be granting them at least second- if not third-level recognition. In an article in *L'Unità* that discussed a meeting of the heads of the coalition parties, explicit reference was made to this general assumption: "At the meeting, the official positions of the parties were taken . . . [which] were steadfastly contrary to any type of negotiation with the criminals which would then legitimate them as 'opponents' of the State."[68] In line with this point of view, the priority of not affording the Red Brigades any, even (perhaps we ought to say, especially) symbolic, political status transformation took precedence over the possibility of negotiating for the return of Moro.

One related notion publicly promoted by these same protagonists during the crisis phase of the Moro social drama was that negotiation would necessarily lead to an exchange of prisoners— Moro in exchange for some (or, eventually, one) state-held Red Brigades member. In fact, whenever the issue of negotiation came up in the statements, speeches, and press releases of the state-defending political parties, the positions taken referred exclusively to the possibility of prisoner exchange. As well, Moro's continuous allusions to negotiation in his letters did focus on the possibility of an exchange of prisoners. However, there was no logical obstacle to the primary protagonists in this social drama choosing to regard the negotiation issue differently, to create their *own* definition of negotiation. What they chose, in fact, was to opt into the terrorist's apparent definition of negotiation, accepting their logic. In doing so, they effectively cut off their other options and closed some major symbolic and real doors in Moro's face. As the following statement of Giannino Guiso, the one-time attorney of Renato Curcio, makes clear, the Red Brigades may not have been as locked into the demand of prisoner exchange as were the political parties and the mass media: "In his [Giuso's] opinion, the counter-move desired by the Red Brigades is not the 'exchange of prisoners' rendered impossible by extant laws. Rather, it consists in a recognition of the Red Brigades as possessing a 'political status' no longer terrorists but declared adversaries. Or else, to recognize the accused in jail as prisoners of war . . . If you wish to save Moro—provided he is still alive, as I believe—it is necessary to make a political proposal, not a moral one."[69] Guiso may have been right in his assessment of what the Red Brigades would "settle" for in the way of negotiation offers,[70] but he misinterprets the animus behind the proposals of the no-negotiation protagonists. The proposal was not moral in nature but was, instead, symbolic.

Here the parallels with the IRA are clear. Terrorist groups often begin with their most extreme demands. Eventually, as the logic of bargaining decrees, the demands can be altered and compromises reached. Just such a process did indeed occur over the course of the almost two months of Moro's captivity. Selva wrote in his diary on May 3: "At the Torino trial, the Red Brigades member Ognibene, during today's hearing, read a long and detailed document, in which the subject of the requests for changes in the prison system was addressed. Is this an indirect indication for those who so endeavor, to save Aldo Moro?"[71]

Thus we find, quite late in the social drama, an opening to a happy ending. We find a Red Brigades member suggesting, albeit obiliquely, that their demands might be redirected from prisoner exchange to prison reform (and this, ironically, presented by a prisoner). We also find a mid-level Christian Democrat director, Luigi Granelli (responsible for the party's foreign affairs sector), proposing to "assign the negotiation to an international organization, to give a wide mandate [to this organization] with the sole exclusion of the exchange of prisoners" (*L'Espresso*, April 23, p. 7). These options, however, were never picked up on by those in the official policy-making positions. (It would, though, be successfully picked up on by the Radicals and Socialists in the D'Urso kidnapping some years later.) But before we leave the issue of negotiation, we need to pose the question: Granted that everyone was having his say about whether or not to negotiate, who, in the final analysis, actually had the power to make the decision? Several scholars have noted the increasing importance of intersecretarial meetings in Italian political decision-making. Indeed, such was the case in the Moro affair. Paul Furlong analyzed this trend: "The increasing importance for the DC of reaching agreement with the PCI has, in concert with other factors, removed real decision-making from parliament and from the cabinet and placed it in the hands of the governing bodies of the major parties. Major policy decisions now tend to be reached by agreement between the party secretaries, who usually come to the inter-secretarial joint meetings of the government parties under clear and relatively narrow mandates from the governing bodies of the parties. So at the time of the Moro kidnapping, the crucial decisions over whether or not to negotiate and what other measures to undertake were not made by parliament or by the cabinet. In particular, the decision not to negotiate was made by a small group of leading members of the national executive of the DC, in conjunction with the prime minister."[72]

Conclusion

We have seen that, in the Moro social drama of 1978, negotiation with the Red Brigades for Moro's release was never a seriously entertained option by those in the position ultimately to decide. The no-negotiation protagonists (the Christian Democrats, the Communists, the mass media, the Catholic church) adopted early and resolute positions. These positions were primarily based on the proposition that negotiation would necessarily elevate the Red Brigades to a status dangerously close to legitimacy if not altogether there. Protagonists adopting the affirmative position vis-à-vis negotiations (including the many groups of the ultraleft and some members of the Socialist party) saw it as the only way to get Moro back but had no power to implement their prospective.

The question remains, however: Why did the no-negotiation protagonists believe that the eventual negotiations with the Red Brigades would necessarily lead to their recognition and legitimation? And, accordingly, in what sense was the threat of the Red Brigades a "real" one. While a more complete response to this question must await the concluding chapter of this study, we may tentatively begin with the idea that we need to develop a reading of the notion of *threat* that is specific to the situation in Italy of 1978. In March of 1978, Italy was not on the verge of a revolution of the type envisaged by the Red Brigades. As previously noted, several analysts have interpreted the Red Brigades' activities as aiming toward provoking a repressive, right-wing reaction and thus, ultimately, in indirectly provoking a revolutionary uprising against this eventual repression. The hard-line position of the no-negotiation protagonists, here particularly the PCI, can then be read as a kind of preemptive strike to prevent such a repressive reaction. The right, however, was, with the exception of the rabidly and constantly anti-Communist journalist Montanelli, preternaturally quiet during the Moro social drama. The fact that at least four neo-rightist trials were proceeding contemporaneously might have had something to do with this quiescence. The right might possibly have been more than pleased to have the nation's attention deflected away from themselves for a while. Given this near silence and given the generally disorganized and ineffective state of the Italian security forces at that time, forces that had been, in the 1960s, actually involved in plots to topple the Italian government in a right-wing coup and, for that very reason, substantially dissolved, we might ask: Were the no-negotiation protagonists fending off mere ghosts and shadows?

There is a way out of this seeming paradox of paranoia, one that can show that the fear of the no-negotiation protagonists, again especially the PCI, was not without basis. Whether or not the actual, immediate threat of a right-wing repression was realistic, it was "real" in the minds and the memories of the Communists, a party that had been, until very recently, the selected victims of this type of repression. For the DC, on the other hand, the idea of being outdone in the defense of the state by the Communists could not be tolerated, particularly in the face of the erosion of their own legitimacy following the Lockheed scandal. Perhaps, the only authoritative and legitimate individual capable of negotiation with the Red Brigades for Moro's release was, unfortunately, Moro himself. In the end, the explanation for the rigidity of those who had the power to make the choice may best be gainsaid by the hypothesis that they were ultimately less worried about unwittingly legitimating the Red Brigades (though indeed this was an unsavory prospect) than they were about delegitimating themselves. In that case, the rhetoric, or better, the lack of rhetoric, would have indeed become "real," had real consequences as, it would have seemed, nobody would have been left defending the state.

Instead, the establishment protagonists were claiming that not only were they not legitimating the Red Brigades, not only were they themselves not being delegitimated, but they were, in fact, being relegitimated through their no-recognition/no-negotiation stance. *Il Popolo* was quite explicit about this point in their March 30 edition. On the second page, they published an article that looked back on the first fifteen days after Moro's kidnapping, days during which the negotiation positions were solidified. The title, something like a summary of the first act, was "The Balance of Fifteen Days of the Drama." And the article read as follows: "But even today we already feel confident in declaring that the terrorists—contrary to what they wanted, have provoked the greatest 'verification of credibility' of the system that we have ever had in these last years."

Finally, the next chapter will present the panoply of "root paradigms" used to symbolically back up the several protagonists' negotiation positions. Here we have developed the stratified paradigm of modes of recognition. In the next chapter the praxis of adopting and justifying these varying recognitions in the Moro social drama will be explored. The engaging of the symbolic justifications constituted the redressive phase of the Moro social drama.

5 Redress: Elaboration of Symbolic Power

In this chapter, the actual construction of the normative bases for accepting or rejecting negotiation with the Red Brigades will be explored. The various stories being told by the Moro social drama protagonists all contained (differentially configured) appeals to what they were positing as the most salient and transcendent cultural values, values the virtues of which would be compromised by either negotiating or not negotiating. As the symbolic weapons in the ongoing action, these appeals—we will want to call the general class of them "root paradigms"—were forwarded by the protagonists as each attempted to lead the drama in a particular direction. The presentation of these appeals was ritual-like, in that the appeals were stereotyped, repeated throughout the fifty-five days, and expressive (i.e., essentially noninstrumental). However, our developing theory of the transposition of the dominant idiom in modern, pluralistic societies from ritual to theater suggests that we examine the ways in which these appeals were, in fact, predominantly framed as theater and not as true ritual.

Clearly, ritual has been defined in many (sometimes contradictory) ways.[1] But certain qualities of ritual appear in many definitions: stereotyped actions, objects or words, repetition, and a nonintrinsic relationship between means and ends. All of these criteria, we shall see, were relevant to the appeals made in the Moro social drama. However, one further criterion, that mentioned explicitly by the philosopher Susanne Langer and suggested in other definitions, is one which a "war of plots and genres" reading of modern social drama would make problematic. That is the criterion of spontaneity or, as Langer puts it, that which "arises without intention."[2] This spontaneity of the *generation* of rituals is extended, by Victor Turner in his analysis of ritual-flushed social dramas, to include a spontaneity of *acceptance*. A spontaneous locking into place of redressive rituals implies an already scripted social drama with a preordained plot which, at times, Turner seems

to accept (he designates the liminal, antistructural times as ultimately being in the service of the social order) and, at times, seems
to reject (given his emphasis on the variable reconciliation/schism
endings of social dramas). On the deterministic side, one which
emphasizes an almost unreflective spontaneity of rituals, is the
following quote from Turner: "Greek tragedy and Icelandic saga
are genres that recognize this implicit paradigmatic control of human affairs in public areas, where behavior which appears to be
freely chosen revolves at length into a total pattern. One has, of
course, to account for the almost instinctual manner in which root
paradigms are accepted by the individual and their social consequences are fatalistically regarded—both in the mirror of literature
and on the stage of history—by the masses."[3] One obviously relevant question here is: Once kidnapped, was Moro's death inevitable, determined by the instinctually felt needs of a collectivity
seeking redress against a crisis? An analysis of the root paradigms
called into service may help us understand the various protagonists'
readings of this question.

We are emphasizing the issue of spontaneity here because of its
critical relevance to the ritual-theater question. Once again, we
must draw upon the simple society—complex society distinction. In
any society with different constituencies (each holding diverse
values, along with ones held in common), there can be no one set of
transcendent root paradigms that sucessfully expresses everyone's
highest order principle. For example, in Italy we find Catholics and
Communists, ultrarightists and ultraleftists, ex-partisans and
revolution-seeking youth, Northerners and Southerners. What
spontaneously generated appeal could address them all? Yet such a
unanimity was precisely the aim of most of the appeals. Sociologist
Joseph Gusfield critiques Turner on just this point. He does this by
referring to the fragmentary nature of modern life: "First, modern
societies are highly differentiated into groups whose experiences,
categories of judgement and criteria of morality as well as economic
and material interests lead toward conflict. Alternate themes and
counter themes exist, both between and within groups, but they are
often held by separate and conflicting communities. In modern
pluralistic 'society' the absolutist order is fictive, problematic and
often illusory."[4]

If, then, the various ritual-like appeals had to be, as they were in
the Moro social drama, custom crafted, reflected upon, expanded

in the aim of greater inclusion, or, less frequently, contracted in the aim of exclusion, does this not represent a self-consciousness and an introduction of choice and substitution (here the commodity-like quality of the liminoid performances discussed in the Introduction is relevant) more relevant to theater than to true ritual?

While we are not saying that theater is essentially or always a degraded form of ritual, we are saying that the two are *different*. Recalling Hermassi's discussion here, we reiterate the claim that theater *can* be as powerful an experience as ritual (in diverse ways, depending on such variables as genre and audience participation). But the difference needs to be marked, particularly as it relates to a social context where the "natural" authority and legitimacy of the governing bodies and individuals has been called into question so dramatically (as was the case in Italy in 1978). One could claim that all contexts of pluralism problematize the concept of transcendent authority. Here we are indicating how this is exacerbated and brought to the surface in a society undergoing a legitimation crisis. By way of foreshadowing, we will develop the argument that some genres of theater (tragedy, e.g.) confront this problem head-on, and some genres (melodrama) ultimately seek to deny it. We will return to this issue.

Terminology

Before turning to the cultural themes hauled out to do battle in the Moro social drama themselves, it is necessary to clarify our use of some of the terms of analysis.

Sherry Ortner traces the emergence of this "cultural theme" concept back to the publication of Ruth Benedict's *Patterns of Culture* in 1934 in which Benedict identified particular axes of variations within and across cultures. The various terms used to describe the general concept during the thirties and forties were "cultural themes" and "cultural configurations" proposed respectively by Morris Opler and Clyde Kluckhohn in the contexts of their studies of native American cultures. Opler described such cultural themes as "a limited number of dynamic affirmations which control behavior or stimulate activity." He went on to add: "Limiting factors, often the existence of other opposed or circumscribing themes and their extensions control the number, force and variety of a theme's expressions."[5]

Finally, Opler was concerned with gauging the significance of particular themes in a given culture and proposed: "Another rough indication of the importance of a theme is the degree to which a group shows concern when its terms are violated. The intensity of the reaction and the character of the sanctions invoked are significant clues."[6] The Red Brigade's act of kidnapping and threatening the life of Moro was portrayed by the various protagonists as opening the door to distinct violations of the terms of several valued cultural institutions, ideas, and historical moments. The potency of these normative items in Italian culture will be gauged as we take them up, one by one, to see what responses their violations evoked during the Moro social drama.

The work of Victor Turner and other contemporary researchers has involved a shift in the analytic orientation to such themes. As distinct from the work of those as Opler and Kluckhohn, Turner's (along with David Schneider's and Sherry Ortner's) analyses focus on the "symbolic units which formulate meaning."[7] In other words, the work has become more semiotic and, as such, is concerned with the interrelations among the various key symbols or root paradigms in a culture; points of opposition as well as points of harmony. Here the view is that the root paradigms or key symbols are referencing, specifically, the social modes of relations and interrelations. Further, the public reordering of the root paradigms in terms of their relative potency within a culture both indicates and helps to create the conditions for reordering social relationships within and between the relevant publics. Lasswell has written that "it is apparent that change in the spread and frequency of exposure to key signs is an exceedingly significant indicator of important social processes. We can follow the dissemination of secular or sacred cults by surveying trends in the geographical distribution of icons and other significant signs found in the whole complex. Similarly, we can establish the presumption of integrative or disintegrative trends within any society by observing sign frequencies.[8]

The original concept of the root paradigm was based on the assumed existence of integrated communities in which meanings and values were shared by all members. The root paradigms connected the past, present, and the future of the community by referencing and reincarnating the traditional scenarios of public pride and pathos. At their most general level, they acted as condensed myths, in much the same way that poems act as condensed prose and, like myths, they "are about events set in diachronic (i.e., allegedly historical) time, but they describe this unique diachronic sequence of past events in terms of a synchronic model valid for all time, the present as well as the past."[9]

The correspondences between the root paradigms and the social relationships that they both reflect and reorder are framed in various ways. James Fernandez, in a response to Victor Turner's discussion of the role of symbols in African ritual, posited metaphor as the most basic unit of analysis. He writes: "A metaphor (and related tropes) is the statement, explicit or implied, of a correspondence between some subject of thought in need of clarification [e.g., social relations] and an object that brings some clarity to it [e.g., appeals to transcendent cultural values]."[10] A sensitivity to the tropes of presentation must, it is clear, be paramount in any study of the structure of emplotted social dramas. Care must be taken, though, not to collapse the different kinds of tropes (metaphor, metonymy, synecdoche, etc.) together (as Fernandez seems to be doing). Thus we will be exploring not only what appeals the Moro social drama generated but also the forms in which these appeals were presented. By distinguishing among these forms, we may be able to discern the significance of the variations. This is akin to what Hayden White has done for historical texts. And we will be drawing on White's analyses. Thus, for example, such aspects of an appeal's presentation as the trope (if any) employed, the level of abstractness or concreteness, its generality or particularity will be gauged. Such an analytic approach may indicate, among other things, the orientation of the appeal toward stasis (a synchronic tendency) or change (a diachronic tendency), toward simplification or ambiguity—issues at the heart of this study.

One final aspect of the engaged "root paradigms" needs to be clarified. The appeals are public in two senses of the word. Those individuals heralding the root paradigms must be seen as doing so in a public capacity. They cannot make these appeals as private citizens with private interests. Further, the appeals themselves must be seen as having a public referent—some segment of the collectivity must be the relevant target. Thus both the appeals and the appealers must be viewed as public in essence. The social must have primacy over the individual. Chapters 6 and 7 will elaborate the way in which Moro's own attempts to call upon root paradigms to back up his claim to continuing authority were largely unsuccessful precisely because he was being denied any further access to the public sphere. His will was no longer recognized as having any relevance to decisions taken in the public sphere by his political colleagues.

It is thus in the service of creating and sustaining legitimate authority in periods of transition and crisis that the protagonists of the social dramas will call up particular root paradigms to provide moral accounts for their actions. As Anthony Cohen wrote in his study of political legitimation in a town in Nova Scotia, such presentations constitute "a picture of the uses and management of political myth which amount to the attempt to 'bridge the gap' between a 'sacred,' rhetorical world of legitimated and unquestioned values and the mundane world of questionable behavior and problematic experience."[11]

The Root Paradigms

A survey of the mass media presentation of the Moro social drama, Moro's letters, the Red Brigades communiques, the various speeches of the political and religious leaders, and other texts extant during the fifty-five-day period has identified six distinct and frequently used root paradigms: the Resistance, the Reason of State, Democracy and Democratic Institutions, the Sanctity of Human Life, the Working Class, and the Party. Not all of these symbolic referents were used by all protagonists: in fact some were anathema to a given protagonist's asserted worldview. But all of the above root paradigms rose to the surface of the public discourse during Moro's sequestration. The task of this analysis is to connect these appeals to the various protagonists who drew upon them and to elaborate the meaning that these themes held for the respective users. In doing so we may reveal something about the protagonist's sense and organization of these symbolic resources.

Unpacking the Root Paradigms
THE RESISTANCE

The presentation of the appeal to the *Resistance* in the Moro social drama was concrete, a combination of historical and mythological and, in tropological terms, was highly metaphorical. It was concrete in referring to a specific historical moment in Italian memory—a moment that was defined in specific ways by specific protagonists. Yet it was engaged in a mythological way, setting up the following logic. Negotiations could not be carried out because they would desecrate the memory and the legacy of the *Resistance*. History was being used in the service of the present order and status quo, not in service of change. Finally, the use of the appeal was metaphorical. The *Resistance,* we shall see, stood for courage in the face of an invasion, sacrifice (this will be an important concept for the protagonists' construction of Moro's role), civility and humanity (versus barbarism), necessary (i.e., defensive) violence and antifascism. The trope of metaphor is, according to Hayden White, essentially representational. The use of metaphor, in this case of the appeal to the *Resistance,* will, it will be shown, create a certain area of ambiguity around the phrase. For metaphors are ambiguous precisely in that they express both similarities and diffences at the same time. Thus the ability to control the meaning and the users of the appeal becomes problematic.

The *Resistance* was, of course, an extremely resonant root metaphor for the Italian social drama. It was a near-universal (with the obvious exception of the ultraright political factions) point of pride for Italy, symbolizing sacrifice, humanity, struggle, and democracy. Roberto Rossellini's movie *Roma: Città Aperta* (Rome: Open City) glorified the character types of the Resistance: Anna Magnani's tough but soft character who is shot running after her arrested "partigiano" fiancé as he is being taken away in a prison wagon, the humane and courageous priest, the Fascist-fighting neighborhood children. All of these characters are portrayed as loving life and each other and as "impegnati" (politically engaged). All root paradigms custom-contour tradition, and the *Resistance* root metaphor provided a most flattering legacy. This root metaphor was used by several of the protagonists to give their positions a moral foundation. Not surprisingly, the Communist party used the legend of the Resistance more than any other protagonist. As well, though, the Red Brigades themselves referred to the Resistance as a moment in history they believed to be analogous to the one they were creating. This metaphoric overlap between the Communists and the Red Brigades was itself cause for a good deal of consternation among the protagonists, particularly the Communists.

In fact, historians of the Resistance movement in Italy have indicated that the Resistance was neither a revolutionary nor even a prerevolutionary movement. While a majority of the Resistance fighters were members of the Communist party (theoretically a party with revolutionary aims), it was Togliatti himself who explicitly refuted the possibility of a revolutionary outcome to the Resistance efforts. Giorgio Galli, a historian of Italy, writes: "The transformation of the Resistance into a socialist revolution would hypothetically have required, on the parts of the parties of the left, the decision to use, towards the end, the over four-hundred thousand armed men at their disposition. It is known that the Communist party, controlling two-thirds of that armed force, excluded, a priori, such a possibility. Togliatti had clarified this at the national council of the party which was held on the eve of the April 25 insurrection, openly denouncing: '. . . that tendency aiming towards a progressive accentuation of the political and class struggles . . . in such a way as to provoke complications and disorder . . .' "[12]

The use of the *Resistance* root metaphor by the Communists was, therefore, both appropriate (in terms of their actual participation in the Resistance) and safe (in terms of their documented, explicit denial of its revolutionary character). Indeed, it was the perfect root metaphor for the Communist party as the selection of the Communist party tradition it represented was one that was universally respected.

References to the Resistance were made continually throughout the Moro social drama by the Communist spokespeople. Enrico Berlinguer, party secretary, often referred to the Resistance as a sort of democratic leaping-off point for the Italian republic, providing it with moral sustenance to endure the Moro trauma: "Italian democracy has demonstrated great strength, the country has held, the citizenry has not lost courage nor allowed itself to be torn by the perverted political designs of the Red Brigades who sought the division of the democratic forces. And, from this we can state that the road of unity is the only just road, the only one capable of strengthening democracy, of rendering invincible the Republic *born of the Resistance*" (emphasis mine).[13]

The Resistance imagery was directly linked in the way that the Communist party "imaged-up" the popular, majority response to the terrorism phenomenon; that being a unified, enthusiastic, a-critical support by the population of Italy for the Italian state.

Thus Alessandro Natta, in a speech in the Senate on April 4, published in *L'Unità* on April 5, spoke of the "unified enthusiasm and engagement with which the overwhelming majority of the Italian population has responded to the insidious ruin of terrorism, spoke of a 'new Resistance' to defend the society and the State. 'It is the Red Brigades themselves who periodically reinfuse the national mobilization campaign with oxygen.' "[14]

Every action or position that the PCI was taking during this springtime of terrorist trials (Torino) and actions was rhetorically cloaked in the sacred garments of the Resistance. In an article from early March, *L'Unità* records with pride the acceptance of another jury member for the Torino trial: "While the activity of the Court of Assizes of forming the popular jury proceeds, the campaign to collect signatures on the document [against terrorism] prepared by the [PCI] Regional Committee intensifies in its affirmation of the values of the Resistance and the principles of the Republican Constitution" *(L'Unità,* March 4, 1978 p. 2).

Thus, as far as the PCI was concerned, the unconditional, "spontaneous," and enthusiastic support for the state in its campaign against terrorism equaled a new Resistance.

However, the Red Brigades, in their own turn, used the Resistance terminology to describe and justify their actions. Alessandro Silj wrote of the group "Proletariat Left," the precurser of the Red Brigades: "In January of '71, in a pamphlet entitled *We Organize the New Resistance,* 'Proletariat Left' proclaims this the moment to instill in the struggling proletariat masses the principle that one cannot have political power without having military power, in order to educate the proletarian and revolutionary left by way of the partisan action, to resistance, to armed struggle."[15]

Even the name that the Red Brigades gave to the mass movement that they imagined already supported them referred obliquely to the Resistance. This movmement of antistate struggle was called the Movimento di Resistenza Proletario Offensivo (MRPO) Proletarian Offensive Movement of Resistance). This name appeared prominently in the "Resolution of the Strategic Directorate of the Red Brigades" that accompanied communique no. 4.

The proprietary use made by the Red Brigades and ultraleft groups of Resistance terminology was of course critiqued by the other protagonists. In Gusfield's terms, the ability of the Red Brigades to attain legitimate ownership of the Resistance legacy was refused by the state-supporting protagonists. The principle quality of the *Resistance* root metaphor was, in fact, its accessibility to protagonists on opposing sides. This may have been due, in part, to the dual nature of the Resistance itself. I am referring here to the fact that the Resistance was both a defensive and an offensive movement. It sought both to preserve and transcend the bourgeois democratic elements in Italy which had been suppressed by the Fascist regime. While, as has been seen, the forces of preservation outnumbered the forces of transcendence in the Resistance, this movement was nonetheless a symbol which could be interpreted as bringing about a new transcendent order.

Another reason for the richness of the *Resistance* root metaphor and its accessibility to the Red Brigades as well as to legitimate political parties was the fact that it incarnated legitimate violence. The Red Brigades, in linking their violent activities to the Resistance legacy, sought to portray these violent acts as justified and, beyond that, required. This conclusion was based on their proposal that all political solutions had been exhausted.

The reaction against all this sliding together of the categories "terrorist" and "partigiano" (Resistance fighter) took the form of public delineations of the phenomenological differences between the two kinds of activists. One Italian commentator, P. Marletti, has written in this regard: "As those who participated in the Resistance know very well, the partisan in no way hides his armed forces from those with whom he lives and by whom, in fact, he is hidden and protected 'like a fish in the water.' He hides his identity only from the oppressor and the oppressor's soldiers. He is clandestine only with respect to them. The clandestinity of the partisan means 'to have roots'—the brigadist's clandestinity, on the other hand, means camouflage, the double life, the appearance of normality with which he fools his own relatives and his fellow workers . . . This model is more Jacobin or Carbonari rather than Leninist."[16]

The Resistance is therefore read as having a public, open quality, with the identity of the fighters known to all but the oppressor, while the terrorists are categorically indicted for hiding their true identity from their intimates and comrades. Their similar activities are, in this way, differentially valued and appraised. The critical variable here is the dichotomy between "identity revealed" and "identity concealed." Here we see parallels with the Geneva Convention clauses on insurgents. Part of Article Three of the Geneva

Conventions required the insurgents to reveal their identity even to their enemies in order to receive convention coverage. This means that the Resistance fighters would not have been eligible for this Article Three coverage if this article had existed at that time, and they would have been, in fact, deemed illegitimate.

The stress on the open character of the Resistance phenomenon was echoed, as well, in the mass media's use of this root metaphor. This was achieved through the reporting of the demonstrations held the day after Moro was kidnapped and the description of these demonstrations as reverberating with the sense of the Resistance.

In the broadcast from Milan, the reporter stated that the demonstrations held in this city had taken place under the aegis of this day's rallying cry; " 'Resistance' . . . a word dense with meaning which sums up . . . a choice of civility rooted in the democratic conscience of the country."[17]

Less enthusiastic use of the rhetoric of the Resistance came from the very few critical sources in the Moro social drama. Author Leonardo Sciascia, the Sicilian Radical party member, identified a more openly cynical use of the Resistance root metaphor: "The Resistance against nazifascism, as indestructable a value as the amount of respect the Christian Democrats have for Aldo Moro, came to be invoked and transposed as Resistance against negotiations to save Moro's life."[18]

The Resistance was not one of the Christian Democrat's finest moments. But, with the help of the Communists, it was quickly becoming a legacy that this party invoked. In the Christian Democrat weekly magazine, *La Discussióne*, E. Gorrieri wrote on March 27, ". . . with an experience shared by many of us; the Resistance. In regard to this, there is no need to repeat that there is absolutely no parallel between the action of the Resistance brigades and that of the terrorists. They are antithetical phenomena." Later in the same article he states: "Let us return to the Resistance. Terrorism has assumed the characteristics of a rebirth of the nazi ideology and practice. There can only be one reply; a new Resistance."[19]

Were the Christian Democrats active participants in the partisan struggles? Not according to journalist and ex-partisan Giorgio Bocca who points this out in a searing critique of the attempt of the Communists to extend the Resistance legacy to cover the DC: "The Communist Youth Federation even proposed, without arousing the slightest scandal, the construction of a single youth organization of all constitutional factions; catholics and marxists, the old flags of the Resistance cover a convenient unanimity. Suddenly we have discovered that DeGasperi's party [Christian Democrats] was the protagonist of the Resistance and the cornerstone of progress and not, as it seemed to us to be, almost totally absent from the partisan battles and most occupied with restoring the old state."[20]

Thus another of the areas of ambiguity expressed by this appeal revolved around its simultaneous reference to a specific set of Italian protagonists and its attempt to represent *all* of civilized Italy, to cover all constituencies.

DEMOCRACY AND THE DEMOCRATIC INSTITUTIONS

In contrast with the concreteness of the *Resistance* root paradigm, *Democracy and the Democratic Institutions* constituted a most abstract appeal. It is time— and spaceless (but can be contextuated in its usage). It is a nonpartisan appeal, referring to no set of protagonists specifically (merely excluding barbarians and dictators). Thus it attached to no overt ideology. It can symbolize change—but only a particular kind—gradual, nonviolent, uncoerced. However, it can also indicate the permanence of an inscribed institution. Tropologically, the *Democracy* reference is more metonymic than metaphorical. It essentially reduces (or elevates—a reduction in reverse) the essence of Italy to *Democracy*. Italy is democracy. Thus if negotiations with the Red Brigades means the negation of democracy, then it also means the destruction of Italy.

The ideas incorporated in this appeal are many. They included popular participation, due process (particularly important when the Torino trial of the Red Brigades was being rhetorically contrasted with the trials of Moro in the "People's Prison"), civil liberties (this also particularly relevant in the light of cries for extended police powers of perquisition, search and preventative arrest, and the ultimate passage of the exceptional laws), representative government, and antifascism. It also expanded outward to signify that which belonged to Western civilization. Thus it departicularized the appeal. For the PCI, it expressed a connection with that which was nondoctrinaire, nontotalitarian. For the DC, it covertly reiterated their claim to be the party of the majority.

The proposition about the potential contaminating effect of negotiations on Democracy was not an exclusive concern of Italian policymakers. Bernard Avishai has maintained a similar position in a review he has written of books on terrorism: "The choice, of course, is not simply between saving hostages and killing terrorists; it is, as the English political writer Rosalyn Higgens recently observed, between possibly saving hostages and *probably subverting democratic practices*. The leaders of democratic states might be more consistent in the face of terrorist blackmail if instead of becoming preoccupied with their managers' efforts to psyche out the culprits, they recognize that *the preservation of abstract laws can be no less urgent than saving lives*[21](emphasis mine).

Italy emerged from a long period of fascist government to find its democratic aspirations intact, if somewhat precarious. In the post–World War II Italian republic, the theme of Democracy became a prominent feature in political debate. As Robert Putnam has written: "One of the most perplexing features of political discourse in Italy is the frequency with which politicians resort to the word 'democracy.' "[22]

The *Democracy* root paradigm is an important member of that set of ideals and values making constant appearance in daily political rhetoric in those societies claiming to be pluralistic. Democracy is a touchstone for a civilized world in which discourse takes the place of violence. *Democracy* as a root paradigm in a social drama, then, stands for the "civilized" world's response and opposition to both violence and fascism. In the case of the Moro social drama, it was posed as counter to the violence of the Red Brigades, as well as to both the putative fascist valence of the Red Brigades and the potential right-wing reaction against the terrorist phenomenon on the part of the conservative elements in Italy. In other words, Democracy was doing more than double duty, responding to actions already completed as well as attempting to stave off actions only potentially being contemplated.

Before proceeding to the analysis of the specific protagonist's uses of the *Democracy* appeal, it is necessary to discuss its constitutional element.

The Italian Constitution, written in 1947, is one of the most "modern" constitutions to have been written and enacted. It is also one of the most politically progressive. The Communist party in Italy, temporarily (before the elections of 1948) legitimized by its Popular Front participation and leadership in the Resistance, had a major role in the framing of the Constitution. As Robert Putnam maintains: ". . . they [the Communists] are committed to the Republican Constitution which, as Tarrow rightly says, 'the Italian Communist Party considers its greatest achievement and the condition of its legal and political survival.' "[23]

One of the major reasons for the Communist's attachment to and reliance on the appeal to the *Constitution* is the gradualist orientation (in terms of bringing about social change) of the Italian Constitution. That is, the Italian Communists view the Constitution as a precedent-setting template for progressive change. The Communists are, however, singular in this view of the Constitution. The parties of the center and the right did not share in this perspective: "For the reformist Left, the Constitution and institutions deriving from it are a bridge toward socialism while, for others, it is a dam against it. The Italian Constitution projects a 'planned capitalism' where private initiatives are to be used toward social goals. But this is impossible, since profit cannot be channeled in the pursuit of social goals by direct state planning."[24]

On the other side, the Christian Democrats were also referring to the parameters of the Constitution. This reference, though, highlighted the constraints (rather than the opportunities) demarcated by that document. Late in the drama, on April 28, Andreotti was interviewed on the second RAI channel about negotiation options. He answered the following: "When the life of new government begins, we swear faithfulness to the Constitution of the Republic, that is, we swear to respect the laws. This is a limit that no one of us has the right to cross."[25]

The *Democracy* root paradigm was favored, in the Moro social drama, by the Christian Democrats, the Communists, the Mass Media, and, to a small extent, the Socialists. Each of these protagonists, though, used this appeal differently as each understood social change through Democracy to mean something different.

The position of the Christian Democrats on the negotiation question was, as noted previously, a steadfast negative one. Their public pronouncements on the issue set their priorities clearly—the democratic institutions and the laws deriving from them were inviolable. Moro's life was valuable but ultimately expendable. "The essential point of reference remains, for us, the democratic state, with its institutions, its laws and its requirements . . . While the

Honorable Moro is undergoing the gravest and most inhuman coercion, the Christian Democrat Party renews its moral and political solidarity with him."[26]

Moral and political solidarity was about as far as his party was willing to go for Moro. The rhetorical strategy involving the use of the *Democracy* root paradigm included the public attribution to Moro (in absentia while he was still alive and in memorium after his death) of the very same priorities. This hypothesized concurrence of Moro was then used to legitimate the no-negotiation stance of the Christian Democrats. The rhetorical flourishes with which this strategy was carried out revealed a high level of political sophistication. Andreotti alluded to Moro's "true" wishes in a speech given to a joint session of the Chamber of Deputies and Senate on the day after Moro's body was found. There Andreotti spoke of the attempt of the Red Brigades "to sap the roots of the democratic system and the respect of the law: those principles to which Moro himself, from his senatorial bench or from his professorial chair had dedicated his activities and convictions."[27]

According to the Christian Democrats, then, Moro was claimed to have virtually dedicated his political and academic life to building the Christian Democrat's case for refusing to negotiate his release from the Red Brigades "people's prison." This claim was sustained despite the torrent of letters Moro wrote in which he adamantly and repeatedly requested negotiation. What might have emerged as a potentially rupturing moral conflict—the Democratic system versus Moro's life—was thus resolved into harmonious agreement. Even Moro was said to have believed the Democratic system to be of a higher existential order than his life.

It was extremely important for those protagonists in the Moro social drama who were taking the hard line on negotiations not to appear, in the eyes of the public audience, callous or indifferent to Moro's fate. Thus, if the content of their decision was not to be altered, at least the form of it could be contoured to project an image of humane, moral concern. The root paradigms, in this regard, could be used as providers of structural, normative constraints temperizing these necessary moral impulses. The Christian Democrat's use of the Constitution, as we have already seen, accomplished precisely that: "In any case, the Republic and the forces representing it, aiming towards restoring Moro to liberty, in the face of a real increase in the use of violence, will certainly know how to find forms of generosity and clemency which are consistent with the ideals and the norms of the Constitution."[28] It is in the last phrase of the above quotation that the constraints on the generous feelings of the republic (read Christian Democrat party for republic here) are made explicit—we can do no more than the Constitution allows us, and, unfortunately, it does not allow us to negotiate with terrorists. Thus our generosity must stop short of that.

The structural position of the Christian Democrats—that of being *the* party of the government since 1948—allowed it a rather untroubled and uncomplicated use of the various root paradigms. As Giuseppe Di Palma has written: "All the center has to do is to exist, to be itself. It may, in fact, need no elaborate and distinctive ideology, beyond presenting itself as the 'defense of the republic.' "[29]

The Italian Communist party also engaged the *Democracy* set. But their use of it had, of necessity, a different valence than that of the Christian Democrats. For the Communists, the crucial theoretical and practical connections to be made were those between democracy and its defense by the workers in Italy and democracy and revolution (". . . it is part of our politics, our successes—that is, being democrats and revolutionaries at the same time."—Enrico Berlinguer).[30] The Communists were maintaining that negotiations with the terrorists would necessarily signify the recognition of these "armed parties" and that this would lead inevitably to the installation of an authoritarian regime.

On April 24, *L'Unità* approvingly reprinted an article, originally published in *La Repubblica,* which had been written by a socialist, Stefano Rodotà. In this article, Rodotà anticipated the political results of negotiating with the Red Brigades: "We would see, first of all, a break-up of the constitutional system which does not allow the existence of 'armed parties' but only 'democratically operating parties' (Article Forty-Nine of the Italian Constitution). Once the existence of an armed party and a situation of civil war were to be recognized, a state-of-siege declaration would be inevitable with all of the consequent suspensions of constitutional guarantees and the passage of power to the military . . . We would, in fact, have a legal coup d'état and the installation of an authoritarian regime."[31]

This catastrophic vision presents a scenario of legitimation of the terrorists through the recognition of them that would be the inevitable result of negotiations. And this recognition would then lead immediately and necessarily to a state of siege where all civil liberties and democratic processes would be suspended. The possibility of negotiating with the Red Brigades while still preserving democracy is nowhere considered.

The Communist party took it upon itself and volunteered its constituency, the working class, to be the staunchest defenders of democracy. Every demonstration, every holiday, every event at which the Communists officiated during the Moro social drama was transformed into an occasion to defend democracy. A *L'Unità* article describing a Communist party–organized demonstration in Cagliari on Sardinia, for example, explained the way in which the recent acts of terrorism had changed the focus of that demonstration: originally it had been organized around the theme of the economic crisis and of the struggles of the Sardinian workers. Now, however, the demonstration was being presented as "a great unitary intitiative to defend democracy." This was a powerful message to the workers from the Communist party. It stated that while indeed there was an economic crisis and indeed the workers were struggling, those issues paled before the specter of democracy under siege. During the entire two-month period of the Moro social drama, all problems of work and the economy were declared to be of secondary importance and were placed on hold for the duration. Everything was to be absorbed into the Democracy-defense campaign. The assertion of the terrorist social problem, then, relegated all other social problems to the sidelines.

During the precarious first weeks of the new government's tenure, it was especially important for the Communists to gain acceptance as a rightful participant in it. This they could accomplish only by being bellicose in the direction of the current (decrying terrorism) and not against the current (decrying the economic crisis which the Communists had claimed was brought on by thirty years of Christian Democrat mismanagement). In this way, the meaning of all Communist-organized demonstrations was transformed into outrage against the would-be destroyers of democracy.

Because the Communist party presented itself as "dalla parte della democrazia" (on the side of democracy) it could claim that it, too, along with Moro, his bodyguards, and the Christian Democrats (as Moro's party) had been personally assaulted.

Alessandro Silj has remarked on the high degree of homogeneity in the Italian mass media responses to the Moro social drama: "The political 'line' of each newspaper appears, for the moment, to lose its traditional specificity and to adopt a homogeneous evaluation [of Moro's kidnapping]. Each views the assault on the President of the Christian Democrats *as an attack on the democratic system.*"[32]

In association with their chosen role as fierce defenders of the democratic system, the establishment mass media, despite their abundant elegies to Moro and editorials of solidarity with Moro's family, emerged as a strong opponent of negotiations. They presented the negotiation issue as one in which an explicit choice between two root paradigms—*Democracy* and the *Sanctity of Human Life*—was posed: ". . . it's a question of sacrificing the life of a man or losing the Republic. Unfortunately, for democrats like us, there can be no doubt about the choice."[33]

When posed in these terms, it would indeed be absurd to sacrifice an entire republic for the life of one of its citizens. There was something obviously dramatic about the idea of losing the republic, so hard won after the twenty years under fascism in Italy. It implied a secular concomitant of the explusion from Eden. The life of a single individual, no matter how exalted and important he or she may be, could not compete as a sacred idea to motivate action.

For the Socialists, who staked out a symbolic territory with their own preeminent root paradigm, the *Sanctity of Human Life* the *Democracy* set was useful precisely as a way to get to that *Sanctity of Human Life* ideal. Bettino Craxi, the Socialist party secretary, framed his party's position in the following way: "In any case . . . the Socialists cannot associate themselves with the triumphant attitude of the saviours of the Republic: Moro's death would mean the defeat of the Republic and the civil and humane principles inspiring the Constitution."[34]

In other words, the Constitution and the republic embodying the Constitution are only sacred because of the principles inhering in them. And, because the principle of humaneness is intimately linked to the idea of the sacred quality of human life, this root paradigm must have precedence. The Socialists, however, were not exactly sure of where to go with their humanism as they entered it in competition with the *Democracy* root paradigm for public primacy. Their self-presentation as the Party of Negotiation was based on their adoption of the *Sanctity of Human Life* appeal as their own.

They could not, however, reject the meaningfulness of *Democracy* or the *Resistance*, for example. They could only deny that they were relevant in deciding how to deal with the negotiation issue.

THE SANCTITY OF HUMAN LIFE

To appeal to the sanctity of human lfe was to appeal, it would seem, to one of the most transcendent values of all. No particular constituency was being singled out—everyone (Red Brigades as well—following upon a first-level recognition) was included. All life was sacred. The historical context of this appeal appeared similarly timeless and transcendent. Yet some of the purveyors of this root paradigm could be making a subtle and perhaps not entirely conscious reference to the particular claim of modern democratic societies in respecting every life. More on this below. Tropologically, the appeal can best be described as constituting a synecdoche—in this case, the whole (humanity) standing for the part (Aldo Moro). Thus both sides of the equation sacralized each other. The obvious meaning of this appeal was that not negotiating with the Red Brigades, and allowing Moro to be killed, would be trespassing on the sanctity of all human life. The engaging of this appeal by the no-negotiation protagonists thus had to be particularly creative in order precisely to avoid this meaning.

The root paradigm of *the Sanctity of Human Life* was handpicked by two protagonists in particular; the already mentioned Socialist party and the various groups of the Italian ultraleft. Other protagonists, including the Communists and the Christian Democrats, alluded only obliquely to this value. These protagonists gave their verbal approval to actions they ambiguously referred to as "humanitarian initiatives" taken to restore Moro to his family. But this approval was always followed by a caveat to the effect that nothing, not even the intrinsic value of Moro's life, could cause the government to give in to the terrorist's request for negotiations. Gustavo Selva, the Christian Democrat–leaning journalist, put this position most succinctly: "Above all, there should be no yielding to the blackmail, as much as this attitude may be painful and humanly difficult."[35]

The *Sanctity of Human Life* root paradigm has rich sociological resonance. Durkheim discussed the development of the cult of the individual in modern societies. In these societies, the individual acquires a sacred quality and the integrity of the individual is inviolable. Durkheim points out an interesting correlation in this regard, that "history gives sound authority for this relation of cause and effect as between the progress of moral individualism and the advance of the State. Except for the abnormal cases . . . the stronger the State, the more the individual is respected."[36]

The fact that the *Sanctity of Human Life* appeal was the currency of the less powerful (in terms of political clout) protagonists of the Moro social drama may indicate something about its relative low status as a cultural theme in Italy.

However, another way of interpreting the rise of moral individualism and, indeed, the interpretation put forward by those who were intransigent against negotiation but recognized the need to reference the sanctity of individuals was, as Durkheim wrote: "It is not this or that individual the State seeks to develop, it is the individual in genere, who is not to be confused with anyone of us."[37] In other words, it was not Moro qua Moro who attained sacred status. It was rather the category of "individual," of which set Moro was a member, that had acquired a new sanctity in modern societies. What this meant concretely was that the hard-liners could give their assent to the categorical imperative while ignoring its practical implications. As Silj has written: "Everyone sensed the need to preface their declarations of intransigence with expressions of solidarity with Moro's family or with solemn affirmations of the value of human life."[38]

On the other hand, both the ultraleft groups and the Socialists emphasized the relevance of the *Sanctity of Human Life*. The ultraleft did so by claiming they were against any form of the death penalty. The ultraleft newspaper, *Lotta Continua* (Continuing Struggle) was the only newspaper to publish an appeal from the newly organized and heterogeneous "Party of Negotiation" (composed of, among others, the president of "Catholic Action"; a number of high ranking priests [indicating a split in the Catholic church hierarchy]; a famous playwright/actor, Dario Fò; the leader of the Radical party, Marco Pannella; and several renegade members of the Communist party). Why did *Lotta Continua* agree to publish this appeal when so many others refused? Because, responded the newspaper to this very question, "the killing of Aldo Moro is against all of the reasons of the struggle in which we are engaged. Because we are opposed to the death penalty, wherever it is applied and however it is justified . . . Because we are radically and irreducibly averse to this state, which in death, in war and in fear seeks the force that it does not have, the authority that it does not have, the legitimacy that it does not have."[39]

Lotta Continua and Democrazia Proletaria, another ultraleft group, held the position that the saving of Moro's life was the bottom line and they were, for this reason, in favor of negotiations. In keeping with their extremely precise and equilibrated opposition to both the state and the Red Brigades, the ultraleft adopted a blanket moral imperative: no life should be spent. Opposed to the state and the government representing it as they were, the ultraleft groups could hardly go with the appeals expressing support for these institutions. Still, as did the other protagonists, the ultraleft groups were structurally required to develop normative resources by selecting one or several root paradigms as their own. They could not simply come out in favor of negotiations—a position which, in its nakedness, came close to resembling third-level recognition of the Red Brigades (i.e., recognizing them as a legitimate enemy). They could only favor negotiations if they located some ultimate value(s) and presented negotiations as the means by which that ultimate value could be attained. In this way, the ultraleft attempted to avoid their own delegitimation and to stave off accusations of supporting the terrorists. By sanctifying the person of Moro, an unambiguous representative of the legitimate state, and by asseting Moro's right to live, these groups sought to deflect the above mentioned accusations.

The other protagonist cashing in the *Sanctity of Human Life* root paradigm, albeit in a prevaricating manner, was the Socialist party led by the party secretary, Bettino Craxi. This employment would turn out to be a politically savvy choice for the Socialist who would receive a small but notable increase in votes in the May 1978 administrative elections. Gustavo Selva noted: "The Socialists assert that the increase in votes is also a prize for the 'humanitarian path' adopted during the Moro affair."[40]

Thus depite the Socialist's minimal political clout in Italy and the high degree of ambivalence with which they presented their campaign supporting negotiations, they would retrospectively view their elective affinity to the *Sanctity of Human Life* root paradigm as a profitable one.

Their ambivalent presentation kept them on just this side of political legitimacy, and it took the following form: "Craxi writes that the Red Brigades' request, that is, an exchange, is absurd and unrealistic, flung against every uncrossable limit of principle and objectively impossible. Nevertheless, the State is able to evaluate if the possibility of an autonomous initiative exists that is founded on humanitarian reasons and which keeps within the sphere of the republican laws."[41]

Toward the very end of April. Craxi proposed a two-point "humanitarian" road. The first point was that the state should release three prisonsers who (a) were not on the Red Brigades list of prisoners *they* wanted released (these appeared in communique no. 8 received on April 24), and (b) could be released without the state being compromised because the prisoners were ill [thus the humanitarian thrust]. The second point was to initiate an inquest into the special prisons in Italy in order to control and abolish "certain conditions."[42]

The Socialist party identified itself during the Moro social drama as "The Party of Negotiation," not to be confused with the other, heterogeneous "Party of Negotiation." A few years later, during the D'Urso kidnapping case of 1980–1981 (Giovanni D'Urso was a High-Court Magistrate), the Socialists would inflate this identification to become "The Party of Life," subtly indicating that those other parties not supporting negotiations somehow desired the death of the hostage.

This special branding of "life-giver" secured by the Socialists for themselves revealed their attempt to leapfrog over the protagonists employing the more "profane" appeals of the *Resistance*, the *Party*, and the *Working Class*, for example, in the quest for the root paradigm representing the most ultimate value. The Socialists presented the *Sanctity of Human Life* root paradigm as the most obviously sacred and in this way staked out the symbolic territory they needed in this social drama in order to regain some exclusive strategic leverage.

The Socialist's attempt to bring about negotiations by way of gaining acceptance for their root metaphor was a good example of a protagonist in a social drama aiming at what Gusfield calls "ownership" of a public problem. The fact that the Socialists occupied a subordinate (though admittedly strategic) position in Italian politics meant that their ability to own a public problem was minimal. As Gusfield says: "At any specific moment, all possible parties to the issue do not have equal ability to influence the public; they do not possess the same degree or kind of authority to be legitimate sources of definition of the reality of the problem, or to assume legitimate power to regulate, control and innovate solutions."[43]

No protagonist went through the Moro social drama without at least publicly acknowledging the presence of the *Sanctity of Human Life* root paradigm. But the solutions proposed by the more powerful participants were never based primarily on this value. In fact, the no-negotiation protagonists generally introduced their positions by first rhetorically asking: What is more sacred than a human life? and then, given their hard-line positions, demonstrating their conviction that there is, indeed, something or things more sacred than a human life. In the independent centrist newspaper, *Il Giorno,* a paper in which Moro frequently published, the major editorial of March 17 asked the following question: ". . . is there anything which is more valuable than saving the life of a man? Is there any price too high for insuring Moro's safety, his health, his liberty? In this terrible moment we cannot repress those anguishing questions which come from the heart."[44]

These questions, however, were left purposely *unanswered* in this editorial as well as in numerous other editorials appearing in the various establishment news organs and in the speeches made by the hard-line protagonists during the Moro social drama.

As far as the two major political parties were concerned, the Christian Democrats and the Communists, the attention paid to the *Sanctity of Human Life* root paradigm was aimed at staving off the criticisms they saw resulting from the way the party membership and the public viewed their hard line. In *L'Unità* on April 24, the following warning appeared: "Let us guard against the division of the country into 'humanitarians' (those who want negotiations with the Red Brigades) and 'stalinists' or 'prussians' (the defenders of the democratic system)."[45]

The phrasing here is interesting. It indicates a dichotomy between those defending democracy and those (favoring negotiations) thwarting democracy. It also states that those who defend democracy, namely, the Communists, are falsely accused of being totalitarian in various ways and that those with such an accusatory vision are simply trying to delegitimate the defenders of democracy.

Sciascia unpacks the division around the humanitarian issue as it developed within the Christian Democrats: "There has been a confused and foolishly ambitious 'negotiating' maneuver on the

parts of the enemies of Zaccagnini. Such figures as Massimo De-
Carolis, who normally play the part of the 'hard' one, the 'cynical'
one, have passed over to the side of the humanitarians solely in
order to place the Party Directorate in trouble. And we have seen
the Barese [Bari is the city of Moro's birth] clientele react in a
sentimental and proprietary fashion, all lined up in an apparently
humanitarian formation, but 'sotto, sotto' [deep down] mercantile
and ferocious, advocating, for example, an exchange of prisoners
followed immediately by a man-hunt and the execution of the
Brigadists."[46]

The very word, humanitarian, grew sticky and unwieldly during
the Moro social drama. Actions that logic would decree were anti-
humanitarian were being called humanitarian actions. As Bernard
Avishai wrote: "The Red Brigades leader, Renato Curcio, called
the killing of Aldo Moro; 'the highest act of humanity possible in a
class-divided society'—not an off-hand remark."[47]

And, as to the way in which the Red Brigades outside of prison
(those carrying out the kidnapping) viewed the humanitarian
appeals, communique no. 7 made this clear: "The 'humanitarian'
initiative is launched by the DC. And here we are in the most
grotesque shamelessness. To which 'humanity' can the various
Andreotti, Fanfani, Leone, Cossiga, Piccoli, Rumor and company
ever appeal . . . The problem to which the DC must respond is
political and not one of humanity."[48]

And, in the other camp, we find, in terms of the structure of the
argument, the same convolutions. The United States Department
of State had sent deputy assistant secretary of state, Steve R.
Pieczenik, a psychiatrist, to Italy to provide psychiatrically strategic
consultation during the Moro social drama. Robert Katz discussed
Pieczenik's view of the relative significance of the *Sanctity of Human Life* root paradigm: "It was . . . essential to demonstrate, he
said, that no man is indispensable to the vitality of the nation-state
. . . This demonstration was particularly crucial because Moro,
according to Pieczenik, was an extremely important member of the
system. In other words, the idea, it seems was to prove that even
Aldo Moro was dispensible."[49]

It was in the way that the *Sanctity of Human Life* appeal was
consistently played off the root paradigms of the collectivity *Democracy*, the *State*, the *Republic*. And, as far as the politically
powerful protagonists were concerned, the collectivity always took

priority over the sanctity of Moro's life. Only one representative of a major political party, Giuseppe Saragat, former President of Italy, actually coupled rather than divided the individual and the collective referents, doing this, however, in a critical way. When Moro was assassinated and his body found, Saragat said that besides Moro's body "there was also the cadaver of the first Republic which had not known how to defend the life of the most generous politician of our time."[50] For Saragat, then, the neglect suffered by Moro at the hands of the government he created came to the same thing as neglecting, and through this neglect killing, the republic.

As far as the workers interviewed at the Fiat plant gates at Mirafiori were concerned, their responses to the various possibilities of saving Moro's life portrayed a basic respect for and acceptance of the relevance of the *Sanctity of Human Life* root paradigm but an unwillingness to hold that referent as absolute. Some examples of the interviewee responses represent the various confrontations of root paradigms found in the workers' attitudes. The individual is played off of the Constitution, the state, and the collective responsibility of political leaders, all of which concepts are presented as reasons to hold off negotiations. A union official made the following statement: "Let's say the exchange possibility is considered. This, on a humanitarian level, is legitimate, but on a political level—no. And even Moro knows this. He chose his own life and has assumed the political responsibilities. Now he has to be consistent to the very end. The State cannot yield, otherwise it will destroy itself."[51] Another union delegate stated: "Well, it's true that the majority of the public, from a humane point of view, is in accord with saving the life of the Honorable Moro, the Italians are hardly a mass of cannibals. But from a political point of view, it's different because if we yield now, tomorrow will be even worse. The Constitution imposes this choice."[52]

THE STATE

The most often quoted sociological definition of the state is that of Weber—"A state is a human community that (successfully) claims the monopoly of the legitimate use of physical force within a given territory."[53] This definition centers on the means by which state power is sustained, revealing physical force to be the ultimate basis of that power.

Modern theorists of the state have elaborated and critiqued this definition in several ways. Some, beginning with Gramsci, have developed the idea of hegemony—the ability of the dominant class to impose its world-view on the subordinate classes through means other than physical force, notably through cultural dominance. It is significant that the ultraleft critique of the Italian state's immediate responses to Moro's kidnapping derived from this theory of hegemony. The ultraleft radio station Radio Città Futura broadcast the following on the afternoon of Moro's kidnapping: "Evidently today, the repressive apparatus of the state is only a reserve structure which is brought to bear only when the processes of political and institutional mediation no longer serve, when they are not sufficient . . . the central element on which this type of power is based is the creation of a vast area of consensus, in determined popular sectors, on which they [the state representatives] then prime a series of operations."[54]

This statement claims that the modern state may still be based on the monopoly of the legitimate use of physical force, but this force may be normally placed on hold as other more political and cultural mechanisms of control operate. The radio commentator went on to say, however, that certain other sectors in Italy, specifically the ultraleft itself, have "seen in person, the 'reserve' repressive apparatus of the state." In other words, when necessary, the force, on which the state is ultimately based, reappears to control belligerents.

Both the Weberian view of the state as well as its Gramscian elaboration only develop one sociological meaning of the word "state." Clifford Geertz has discussed the several etymological and social themes condensed within the one word. He sees three possible readings: "status, in the sense of station, standing, rank, condition-estate . . . pomp, in the sense of splendor, display, dignity, presence stateliness . . . and governance, in the sense of regnancy, regime, dominion, mastery-statecraft . . . And it is characteristic of that [state] discourse, and of its modernness that the third of these meanings, the last to arise (in Italy in the 1540s . . .) should have come to dominate the term as to obscure our understanding of the multiple nature of high authority."[55]

What is interesting about the Moro social drama protagonists' uses of the state root metapor is that they encompassed Geertz's second meaning of the word: splendor, stateliness, and display along with the third meaning of governance. A high level of pageantry was sustained throughout Moro's captivity. There were frequent demonstrations and rallies "in support of" the State or Democracy or the Resistance. The major political figures were engaged in vigorous speechmaking at these public assemblies, all speeches circling round their negotiation positions and moral imperatives. The media reports of these demonstrations always spoke of the party flags waving aloft and the enthusiastic responses of the large crowds. There was the consciousness of publicly making history, the kind of consciousness that the narrative historians only attribute to the retrospective analysis of the historian. In this case, as Italian journalist Ida Magli claims, the historic consciousness actually worked, ironically, to suppress historical evolution. An event is declared "historical" and the actual work of history, in this case the substantive ratification debates in Parliament, is preempted: "Affirming that, in Moro, [the Red Brigades] had also struck the 'heart of the state,' calling everybody out into the piazza in response to an incident which for all its gravity and sadness, had become 'history' only because it had been treated as if it were history, hurrying to silence the substantive [as opposed to formal] 'confidence debate' in Parliament, in the anxiousness to declare that this is the historic response to an act which, for this reason and only for this reason, had become historic."[56]

I am not presenting here a theory of an Italian theater-state as Geertz has done for Bali, in which the great mobilizations of the population "were not means to political ends, they were the ends themselves, they were what the state was for."[57] Geertz's Balinese theater-state was, after all, highly metaphysical. Rather, the modern Italian state seems to be a strange combination of a theater-state and a governance state. The public ceremonies both stand on their own and act as means to the achievement of the political agendas of the protagonists of the spectacles. The Italian state partially builds its strength from its ability to mobilize hundreds of thousands of people to attend a demonstration.

Several protagonists of the Moro social drama dealt in the currency of the *Reason of State* root paradigm. This essentially entailed the refusal of negotiations with the Red Brigades because of an alleged *Reason of State* (Raison d'État).

The history of the Reason of State concept is a long one—its most famous expositers including Machiavelli, Frederick the Great, and Hegel. Specifically, the Reason of State argument proposes: "The well-being of the State and of its population is held to be the ultimate value and the goal."[58] And, Meinicke, the great analyst of the Reason of State argument, goes on to say that "it is an essential part of the spirit of raison d'état that it must always be smearing itself by offending against ethics and law . . ."[59]

In other words, the *Reason of State* root paradigm will invariably come into conflict with other root paradigms appealing to different orders and systems of morality. In the Moro case, as has been shown, the *Reason of State* argument came most directly into conflict with the *Sanctity of Human Life* appeal. According to Meinicke, Machiavelli was responsible for first elaborating and defending this theory of the Reason of State in which the state's contravening of the moral law "freed the political sphere from all unpolitical restrictions."[60] So while the Enlightenment-developed system of ethics declared that an individual life was more valuable and, as it were, sacred than the political integrity of a state, those using the *Reason of State* argument reversed the order of these values. Nothing could transcend the state, not even the life of one of its most important representatives. Here the ideas of the Enlightenment came up most directly against the reality of the power state.

An important theme running through the historical discussion of the Raison d'État is that the state rulers, when placed in a position to do so (e.g., by being captured by the enemy), were required to sacrifice themselves for the state. As Meinecke wrote: "One sees clearly what is the real central idea in Machiavelli's life: namely, the regeneration of a fallen people by means of the virtue of a tyrant."[61]

The following chapters analyze the unsuccessful campaign on the parts of several protagonists to induce Moro to adopt the *Reason of State* root paradigm as his own and to voluntarily serve himself up to preserve the integrity of the Italian state. Moro, however, persisted in attempting to regain his freedom.

The options were being presented as crystal clear—either Moro's life would be saved through negotiation with the Red Brigades, or the life of the state would be ensured through the *refusal* to negotiate. Not only that, but the two alternatives were not permitted to be considered as essentially different (i.e., existing in mutually exclusive moral universes as in Isaiah Berlin's analysis of *The Prince*) but equal ultimate values. Rather, the *State* root paradigm was publicly configured as incorporating the *Sanctity of Human Life* root paradigm in that the state itself was held to be responsible for the preservation of so many other lives. Such a formulation helped to ward off the accusations being leveled against the hard-liners of apparent callousness in the face of Moro's plight. Andreoni, a Christian Democrat deputy from Milano, when asked if there were any circumstances under which his party would consider negotiations (this question being posed the day after Moro was kidnapped and before the Christian Democrat positions was hardened into place), replied: "That's a question capable of killing a man. The state cannot yield to any blackmail—besides from the fact that the people would never understand saying yes for one politician and no to another."[62]

The Christian Democrats demonstrated their conviction that the Red Brigades had one primary, double-edged aim; to humiliate Moro (by making him do such face-losing behavior as introduce and lobby for negotiation in his letters) and to provoke a crisis of the state. In fact, according to many Christian Democrats, Moro did not, for whatever reasons, demonstrate a sufficient sense of the state in his letters.

But adopting the *State* appeal and *being* the State were two different things. In this regard, discussing the general alienation and extraneousness of the public to the Moro social drama, Ida Magli wrote: "Our extraneousness is born of our understanding that the men of power, at the slightest tug at the cord, reveal that they identify the state in *themselves*, that *they* personify and live through the institutions. They have, in other words, a sacred vision of power."[63]

The Christian Democrat's unbroken rule in Italian politics, which by 1978 had proceeded for thirty years, had allowed them to develop and cultivate their sense of selfhood and statehood. As far as they were concerned, they *were* the state. In this way, the path was clear to their interpreting any attack against the party as an attack against the state and any attack against the state as an attack against the party. And, since Moro was the president of the Christian Democrats, the attack on him could easily be read as an attack on the party. The Christian Democrats, then, were revealed as believing themselves to be the veritable owners of the state apparatus and of all public problems threatening it.

Along with the Christian Democrats, the numerous organs of the establishment Mass Media displayed their enthusiasm for the *Reason of State* root paradigm throughout the Moro social drama, as we have already seen. Publications spanning the political spectrum lined up behind the major political parties' no-negotiation position and did so, for the most part, by asserting that negotiations would clearly jeopardize the effectiveness and very existence of the state.

Some examples from this mass media solid front follow. From *Il Giorno*, we find an editorial of March 17 which reads: "As a response to this assault on the institutions, we must obviously prepare ourselves to resist and to act so as to defend the dignity, the authority and the very life of the State."[64]

Indro Montanelli, editor of the right-wing *Il Giornale Nuovo*, presented an explicit position on the possibilities of negotiation and its impact on the state: ". . . the Honorable Moro is not, nor can he be an object of barter for the Red Brigades. However important the person is, however great the respect we nourish for him, not even his head is worth the capitulation of the state . . . The more important these [kidnapped] leaders, the more necessary it is that they subject themselves to the community's laws—there can be no negotiations with delinquents."[65]

On the other end of the political spectrum, *La Repubblica's* editor, Eugenio Scalfari, an independent socialist, was saying what amounted essentially to the same thing: "Moral energy, a sense of the state, public and private rectitude, these are the grand responses necessary to solder the populus and the institutions together in a non-dissolvable pact. The terrorism of these killers is a disease which can attack a body with some hope of success only if the body is already corroded. If the body is vital and healthy, the criminals will not prevail."[66]

Regardless of political placement, then, all of the independent (nonparty affiliated) newspapers and radio and televison stations (with the exception of the ultraleft and ultraright organs) followed the government's hard line against negotiations. Moreover, most did so by presenting *Reason of State* pronouncements.

This nearly automatic and unanimous lining up of the mass media behind the government appears somewhat problematic. The traditional role of the press in democratic, pluralistic countries, has been one of critical analysis and, often, opposition toward the standing bodies of government. And, indeed, this had generally been the case in Italy. The Italian press (both left and right) has, at least since the late sixties, generally adopted a critical stance toward

the many Christian Democrat–led governments and has put forward the notion that the Italian state was, at the minimum, weak
and, at the maximum, self-serving and corrupt. The task, during the
Moro social drama, was to develop some way of supporting this
state that had been decried as being so weak and now was being
touted as strong. In other words, the media had to come up with
some way to deal with the government's contention that negotiating
with the Red Brigades would be tantamount to admitting that Italy
was a weak state and that not negotiating signified that Italy was a
strong state and *still* sustain their critical stance toward this state.
Eugenio Scalfari hit upon the perfect formula out of this quandry. It
involved the following sophisticated dialectical reasoning: ". . . the
law must be equal for everybody . . . terrorists are common criminals . . . they fall under the jurisdiction of the law (as does everyone) . . . These principles do not belong specifically to *this* state, so
little worthy of respect and defense, according to the opinion of
senator La Valle and also my own, but rather are those of every
human cohabitation."[67]

The contemporary Italian state, then, merits no particular loyalty or support. Silj explicates this type of reasoning quite succinctly: "It is not, therefore, in the name of *this* state that we must
refuse to negotiate with the terrorists but in the name of an ideal
state that today does not exist, in the name of the universal laws that
regulate every 'human cohabitation.' "[68]

By sidestepping the real Italian state and pointing to some sort of
ideal, universal state, Scalfari and company could justify their use
of the *Reason of State* root paradigm and not lose face in terms of
their journalistic mandate to be critical.

Having assessed the Italian state and found it lacking in basic
legitimacy, the ultraleft media organs could not fall in line behind
the government's no-negotiation position. Also, from a dramaturgic point of view, any appeal publicly engaged by this political area
would have to be clearly opposed to the *State* root paradigm. Only
the *Sanctity of Human Life* as an ultimate value had the capacity to
transcend the broad and patriotic root paradigm of the *Reason of
State*.

We have seen how *Lotta Continua,* in publishing the "Appeal of
the Party of Negotiation," affirmed this value. Another newspaper
of the left, this somewhat closer to the Communists, however, *The
Daily Paper of the Workers,* critiqued the *Reason of State* line of

thought from a different perspective. What they critiqued was the official Communist party elaboration of the *Reason of State* root paradigm. Here the issue was the very concept of the state in marxist thought and the differences in interpretation that had developed between the party rank and file and its leadership: "The Communist Party, on the other hand, while it conquers on the field, with its capacity for popular mobilizations, a further legitimation as a governmental party (however much subordinate), must deal with the fact that within the working class, the consciousness of 'being the state' is understood differently from the way its historical party understands it."[69]

Here the critique is aimed at the zealous state-supporting activity of the Communist party during the Moro social drama. The status of quasi-participant accorded the Communist party in the new coalition government had, according to these leftist critics, allowed the Communist leadership to develop a different way of conceiving the state, one which was closer to the Christian Democrat way of conceiving and constructing the state than to the way it was conceived among the rank and file of the Communist party, particularly in the working class.

In general, the ultraleft presented the *Reason of State* root paradigm as a foil against which they could assert their own appeals—those being the *Sanctity of Human Life* and, still to be discussed, the *Proletariat*.

The Communist party, on its part, developed an individualized reading and presentation of the *Reason of State* appeal. It was not one of their most often or most emphatically presented symbols, but it did have a place in the Communist rhetorical lexicon. The crucial point is that every time the Communist leadership claimed that their actions were aimed at preserving the state, they would link the *State* appeal with another, most often with the *Resistance*. An example of this symbolic strategy comes from an April 24, 1978, *L'Unità* editorial which discussed a rally held that day: "The word of the day in every assembly, in every mass meeting is a call to the steady struggle for the defense and renewal of the democratic state born of the Resistance."[70]

Here the state is doubly qualified by concepts toward which *L'Unità's* readership is naturally sympathetic; democracy and the Resistance. The Communist constituency, still used to considering its party as a party of the opposition, was not yet fully comfortable with a wholehearted, unproblematic defense of the state as that state had developed in postwar Italy. Thus there was the need to present this particular root paradigm in tandem with other, safer, appeals. The question remains, however: Why did the Communists feel the need to use this root paradigm at all when it had so many others in its arsenal? Apparently the need to be recognized as a legitimate political party determined the choice of symbolic appeals, and using the Reason of State argument to back up their no-negotiation stance put the Communist party in the role of a *defender* of the legitimate state. It provided a relatively safe perch in the politically volatile and precarious time of the Moro social drama.

The *Reason of State* root paradigm was used, then, most consistently by those protagonists opposed to negotiation with the Red Brigades. In fact, these protagonists consistently questioned the patriotism of those who sought to understand terrorism without prefacing their analyses with laudatory comments regarding the extant Italian state. In the introduction to the book *Dimensioni del Terrorismo politico* (Dimensions of Political Terrorism), Barbano describes this process of polarizing the responses to terrorism and delegitimating any truly critical discourse about the terrorist phenomenon that took place during the Moro social drama: "At the culmination of the Moro affair, the polarization between the [public] attitudes of condemnation [of terrorism] because of a Reason of State—and a whole genre of judgements seeking to understand terrorism by way of determined conditions of analysis was completed, and the latter stigmatized as 'sociological justification.' Certainly, this polarization did not mirror a reality in which whoever was not with the state was with the Red Brigades, or, put otherwise, whoever was against the Red Brigades was all for the state."[71]

THE PROLETARIAT

The appeal to the *Proletariat*, along with the final appeal to the *Party*, was concrete, particularistic, and metonymic. The *Proletariat* stood, in the eyes of those engaging in it, for that which was the best in humanity. The general strike announced and held the afternoon of Moro's kidnapping symbolized the kind and level of rhetorical inclusion of the Italian worker in the Moro social drama. The proletariat played the role of the walk-on in the crowd scenes of this theatrical event, the subjects on whose behalf and in whose name the other protagonists waged their symbolic war. This involved a rather sudden change of valence from opposition to Moro and the ruling Christian Democrat Party to one of support for them.

What then was involved in the major protagonists' turn to the proletariat? How did the *Proletariat* function as a root paradigm, and for whom?

The *Proletariat* root paradigm brings up, most explicitly of all of the appeals, the issue of protagonist constituency. It addresses the question: How broad-based can the symbolic appeal of a root paradigm be? For the Communist party, the historic party of the working class, the naturalness of the *Proletariat* root paradigm is obvious. In a way, the Communists "owned" its proletariat constituency and could easily have limited itself to addressing that portion of the population exclusively, the Italian electorate being for the most part differentiated along class lines. That this electorate is highly differentiated and that the different political parties have elective affinities with the various segments is echoed in the following statement of a Communist senator being interviewed by an American researcher: "You keep talking about parliamentarians and the electorate as if they were some sort of undifferentiated and disembodied entities floating in midair . . . I don't know any such thing as the electorate in general. I know there are electorates of each party, each with its own . . . demands and aspirations, and this is the reality which we recognize."[72]

Appeals to selective constituencies though are problematic in two ways. On the one hand, if the appeal is too circumscribed, the ability of the appeal-making protagonist to present itself as a legitimate representative of the general interest of the society will be undermined. On the other hand, if the appeal is too general, the appeal-makers' specific constituency could end up by being alienated. The Communist party faced precisely this double-edged dilemma in its use of the *Proletariat* root paradigm. Its overriding concern with being accepted as a legitimate political party of the government caused it to temper and rework its use of the *Proletariat* root paradigm. The great mobilzations/demonstrations organized by the Communist party were accomplished in such a way as to both single out the party's chosen constituency, the proletariat, as well as to include the wider population of students, housewives, and "Italian citizens." In other words, everyone but the terrorists and the fascists were to be identified as "defenders of the Republic."

The theoretical issue here is that of representative authority staying in touch with its social base. Geertz writes of this in reference to the situation of the divine king in Bali: "The sphere within which any particular lord could actually play the divine-king game was circumscribed by the points where he lost touch with his social base if he became too grand; yet the threat of falling behind in the spectacle race if he failed to stay grand enough kept pushing against those limits."[73]

The back-and-forth movement of the Communist party from the particular to the general, from its traditional working-class constituency to the near-entire population gave a special cast to the Communist's proletariat appeal. The nature of the *Proletariat* root paradigm, as used by the Communist party, consisted of asking the proletariat to participate in the general defense of the other Communist-utilized appeals; the *Resistance, Democracy,* and the *Constitution.* The proletariat, in other words, was being appealed to as the protector of the sacred possessions of Italy. The historic struggles of the worker's movement were to be interpreted purely as struggles aiming to safeguard these anti-Fascist attainments and not as movements against a particular capitalist class and aiming at revolutionary change. Berlinguer was explicit about this in a speech he made at the above-noted workers' rally on April 24: "They [the workers] know and feel that this democratic state, as devastated as it is by so many ills that must be extirpated, remains forever marked by the stamp that they gave to it with the Resistance, with the republican Constitution, with their thirty-year long stuggles."[74]

Alessandro Silj has noted that all of the articles dealing with trade unions during the period of the Moro affair dealt solely with the fact that "the unions wish to take the role of plaintiff against the Red Brigades."[75] All other union-relevant issues virtually disappeared from the organs of the press during this period.

As far as many of the workers were concerned, however, their symbolic recruitment to the cause of what they reviewed as essentially defending the Christian Democrats was problematic: "It's obvious that the worker—and there does exist the Christian Democrat worker as well—the worker is not very interested in this Moro event. It's not that he's not interested, he's interested but I think that this Moro thing is really a little too much playing the game of the Communist Party. They want to be the interlocutor of the Christian Democrats, by way of the Historic Compromise. Also because by now—do you remember the last [union] assembly we had? In these meetings we don't discuss the problems we have in the factory anymore—by now all discussion in the meetings is about the Red Brigades, about Moro."[76]

This general disinclination to direct involvement in the Moro social drama was expressed by many workers along with the dissatisfaction with the way other problems, more specific to the factory and the unions, had been abandoned. The whole process of involving the proletariat in the "saving of democracy" was viewed by a significant number of the interviewed workers as a diversion from the more purely economic and profound problems faced by them in their workplace. Further, the *kind* of involvement that the proletariat was to have in the whole Moro affair was the kind of involvement expected from the audience of a melodrama. They were not asked to participate in policy formation or even to participate in a discussion of the meaning or sources of the Red Brigades or the significance of Communist participation in the government at this historical moment. Rather, to quote the words of PSI secretary Craxi, the workers (in this case extended to include all citizens) were being asked to "collaborate" with the state; to let the hero know when the villain is on stage (i.e., terrorist infiltration in the factories): "Defend democracy and the State, to this end mobilize all of the energy available to obtain the liberation of Honorable Moro, ask for the active collaboration of all of the citizens" (*L'Unità*, March 17, 1978, p. 2) Underlying much of these laudatory references to the defense work of the proletariat was some concern about the presence of Red Brigades sympathizers in the factories. Bocca writes about the varied reactions on the day of Moro's kidnapping and includes the following: "In Milan, for example, in some sections, in front of Unidal, an occupied factory, in Novate, in Giambellino, the communist workers meet and uncork bottles of wine for a celebration: [political] pamphletting becomes easy, it climbs from six-hundred copies, normal for Milan, to four-thousand. There are those comrades who know some BR 'irregulars' and murmur to them, 'Ask him about the Montesi scandal.' 'Interrogate him about Cippico.' Old stories that the BR youth ignore."[77]

The only other protagonists to use the *Proletariat* appeal were the groups of the ultraleft and the Red Brigades themselves. The ultraleft groups' use of the *Proletariat* root metaphor consisted in a kind of metacritique of the ways in which both the Communists and the Red Brigades developed the proletarian appeal. They accused the Communist party of muting and distorting the history of the working-class movement in Italy, presenting that history as substantially less violent and less oppositional (toward the state) than it actually was. On the other hand, they accused the Red Brigades of attempting to legitimize themselves by asserting that they were the rightful heirs to that working-class movement. In this regard, Mantelli and Revelli wrote: "Now, [the real history of the working-class movement] seems to have disappeared, annulled by two converging attacks. From one side come the attacks of a 'statism' of the left that sacrifices the most beautiful part of the history of the workers' movement to an institutional compromise, that attempts to uproot the memory of the contents of the rupture and the very class in order to represent the past as a legitimation of the present, that reads the history of the workers' movement as the story of one institution among other institutions. And, from the other side, come the attacks of a terrorism that immiserates and annihilates the history of a class in the attempt to reduce it to the improbable source of its [terrorism's] own identity."[78]

At the "Automonia" group's meeting at the University of Rome held on May 6, 1978, to determine how to respond to the Red Brigades' latest communique in which the Brigades had announced Moro's death sentence, the general opinion was one of condemnation of the Red Brigades as revealed in the statement released: "The proletariat communists do not kill political prisoners."[79] In other words, these ultraleftist students were saying that *real* proletariat communists would not do such things, and it was left up to the Red Brigades to decide if they were, in fact, proletariat communists or merely imposters.

As for the Red Brigades themselves, every document they issued, every communique sent to the newspapers made specific reference to their chosen constituency, the proletariat.

In a section of communique no. 2, received on March 25, titled "The Imperalist Terrorism and the Proletariat Internationalism," the Red Brigades wrote that "we hold that the effective action of the PROLETARIAT INTERNATIONALISM must begin today also making clear among the Combatant Communist Organizations that the European proletariat has expressed a relationship of profound political confrontation, of effective solidarity and of a concrete collaboration."[80] In communique no. 3, they go on to assert: "The proletarian initiative has not halted, rather it has extended itself and assumed the form and contents of the Revolutionary Class War."[81]

In fact, the Red Brigades proclaimed themselves to be the only truly proletariat party in Italy. Thus every action they took was taken "in the name of" the *Proletariat*, this root paradigm serving, in their eyes, to legitimate their—what others would call terrorist— activities. As Renato Curcio cried out from behind the bars of his cage in the Torino courtroom: "Moro is in the hands of the proletariat."

THE PARTY

The last root paradigm to be discussed, the *Party*, did not figure dominantly in the presentations of the protagonists of the Moro social drama. The logic of its subsidiary status is understandable. Its particular appeal was much less global, much less metaphysical than such other root paradigms as the *Sanctity of Human Life* or the *Resistance*. And, as a metonymical device, it was essentially reductive. Only two protagonists attempted to utilize this appeal: the Christian Democrat party and Moro himself. Moro's attempt to use this appeal effectively will be taken up in the following chapter.

The Christian Democrat's use of the *Party* consisted in their identifying the interests of their party with the interests of Italy generally. This strategy, as will be recalled, was critiqued by Ida Magli in her exposition on the "men of power." If the Christian Democrat party was the same thing as Italy, then it indeed could be regarded as a "sacred" institution which, potentially, negotiations with the terrorists could transgress and contaminate. This identification did, however, effectively disenfranchise the more than two-thirds of the Italian electorate *not* identifying the Christian Democrats with the whole of the country. Leonardo Sciascia commented on this Christian Democrat strategy: "To this Christian Democrat party which finds its unity and solidarity in the defense of the individual Christian Democrat, to this party-family, to this party that interprets and represents the 'general will' of the Italians even if arithmetically it represents only a third of it, Aldo Moro addressed himself from the 'people's prison.' "[82]

The Red Brigades themselves, in their second communique, commented ironically on this DC strategy and, taking it a step further, claimed that the Andreotti-led government had ended up negating parliament altogether: ". . . the special laws just passed are the accomplishment of the most complete acquiescence of the parties of the so-called 'constitutional arch' [here we see the Red Brigades engaging in their own bracketing of reality in quotation marks] to the imperialist strategy, directed exclusively by the DC and its government. Thus have we passed from the State as the expression of the parties, to the parties as a pure instrument of the State."[83]

The use of the *Party* root paradigm, then, expressed an attempt to negate the other political parties' representational rights. (The most obvious target was the Communist party.) And it accomplished this by proposing the Christian Democrat party as the special and unique target of the Red Brigades. Significantly, though, by presenting their party as the political incarnation of all of Italy, the Christian Democrats could avoid the appearance of particularism in their use of the *Party* root paradigm.

Conclusion

At the heart of Victor Turner's discussion of the social drama of the fatal conflict between Becket and Henry II is the following passage: "At any rate, the real issue was not the breach of this or that rule, but of who was master . . . Each contestant was cashing in his resources of power, influence, prestige, wealth, numerical following, organization, prestige, internal and external support of every type in a trial of strength."[84]

In this dramaturgic analysis of the Moro kidnapping, we are beginning to see how such "trials of strength" in the Moro affair were essentially trials of legitimacy. Turner's contention that the "real" issue in a social drama is not the breach of "this or that rule" but is, instead, the determining of the "master" of a situation, names the central problematic of the dramaturgic approach to social life. There *was* a contest of mastery taking place among the several protagonists of the Moro social drama. And, in this case, the mastery consisted in being recognized as legitimate authority in one's own relevant arena of operation.

In this regard, it is vital to keep in mind the enduring precariousness of the Italian governing bodies,the numerous governmental changes, the many national scandals cutting across institutions, the residual fear of fascism, and the contemporaneous fear of a burgeoning communism. To be recognized as a legitimate ruling authority in this context was, then, no mean task. For the Christian Democrats it meant reasserting its traditional dominance at a time when the Communist party was edging into the arena of duly constituted authority. For the Communists, it meant making a qualitative leap from being generally regarded as suspect to being recognized as the legitimate constitutional representative of one-third of the population. As well, the Communists were adamant in their denials of any association with the putatively "Red" Brigades. The Socialists had no particular problem with legitimacy; rather their problem had to do with their lack of authority. In other words, they wanted to emerge from the Moro social drama as a political party that the Italian people and the other parties took *seriously*. The ultraleft quest for legitimacy deviated from the others in that generally the ultraleft groups sought recognition from only a portion of the Italian population—that of students and workers. However, their particular overriding need during the Moro social drama was to avoid criminalization—to avoid (which they were ultimately unsuccessful in doing) the terrorist or prototerrorist label themselves.

Thus, while for the Christian Democrats and the Socialists the emphasis was on the *authority* part of the "legitimate authority" formula, for the Communists and, much more, for the ultraleft, the emphasis was necessarily on the *legitimacy* aspect.

The satisfaction of all these needs constituted the not-so-hidden agenda of the root paradigm campaign of the Moro social drama. While the apparent preoccupation and consideration responsible for motivating the protagonists' negotiation/no-negotiation choices was the possibility of involuntarily recognizing the Red Brigades as legitimate enemies, it is the claim of this analysis that the deeper and central preoccupation of the protagonists was the fear of their *own* delegitimation and their concomitant loss or nonattainment of authority. In their anxiety, the protagonists forged hard-line decisions and never altered them throughout the Moro social drama.

For our purposes, the most significant feature of the protagonist's process of taking positions was the fact that no protagonist merely adopted a position without backing it up with considerable symbolic references. In other words, merely stating, for example, that negotiating with the Red Brigades would summarily legitimate them as political opponents was obviously considered to be insufficient justification for taking the decision not to negotiate. Rather, what was demanded in this Italian social drama was the further explication that by legitimating the terrorists the "legacy of the Resistance" or the "ideas and ideals of Democracy" and so on would be desecrated. Or, alternately, for those adopting the yes-negotiation stance, that refusing to negotiate would constitute abandoning that highest of values, the "Sanctity of Human Life." In this way, the root paradigms were portrayed as a series of first-movers, inspiring and guiding the choice of the actors. The references had to be lofty, the values deeply rooted in the Italian collective conscious. Much was at stake here, not the least of which was Moro's life. The protagonists, then, cashed in their resources, both the instrumental type Turner mentions—numerical following, organization, power—and the symbolic type of prestige and internal and external support. The symbolic resources derived their strength and effectiveness in turn from the pantheon of root paradigms at the disposal of the protagonists. The masterful deployment of them was a testament to the Italian sense of the dramatic, that not even the desperate and reasoned voice of Moro could vanquish. This sense of the dramatic was not, however, the same thing as good drama. The images of the world of ultimate values and symbolic touchstones were consistently polarized images. Either the State or the Sanctity of Human Life. Few were the attempts at reconciling or transcending claims, although a few of the appeals, such as that of the *Resistance*, did open up a space of ambiguity. While most were trapped in a melodramatic vision of what was at stake, only the ultraleft in its tortured neither/nor position and the Socialist party in its attempt to kill two birds with one stone (regain political leverage and be consistent with its libertarian philosophy) publicly sought paths to a "happy ending." The great majority of the other protagonists, including the Red Brigades, were trapped within a villain-victim rendition of the Moro social drama and subsequently, as we will see in the next chapter, redefined the "happy ending" as consisting in Moro's Great Sacrifice for Italy.

6 Reconciliation or Schism: Theory

> While Anglo-Saxon political culture values pragmatic solutions, informed by facts and experience, tentative and adjustive in style and validated by empirical testing, Italian political culture values rationalistic solutions, informed by ideas and abstraction, definitive and fixed in style and validated by logical consistency.
>
> GIUSEPPE DI PALMA[1]

> Was help at hand? Were there arguments in his favor that had been overlooked? Of course there must be. Logic is doubtless unshakable, but it cannot withstand a man who wants to go on living.
>
> FRANZ KAFKA[2]

Every social drama has its final act. And it is in this act that the final unmasking occurs. (The "truth" of this unmasking may, of course, never be universally accepted.) It is at this point that the drama's heroes and villains are most categorically recognized and, respectively, hailed or denounced. As well, most significantly for the society embroiled in the social drama, the final act declares the ultimate outcome of the initial breach as the society either joins itself back together or establishes the fact of an irreparable rift.

In this chapter, the Aldo Moro social drama's final act will be dramaturgically analyzed. The inspiration for this chapter's "plot" is Moro's personal campaign, conducted from within the "People's Prison," to obtain his own release. This campaign began on March 30 with the publication of Moro's first letter, received by newspapers the day before. It ended with Moro's own private funeral on May 10. It is particularly at this point, then, that this Italian social drama also can be read as Moro's personal drama. Forty-nine (known) letters emerged from the "People's Prison" with the signature of Aldo Moro. Nine Red Brigades communiques also were issued during the two-month-long affair. These documents acted as diacritical marks, dividing the period of Moro's imprisonment into Red Brigades determined chapters.

The next chapter will develop an analysis of the above-mentioned documents themselves. Of central concern are the variable ways in which these documents were "read." But before a direct approach to the documents can be taken, it is first necessary to address the twin issues of text attribution and text interpretation. Once a text leaves the hands of the author, nothing may be assumed regarding its form, content, style, or validity. As Paul Ricoeur, philosopher of the text (and of society as a text) has written: "But the text's career escapes the finite horizon of its author. What the text says now matters more than what the author meant to say, and every exegesis unfolds its procedures within the circumference of a meaning that has broken its moorings to the psychology of its author."[3] And, in fact, the several protagonists of the Moro social drama adopted separate, specific interpretative strategies for reading the "texts" appearing at intervals during the Moro affair. Thus this chapter will concern itself with the issue at the very heart of all interpretative activity, whether it be oriented toward a painting, a letter, a speech, or a gesture. That issue is the issue of identity, the attribution or nonattribution of authorship.

The Authority of Authorship

That attribution of authorship is always a matter of judgment reveals both the shifting nature of identity and the existential creativity of the interpreter's endeavor. In other words, interpreters participate in the processes of creating, shaping, sustaining, or denying identity. These activities lie at the center of the sociological discipline and compromise the "stuff" of the sociological concept of role. It runs through strict sociophilosophical discussions of individual identity, through discussions of mental health competency, and through discussions of identity transformation (rites of passage).[4] Some of the most keen sociological writing on identity transformation has, in fact, focused on the process of denying a certain positive identity to the social deviant. Kai Erikson describes the transition ceremonies accomplishing the downward and/or outward (out of the boundaries of the relevant society—a kind of literal or metaphorical exile) transition of the deviant: "They [the ceremonies] supply a formal stage on which the deviant and his community can confront one another [as in the criminal trial]: they make an announcement about the nature of his deviancy (a verdict or diagnosis, for example); and they place him in a particular role which is thought to neutralize the harmful effects of his misconduct (like the role of prisoner or patient) . . . It should not be surprising . . . that the people of the community are apt to greet the returning deviant with a considerable degree of apprehension and distrust, for in a very real sense they are not at all sure who he is."[5]

The relevance for the Moro social drama of such ceremonies as Erikson describes, and of the mistrust a community has of a returning deviant, will be explored in this chapter. We must confront the question: How did Aldo Moro, president of the Christian Democrat party, former prime minister of Italy, "become" a deviant? Part of the answer will be found in an exegesis of the many roles that Moro enacted, in absentia, during his sequestration. Some were roles that Moro chose to embody, some foisted upon him apparently against his will. It is also necessary to trace the processes by which authorship of Moro's own identity was gradually but systematically denied to him. Accordingly, the process of imposing alternative identities on Moro was carried out by several of the protagonists and was advanced by way of a series of ceremonial and ritual panegyrics and denunciations.[6]

Together, all of these activities comprised the fourth Turnerian phase of the social drama, that termed "Reconciliation or Schism." So, before analyzing the developments specific to the Moro social drama's final phase, we will first elaborate Turner's notion of "Reconciliation or Schism."

The Final Act
Of the social drama's final stage, Turner writes that it may consist of either of two movements—a rejoining together, or a permanent moving away or separation. In other words, a "social recognition of irreparable breach between the contesting parties, sometimes leading to their spatial separation"[7] or a social recognition of reconciliation. It is important to note the necessary presence of public ceremony or ritual in this phase. Such public actions symbolize the resolution of the social drama—regardless of the end result. Significantly, the Moro social drama represented an attempt to have it

both ways. The representatives of the newly installed government, the major political parties, the establishment mass media, and the Catholic church hierarchy enacted and attended public ceremonies of reconciliation. These ceremonies were to symbolize Italy's reunification, made possible by Moro's sacrifice.

In spite of this thrust, Moro's family and the "Moro"[8] of the letters proclaimed a profound and irreversible schism and enacted their own pointedly exclusive public rituals of separation. Here we discover that the focus of the social drama—the pivot of the action—has shifted from the original precipitate of the breach, described in an earlier chapter as consisting essentially of a rift between the older, established generations of the political class and the unabsorbable political youth, to a whole new breach, that opening up between Moro and his own cohort. As this chapter proceeds, it will become clear why the rift between Moro and his own colleagues constituted a second breach in the Moro social drama, one that split along a different axis from that of the first breach. Here it is important to note that one interesting and surprising effect of this shift in focus was the severe diminution of the Red Brigades' role in the social drama. While the police continued to search for Moro's abductors and the various media organs continued to publish and publicize the Red Brigades communiques, the central stage of the drama was given over to the dialogue between the Moro of the letters and the state-supporting protagonists. And, it was primarily by way of this dialogue that the dialectic of the drama progressed.

In retrospectively analyzing a social drama into its component parts, those actions or events which moved the drama along are easily discerned. Here, however, we are also interested in imagining alternative actions that, had they occurred, could have cleared the way for the drama's (earlier or alternative) completion but were, instead, suppressed. In the case of the Moro social drama, the most obvious nonoccurrence was the locating and releasing of, or the negotiating for and having released Aldo Moro. The social drama's ending would have been very different if either of these modes of redemption were employed. It is the claim of this study, however, that, for reasons which will now be explored, such a scenario was unlikely at best and most probably impossible. That Moro, in his letters, specifically lobbied for release via negotiation meant that he would end up going against the dominant plot of the drama. Before we can discuss the ways in which his dissonant voice was dealt with, we should first analyze the several imperatives, coming from diverse ontological realms, that pushed the drama in the direction it ultimately followed.

A Case of Structural Convergence

Lucrezia Escudero, an Italian linguist, has commented on the multiple readings to which the Moro affair lends itself. She has claimed that it may be read as a political crisis, as an issue of law and order, as a familial tragedy, and as a linguistic event. To these readings, I would add that the Moro affair may be regarded as an event structured in accordance to both anthropological and aesthetic concerns. This study asserts that there is a high degree of structural congruence among the many levels of a social drama. If this is true, the contours of these synchronized layers of the social drama could, then, be explored in terms of the way they propel the drama in one direction rather than in another.

With the above in mind, we may now ask the question: Why was Moro's discovery and release a most unlikely occurrence? The most obvious reason for the continued sequestration of Moro was the (broadly acknowledged) inefficiency and unpreparedness of the Italian police.[9] Despite the thousands of polizia, carabinieri, and military personnel performing house-to-house and car-to-car searches, neither Moro nor his abductors were found. What results that were obtained, the discovery of some Red Brigades arms and documents, were scanty at best and, as we have seen, even these were the result of serendipity.

Of even more significance for this analysis, though, was the public's singular lack of surprise at this scantiness of results. The Italian public generally expected the military operation to fail. As a check on this, it is useful to note the immense pride and genuine surprise evinced by General Dozier's release recently by an Italian antiterrorist team. Still, even when the traditional low level of military and police organization and efficiency are controlled for, we must acknowledge that these forces had fifty-five days to uncover Moro's whereabouts, a long time for such minor success.[10]

This incongruity suggests that there may have been other possible reasons why Moro was not discovered and released. Before investigating these reasons, it is important to reiterate that a case is being made here for the ultimate ending of the Moro social drama having been determined by a general convergence of motives and forces (as opposed to there being only one cause)—all levels of causes and a variety of motives together pushing the drama in one direction rather than in another.

Keeping the above in mind, we are now in a position to indicate the *political* reasons for Moro's continued sequestration. The approach to the political sphere here must be somewhat speculative. As mentioned in the discussion of the negotiation question (cf Chapter 4), it is still mere speculation to develop a theory of there having been an explicit conspiracy against Moro, assuring his not being returned alive. However, a reasonable case can be made for the political expediency of having Moro "out of the picture."[11] It will be useful, at this point, to detail those aspects of Aldo Moro's personality, history, and relationship to his political colleagues that may have diminished those colleagues' collective animus to find him and/or have him returned.

Moro's Career

The basic outlines of Moro's political career have been drawn in the opening chapter of this study. Moro had been a consistent figure on the Italian political map since 1948 when, at the age of thirty, he entered the newly constituted Italian Parliament. Actively identifying himself during the entire period of his political life as a Christian Democrat,[12] Moro was thought of, in the words of Sciascia, as the "least implicated of them all." In 1978, the year of the Lockheed affair, the Christian Democrat party was ridden with scandals and had been consistently so throughout its history. Moro had often found himself in the onerous position of having to defend a fellow party member who had been accused of some misconduct. In fact, in the week prior to Moro's abduction, he had made a speech in Parliament defending the Honorable Gui, a fellow Christian Democrat, who had been accused of involvement in the Lockheed scandal. Moro's own divagations vis-à-vis the Lockheed affair were, at that point, in early 1978, highly speculative and soon repudiated. Because of his relative lack of involvement in scandals, because of his consistent leadership and steering role, and because he alone was given credit for perennially reconciling the warring

Christian Democrat factions, Moro was recognized to be the "most eminent statesman of the Christian Democrats after or together with De Gasperi."[13]

But while he held himself above the general rabble of the politically corrupt, Moro did not hesitate to defend those of his party who did not so restrain themselves. This double standard of Moro's has been explained by one biographer, Aniello Coppolla, as a tendency of Moro's to identify himself with the entire Christian Democrat party: "He tends to present himself as the representative of the entire Christian Democrat universe, including that part which claims and receives penal and political impunity for its dirty dealings."[14]

It was in this sense, then, that Moro was a paradoxical political figure, attempting to reconcile the purity of his vision of the party with the impurity of the reality of the party. In fact, Moro consciously held himself aloof from the material reality of his party, and, extrapolating now from the theoretical animus of this study, this aloofness may have itself contributed to his ultimate expulsion. I am building a case here for the existence, within the Christian Democrat party, of a fair measure of "ressentiment" toward Moro. His bias in the direction of the harmonizing intellect and his disinterestedness regarding the material reality of the stratification of interests in the DC (Christian Democrats) frustrated his colleagues and alienated him from them. Coppolla describes Moro's particular political vision as follows: "His evolutive vision, and his preference for the logic and techniques of the Enlightenment—this is the other face of his contempt for the empirical controllers of the levers of command. As well, his minimal concern for the material existence of the stratification of interests, his lack of comprehension of the motives behind the aggregations of the social forces, derive from Moro's profound conviction that politics, above all, is the *projection of a system of ideas*. For Moro, to lead is to persuade; to command signifies to affirm the superiority of the intellect."[15]

Thus, just as we have seen how the DC identified itself with the whole of Italy, so Moro identified himself as embodying and representing the whole of the Christian Democrat party. In this regard, Moro, as part of his letter-writing campaign to inspire negotiations, wrote on April 21 to Zaccagnini, friend and DC secretary: "I am thinking of the many, many Christian Democrats who, for years, have been accustomed to identify the party with me . . . would not be able to accept this tragedy."[16]

Moro Public and Moro Private

This firm belief of Moro's that he *was* Christian Democracy was often expressed by way of a typically Italian idiom—that of the filial relationship. As previously noted, in the earlier analysis of Prime Minister Andreotti's postkidnapping speech on Italian national television, the use of the word "family" as signifying both the biological entity and the figurative entity (family as a metaphor for the party, the nation) was frequent and not surprising. Moro himself was a particularly practiced employer of this hybrid term and quite sincerely viewed himself as the father of the DC. In this light, we can better understand Moro's drive to keep party/family unified regardless of the very real internal divergencies. Coppolla concludes: "There is one constant in the thought and practice of Moro: the Christian Democrat unity. To this filial relationship with the DC, Moro sacrificed even his great love—the 'centro sinistra' (center-left coalition organized by Moro in the sixties)."[17]

As a basic social unit in all societies, family is indeed both a universal experience and a concept with which, as Levi-Strauss has claimed for totems, it is "good to think." In Victor Turner's dramaturgic analysis of the Becket-Henry II conflict, Turner quotes Robertson's report that Becket, in his reply to the other bishop's attempts to persuade him to resign and ask for Henry's mercy, proclaimed: "The sons of my own mother [the church] have fought against me."[18]

The use of the familial idiom indicates the attempt of the speaker to claim familial ties and thus the obligations that go along with them. This attempt can be either successful or unsuccessful, and this in two distinct ways. First, the claim can be either upheld or denied. Second, the obligations of an upheld claim can be, according to the institutional prerogatives of the family in a given society, profound or minimal. Terence Turner, in his analysis of the Oedipus myth, the archetypal drama about the relationship between familial relations and social relations, situated the emergence of the Oedipus myth in a historical period in Greece which was "a time of social change and instability in which the old normative social and cosmic order of the polis, based on a class-stratified descent structure, was being undermined by more universalistic (non-kin based) forms of organization. The struggle between kinship based and non-kin based modes of social organization, and the resulting instability of patrilineal succession and continuity, was a central theme of the class struggle that marked the historical development of the polis. This struggle is also, as [this] analysis has shown, the central theme of the dialectical structure of the Oedipus tale."[19]

Turner is making a case for a general diminution of the institutional prerogatives of kin-based modes of social organization in the Greece of the Oedipus myth. Perhaps one might make a similar claim for the Italy of the Moro social drama. Moro quite explicitly focused his pro-negotiation campaign on the needs of this "family" (placed between quotation marks here because of its twofold nature). In almost every letter, he made this reference. In his April 5 letter to Zaccagnini, he wrote: "If I did not have a family that needed me so much, it would be a little different."[20] Later, in the April 21 letter, he stated: "And, in fact, along with the problems of the country, there are those concerning me and my family."[21] Finally, on May 4, five days before his assassination, a letter from Moro was received by the president of Italy, Giovanni Leone, in which Moro asked to be "returned to my family which has grave and urgent need of me."[22]

The apparent reference, in these excerpts, is to Moro's biological family, but Leonardo Sciascia gave it a different reading, one which tallies more with the accepted biographical view of Moro: "The State which worried him, the State which occupied his thoughts in an obsessional way, I believe he signified in the word 'family.'"[23] Indeed, this may well have been Moro's intention—to refer to the Italian state as his "family" and to remind the leaders of this "family" of its overwhelming need of him.

These two ways of reading the word "family" indicate the analytic distinction between *public* (family as the party, the state, etc.) and *private* (family as biological kin group). As previously noted, this was a most salient distinction in the Moro social drama. Moro was alternately granted and denied public, collective status. When so granted, he was either praised or criticized in terms of his performance as a public figure: when so denied, his actions (such as they were, entirely epistolary) were judged as one would judge any private individual who had been kidnapped. Here we shall foreshadow a bit the discussion (further developed later in this chapter) of the structural imperatives of all dramatic narratives in order to quote Terence Turner on the public/private distinction: ". . . the synthetic aspect of narrative form is a cultural model for the process of interaction between another pair of antithetical elements: the individual and the collective order."[24] Turner is indicating that the public/private distinction is basic to social life and is thus reflected, on the level of culture, in narratives (such as the Oedipus myth, e.g.) that present this distinction as conflictual.

As far as Moro was concerned, the various protagonists of the Moro social drama drew on and worked with this distinction often to justify their positions on the negotiation issue. An April 3 *L'Unità* article referred to the Communist party attitude of firmness against negotiations but allowed that "private initiatives and responses that aim at saving the life of the 'sequestrato' (sequestered one) should not be excluded."[25] Moro, here not even referred to by name/or title but merely called the (anonymous) 'sequestrato,' has sunk, rather ignominiously, into the private sphere. Even in the statements issued by members of his own party, Moro's public personality has been all but expunged. Moro's close political colleague Zaccagnini exemplified this strategy in an April 23 statement to the press: "I want to sincerely thank all of you journalists for the active participation with which you have followed these, our hours of anguish, over the life of our friend Moro."[26] From incumbent president of the DC party and several-time prime minister, Moro has become simply a "friend." The Christian Democrats, severe no-negotiators, could not allow Moro to be thought of as meriting special, public privileges.

Such a retreat from public to private, however, could slice both ways. While fellow political leaders used this strategy of privatization as part of what we shall see was a general process of degradation, many of the workers interviewed at the Fiat Mirafiori plant (located in Torino) during Moro's sequestration gave a more sympathetic reading to Moro the private citizen than to Moro the public figure. Many were unwilling to simply abandon Moro the human being and, significantly, familial head to a decidedly fatal end: "Politics is one thing, but even if he has made mistakes, he is still a man. If he could be saved, it would be better,"[27] indicated one of those interviewed at the factory gates.

Congruent then with their decision to approach Moro as a private citizen, Moro's colleagues chose to read Moro's references to "family" as indicating his biological dependents—not his political dependents. And thus they denied any filial obligations on their parts. As well, given this singular indifference to Moro's familial claims on the parts of his political associates, we may hypothesize that kin-based modes of social organization, modes with which Italy has always been strongly identified, have been undergoing a weakening of their institutional prerogatives in that country. In fact, the DC-sympathizing journalist, Gustavo Selva, in a statement written after Moro's body was discovered, implied precisely that: "Reason and also sentiment must comfort us, giving assurance that the State, the DC and the government did everything possible to restore Moro to his family."[28] The comfort Selva felt may strike us as rather inappropriate and unmerited. The reference to Moro's family is almost off-hand. It is as if Selva were saying, "We tried our best, but after all many families lose relatives to terrorists." Perhaps most significantly, Selva involuntarily offers up a theme *not* developed; the restoration of Moro to the state, to the DC, to the government. In neglecting to develop such a theme, Selva implicitly asserts that, as far as these institutions were concerned, Moro was expendable. Indeed, this expendability issue is the key. Moro's entire letter-writing campaign carried the burden of proving that Moro was not expendable, that his party needed him, that the fledgling government needed him, that Italy needed him. This was why Sciascia read Moro's references to "family" as, in fact, references to these collective institutions—the bond, according to Moro, was just that organic. However, such an assumption on Moro's part must strike anyone familiar with DC politics as either willfully naive or simply desperate. This because Moro had already been indicated as expendable once before by his party. A precedent had already been set for Moro serving as party scapegoat, and it is to this episode that we will now turn.

A Precedent for Expulsion

In the national elections of May 1968, Moro's center-left coalition suffered a clear defeat, and the Communist party saw a significant gain. Moro soon after experienced a marked emargination within his own party. He was no longer a ubiquitous public presence, he was removed from his position as president of the "Consiglio nazionale" (the main leadership organization of the party), and his previously prolific writings in *Il Popolo* all but disappeared. In short, Moro had almost entirely vanished from the leadership. However "at the end of the year [1968] he suddenly returned on the scene in order to announce his polemical reflections to the directorship that had had the illusion of being able to exorcise their failure with the sacrifice of this scape-goat. The occasion for this speech was provided to Moro by the convening of the National Council of the party . . . Excluded from the levers of command he [was] ostentatious enough to express his confidence, in contradistinction from the others, in the force of his own political discourse."[29]

In 1968, Moro made a successful comeback. In 1978, he would not be so successful. And, we are now in a position to clearly identify the structural weakness of Aldo Moro, the political figure, to understand why he was such ripe material for sacrifice.

Since the fall of the center-right coalition in the early sixties, Moro had consistently looked left. He had "recognized" first the Socialists and then the Communists as being fellow human beings with autonomous political organizations approaching, but in an asymptotic fashion, a state of legitimacy. They were still enemies, but he recognized them enough to talk to them. In fact, the inauguration of a dialogue was, for Moro, the highest interparty political goal: "I have served in the positions entrusted to me with a great sense of liberality, both internally [the party] (refusing every form of personal power) and externally where the open acknowledgement of my political creed has never prevented me from being profoundly respectful of the positions of others and from fighting for a democratic debate, without either compromises or hidden interests, but truly civil and clear."[30]

But even "talking" to the left was considered heresy by some in the DC leadership, and they were willing to grant Moro his license to talk with the left only as long as the left reaped no political benefits from such dialogues. The moment such benefits were accrued, Moro was "revealed" as responsible and would be, subsequently, politically exiled. We may now understand the inauguration of the Andreotti-led government, *with the Communists in the majority* as another moment of the left reaping rewards from a Moro-conceived plan.

Another aspect of Moro's political personality that made his colleagues ambivalent about him was manifest in his constant pronouncements against what we might call "politics as usual" or "power for power's sake." In other words, Moro had understood his political role to be that of statesman, and while his fellow Christian Democrats could point proudly to Moro's statesman-like prestige they could also suffer from his pride. In this regard, Alessandro Silj has located a particularly revealing editorial statement in the March 19, 1978, edition of *La Repubblica*. Here we find that Moro's very prestige has become his political and personal liability. Reflecting the public/private distinction, *La Repubblica* claimed that "Moro, then, in exchange for his physical salvation [the result, here, of hypothetical negotiations], would be underwriting . . . his own political suicide. And it is precisely this that revolts us. We cannot allow ourselves to accept this or to believe it possible."[31] The strategy of the mass media and of Moro's political colleagues for confronting this alleged political self-destruction of Moro's was, as will be shown later in this chapter, to echo the author/narrator of a Unamuno novel *(Niebla)* who does away with a suicidal character, to "kill" Moro politically *before* he committed political suicide.

Thus while it remains, for the present, in the realm of speculation, the hypothesis being presented here—that it made "political" sense that Moro *not* be located and released—does not contradict either the history of Moro's relationship to his party nor the logic of the political scapegoat role.[32]

The Need for Purification

The introduction of this concept of the scapegoat role directs us to an examination of the *anthropologically* coherent (coherent, i.e., with the structure of the other layers of meaning of this event) structure of the Moro social drama.[33] We have already seen how this, the last phase of a social drama, Reconciliation or Schism, depends on the presence of public ceremonies and rituals to determine the direction in which the drama will end. The focus is inevitably on the *community* as a whole, and the general anthropological analysis of broad-based social crises declares that the society in question has been contaminated either by internal sources or external sources. Thus the public rituals that will be relevant to the last phase of social dramas are rituals of purification, in other words, of sacrifice. Some object or some person must gather into him/herself all of the dangerous and divisive impurities that have infected the social system and, in curative fashion, remove them. Only if this happens can the social order be purified and made "whole" (wholeness here indicating health) again.

Anthropologists have paid particular attention to the sacrificial theme since the days of Tylor. Tylor believed sacrifice to be a gift offered to supernatural beings to propitiate them or to gain some favor from them. The analysis of the role of sacrifice has shifted over time, but the etymology of the word "sacrifice" (Latin sacrificium; sacer—holy and facere—to make) indicates a basic, universal character. The sacrificial object is transported from the realm of the profane to the realm of the sacred, all this in the service of the collective being performing the sacrifice.

Translating rituals that anthropologists have identified in primitive and archaic societies into a modern idiom is an enterprise involving some risk. The dramaturgic perspective being taken here claims that it is possible to locate the "sacrificial principle" in modern societies but that this principle is no longer found only under the aegis of obviously religious institutions. As Kenneth Burke has written: "Dramatism, as so conceived, asks not how the sacrificial motives revealed in the institutions of magic and religion might be eliminated in a scientific culture, but what new forms they take."[34] Thus at the heart of the dramaturgic approach is this search for the sacrificial principle in modern societies.

As regards the Moro social drama, we can hypothesize that some form of sacrifice was not only desired but pivotal. As we shall see, many of the protagonists, including the Communists, the Christian Democrats, the establishment mass media, and the Catholic church hierarchy, would have preferred an eventual *self*-sacrifice on the part of Aldo Moro. In this version, Moro would have recognized his symbolic destiny and willingly have donned the martyr's mantle. Unfortunately, Moro would not encourage his sacrificers, and his refusal of the role of martyr will be explored in detail below. This refusal introduced an entirely new element into this social drama, causing the original narrative flow to detour and find new paths. It is important to note that, in refusing to proceed with his own self-sacrifice, Moro placed the sacrificing action squarely in the hands of his community. Joseph Gusfield has suggested that, in fact, this act of purification based on sacrifice is one of the creative principles of social order: "Following Kenneth Burke's provocative analysis, I look for a sacrificial principle as a dramatic theme in creating social order. That is, when an image of social order is conveyed, its opposite—disorder—is also portrayed. The drama consists in seeing some players as victims, others as villains. Order is obtained through sacrifice so unity is derived."[35]

During the course of the Moro social drama, several Italian journalists proposed the sacrificial role as an appropriate role for Moro to adopt. Selva wrote that "they [the Red Brigades] have the brute force to break Moro's life, but they are up against a free citizenry that in this hour, as in the great moments of history, elects Moro as its symbol: there is no more division, no more reservation around that which Moro represents today."[36] The social efficacy of Moro's potential sacrifice is stressed over any consideration of the tragedy of Moro's death. Selva admits that Moro may die, but that possibility is not presented as a salient issue in itself. We may wonder at this nonchalance, but it does make good anthropological sense. Someone had to absorb the contamination and purify the Italian nation. Aldo Moro was the anthropologically logical choice.

We are now in a position to approach the question of how Moro's refusal of the sacrificial victim's role affected his structural location in the Italian moral universe.

Anthropologists have identified several types of sacrifice, including two particularly important ones: the communal sacrifice, and the expiatory sacrifice. In the communal sacrifice, communion is achieved among the community of devotees themselves. The expiatory sacrifice involves the casting out of the (contaminated) sacrificial victim for the purpose of removing whatever impurity is extant in the society at large. However, in Hubert and Mauss's critique of Robertson Smith's attempt to categorically distinguish between these two types of sacrifice, they state that "for Smith, it is in these communion rites themselves that the purifying force of these kinds of sacrifices resides; the idea of expiation is thus engulfed in the idea of communion. Undoubtedly he discovers in some extreme or simplified forms something that he does not venture to link with communion, a kind of exorcism, the driving out of an evil spirit . . . One of the aims of this work is to demonstrate that the expulsion of a sacred spirit, whether pure of impure, is a primordial component of sacrifice."[37]

There is an obvious paradox here, and Jane Harrison, in her study *Ancient Art and Ritual,* addressed this paradox when she described the springtime sacrifice of the bull: "The bull is sacrificed and why? Why must a thing so holy die? Why not live out the term of his life? He dies because he is so holy, that he may give his holiness, his strength, his life, just at the moment it is holiest, to his people.''[38] The relevance of this paradox to social dramas in general is that for a sacrificial object or person to be effective in purifying the society in crisis and in bringing about a general reconciliation, that object or person must be powerfully "holy." In terms of the particular social drama under investigation here, this means that some object or some person has to be sacrificed in order that Italy might reestablish social and political harmony. Moro, because of both his eminent persona and his (albeit involuntary) status as "innocent" victim,[39] was in a position to be sacrificed or "made holy."

Moro's Moral Passage

In our discussion of the anthropological principle of sacrifice, two relevant axes of ontological differentiation have emerged. They are the axis of *sacredness,* indicating relative degrees of participation in the sacred, and the axis of *purity,* indicating relative degrees of cleanliness. The axes are framed here as continua rather than as two sets of dichotomies: sacred/profane, and purity/contamination. This framing emphasizes the shifting nature of the respective domains and indicates the existence of marginal and mixed areas. Such an approach follows Mary Douglas's discussion of such states in her book *Purity and Danger,* in which she stresses the "energy in the margins and the unstructured areas."[40] It is, then, useful to calibrate Aldo Moro's several moral locations along these two axes of variation, before, during, and after his abduction. That he fell outside the boundaries of the structured areas determined by the poles of these axes of variation has already been established. But, by identifying and analyzing the specific route taken by his "moral person," we may locate the key to the modern translation of the sacrificial idiom.

On March 16, 1978, Aldo Moro was on his way to Parliament to ratify the new government that he had so painstakingly constructed. In the eyes of his political colleagues and the establishment mass media, he embodied reasoned statesmanship and prestigious, untainted leadership. Still, he was clearly a "politician" with a particularistic (i.e., Christian Democrat) orientation and loyalty.

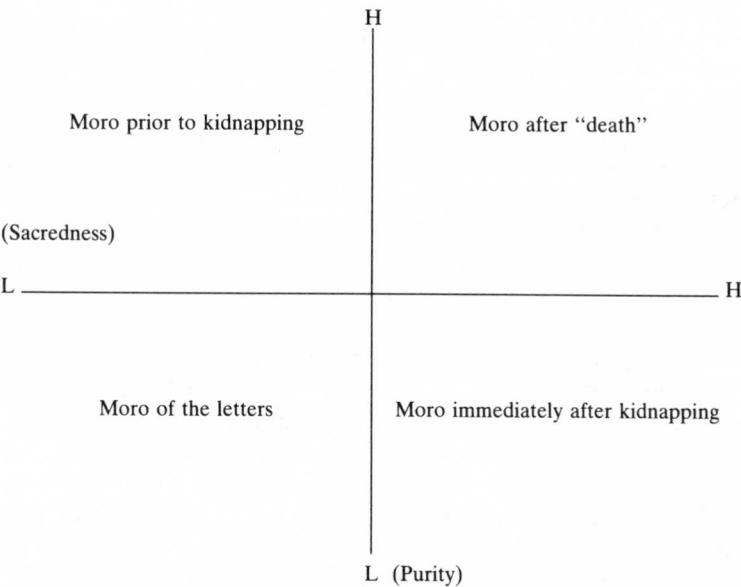

Given such an orientation, "Moro prior to kidnapping" can be regarded as high on the Purity dimension and low on the Sacredness dimension.[41]

In the immediate aftermath of Moro's kidnapping, Moro was the subject of both exaltation as the symbol of democratic Italy (described in the chapter dealing with the redressive phase of the social drama) and very tentative critical speculation. The exaltation took the form of panegyrics both in the press and in the sermons of the Catholic church clerics. In fact, in such "eulogies" (for that is the impression one has in reading them—despite the fact that Moro was not yet dead) Moro's religious faith and religious connections are highlighted. In *Il Giorno* on March 17: "It is atrocious to imagine the clash between the physical force of the terrorists and the pure, spiritual force of Moro."[42] In a similar vein, Selva wrote the following Easter (March 26) message: "Aldo Moro will know how to make the significance of the Resurrection, symbol of peace and real liberation, live again with his religious faith [even] in this terrible condition."[43] And finally, in a rather bizarre quotation of Francesco Grisi's (president in 1978 of the DC-linked Free Writers Union) published in *Il Popolo* on March 21, Moro's spiritual purity and transcendent quality is already being proclaimed as the reason that he is a fit subject for sacrifice: "Our choice is that the State cannot negotiate with the Red Brigades [this comes nine days before Moro's first letter arrives in which the subject of negotiation is brought up for the first time]. The painful eventual death of Moro, killed by the Red Brigades, signifies the everlasting quality of his testimony in the golden dawn of liberty. Often, immolation precedes the resurrection of truth . . . Maybe for Moro there is, yes, the problem of the PCI but it is the problem, above all of the communion of the saints. The discourse is metaphysical, theological, even if it is apparently political and constitutional . . . It seems strange that the man most engaged in our Italian history in reality is the man most 'disengaged' " (*Il Popolo,* March 21, 1978, p. 5). Thus, as Moro is already operating in some metaphysical sphere, there is really no need to try and drag him back into the mundane world of Italian politics. Clearly this was an extreme rendition of the "Moro spirituality" school of thought. But in its extremeness it goes to the heart of many of the protagonists' (DC, PCI, Catholic Church, Mass Media) expectations for Moro. He will be sacrificed. (This much was not questioned by these protagonists despite the fact that the front pages of so many newspapers were awash with photos of the security forces tracking Moro down.) He will be resurrected (as a martyr), and along with him will be resurrected the Italian state. And finally, the "Problem of the Communists" will be remanded to the sphere of discourse, not political discourse, but the communion of the saints.

On the other hand, the critical speculation emanated from a consideration of the possible effects of Moro's close proximity to the terrorists on Moro's physical, psychological, and, most important of all, moral person. A *Corriere della Sera* article on March 30, approximately two weeks after the kidnapping, expressed this opinion. The article has a premonitory admonishment in it: ". . . the total physical dependence of the hostage on his kidnappers often brings him to a state of total psychological introjection. In other words, he finds himself in the same situation as that of a baby who needs help and who, given this, identifies with his parents. Like a baby, the hostage finishes by identifying himself with his kidnappers."[44] The infantalization of the hostage, as "noted" by a set of concerned observers, suggests the idea of *contamination.* The hostage's close proximity to the kidnappers and his dependence on them is interpreted as being dangerous to the hostage in several, not merely physical ways. Lietta Tornabuoni of the *Corriere della Sera* wrote, on March 24, of Moro's fastidious nature and of the way in which his proximal relationship to the kidnappers would be suffered by him as a kind of suffocating dust. Moro "may suffer from the lack of physical privacy . . . he does not like physical contact, hugs or walking arm in arm. It upsets him to be touched . . . He starts with fright if someone gets dirt on his sleeves." Further, discussing his quotidian habit of reading many newspapers, she states that "the reading of newspapers is a sort of daily drug for him."[45] Here we have even the introduction of the theme of "Moro drugged." This reference is metaphorical, but a few days earlier another *Corriere della Sera* article noted Moro's knowledge of military secrets and immediately segued into a discussion of what the Red Brigades could do to Moro with drugs (March 19, 1978, p. 4). Thus it is not surprising that it is at this point that rumors of Moro's delicate and poor health begin to circulate. This is a form of internal contamination, one that would make Moro little able to resist the questions and demands of the terrorists. Such was the loudness and persistence of these rumors that Moro's family finally had to indicate, through Moro's secretary, Nicola Rana, that there was no basis to them. *Il Popolo,* on March 21, published an article titled "The News about Moro's Health is Without Foundation," which contained Rana's statement: "The family of the Honorable Aldo Moro, that up to today held it opportune to abstain from giving any information on the condition of the health of its loved one, must now respond, given the ceaseless propagation of the unfounded news. Thus, the family wishes to make clear that Moro has not had an operation, that he thus has no need of therapy that would be subsequent to such an operation and that the condition of his health, at the moment of the kidnapping, was satisfactory. He needed no medicine. In any case, the Honorable Moro would be utterly capable of indicating anything that he might need" (p. 2). Contrary to popular opinion, then, Moro was both healthy and an adult, competent to ask for specific medicines.

Finally, Marletti, in his essay in the book *Dimensioni del Terrorismo Politico (Dimensions of Political Terrorism)* has referred to the phenomenon of the contagiousness of evil and has added another dimension to this discussion, that being the imputation of guilt, by way of association, of the hostage: "The horror that the victim inspires must also make us ponder. We are led to think that that which has befallen him must have some explanation. The victim must be guilty of something. It begins thus—at the very same base as that of the horror—a process of removal, of distancing that leads to a kind of ambiguous [imputation] of complicity . . . thus . . . if they [the terrorists] have done all of this to the victim, it must mean he deserved it."[46]

Thus, "Moro immediately after the kidnapping" was viewed by the above-designated protagonists as being high on the Sacredness dimension but fairly low on the Purity dimension. He is on his way to becoming unpure. Here it is important to recall the "ressentiment" of his colleagues as well as his prior experience as party scapegoat. However, as the immediately relevant level of analysis concerns the anthropological interpretation of sacrifice, we must highlight that which seems to be a case of a designated sacrificial victim beginning (albeit involuntarily) to absorb the extant contaminating evil into himself in preparation for the sacrifice.

As the victim of the incipient sacrifice had, up until March 30, no voice of his own, the process of creating a sacrificial being was developing smoothly. However, the Red Brigades, having already issued two communiques, had imparted the news that Moro was going to be tried by a "Tribunal of the People." Thus, while Moro had not yet said anything himself, the idea that he could conceivably "talk" in this trial began to take hold. And his colleagues therefore became alerted to the possibility that resistance to accepting the sacrificial role, on the part of the hostage, could occur.

According to the Spanish priests observing the Aztec rituals of human sacrifice, the sacrificial victim, called Tetzcatlipoca after the diety, would, after having spent a year literally being the god, calmly accept his own demise. Moro was not quite so willing. His repeated proposals of negotiations in his letters constituted his resistance to his designated anthropologically logical role. And it is at this point that we can begin to unravel the dynamic of the modern translation of the sacrificial idiom. We have already seen how the issue of contamination figures in sacrificial rites and, more specifically, had begun to play a part in the Moro social drama. What happened as a result of Moro's nonacceptance of his role was that two Moros were proposed in the place of the original—a Bad Moro and a Good Moro. And the process by which this bifurcation was made possible consisted of a degradation of the "Moro of the

Letters" and an elevation of the (putative) Moro of the uncontaminated soul. This latter Moro, as evidenced in the Grisi quote, was relegated to the world of pure spirit. In other words, for this elevation to take place Moro had to be assumed dead. Only in this way could he be hailed as a martyr.

With the above in mind, it is now possible to locate "Moro of the Letters" as being low in both Purity and Sacredness. And the key to this moment of his moral passage was his degradation. This was accomplished by way of the above-mentioned imputation of contamination. By advancing the propositions that Moro had been drugged, tortured, or, at the very least, humiliated and thus transformed, the no-negotiation protagonists could discount and discredit his letters. Full analysis of the salient features of these letters and the precise way in which they were "handled" will be developed in the next chapter. Here we can begin to explore the responses to them in terms of the profane-contaminated category into which these responses thrust the "Moro of the Letters."

On April 14, after a series of letters signed "Aldo Moro" had emerged from the "People's Prison" requesting some form of prisoner exchange, or, at the least, negotiation, Piazzesi of the *Corriere della Sera* wrote about Moro's changed moral status. Speaking about the possibility of Moro's release: ". . . in no case, however will he [Moro] still be the Christian Democrat leader of great authority and prestige, nor even a secure reference point for all the other parties, including the Communists . . . saying this, we do not intend to advance any simple judgment on the way in which the president of the DC is surmounting the trial he is undergoing. We are limiting ourselves to acknowledging, with a realism equal only to the bitterness, that certain wounds inflicted by kidnappers and guards can never be completely removed."[47] This passage is a rich one. Piazzesi is saying, first, that Moro is no longer to be considered a collective figure, for his party or for anyone else. His authority and prestige have been removed. Even if he were to return alive, he would be a mere private citizen. As well, Piazzesi puts forth the idea, delineated above, that proximity to terrorists inevitably causes contamination.

Many of the statements issued by political colleagues and journalists indicated that Moro had been or was about to be stripped of his collective post. Often this was performed by way of comparing his captivity to the real or possible captivity of other "citizens."

When Moro asks to be exchanged for other, state-held, prisoners, Selva writes: "That which Moro invokes involves really stretching a point. It is a wrench having a precise weight; the liberation of a certain number of prisoners who are in prison for committing some of the most horrendous acts of terrorism in our country. It is a liberation or an exile that would eradicate any force we have in the struggle against terrorism . . . that would place other victims of kidnapping in a condition of inferiority, because the same price had not been paid for them. And, after this [price paid for Moro] it would be necessary to do the same for everybody."[48] Selva believes that Moro ought not be treated as if he were, in any way, special and should not have his requests for special privileges entertained. However, he goes on to write: "It is understandable and absolutely necessary that Moro and his family humanely struggle against death, a death that would be an assassination."[49] The public/private distinction is succinctly stated here. Moro is not to be considered a public figure any longer. He no longer qualifies for the perquisites of office. He is merely a (certainly unfortunate) private citizen. As such, it is more than comprehensible that he and his family should seek his release. But the approaches appropriate to this end should be limited to those the state would follow in any attempt to have any private citizen released. Recall here, as well, *L'Unità's* reference to Moro as the "sequestrato."

Once Moro had suffered the first type of identity degradation, that being the demotion from collective figure to private citizen, he was prepared for the second type of degradation; the discrediting of Moro as a full-fledged participant in civil society. We should expect either or both of two relevant rituals to occur in this case: (1) the public denial of the person's ability (for whatever reason) to competently carry out the responsibilities of his or her institutional role(s), (2) the public declaration of the person's "civil death." This latter is, of course, simply a more extreme version of the former. In fact, the two can be distinguished in terms of the possibility of reversal built into the logic of the former and the lack of this possibility built into the logic of the latter. The first variant carried within it the concept of *career* and the individual's ability to alternately don and remove its mantle at will. Of this broadened concept of career, Goffman has written: "One side is linked to internal matters held dearly and closely, such as images of self and felt identity; the other side concerns official position, jural relations and style of life, and is part of a publicly accessible institutional complex. The concept of career then allows one to move back and forth between the personal and the public."[50] As has been shown, it was this very fluidity, this freedom of movement between these two spheres that Moro was being denied.

Various strategies exist for denying career competency. These strategies, already noted, include infantalization, mortification, and involuntary imposition of the sick role (signifying either physical or mental health). In the discussion of the various protagonists' responses to Moro's letter that will follow in the next chapter, we shall see the ways in which all of these strategies were indeed used. Here, the contours of the strategies will be systematically presented.

Silj, in his discussion of the "removal" of Aldo Moro and the Red Brigades as problems worthy of serious consideration, by the establishment mass media, noted the process of infantilization: "It is thus that the Red Brigades become 'beasts' (*L'Unità*, March 26, 1978) and Aldo Moro a 'baby' (*Corriere della Sera*). Animals and babies, it is known, don't in fact engage in politics. Rather they are capable of inspiring horror or pity."[51] Victor Turner, speaking of the process of ritual initiation into adulthood of tribal adolescents, gives theoretical grounding to Silj's insight: "The hard saying 'except ye become as a little child' assumes new meaning. Unless the fixing and ordering processes of the adult, the socio-structural domain, are liminally abandoned and the initiand submits to being broken down to a generalized prima materia, a lump of human clay, he cannot be transformed or reshaped to encounter new experiences."[52] Moro, then, was losing his "adult" status. And by way of this loss, two separate but interconnected things were happening to him. First, he was being denied his rights to participate in political decisions, such as those regarding his own life. Second, he was being prepared for some kind of transformation. This transformation would have more to do with the quality of innocence, associated with babies, than with the other infantile quality, already mentioned, of incompetence. (This transformation involved the above-noted splitting of Moro into two beings and will be described below.) The contention that Moro was acting and speaking "foolishly" eliminated him as a person competent to judge the ramifications of his or any other protagonists' actions. The accusations that Moro had been drugged, brainwashed, and/or beaten, accusations that, during the period of the letter writing were totally speculative and vanquished after the autopsy, in essence reduced Moro to a kind of foolishness. It would be claimed that he no longer knew what he was saying. And, not surprisingly, these claims came exclusively from the no-negotiation camps.

Thus far, Moro has been viewed as both a child and a fool. The final modern mode of civil degradation is that of transforming a healthy adult into a "sick" adult. This process depends upon the calling into service of the medical model. Moro the hostage was transformed into Moro the patient. In this regard, Goffman has outlined the mental patient's career: ". . . in terms of an extrusory model; he starts out with relationships and rights and ends up, at the beginning of his hospital stay, with hardly any of either. The moral aspects of this career, then, typically begin with the experience of *abandonment* [emphasis mine], disloyalty and embitterment."[53] Moro used precisely these words in his later letters (April 5, to Zaccagnini): "And, to tell the truth, I also feel a bit abandoned by you all."[54]

Once again, that which is most sociologically impressive is the fluidity of the self, and the final word of this section goes to Goff-man: "The self then as a performed character is not an organic thing that has a specific location, whose fundamental fate is to be born, to mature, to die. It is a dramatic effect arising diffusely from a scene that is presented and the characteristic issue, the critical concern is whether it will be credited or discredited."[55]

The last position of the diagram on page 221 to be considered is that of "Moro after 'death.'" In this position, Moro is high on both the *Scaredness* and the *Purity* dimensions. Of course, the "death" is as metaphoric as it was ultimately real. It was noted above that an extreme form of civil degradation is the issuing of the sentence of "civil death." And, it was by way of such a sentence that the Bad and Profane Moro who was writing the letters was successfully split off from the Good and Sacred Moro that Italy adopted as a martyr (Italy here a shorthand for the no-negotiation protagonists). Sciascia wrote about this enthusiastically embraced solution to the "problem" of the letters: "The independent [nonparty affiliated] newsapers, the party organs, the weekly magazines, the radio, the television; they are nearly all lining up to defend the State, to proclaim the metamorphosis of Moro—his civil death."[56] Montanelli, the right-wing journalist, exemplified Sciascia's description when he wrote, after the false alarm that Moro was dead at the end of April: "If we allowed ourselves to be bartered with, Moro would be more "dead" than he would have been if we had found his body at the bottom of the Duchess Lake."[57] The advancement of the idea that it would be better, that is, less morally dissonant, to think of Moro as if he were dead, was frequently framed as *concern* for Moro's own sense of himself. Further, a hierarchy of concern was developed in which Moro's physical life was assumed to be of minor importance. An April 27 article in *La Stampa* (the Torino-based daily) expressed precisely this sentiment: "The moral destruction of Moro's person carried out to that end [destroying the politics that he promoted] is even more important than his physical elimination."[58]

Silj has claimed that the "Moro is not Moro" operation, which included the publication of a petition signed by fifty of Moro's "friends" stating that the Moro who wrote from the "People's Prison" was not the same Moro they had known (this petition will be analyzed in terms of its symbolic significance as judicial evidence in the next chapter), was completed by March 31. This was the date of the publication of Moro's *first* letter.

Moro's own party published an article in *Il Popolo* on March 31, 1978, which revealed this virtually overnight transformation: "Vivid emotion in the Country—The forces of democracy are united"; ". . . We hold, however, that we must reiterate with conviction well thought through, that it is not possible to accept the blackmail of the Red Brigades [negotiation—which was not mentioned in any Red Brigades communiques yet]. . . Yesterday, most newspapers made reference to the conditions of torture and moral and psychic oppression in which Moro finds himself. And the anguished question is raised: how much must these conditions weigh on and influence Moro's behavior in spite of his moral and political stature? This letter [of Moro's], even though it is signed, has little of the usual modes of expression of the man" (p. 1). *L'Unità* joined in to cast suspicion on Moro's letters. On March 31, the PCI paper printed one article that accepted that Moro had written the letter but indicated that perhaps he had not conceived it: "Point by point the investigators analyze the letter of Moro—little doubts about the handwriting, many about the contents" (this distinction is crucial as the next chapter shows). *L'Unità* also printed another article that essentially rejected not only the letter just received but also any other letter, signed Moro, that might be received in the future. Essentially they were preempting the script: "No one has doubts. Moro's letter (if one can actually speak of Moro's letter) was written in a state of moral and physical constriction such as to remove any authenticity and thus every significance and value from the statements it contains. And this is not only true for the message of yesterday, in which the signs of this inhuman torture are clearly visible. It is true also for other documents written with the same handwriting that, unfortunately, we must already await from the kidnappers" (March 31, 1978, p. 1).

The celebration of the new Good Moro took a bit longer to inaugurate and, in fact, left a period of about two very muddy and dissonant weeks during which Moro's letters continued to pour out of the "People's Prison." In order to be declared civilly dead, Moro had to be accused of the greatest possible shameful or "sick" act—treason. And, in fact, after the highly polemical April 10 letter of Moro's, in which Moro harshly criticizes his party for rigidity, the accusation of treason was made: "'Hypnotized or convinced, by now Moro speaks as one of the Red Brigades.' This is the thesis that falls like a huge stone on the living, combative and acute man that Moro, in the 'People's Prison,' still is. This [villification] while the celebration of the Moro already 'dead,' the Moro to monumentalize . . . begins."[59]

So began the development of a new, heroic Moro, a Moro who would never accept being part of a prisoner exchange. It was assumed that Moro, in his lucid and articulate moments in captivity, would have been in perfect agreement with the no-negotiation protagonists' complex denials of the validity of his letters. Toward the end of the period of the creation of the Moro-martyr, he was no longer viewed as an *individual*. Moro, depersonalized, was finally ready for this pseudoritual sacrifice.

We have followed Moro's passage from profane to sacred, from pure to contaminated and back again as he "became" an ideal sacrificial victim. In its structural symmetry, this passage was an anthropologically perfect model of its kind. Moro, like the bull, gave his life at the very moment he was the most holy. The sense of inevitability about Moro's death, then, is, at least in analytic retrospect, striking. And the no-negotiation protagonists, attempting to adopt this ritual frame, could exploit this sense of inevitability to attain their dramatic end.

Aesthetic Imperatives

One reason for describing a social event as a "social drama" rests solely on the notion that the event is "dramatic" in the sense of being exciting or surprising. Such reasoning does little, however, to explain the event's actual structure. As developed in the Introduction, my use of the concept "social drama" refers specifically to the expectations of the protagonists and those of the audiences of these events. Now we need not forget that dramatic performances are the imitations of actions and that Moro's death was, sadly, real life. The point of the dramaturgic perspective is that it reminds us that the barrier between reality and imitation often breaks down in the moral imagination of the political protagonists of a social drama who can forget that they are not "in a play." Why can they forget this? Part of the answer can be found in their surround. The major protagonists of a social drama are almost constantly surrounded by cameras and tape recorders, journalists and microphones, crowds and institutional settings. Too many stages are available for the protagonists not to feel that they are constantly "making history." Further, the ubiquity of mass media screens in our society have induced us to absorb the serial narrative mode—we are constantly being provided with acted-out scenarios. In fact, we have been culturally trained to expect a certain formal sequencing from dramatic presentations. Dramatic critics since Aristotle have elaborated rules for proper dramatic progress. When we go to a play, we anticipate development of conflict, denouments, the experience of catharsis. Thus, in like manner, the idea of a social drama proposes that we have precisely the same kind of expectations about the social events of our "real" (as opposed to fictive) world, that we "read out" of and "read into" a social event a certain definite dramatic structure. James Peacock has written that this dramaturgic view "imagines and treats behaviors as if they were organized 'aesthetically' as in a play that arranges its scenes poetically and climatically to evoke appreciative and cathartic responses from an audience."[60] Thus the techniques used by the literary critic to analyze narratives and dramas are applied with equal relevance to social texts.

A common denominator of all of the analyses of dramaturgists has emerged. That is, the issue of order (or equilibrium) appears at the center of all dramaturgic approaches. In fact, this concept has provided the theoretical foundation of the dramaturgic enterprise.

Essentially, all analyses of social dramas resolve down to one basic drive—to return back from a state of disequilibrium, disorder to equilibrium or order. Such a drive has been identified as well by structuralist critics of folktales. Todorov has, in fact, indicated that a minimal complete folktale plot consists in the passage from one equilibrium (the initial situation) through disequilibrium, back to another equilibrium. Victor Turner's own social drama model revolves around just such a passage. The critical issue here, in the discussion of the final phase of the social drama, is the *means* by which this passage is accomplished. And, in this discussion of the aesthetic structuring of the Moro social drama, we must locate the narrative moves tending in that direction.

We have already seen how the anthropological impulses of the Moro affair led to the sacrifice of Moro. And it would not be unwise to look for a similar tendency in the realm of aesthetic prerogatives. In fact, Frye has claimed: "The archetypal analysis of the plot of a novel or play would deal with it in terms of the generic, recurring or conventional actions which show analogues to rituals: the weddings, funerals, intellectual and social initiations, executions or mock executions, the chasing away of the scapegoat villain and so on."[61]

Now, it is one thing to indicate that literary critics use the methodology of text interpretation to analyze a social event to the point of calling it a "social drama." It is quite another, and ultimately more meaningful, thing to say that the protagonists of the social drama had a dramatic self-consciousness. Indeed, the assertion of this self-consciousness counters any claim that these dramatic sequences and moves automatically lock into place after the initial order is disrupted. We are now in a position to ask: Who of the protagonists displayed a dramatic self-consciousness? And, what did they do with this self-consciousness?

That the Moro affair protagonists were conscious of and working with the dramatic progress of the event is patently clear. The press was a protagonist particularly keen to exploit the "inherent"drama. However, they were not alone. The Red Brigades, Moro's political colleagues, and the ultraleft all speculated on and contoured the aesthetic mode.

Lucrezia Escudero has remarked upon the recognition of the narrative character of certain political events: "The press has constructed the Moro case as a macabre story of homeric heroes who

lose their judgment . . . of unrecognized or hidden letters, in sum
[they have constructed] a mystery novel."[62] An example of this
dramatic speculation in which the press participated is revealed in
the following excerpt from a *Corriere della Sera* article: "It doesn't
seem accidental to us that Moro was kidnapped just as he was in
transit from the church to his activity of politician. There are, in
these occurrences, signs that signify beyond our intelligence capacities. Here, for example, the perpetrators of the assault have involuntarily rendered homage to the Christian."[63] Not only does this
excerpt reveal the attention the press paid to dramatic symbols
(here, the symbolic location of the victim at the time of the kidnapping) but it also reveals their participation in the creation of these
dramatic moments. As noted in the earlier chapter describing the
Breach phase of the social drama, and as Silj notes in a footnote
relating to this quotation, Moro was actually only on his way to the
church when he was kidnapped. However, in the interest of aesthetic symmetry, the writer got the information wrong and placed
Moro midway between Church and State.

At rare intervals, the newspapers exhibited a keen sense of the
varieties of modes of presentation that they themselves were working with. A front-page *Corriere della Sera* article on April 27 revealed such a self-consciousness to a high degree. Yet the meaning
of the commentary is, as will be seen, most ambiguous. The title of
the piece was "Zaccagnini, the Drama between Respect for the
State and Private Mercy," and the key passages read as follows: "In
the events linked to the Moro kidnapping there are, apparently,
many elements of classical tragedy. First of all there is the lacerating
conflict between the Reason of State and private mercy. Great is the
tension of the illustrious emotions of the prisoner, threatened with
death. High and noble are the voices that invoke his salvation . . . The public waits, thus [we have] demonstrations appropriate to heroism in a circumstance such as this: as much on the part of
the politicians as on the part of the prisoner . . . But Zaccagnini
cries and prays. The Christian Democrat chorus, gathered under
the flags of firmness cries and prays. More than a tragedy, this is a
miracle play: it's not the result that counts, but the faith and the
level of emotional involvement that the protagonists succeed in
demonstrating."

Interesting on several counts, this article seems to veer from the
solemn to the ironic and the cynical. It draws attention to the

semiotically marked tears of the DC secretary Zaccagnini, recipient of several harsh letters from Moro. These tears were most often referred to in the press as proof of Zaccagnini's intense concentration on bringing about Moro's release—a most noninstrumental kind of cause and effect. The article is also conscious of the public/ private distinction and the salience of this for the tragic mode. But immediately the relevance of this genre to the Moro affair is called into question, not by the strict structure of the event itself but by the actions of some of the protagonists, notable the DC. From tragedy we move to a miracle play. The key to the distinction, in this article, seems to be the respective emphasis placed on *results* in tragedy and *faith* in the miracle play. It is a difference in genre. The author marks this difference along the axis of efficacy: what can human beings do in the dilemmas that strike them. Tragedy, he intimates, provides room for human action. Miracle plays, with their sacred undertones, accept only faith. Here we need to recall the Christian Democrat links with the Catholic church and the ability of this party to draw on its catholicism in moments of crisis.

More generally, the newspapers adopted, and only intermittently self-critically commented on, a type of Dickensian serialization of the Moro case. One example of this infrequent self-commentary came from Pignotti of *L'Unità*: "The public is now primed to wonder: what will be the next move, the next 'installment'? Will it be a move made by the Red Brigades or by the police?" Pignotti is decisively *not* saying that the press must reject this narrative format. Rather, he is merely saying that it is important for journalists "not to, themselves, move the terrorist plot along."[64]

Many analysts of terrorism have noted the interaction between the terrorists and the press: the terrorists write the script and the newspapers provide the stage. It is not surprising then that the Red Brigades exploited the narrative flow by "issuing their messages on the days of major distribution of the daily newspapers."[65] Nor should we be surprised that the newspapers registered this coincidence and remarked upon it. We seem to have an infinite regress of consciousness of dramatic self-consciousness. Finally, the dramatic self-consciousness of the press is underscored by the coverage of the discovery of Moro's body: here we have a paradoxical sense of deja vu. In the newspapers printed on May 10, the only real new fact is the photograph of Moro's body.[66] In other words, the script, with its

unhappy conclusion, had been written for some time. It is, as Sartre
has Roquentin say in *Nausea*: ". . . things happen one way and we
tell about them in the opposite sense. You seem to start at the
beginning . . . and in reality you have started at the end . . . The
end is there, transforming everything."[67]

The suggestion that the drama might have ended differently was
not explored until, in a post hoc "revelation," Craxi, the Socialist
party secretary, was interviewed by the German magazine *Stern*. In
that interview Craxi indicated that, on the very eve of the drama's
conclusion, the president of Italy was considering an act of clemency toward the terrorists. That such an action was not taken
cannot, at this stage of our analysis of the logic of the social drama
under investigation, surprise us. What is striking is the melodramatic presentation of the eleventh-hour, nick-of-time proposal.

The theoretical model of sacrifice, described in the last section,
ideally involved a willing sacrificial victim. It was seen how Moro
impeded the natural progress of the ritual by refusing his role.
Similarly, we must confront the issue of narrative "point of view" in
our discussion of the aesthetic progress of the Moro case. From
whose point of view was the story being told? Through the working
out of this question, we will also be able to suggest the generic
tendencies of this particular social drama. (This issue will be most
fully developed in this study's conclusion).

The issue of point of view is a critical one for the structural
analysis of a narrative. Of point of view, Juri Lotman has written:
"[It is an] element of structure which we become aware of as soon as
there is a possibility of switching it in the course of the narrative."[68]

Thus Moro *forced* the other protagonists and the audience to
become aware of the point-of-view issue by radically switching the
drama's point of view (from that of the no-negotiationist's to
Moro's own) in midstream. Essentially he was saying: There is
another route this story can follow, one which will lead to my
release rather than to my death. We can look at the terrorist
demands and the government's options from another point of view.
The detour Moro hoped to erect consisted, we will see in the next
chapter, in adopting a less drastic, more flexible point of view.
Lotman goes on to claim that, in fact, "point of view can be
aesthetically active only as long as it is anti-system."[69] This is the
assertion of the antihero, a specifically modern dramatic character,
one usually resentful about having to shoulder the burden of the

narrative progress. He is the thoroughly modern hero/victim. Lapan has written of this modern victim and of his novel position: "Now in contemporary literature, the 'heroes' are also ordinary people, often wretches, certainly people of no consequence. They feel themselves to be victims, and what is more, they feel that they are being sacrificed, and that in the sacrificial process they are being reduced to utter nonentity, to utter nothingness. But a novel like *The Trial* or a play like *Waiting for Godot* differ, in what they make manifest, from an ancient sacrificial rite in that the sacrificial process is also seen from the point of view of the victim."[70]

Now whereas Moro was attempting to assert that he was quite the opposite of an ordinary wretch, we have seen that the no-negotiation protagonists have claimed precisely that "ordinary" status for him. Nevertheless, we still have access, by way of the letters, to this new perspective on the sacrificial process: the victim's perspective.

In terms of genre, this possibility of switching the point of view from the society's vision to that of the victim indicates a case where irony is brought to bear. Thus there is a convergence of literary description of the ironic mode and the reality of Moro's destiny: "Irony" says Frye, "descends from the low mimetic: it begins in realism and dispassionate observation. But as it does so, it moves steadily towards myth, and dim outlines of sacrificial rituals and dying gods begin to reappear in it."[71]

Frye claims that a leader's relation to his society is ironic, for, even prior to undergoing a tragic fall of the sort we instantly relate with Oedipus, the leader is, in a very real sense, isolated from that society. In Moro's case this was all made just that much more explicit and extreme.

But what about this hero whom we have seen degraded and, ultimately, expelled? What did the other protagonists want from Moro? What were their aesthetic expectations? It is useful to begin with the idea of a "day of reckoning," the hero alone, or alone before his maker (depending on the idiom).

The hero does not usually get to choose his day of reckoning and may, as in Moro's case, refuse to recognize it when others say it has come. The journalist Selva made his ideas regarding Moro's existential moment explicit: "This then is realistically the situation in which the drama of Moro's family, as the other families in Italy waiting for the return of their kidnapped relatives, brings everything back to the measure of the man, who, at the end stands alone before the themes of his existence and of history."[72]

Moro, it was soon evident, was not performing the stalwart, self-sacrificing role that the no-negotiation protagonists wished upon him. Moro's appeals were all, at least on the surface, oriented toward self-survival. How discomfiting this was to the no-negotiation protagonists can be read in this statement of Alessandro Galante Garrone, former judge and, at the time of the kidnapping, a history professor: "Certainly, we can't ask anyone to be a hero, but at least we can expect them to conquer fear, and even to have a little shame, to pay heed to certain obligatory elements that take priority even before the laws, that derive from the popular conscience."[73]

From the left, we get a similar reading, but this is given a different judgement: " . . . the image of Moro as prisoner, his letters—pathetic, quasi-literary testimony of a tragedy without a tragic hero—were used without scruples in the underground battle that raged in the bowels of a mediocre and cynical political class."[74] Here Mantelli and Revelli drew attention to the way in which Moro's letters were manipulated to suit purposes other than those of Moro. We have seen how, in order to pull this off while not appearing to detach their purposes from Moro's own, it had been necessary for the no-negotiation protagonists to create two Moros—the Bad/Contaminated Moro and, the Good/Pure Moro. If the letter-writing Moro would not "act in character," a new Moro would be created who would. How realistic was it for the no-negotiation protagonists to expect Moro to act the hero part, to bravely face his other-determined day of reckoning and die at the appropriate moment? One might reply—not very, if sociologist Franco Ferrarotti is correct in his analysis of the expectations of the establishment political protagonists during the Moro affair. He writes: "The fans of the Italian political melodrama were waiting for a Moro steadfast statesman, a Tommaso Moro [Thomas More] who would lay his neck on the axe of the butchers . . . Moro instead spoke and wrote as the Red Brigades: the subtle and untiring mediator searches, with the meticulousness of which desperation is sometimes able to achieve, to mediate and resolve the ultimate match."[75]

But even Ferrarotti does not seem to realize how on the mark he actually is for, in an eerie example of life imitating the interpreting text, on March 6, 1978 (ten days before Moro's kidnapping), *Il Popolo* printed an article reviewing the life of Thomas More and discussing the lessons of this life for Italy: " . . . man of law, famous humanist, politician attentive to the affairs of his time, not less complex than our own. Chancellor to the King of England, called on to cover the most important public positions and ending up on the gallows for having stayed faithful, up to the extreme sacrifice to the requirements of his own conscience with unflagging moral coherence" (March 6, 1978, p. 3.) Aldo Moro must not have been reading his own party's newspaper.

This peculiar dramatic circle, from life to art to life again, came full round as an attempt to reestablish equilibrium was made. This attempt incorporated an element that had broken the circle: Moro's death. Thus Italy's governing coalition planned and held, despite Moro's preemptive protestation and refusal, a public state funeral ceremony on May 13, four days after his body was found. In attendance were all of the leaders of Italy's major political parties, all ministers of the government, and approximately one hundred foreign dignitaries. Presiding over the ceremony was the spectral figure of the ailing Pope Paul. The funeral was held in the great Basilica of San Giovanni in Laterano in Rome, thus breaking a two-century precedent in papal attendance. All funeral services in the past two centuries, presided over by a pope, took place in the Vatican basilica. Pope Paul, symbolically bowing to the reason-of-state victors, reversed the precedence of Church and State in this matter of transition from this world to the next. However, something jarred this symbolic ritual of reconciliation. Neither Moro's family nor the body of Moro itself was present. Reconciliation was attempted over an absence.

7 The Praxis of Reconciliation and the Praxis of Schism

Symmetrical Trials

Who wanted to negotiate for Moro's release? Moro, his family, sections of the ultraleft, sections of the Socialist party, and the Red Brigades. Who rejected negotiations? The DC, PCI, the Mass Media, the other coalition parties, and the Catholic Church hierarchy. We can best comprehend the dynamics of challenge and power between these two umbrella groups if we regard the Moro social drama, in this chapter, as being composed of a series of interlocking and cross-referencing trials. These trials were each composed of relative degrees of instrumental and symbolic efficacy and potency, and together they constituted the praxis of the protagonists as they vied with each other for dominance over the path of the social dramatic plot. The trials, separately and together, determined issues of life and death, guilt and innocence, weakness and strength, and freedom and imprisonment. We will be attending to the organizational apparatuses of these trials, to their goals and procedures, and to their notions of evidence and proof.

The trials then consisted of (1) the state-organized trial of the forty-nine Red Brigades historic leaders in Torino, fifteen of whom were actually present at the trial. It is important to note that this "master trial" was really an agglomeration of seven separate trials, with judges and defendants hailing from three different cities. Three trials were originally under the aegis of Judge Caselli in Torino, two were under Judge Lombardi from Milano, one under Judge Armati from Milano, and one under Judge Ziniti from Rimini. These Red Brigades members were being tried for having formed an armed band, the goal of which was, according to the accusation, to "subvert the laws of the state." The official accusation was "Constitution, organization and participation in an armed band having, as its goal, the suppression or the violent subversion of

the economic, social and political systems of the Italian state."
Having begun two years earlier, in May of 1976, this trial had
suffered stops and starts ever since. Jurors were not easy to find,
and the logistics of trying so many people together were formidable.
Further, the trial had ground to a halt after Genova Attorney
General Coco was assassinated by other Red Brigades members (he
had reneged on a prisoner exchange deal with the Red Brigades at
the time of the kidnapping of Sossi) and had finally recommenced in
May of 1977 only to be halted once more. It was scheduled to finally
proceed in the spring of 1978: (2) The Red Brigades initiated and
oversaw the trial of Moro in the "People's Prison," the purpose of
which was "to clarify the imperialist and anti-proletariat politics of
the Christian Democrats; to distinguish the international structures
and national affiliations of the imperialist counter-revolution with
precision; to unmask the political-economic-military personnel on
whose legs march the multinational projects; to ascertain the direct
responsibilities of Aldo Moro for which, guided by the criterion of
PROLETARIAN JUSTICE, he will be judged."[1] (3) the trial of
Aldo Moro, outlined in the preceding chapter, as initiated and
overseen by Moro's political colleagues and the establishment mass
media, to determine Moro's sanity, credibility, health, loyalty, and
general competence.

The Torino trial and Moro's "People's Prison" trial confronted
each other as mirror images. Their respective sets of interrogators
viewed only their own trial as "real" and possessing authority. We
here recall the characterization of the "People's Prison" trial in the
press of the DC and the PCI as a "tragic farce." By reciprocally
denying reality to each other, these protagonists were asserting
their claim to be the only legitimate authority. By the same token,
both sets of defendants regarded their own inquisitors as illegitimate, usurping a power and authority not rightfully theirs. The
simultaneity of these two major trials was noted and exploited by
the press as the constant comparative assessments bolstered the
no-negotiators case.

Trial in Torino
The Red Brigades trial was being held in Torino, a Northern city of
heavy industry, dominated by the Fiat company and Communist
local government (at the time of Moro's kidnapping). The Com-

munists had labored long and hard in an atmosphere of fear and alienation to get the trial off the ground. It was an uphill battle. Already a judge, Riccardo Palma, who had come to Torino to inspect the prison where the defendants were being held, had been assassinated on returning home to Rome on February 14. Police chief, Francesco Berardi, also had been assassinated in Torino on March 11 during the period of jury selection, making the "normal" judicial process even more fraught with tension. A large demonstration had accompanied Berardi's funeral cortege which the Communists had been active in organizing. Berardi's assassination had occasioned the writing and distribution of the Red Brigades defendants communique no. 9 (not to be confused with the communiques that Moro's kidnappers would send some weeks later). This document was read in the court and, as a *L'Unità* writer reports (one cannot tell if with irony or not), xerox copies of it were distributed to the press: all must have a copy of the script. The communique read: "The mastodontic apparatus of men and means, this monster-spectacle of 'terrorism of the State' in which the military function does not succeed in dissembling that of the psychological war, has not been able to prevent an armed nucleus from bringing another director of the local anti-guerilla forces to justice" (March 12, 1978, p. 2).

Here we cannot regard the choice of the word "spectacle" as accidental: the Red Brigades saw their own actions as necessary guerrilla actions and the state's actions as spectacle, while the state viewed the Red Brigades rhetorical flourishes and grandiose military operations as spectacle and its own actions as necessary defenses of democracy. Lietta Tornabuoni, *Corriere della Sera*'s on-the-scene reporter, gave the following appraisal of the trial: "For them [Red Brigades] the trial is only a theater of confrontation and political propaganda and perhaps, as for all defendants, an occasion to socialize . . . For the State, it is justice, for the political forces and the city of Torino, the trial has been given the symbolic value of a struggle between institutions and eversion and of an exorcism of the specter of terrorism" (March 10, 1978. p. 2). Each side was caught up in a reified vision of good and evil in which the evil forces encouraged the spectacularization of the trial.

Each day in March prior to Moro's kidnapping on March 16 had seen a front-page *L'Unità* story devoted to the Torino trial. Problems of juror selection were discussed, and the PCI "proletariat" root paradigm appeared in their analyses of this issue in a most telling way. A February 23 *L'Unità* article put it as follows: " . . . it was necessary to wait for the only worker included in the list of people summoned yesterday to the second sitting for the formation of the jury of the 'Red Brigades' [note quotation marks] trial, in order for the president Barbaro to receive the first and only positive response yesterday to the question: "Are you willing to accept this task?" (p. 2). Foreshadowing the demonstrations of March 16, the PCI presents the "workers" as the true "defenders of democracy." Jury selection was indeed a sticky and polemicized issue in the Red Brigades trial. Much press space was devoted, throughout the month of March, to the difficulties involved in getting a complete jury. Prospective jurors presented an embarassing array of reasons why they could not participate. The fear was palpable and motivated. Late in 1977, before the last postponement of the trial and soon after the killing of Carlo Casalegno, a message had been received by the news agency ANSA in Milan with the following warning: "Let the judges, the jurors, the lawyers and their relatives think carefully. The Red Brigades trial will not proceed tomorrow or ever." This message was reprinted on March 5, 1978, in *Corriere della Sera* as a reminder of the pall under which jury selection proceeded. As if this were not enough, the Red Brigades defendants included a new threat in their communique no. 8, read in the courtroom on March 9.

In the end, the magistrates decided to stop at fourteen popular jurists rather than struggle on to achieve the specified number of sixteen, and the Red Brigades trial proceeded.

There was turmoil when news of the day's event reached the Torino courtroom on March 16. "This is a political trial," screamed Red Brigades member Franceschini, while in the hall pandemonium exploded. Curcio, in his turn, broke in screaming: "The trial will be held, and very seriously, somewhere else. We are a combatant organization." While the brigatisti abandoned the cage in protest, Curcio said: "We will try the entire DC. Moro is in the hands of the proletariat" (*L'Unità*, March 17, 1978, p. 1). Here we see the Red Brigades members asserting many things at once: they are political, the Torino trial is a farce, the real trial will be held in the "People's Prison," the defendant of that trial is not only Moro but the whole DC, and the true judge of that trial will be the proletariat. Never was the name of the proletariat dragged around more than in the Moro social drama. The PCI were claiming that the workers were responsible for resurrecting the Torino trial, and the Red Brigades were claiming that the proletariat was the animus for the "People's Prison" trial.

The DC, for their part, were somewhat ambivalent about the Torino trial. Not that they did not heartily approve and believe that much was at stake, including their own legitimacy, in being able to bring about the convictions of the historic leaders of the Red Brigades. But they were not keen on the PCI getting the credit for "pulling it off," and this ambivalence revealed itself in an *Il Popolo* article about the trial that somehow got around to the subject of the spectacularization by the PCI of the various scandals and political issues extant in Italy (many involving the DC). The passage is worth quoting again: "The left utilizes the press, the cinema, the television, the narrative, the essay, the theater, the magazine, the cabaret, popular music to give everybody the idea that Catholics [read Christian Democrats] are corruptors, corrupt and corruptible. On the contrary, we are determined to create the institutional conditions that will eliminate the motives of scandal, that do not constrict the space, in fact, that enlarge the efficiency of the controls in the various passages of the administrative life" (March 7, 1978, p. 3). In the context of an article about the Torino trial, one can only interpret the sentiment as being one of resentment: the PCI was simply getting too much press and credit for organizing the trial. The PCI was resented for having a dynamic way with the life of demonstrations and festivals, and the DC were waiting for an opportunity to join in the active choreography of its own political agenda. Being politically dominant, in these days of great and dramatic gestures of "patriotism" and other ultimate values, no longer sufficed.

On the other hand, bringing the Red Brigades to trial was surely something the DC wanted to accomplish. The frustration attached to the lack of success in doing so up to now was quickly becoming embarrassment. According to *Il Popolo*: "The Prestige of the State Is at Stake": "The Torino trial, even more than that of the neo-Fascists taking place in Florence, has by its very nature the force and intensity of a symbol of the judicial arm of the Republic, objectively weakened by many factors and drawn-out experiences. It will either succeed or not in ministering justice to those who, like the Red Brigades, have repeatedly and directly assaulted the Republic" (March 9, 1978, p. 1). Oh yes, there was the Fascist trial in Florence going on.

And here we need to explore the presentations of this and other ultraright trials proceeding during this period in Italy. We need to gauge the differential emphases placed on these trials and the Torino Red Brigades trial—to see how the realities of these different trials were being constructed. First, it is useful to clarify the numbers and types of concurrent ultraright trials.

I have been able to identify at least four trials of ultrarightists—in Florence, Rome, Catanzaro, and Bologna—that were in session in early 1978. The Florence trial involved the 1976 assassination of the judge Vittorio Occorsio, a judge who had been investigating the neo-Fascist groups. During this trial, both the president of the court and the public prosecutor received threats from the neo-Fascist "Ordine nuovo" (New Order) group. The Rome trial focused on the 1970 attempted coup d'état by ultrarightist Prince Valerio Borghese and on the various links between this attempt and the (now-defunct) SID branch of the Italian secret service. This trial was mired down because eleven reels of tapes possessed by SID, of conversations in which Remo Orlandini, "right arm of the black prince," took part, were missing. The Catanzaro trial was one of several that had dealt with the 1969 bombing in Piazza Fontana in Milan. That bomb had killed fourteen people and injured eighty. While this trial, with ultrarightist defendants, was proceeding, Pietro Valpreda, the anarchist originally tried and, after nine years of imprisonment, acquitted in this case, was bringing his testimony of the differential treatment of anarchist and neo-fascist defendants in Italian legal proceedings before the European parliament in Strasberg. Finally, the Bologna trial, with eighteen "Ordine nero" (Black Order) defendants, was hearing testimony on the train bombing of 1974. That bombing had resulted in the deaths of thirteen people and the injuries of one hundred. These were, then, clearly not the investigations of small-time capers. By comparison, it is useful to recall the charge against the Red Brigades defendants in Torino, most of whom had been in jail since 1974. While the Red Brigades member Roberto Ognibene had, in a previous trial, been indicted for murder and given a twenty-eight-year sentence, the present Red Brigades trial included no accusations of murders. Recall that the charge was constitution of an armed party.

The front pages of the major newspapers were flooded with stories about the Torino trial. By contrast, to select one paper, the *Corriere della Sera* included stories about the ultraright trials only deep inside the paper in its "Internal News" section. These articles were invariably small and sketchy. We have already hypothesized somewhat on the possible reasons for such an extreme divergency between the coverage and general media and political concern of the Torino trial and those of the ultraright, even, and significantly, before Moro's kidnapping. The "threat" of the day was being constructed as coming entirely from the ultraleft, and this reading of contemporary history was being developed as much by the center as it was by the right itself (the MSI party). The PCI's variant of this involved, as will be recalled, the imputation of a fascist orientation to the Red Brigades. Thus not even they focused their rhetorical zeal on the neo-Fascist trials. The imperative to distance themselves as far as possible from the Red Brigades and other ultraleftists was far the most important. The legitimacy of the party seemed to hinge on such a distancing. As the DC were not unhappy to have the Lockheed scandal temporarily disappear, the ultraright were not unhappy to have the country forget the recent complex network of neo-Fascist/secret service co-involvement and the current incarnations of the New Order and the Black Order organizations. Torino was the chosen focus of nearly all the protagonists of the Moro social drama.

The Torino trial was massive, requiring abundant armies of judges, lawyers, and police.[2] It had been elaborately and approvingly publicized as a major show of strength against the terrorists. Some discordant notes were struck, however, by Torino's own mayor, Novelli, who alluded to the spectacle-like atmosphere of the trial. In a sense, he was accusing the organizers of the trial of being more preoccupied with making "una bella figura" than with establishing effective justice. In an interview with the press he stated that "the idea of trying so many defendants together and of simultaneously hearing so many different charges has transformed this trial into a sort of ungovernable judicial monster. It benefits neither justice nor the public order nor anyone."[3]

The general atmosphere in Torino and in the courtroom was chaotic, tense, and bordered on the surreal. In the city, noted Lietta Tornabuoni: "Everything is normal on the eve of the Red Brigades' trial. Sudden road blocks appear, unexpected searches, uniformed patrols and patrols in streetclothes. Carabinieri march back and forth in the tribunal halls."[4] In the courtroom itself, the defendants, manacled together, were placed in a metal cage and were ringed around by carabinieri. The journalist Giorgio Bocca observed that "this event, with all its deaths, its ferociousness, its fanaticism, its hopes and its authentic sufferings continues to seem gratuitous, almost a dream—it's not clear whether good or bad—from which everyone still believes it is possible to awaken."[5]

As we compare these two trials, the Torino trial and the "People's Prison" trial, it will be useful to keep in mind certain relevant dimensions regarding the very notion of a trial. These dimensions are: (1) locale, (2) adjudged authority of the interrogators, (3) procedures, (4) evidence.

We have already seen how significant locale of the trial can be. Torino had been turned into a kind of representative symbol of all of Italy. Structurally, it is important to identify a trial's locale according to the public/private distinction, so relevant for this study. The Torino trial was certainly public. The exact location of the proceedings was known. The trial was taking place in what was being called the "bunker" courtoom. The building in which the courtroom was created was an ex-military barracks. The "bunker" effect was highlighted by the presence of an enormous cage in the middle of the room, ringed around by carabinieri, in which the defendants were placed for the duration of the trial. Some journalists, however, complained that not much of the public actually could enter the courtroom and witness this "public" trial: "When the reading [of the Red Brigades communique] began, there were, in the room, the lawyers, some few journalists and other journalists (among whom we figured) continued to be incomprehensibly held back, bent over each other like sardines in the entrance, and no public" (*L'Unità*, March 10, 1978, p. 1). Friends, relatives and cameras were granted entrance, however. The daily statements of the defendants were dutifully reported on the evening news. This trial was accessible to public consumption, if not to any bonafide public scrutiny. In direct contrast to this publicity was the secrecy surrounding the locale of the "People's Prison" trial. No one but the active members of the Red Brigades knew where the "People's Prison" was located or what Moro's physical placement within it looked like. Whatever information there was to be had of it came from the letters of Moro and the documents of the Red Brigades.

As noted in previous chapters, Moro was to be tried both as an individual, high-ranking Christian Democrat, and as a proxy for the entire Italian political class.

The specific charges leveled against the respective defendants lead us to a consideration of the adjudged authority of the interrogators. The issues here are complex. First, it is legitimate to ask if the very identity of the interrogators is known. Are their names, credentials, and histories in the public domain? Are their faces uncovered? Are they representatives of "legitimate" institutions? Do they represent the will of the collectivity? In other words, are these people considered to have the right to judge the guilt or innocence of a defendant?

Relevant to the above is the next issue, that of procedures. The concern here is that correct procedures are followed, that defendants have counsel, that "both sides" are heard, that innocence is not punished.

Finally, we must pay particular attention to questions of evidence. What is accepted as admissible evidence? How is the authority and authenticity of this evidence determined?

Each of the above issues was, at various points during the Moro social drama, cited as problematic by one protagonist or another. In the following discussion, precisely these moments of debate will be highlighted. The decision to credit or not to credit a particular judicial procedure had gross ramifications. Such a decision could determine the fate of a person's life.

The Trial in the People's Prison

The response on the parts of the establishment mass media and Moro's political colleagues to the trial taking place in the "People's Prison" was to immediately set about to discredit this trial. All but two daily newspapers in the vast panoply of Italian papers printed the word *trial* between parentheses every time they were referring to the "People's Prison" trial.[6] Selva referred to this trial as "absurd," and Arrigo Levi, editor of *La Stampa*, viewed it as a trial in which democracy was the, obviously abused, defendant. An April 23, 1978, *L'Espresso* editorial made the contrast rather stark as it presented the establishment protagonists' point of view. The crux of the difference lay in the opposition between the primitive and the civilized: "The single fact of having tried and condemned

(Moro) according to the rules and rituals of a tribal tribunal precisely when Curcio and the other Red Brigades exponents fully utilized the guarantees of a constitutional state that they publicly challenge and whose functionaries they kill, reveals the level of ideological perversion and moral distortion that animates the protagonists of the terrible undertaking" (p. 5).

At the same time, the Red Brigades defendants in the Torino trial were rejecting the Italian authorities who had indicted them. An illustrative piece of courtroom dialogue reveals this Red Brigades rejection of the Torino trial. The president of the court, Guido Barbaro, against the wishes of the public prosecutor, decided, on March 13, to allow the defendant Paolo Maurizio Ferrari to speak: "Barbaro: Let us hear what Ferrari has to say. Ferrari: Communique number ten. We have refused this farce . . . Public prosecutor: I object. Farce is an insult. This trial is not a farce" (*Corriere della Sera,* March 14, 1978, p. 7).

The characterizations of these trials are themselves of much interest for this study. The "People's Prison" trial is likened to a primitive ritual. The Torino trial is a farce. The delegitimation of the former rests on its association with the world of the primitive, the preconstitutional. The delegitimation of the latter rests on its lack of seriousness, its unreality, or, given the generic characteristics of farce, its burlesque turning of the world upside-down.

Why did the Red Brigades bother to activate the judicial processes and "try" Moro when, as anyone with any knowledge of the modes of terrorist actions would know, the verdict was predetermined? The answer, following sociologist Georg Simmel's analysis of nineteenth-century secret societies, lies in the fact that secret societies structure themselves as mirror images of the dominant society: "The secret society makes itself into a sort of counterimage of the official world, to which it poses itself in contrast."[7] Thus, if the Italian state was placing the Red Brigades' leaders on trial, the Red Brigades' antistate would place the Christian Democrat leaders on trial. Symmetry, in this sense, was being proposed as a kind of substitute for parity, legitimacy, and effectiveness.

We have seen, during the course of this study, how the issue of recognition was a constant one during the course of the Moro social drama. Here, it is interesting to note how much rhetorical time was made with the idea of the defendants' (alleged) recognition or nonrecognition of their own interrogators. And, once again, there was a mirroring of Moro's and the Red Brigades' leaders emphatic rejections of their respective interrogators. The symmetry became somewhat complicated, however, by the commencement of a third trial—the trial of Moro as overseen by his political colleagues and the mass media. The seat of this trial was in the newspapers and on the television screens of Italy where the *evidence* was presented and dissected by the relevant protagonists. In order to unravel the strands of the several trials, their procedural sticking points, and their interconnections, it will be useful to focus on the issue of Moro's relationship to his captors.

In the last chapter, the logic of the last phase of the Moro social drama was revealed as containing a degradation/sacrificial imperative. Further, it was shown that Moro was the individual ideally positioned to fill this role. We can now begin to see *how* this was effected.

The leaders of the Red Brigades, on trial in Torino, rejected the authority of their Torino-based interrogators out of hand. One would assume a similar rejection on the part of Moro vis-à-vis his own interrogators. Moro's first letter to Cossiga, minister of the interior, indicates that he viewed his incipient trial as potentially dangerous and wrote that he found himself a victim subjected to "full and uncontrolled domination"; further, that he was running the risk of being "forced to speak in a manner that could be unfortunate and dangerous."[8] Leonardo Sciascia, developing a retrospective, sympathetic reading of Moro's attitude, wrote that Moro was waiting for " 'his friends' [to] initiate negotiations and the police to move. His own proposal was to resist the trial, to reject it—an attitude parallel to that of the Red Brigades before the court of Torino."[9] However, Sciascia's reading was not that favored by most of Moro's political colleagues and the media. In fact, the no-negotiation protagonists claimed that Moro had indeed accepted the authority of his interrogators, that this acceptance was the manifestation of Moro's contamination (the so-called Stockholm syndrome) resulting from his proximity to the terrorists and his dependence on them. They claimed that the evidence for this was plainly visible in Moro's letters.

It was the Red Brigades' intention that the letters Aldo Moro wrote inside the "People's Prison" would ultimately be rendered public, this despite what appears to have been Moro's desire to keep several of them private. The Red Brigades' refusal of Moro's wishes is documented in their communique no. 3: "He has asked to be allowed to write a secret letter (the occult maneuvers are the norm for the Christian Democrat mafia) to the government and, in particular, to the head of the 'leatherheads,' Cossiga. This was granted him but, as nothing can be hidden from the people and as this is our custom, we render it public."[10] Thus Moro's letters were all bound for the public domain, were all bound, in other words, for publication in the daily editions of the Italian press.[11]

The Interpretation of Evidence

We may now recall the discussion of interpretation, introduced earlier in this study. Interpreters, it was claimed, possess a specific type of power. They are able to credit or discredit whatever object or person is before them for analysis. As well, it has been suggested that the modern mass public relates to public events through the official interpreters' translations of them, that the events are grasped and engaged in a mediated way. These modern official interpreters consist of government representatives, the media elite, and intellectuals (both within and outside of political parties). In the Moro social drama, the hermeneutic skills of the official interpreters were sharpened on the most fertile and abundant precipitates of the drama—Moro's letters. As Lucrezia Escudero has pointed out, Moro's letters became the main locus of interpretation in the Moro affair. We will also analyze the two photographs of Moro that surfaced during the social drama.

In order to understand the way in which the letters were exploited as "evidence" in the service of the event's developmental imperatives, identified in the previous chapter, we must first answer the question: With what specific questions did the interpretors approach their data? In other words, what did they believe the letters *could* reveal?

At the most general level, it was proposed that these letters could reveal something about the condition of Moro. The specific questions addressed to the letters were the following. Was Moro really the author of the letters? If yes, was he a lucid author or had he been drugged or tortured? If no, who had written the letters? On the other hand, if Moro was the lucid author, was he also a clever lucid author, writing in code, transmitting secret messages? Or, worst case of all, was Moro a lucid author who had gone over to the other side, writing not merely with a terrorist's pen but with a terrorist's mind?

Performance and Competence

To understand the mechanisms involved in answering such interpretative unknowns, we must first understand the interpretative assumptions upon which these mechanisms rest. These assumptions have best been analyzed by A. J. Greimas in his work on *discourse linguistics*. Discourse linguistics proposes that there are certain organizational principles at the base of any moment of discourse. Here we are interested in one specific aspect of discourse linguistics—the study of the relationship between *performance* and *competence*. Greimas has written: "The concept of performance naturally . . . evokes that of competence . . . according to presuppositional logic, the performance, or doing (le faire performateur) of the subject implies a prior competence to act. That is why . . . narrative semiotics was led to interpret competence as a set of modalities of doing. Hence, on the pragmatic level, the introduction . . . of at least three fundamental modalities (among other possible ones): those of volition-to-do . . . cognition-to-do . . . and power-to-do."[12]

We may now say that the Moro letter interpreters proposed to distinguish the performance (the production of the letters) from the imputed competence (or lack thereof) of the author. Further, they claimed to be able to qualify the kind of competence producing the performance along precisely the lines Greimas has delineated. In this regard, Silj noted simultaneous but contradictory negations of the legitimacy of Moro's letters and of that other "locus of interpretation," the Red Brigades' communiques. He wrote: "Many are the messages of the Red Brigades and many the letters of Moro. But the articles pretending to describe them are all invariably the same, and this for one very simple reason: legitimacy is denied equally to both. Thus it is never the analysis of the actual contents that really matters; that which matters is to repeat every time to the reader that the Red Brigades are capable of intention and will but don't have human or political dignity and that Moro is a great man and a great politician but is no longer in a condition to intend or to will."[13]

Moro was, thus, being tried not only in the "People's Prison" but also on the pages of the government's no-negotiation line supporting press. Turning the interpreting eye on Moro's letters to discover how much of Moro was left, to calculate his current level of competency, had the effect, then, of breaking apart the "natural" coupling of performance and competence or rather, as the more philosophically minded would term it, of action and will.

Read in reverse, the Moro letter interpreters viewed the producer of the letters as possessing the power to act but lacking the capacity to will. Simply, Moro was not himself. A further wrinkle was added to the dialectic of interpretation: Moro, hidden away in the "People's Prison," was made aware both of the interpreters' business and of their grim and critical conclusions. His response was tense and ironic: "It is true; I am a prisoner and not in a happy state of mind. But I write with my own style, however ugly it may be. I have my usual calligraphy. But I am, it is said, another and don't deserve to be taken seriously. And so, to my various arguments no one even responds."[14]

There are many ways to discredit written, discursive evidence. One can confront its form, its content, its context, or its author with a suspicious interpretative eye. In order for Moro's letters to have received complete accreditation, they would have had to be recognized as having been written by a lucid, competent, sincere, and consistent Aldo Moro, with his own hand. The fact is that all such character-integrity imputations had to be extracted from "mere" written text. Moro was unavailable to all but his prison wardens.

Photos of Moro were available to the public, however. The first photo, in which Moro sits in front of a large Red Brigades star symbol, was published in the newspapers on March 18. *L'Unità* reproduced the photo on its front page with the following explanation/interpretation (the caption read "A tortured man"): "The emotion with which we are forced to reproduce—as the piece of news that it is—the photo of Aldo Moro in the hands of his jailors is very sad. We do it with the disgust of those who touch a document handled by assassins . . . Look at this photo. It is the image of a man whom his kidnappers intend to martyr in one of those tragic farces to which they give the name trial; and that to make endure the challenge to Italian democracy and the honor of this Republic" (p. 1).

Thus Moro, already the projected martyr three days after his kidnapping and still mute (his first letter arriving on March 30), is displayed in this contaminated and troubling photograph. The DC response to the photo was equally if differently active. "We have experienced a great emotion," said a vice-secretary of the party, "seeing him like this, in good health, and with his usual serene and melancholy air" (quoted in *L'Unità*, March 19, 1978, p. 1). Melancholy because pessimistic (Moro will know better than to ask for negotiations), serene because he has accepted his destiny as symbol of Italian democracy.

Much was also made, as we noted in a previous chapter, of the fact that Moro was in his shirt-sleeves in the photo. This stripping of Moro of his authoritative apparel of suit and tie was striking, and it revealed the leveling of the high that the Red Brigades wanted their trial to accomplish.

The second and final photograph of Moro was received by the press on May 6, just three days before Moro would be killed. This photo was arranged in such a manner, with Moro sitting in back of a copy of *La Repubblica* of a few days earlier, to prove that he was still alive. The *La Repubblica* edition had the front-page headlines "Moro Has Been Killed," and this macabre photo defied precisely that. But rather than take the optimistic reading, the press decided that *La Repubblica* was at least metaphorically correct and that it was just a matter of narrative time: "Even at the State Department yesterday evening there was much pessimism: Unfortunately—said an administrator—at this point we think that all there is left to do is to wait for a last tragic piece of news" (*L'Unità*, May 6, 1978, p. 1). *L'Unità*'s front page was dominated by two photographs of Moro, a "before" and an "after" shot. The "before" shot is a full-face, close-up shot, very clear and sharp. This shows Moro as he used to be. The "after" photo is the Red Brigades one and is reproduced in a very blurred manner (this photo was reproduced in other papers as being much clearer). Here we have a clear imaging for the Italian public of the Good Moro and the Bad Moro. And to the latter one need not even attend.

The Letters as Evidence

There is a logical hierarchy of conditions in the interpretation of written "evidence." Before the content or tone may be deciphered, the identity of the author must be determined or vouchsafed. Of course, this process is based on an interesting dialectic. That is, authorship is read out of a piece of writing only when the content and style have already been "recognized" as consistent with the ways of thinking of that author. In Moro's case, accepting the letters as Moro's could constitute the first step toward crediting the *messages* embedded in the letters. Not surprisingly, such acceptance was largely withheld. The no-negotiation protagonists from the establishment mass media spent much editorial time withholding credit. *L'Unità* articles, appearing during the term of Moro's sequestration, produced the phrase "letters signed 'Moro,' " to indicate what we are here calling Moro's letters. *L'Unità* was not alone in this display of skepticism. *Il Popolo* referred to the "letters" of Moro (March 31); *Corriere della Sera* speculated: "The letter signed Moro was perhaps written under dictation" (March 31); *La Stampa* indicated their doubt by following the word *letter* with the qualifying "(true?)" (March 30).[15]

With equal intensity, Moro's colleagues participated in the campaign to cast doubts on the authorship of the letters. Escudero writes that in an April 10 letter "Moro, on his side, polemicizes with Taviani, member of the Christian Democrat party leadership . . . He asks if, in this "hardness" [against Moro's suggestions of an exchange of prisoners] there is some American or German influence. Taviani makes it known that he "does not respond to the texts of the Red Brigades."[16] Taviani's verdict on Moro's letters, then, is that of forgery. The verdict is quite straightforward and simple. Thus no one need even consider the letters' messages and proposals.

Handwriting experts as well as those familiar with Moro's particular discursive style complicated the matter by coming up with the judgment that the letters had actually been *scriven* and at least largely *composed* by Moro himself. Moro's arcane style was clearly evident in the published letters. Thus it seemed that Moro was actually the author of the letters after all. Something else was needed then to still the waves created by Moro's dissonant voice, something in the way of a more elaborate and subtle delegitimation. If the letters were to be recognized as the products of Moro's pen, at least they did not need to be received as the products of Moro's (unsullied) mind. "Who has written this letter?"—the *Corriere della Sera* asks rhetorically—"Has this letter been written by Aldo Moro, president of the Christian Democrats, statesman, maximum mediator and inspiration of Italian politics, cautious strategist? Or, has it been written by a man who has the same name, the same face, still Aldo Moro, but reduced to impotence by a cruel imprisonment, isolated and perhaps dulled by drugs . . . There is no doubt that Aldo Moro, in normal conditions, would never have suggested . . . the yielding to terrorists."[17]

Thus began the campaign, the outlines of which were drawn in the previous chapter, designated as the "Moro is not Moro" campaign. On April 5, six days after Moro's first letter was received by the minister of the interior, and barely three weeks after the installation of the government designed by Moro, Prime Minister Andreotti made a speech in the Chamber of Deputies in which he indicated that Moro's letters could not be "morally ascribed" to him. In a very real sense, the third trial of the Moro social drama, that claiming to be capable of and authorized to pass judgment on Moro's present moral state and competency had begun. Silj described the press positions in this trial: "First it is said that perhaps the letter is not authentic, 'many are the doubts, great the perplexity.' Then, in the very moment in which the news breaks that the doubts have been vanquished, they [the newspapers] begin to speak of merely graphic, technical authenticity. The 'substance' of the letter is false. Is it false because the affirmations made in it do not correspond to the truth? . . . The question is irrelevant. The letter is false because it has been extorted."[18]

The most paradoxical and the sharpest moment in this campaign of moral degradation came when a group of some fifty figures from the Catholic hierarchy published a document that figured as a kind of petition. This document asserted: "The Honorable Moro we know, with the spiritual, political and judicial vision that inspired his contribution to the drawing up of the Republican Constitution, is not present in the letters addressed to Zaccagnini, published as Moro's. They constitute an attempt to destroy Moro's physiognomy, as insidious an attempt as that threatening his life . . . the irremediable sin of such an absurd homicide will fall back solely on the actual executioners and planners of it. The Red Brigades should not delude themselves into believing that they can unload onto others the weight of a death penalty that the Italian State does not recognize as applicable in any case."[19]

The clerical "position paper" accomplished several things. First, it constituted a testimony given, by "friends" of the defendant, *on behalf of the prosecution*. It implied that the signers of the petition (religious figures all)[20] would have liked to have been able to be character witnesses for Moro but that they no longer recognized Moro as the owner of his former character. Here it is necessary to remark that Moro's relationship with the Catholic church had not always been a smooth one. In the early years of the sixties decade, Moro was subject to much criticism from the church hierarchy for his idea that the state ought to be autonomous from the church and for his, albeit much qualified, opening to the Socialist party. Still, Moro was a Christian Democrat, a man who went to church daily, and a personal friend of Pope Paul. Thus, when the clergy refused to acknowledge the Moro of the letters they were, in a sense, dispossessing themselves of one of their own.

The petition accomplished something else as well. It specifically denied that the no-negotiators' camp, in which they were lodged, need claim any responsibility for any harm that ultimately may have befallen Moro. So that, ironically, in the very act of judging Moro, these "friends" were denying that they had anything to do with his sentencing and *that* on the basis of the technicality that Italy did not have a death penalty. (Moro best answered this technical objection in a letter to his personal secretary, Rana. There he said, "To apply all the normal peace-time laws here makes no sense. And then, all this rigor in a country as discombobulated as Italy is.") Finally, the idea of comparing the destruction of Moro's (moral) physiognomy with the destruction of his life may strike the reader as self-righteous and strangely distant. Nothing is said of the *content* of Moro's letters in this petition, of Moro's references to his past position on terrorist negotiations, of his recommendations regarding his own fate. Nothing of the bitter sorrow we would expect from friends of a condemned man is present in this document.

The truly tragic quality of this document, and the assumptions about what Moro ought to do behind it was best articulated by one figure in the Catholic world who did not share the document's view of Moro of the letters. Father Turaldo, in an article in the April 23 edition of *La Repubblica,* asked: "Why have they signed this document, a document that, in essence, says yes to Moroism, no to Moro? That is, yes to the ideology, no to the man . . . It is simply this: their idol has been smashed and, in the place of the idol, a man has emerged, a man who wants to live, who is asking to live and to be saved. [This] because he has affections, a family, children, and because he sees other political possibilities . . . their idol has been smashed and in the place of the idol, a man has emerged, a man of profound familial sentiments. A man has emerged, a simple man, the authentic being, the creature for whom even God moves . . . I believe that Moro's letters contain the most truth in the flood of all our words . . . Thus I believe in the authenticity, not only semantic, of Moro's letters. He seems, finally, the only sincere character in this tragedy."[21]

Father Turaldo was not completely alone in his rejection of the no-negotiation hard line. Ten Italian high-ranking clergy had, we should recall, signed the "Party of Negotiation" petition in *Lotta Continua*. As well, the Conference of Italian Bishops came out, toward the end of April, agaist complete intransigence. Yet the Vatican bureaucracy remained firm in its no-negotiation stance, and such divisions as there were were muted. It should be noted here that Pope Paul, a personal friend of Moro's, was very ill during this entire period with the flu. Thus one can imagine that his ability to act autonomously of the Vatican curia was diminished.[22] The Church was ultimately, despite the several protests, going with the State.

Father Turaldo's missive represents an attempt to reverse the direction of Moro's moral passage, to return him to his prekidnapping condition—that being high on the purity dimension (a good, religious, family man; a clean politician) and low on the holiness dimension (a simple man among men, not a god or a hero). But a heroic martyr was on the order of the day, and all the available evidence seemed to imply that Moro would not come through. He persisted in attempting to be recognized as a politician with political prerogatives, writing political letters.[23] Umberto Eco, in his analysis of the mass media response to the letters, describes the media activity during the early and the final acts of the Moro social drama as the construction of a myth of a superman or—in the terms of this study—a pure and sacred Moro able to withstand and, more important, to transcend any coercion or torture. (During the middle act, incorporating the period we have designated as being dominated by "Moro of the letters," the superman temporarily became a "mere" man and [nearly] a traitor.) The no-negotiators wanted this superman to adopt a "Reason of State" root paradigm as his own. Moro, however, was claiming the logical priority of the "Sanctity of Human Life" root paradigm and continued to press for negotiations in his letters. The no-negotiator's idea of ideal behavior is best exemplified by an interesting historical precedent which, we can be sure, this group would have referenced if they had known of it. It involved the ideas Frederick the Great held about the "Reason of State" concept. In a letter he wrote on January 10, 1757, to his minister Count Finckenstein, Frederick stated his position: "If it should be my fate to be taken prisoner, then I forbid anyone to have the smallest concern for my person, or to pay attention to anything I might write from my place of confinement. If such a misfortune should befall me, then I shall sacrifice myself for the State, and everyone must then obey my brother; I shall hold him, and all my ministers and generals responsible with their heads for seeing that neither a province nor a ransom is offered for my release, but that the war is continued and every advantage seized, just as if I had never existed in the world."[24]

Frederick is saying "discount what I might write. I shall no longer be credited with political savvy nor any longer have political authority." Moro, quote to the contrary, had left no similar previous instructions, had, in fact, left a record of being a grudging scapegoat. In his letters, Moro constantly asserted his continuing political authority and party role. He attempts to activate this role by calling for the convocation of the Christian Democrat National Council to discuss his negotiation proposals. In the April 21 letter to Zaccagnini: "I address myself to you and, in so doing, I mean to address myself, in the most formal and, in a certain sense, solemn, way to the entire DC party, which I permit myself the privilege of still addressing in my capacity of Party President."[25]

No one in Moro's party, however, did permit him the privilege of political action. The only response he received was the usual DC statement, made repeatedly since March 31: "While the Honorable Moro is subjected to the gravest and most inhuman coercion, the DC renews its expression to him of its most profound moral and political solidarity" (published in *Il Popolo*, March 31). Hermeneutic skills are not needed here to translate this response. Essentially there was no response to Moro's requests. Just as the Red Brigades spoke of "invalidamento" (invalidation—killing of a target), we may say that the no-negotiation protagonists had undertaken their own form of invalidation of Moro, one that was equally effective.

Thus far we have seen how the *contents* of the letters were either disregarded altogether or were delegitimated. The posture implicit in these approaches was reinforced by the decision, publicly communicated, that Moro was no longer Moro. The decision to "invalidate" Moro was typically explained by the no-negotiation protagonist's conviction that Moro had been drugged, tortured, dictated to, or brainwashed. A more subtle "invalidation" was formulated by Eugenio Scalfari, editor-in-chief of *La Repubblica,* which he reiterated (in case there should be any residual doubts) a year later, in May 1979: "The letters were his, from the material point of view, and, from what it is possible to understand, they were not written in a state of psychic alteration, nor obtained with psychotropic drugs . . . That which was radically changed was Moro's relationship with reality. For 55 days, Moro saw Italy, the government, the DC, himself by way of the deforming perspective of the prison in which he was closed. His letters are authentic from the point of view of that perspective. But as that perspective was imposed upon him artificially, by way of the violence of the kidnapping, it follows that the letters are not authentic, that is, do not correspond to the Moro who existed before March 16."[26]

Scalfari is saying, essentially, that any trauma, imposed change of scenery or conditions is sufficient, *without any further evidence,* to radically alter one's ability to perceive things realistically. Thus, reading backward, from the letters to the imputed altered state, leaves the letter writer very little room to maneuver.

The final phase of the no-negotiators' letter interpretation process, that, corresponding to the fourth phase of Moro's moral passage (high in purity, high in sacredness), consisted of an overvaluation of the contents of these letters. And, as such, it marked a return to the superman reading. Here, the hypothesis of a secret code embedded in the letters was developed by the no-negotiation protagonists. The journalist, Selva, in his daily diary, recorded the following rumination on some of the phrasing found in the "Moro" letters: "One digs down into the words written by the DC president. There are those who maintain that the response 'no' to the blackmail is supported by the very prisoner. That having stressed the 'complete and uncontrolled domination' [and] the phrase, addressed to Cossiga, 'having awareness of all your responsibilities'; the invitation to 'reflect well on what to do' would be significant proofs to this effect."[27]

Thus, Moro, while appearing to solicit swift and decisive negotiation, was now being read as actually refusing the very negotiation option he was "being forced" to suggest. Silj provides some further examples of text exegetes developing this line of approach: Not only did Moro not agree with the text of the letter (when he writes "I must [devo] think that the great charge levelled against me" he was about to write "tevo" with "t" in place of "d"—"it is a sign of rebellion"), but he may have indicated to his friends that they ought not heed the appeal ("The sacrifice of innocents in the name of an abstract legal principle . . . is inadmissible") that he is making to them. In fact, "While writing the word 'legal' Moro made his pen slip." Pesce [a Christian Democrat journalist] deduces from this that that word was "imposed" upon him and that Moro, instead, "intends to sacrifice himself and inside himself refuses the exchange [of prisoners]."[28]

The discourse interpreters from the no-negotiation camp shifted back and forth between a reading that underestimated the author's ability to think clearly and freely and to communicate such and a reading that overestimated these very same things. The one reading they never, during the entire period of Moro's letter-writing campaign, adopted was that of taking the letters at face value, that is, the letter-writing Moro, consistent in handwriting, style of writing, and ideas with his past epistolary productions, saying what he wanted and meant to say. Certainly, Moro had never written an "easy" Italian. Pasolini, the famous poet and filmmaker, had called Moro's way of using Italian that "completely new language." In this regard, Sciascia makes the uniqueness and difficulty of Moro's latest task explicit: "But before they assassinated him, he was forced to live an atrocious contrapasso for almost two months; on his 'completely new language,' on his new, incomprehensible as it was ancient, Latin . . . he had to speak with the language of non-speak, to make himself understood using the same tools he adopted and experimented with in order to make himself *not* understood."[29]

Now, before exploring the quite different response to the letters of those who favored negotiation, it will be useful, bearing in mind the trial idiom being presented here, to reference any precedents or other data that might bolster the case of accepting Moro's letters as straightforward evidence supporting the defendant. One extremely significant precedent was the case of Mario Sossi, a victim of a Red Brigades kidnapping some years earlier. We have already discussed this case in a previous chapter in terms of Sossi's après-kidnapping recognition of the terrorists as intelligent and not unkind. Here we are interested in Sossi's further claim that he had written all of his own letters, likewise mailed from a "People's Prison," autonomously and had suffered no coercion in doing so. This absolutely relevant piece of data was, however, ignored by the determinedly skeptical no-negotiators. As well, it was certainly true, as anybody willing to do a little research would discover, Moro's position on hostage negotiation in his letters was consistent with positions he had taken on his preabduction past. The irony of Moro's most recent admonishment to his party (February 28, 1978) to act with "constructive flexibility" regarding the evolution of political relationships (here referring implicitly to the Communists) must strike us as precisely his party's *rigidity* in this social drama that undermined all his efforts.

Other evidence that Moro had not either lost his mind or gone over to the other (terrorist) side came, paradoxically, from the documents from the Red Brigades. In the very communique in which they announce that Moro is condemned to death (communique no. 6) they declared, quite forthrightly, and seemingly without a sense of tragic irony: "There are no clamorous revelations." In other words, Moro had *not* talked after all. Finally, in the aftermath of the long ordeal, the autopsy of Moro revealed no injuries (other than a by-then healed flesh wound from a stray bullet from the March 16 volley of machine guns), no trace of drugs or poisons in his system. His general physical condition was good despite some weight loss. Thus, all strictly empirical data points in the direction of Moro having been a lucid, competent, rational author. Yet his letters were systematically rejected as carriers of rational political discourse.

All this may seem theoretically problematic, but it ought not surprise us. Simmel illuminated the particular accessibility of letters to seemingly illogical interpretations: "As a matter of fact, however, the recipient does not usually content himself with the purely logical sense of the words which the letter surely transmits much less ambiguously than speech . . . For this reason, the letter is much more than the spoken word, the locus of 'interpretations' and hence of misunderstandings—despite its clarity, or more correctly, because of it."[30] It is, then, not surprising that when the final verdict (from all of Moro's trials) was handed down, Moro wrote to Zaccagnini: "I repeat, I do not accept the DC's iniquitous and ungrateful sentence."[31] According to a much embittered Moro, his own party (at least) shared the responsibility for his conviction with the Red Brigades and would, he clearly communicated, share responsibility with them for his death.

But what was Moro actually saying in his letters? First he was saying, as we have seen, that he was not in a happy condition. This was obvious, if unfortunate. Next he was saying that the Italian government should attempt to initiate negotiations with the Red Brigades. Moro's own initial attempts at communicating this message were consistent with his role as Christian Democrat politician—the negotiations were to be secret. From his March 29 letter to his personal secretary Rana: "My idea and hope is that this line of communication [between Moro and Cossiga], that I hope to connect, will remain secret as long as possible, outside of dangerous polemics. That means that the response, or the first response, when it comes, must not pass through the newspapers but via a letter or communication sent to you by the Minister [Cossiga]." Thus Moro anticipated that he would have first to negotiate with his own (a "first" response) before his own would negotiate with the Red Brigades. He also hoped to sustain his authoritative prerogatives in directly communicating with the rulers of Italy. He also wished to avoid the public.

One last interesting note about the above letter is that he used the formal pronominal form with his personal secretary. This form, in such a case, asserts distance and hierarchy. With the president of the republic, Moro would be more familiar.

In the above-referenced letter to Cossiga, Moro intimated that some kind of prisoner exchange was not only thinkable but also, for reasons of state, necessary: "Above all, this reason of State in my case signifies . . . that I find myself under full and uncontrollable domination, subjected to a popular trial . . . with the risk of being called to or induced to talk in a manner that could be unfortunate and dangerous in determined situations . . . All of the States of the world have adopted positive measures, with the exception of Israel and Germany . . . And it is not necessarily true that the State loses face because it has not known or been able to prevent the kidnapping of a high personality who is significant in the life of the State. Turning a moment back in history, I remember the exchanges between Breznev and Pinochet, the many spy exchanges." Here Moro is still thinking as the DC mediator that he was, bringing as evidence the various precedents of past exchanges between enemies, viewing himself as a collective responsibility, linking his own fate to the fate of the state.

With the immediate and never-to-be-altered position of "no-negotiation" coming from his own party and the PCI, Moro had to confront the reality of his *changed* situation. The underside of his treatment by his party begins to come to the surface. In a letter to Zaccagnini, friend and party political secretary: "And it is even necessary to add, in this supreme moment, that if my escort had not been, for administrative reasons, completely unequipped for the exigencies of the situation, perhaps I wouldn't be here . . . I am a political prisoner and your brusque decision to close every discourse relative to other similar persons, puts me in a situation difficult to sustain."

As for the Communists, Moro had no illusions about them. In a letter of April 7 to his wife he wrote that "the Communists have been very hard, being, as they are, in the game for the first time as a part of the government."

By April 10, Moro is beginning to view his party, as if for the first time, as a rigid and anxious party of the state. In a response to the declarations of DC Senator Emilio Taviani that, to the contrary of what Moro had written in one of his letters, Moro had not, in fact ever spoken to Taviani about being in favor of prisoner exchanges in the past. Moro writes: "Why this denial? There is only one explanation: excess of zeal, that is, fear of taking the risk in these circumstances of not being in the front row in defending the State." Moro proceeds in this document to outline the zigzagging career of Taviani and ends with the following: "In both of the delicate posts [Taviani] held [minister of defense and minister of internal affairs], he had direct and entrusting contacts with the American world. There is, perhaps, in the hard attitude against me, an American or German indication?"

All of the while, as noted previously, Moro makes continual references to the needs of his family and of his party for his return. The bitter truth that his party does not recognize its need for him clears and complicates his vision at the same time. In a late letter to Zaccagnini: "Of these problems, terrible and anguishing, I don't believe you will be able to free yourselves, even in front of history, with the facility, indifference and cynicism that you have exhibited up to now in these fifty days of my terrible sufferings. With profound bitterness and disbelief, I have seen, in a few minutes, the assumption of a rigid and closed attitude without any serious human and political valuation . . . I don't wish to indicate anyone in particular but I address everyone. But it is most of all to the DC that the Country turns as responsible, for the way in which the DC has known how to always wisely moderate between reasons of State and reasons of humanity and morality. If you fail now, it will be for the first time." Here Moro still claims for his party a history of complex and thoughtful weighing of alternative and competing moral claims. Whether or not we share Moro's assessment of the DC, it is noteworthy that in the midst of this melodrama and of polarized good and evil Moro is stressing the need to acknowledge something in between, some shades of gray.

Finally, responding to the accusations that have filtered back to the "People's Prison" from the establishment and party press, that Moro is now just speaking with the voice of the Red Brigades, Moro writes in an open letter to his party: "Why this conviction of my non-authenticity? But between the Red Brigades and me there is not the minimal commonality of viewpoint. And my position, that I have sustained from the beginning (as I demonstrated many years ago) in accepting, as occurs in war, an exchange of political prisoners, does not amount to an identity of viewpoint . . . For my part, I have said and documented the things that I say today in the past in a totally objective condition. Is it possible that there is to be no statutory and formal meeting, whatever may be the results of such a meeting? Is it possible that there are no courageous ones who request it, as I request it with full lucidity of mind? Hundreds of parliamentarians wanted to vote against the Government. And now no one poses the problem of conscience? . . . If all is decided, it is the will of God. But no one who is responsible can hide behind the fulfillment of a presumed duty. Things will be clear, they will soon be clear."

The Benign Interpretation
What resistance was there to the no-negotiation camp's reading of Moro's letters? Who pleaded the case for the defense? Those favoring some kind of negotiation were, as we have seen, Moro's family, the ultraleft, the Socialists, the Red Brigades captors, and Moro himself. Here, as well, we must, in a qualified way, add the "general public" for, in the only national poll on this question taken

during Moro's sequestration, "sixty percent of Italians polled were in favor of negotiations with the Red Brigades as long as the government was not involved."[32]

This poll, and its interpretation, requires some comment. The poll was commissioned by the weekly news magazine *L'Espresso* from the DOXA polling institute. It appeared, in a much abridged and fragmented form, in the April 23 edition of the magazine. This was, to repeat, the only national poll taken during the fifty-five days of Moro's captivity. The first question we might pose is: Why, in the midst of such a storm of rhetoric about the inclusion of the active and concerned citizenry of Italy in the defense of the state against terrorist violence, was the actual public opinion not more actively sought? Here an illuminating comparison might be cited. While the American personnel in the embassy in Iran were being held hostage for over a year, numerous national polls were taken. The polls focused on many of the same issues that plagued the Moro case. From the Gallup polls, taken on the average twice a month for the duration: "Do you think the hostages will be released or not?" "What, if anything, do you think the U.S. should do about the situation?" One of the response options of the latter was: "Continue negotiations; wait it out."[33] Many of the major television networks, such as CBS, also took similar polls. And, of course, the results of the various polls appeared frequently in articles in such papers as the *New York Times*. Yet, in the Italy of the Moro affair, only one poll was taken and, rather scantily, reported. While the fact of a more active and socially inscribed polling industry in the United States partly explains the discrepancy, it does not explain its magnitude.

Perhaps one way to get at the reason for the single poll can be found in the mode of presentation of the results of that poll. The *L'Espresso* article presenting these results framed the issue in the following way: "[Will the people] share the considerations expressed by the press, the television and the radio, and understand the reason of State that prevents negotiation with the brigatisti? Or, instead, [will] all these arguments be clouded by the drama that Moro's family is living?" (*L'Espresso*, April 23, 1978, p. 12).

Let's unpack these questions. First, the "majority" opinion of no-negotiation is clearly the correct one, in the sense that it is the decision made of a lucid, reasoned comprehension of the requirements of the state. The alternative—unspoken—of negotiation can derive only from an obscured vision and an emotional involvement in the Moro family drama. Once again, the state is pitted against the family. And, interestingly, the state reasoning is portrayed as objective, and the family imperatives are portrayed as "dramatic." Yet note that the state's interests are only known via the mediations of those drama-creating channels of the mass media.

What about the questions and results of this poll? As framed by *L'Espresso* (the only public access to the poll results), the poll appears to have incorporated many questions: "Should the government negotiate and accept an exchange of prisoners?" "Should the government negotiate on other [not clarified] grounds?" "Should others [the family, the Holy See, other private organizations] negotiate?" The responses to these questions are presented in a very confusing manner, for only a portion of the possible responses are cited. For example, to the question: Should the government negotiate on other grounds? we are told that 23.3 percent of those interviewed are in favor of such negotiations. But we are not told what the other responses were (absolutely against? don't know? only in certain circumstances?). This same lack of completeness is true for several of the other questions asked. We do not find, in the article, a complete interview schedule and thus know nothing of the number of questions asked, the order, or the response options. However, *L'Espresso* has interpreted the results of the DOXA poll as indicating that a majority (approximately 60 percent) of the people would favor nongovernmental negotiations. But, as the introductory remarks to the article indicate, *L'Espresso*'s attitude toward this "humanitarianism" was, at best, most ambivalent. The article confusing, the results not, perhaps, completely pleasing to the government, this was the first and last poll of the Moro social drama.

By April 15, the day on which the Red Brigades communique no. 6 was issued, it was clear that Moro had made no startling revelations to his captors. This left, as it turned out, almost a month for improvisation in negotiation options and a month for Moro to intensify his letter-writing campaign. The general public, amply exposed to the contents of both the letters and the communiques, responded in a measured and sympathetic manner to Moro's pleas: "The readers . . . did not share the point of view of the Christian Democrats—even if it ws a point of view shared by the large circulation newspapers and by the radio and television. Regardless of whether or not they approved of the behavior of the Honorable Moro, the readers could not understand why one had to judge 'out of himself,' not in a condition to will or to desire, a man who did not want to die and who turned to his own party to redeem him with means that, while electorally risky, were not impossible."[34]

Here, however, we must recall that, in this as in most contemporary social dramas, the general public played more the role of audience than that of an active protagonist in its own right. Having largely attained the status of C. Wright Mills's mass, the Italian public had very few channels through which to respond to the government's hard line. (One of these, as noted previously, was the election to come in late May. In these elections, the no-negotiators lost a few percentage points while the Socialists gained a few. Many read this as an expression of the public's dissatisfaction with the handling of the Moro affair.) This seemed to be a significant case of the kind of limited action permitted to citizens of formal democracies identified by Habermas: "The arrangement of formal democratic institutions and procedures permits administrative decisions to be made largely independently of specific motives of the citizens. This takes place through a legitimation process that elicits generalized motives—that is diffuse mass loyalty—but avoids participation . . . [these individuals] enjoy the status of passive citizens with only the right to withhold acclamation."[35]

Chapter 6 describes the way in which so much of the dialectic of this drama hinged around the distinction between public and private. So many protagonists developed their parts in terms of this distinction. Some proposed that Moro be viewed as a collective figure—a proxy for Democracy, for the entire Italian republic, or, simply, for his own entire party. Not all of those who saw him thus were opposed to negotiating for his release. Notably this group favoring negotiation included the ultraleft whose adherents viewed Moro's letters as *political* documents, that is, as Escudero claimed, capable of persuading. In one comment in the ultraleft newspaper, *Lotta Continua,* one of Moro's letters is called a "political last will and testament."

There were those protagonists who rejected the public Moro, claiming for him, instead, the status of "un uomo qualunque," Biedermann, Anyman, with only the rights and privileges of an average citizen. Still others shifted back and forth, as befitted the moment, now viewing Moro as a citizen, now as a collective hero.

This last was the particular province of the strict no-negotiators (the Christian Democrats, the Communists, and the establishment mass media). As described, these protagonists led an unwilling Moro through a moral passage during which his role changed from private person to public hero to private incompetent to, finally, public saint.

There was a startling amount of symmetry in the Moro social drama. We had two trials that opposed and reflected each other—the one held in the Torino courthouse, the one in the "People's Prison." There were to be two antagonistic funerals. And here, as well, regarding Moro's moral passage, we find an example of, as William Blake would say, "fearful symmetry." What I am referring to here is the way in which Moro was regarded by his Red Brigades' captors during the course of Moro's trial(s) and aftermath. Their perspective was a direct counterpoint to that of the no-negotiators.

Prior to and during Moro's Red Brigades trial, all references to Moro in the Red Brigades communiques (nos. 1–6) concerned his antiproletariat, imperialist activities, the conciliations he made in his public career to the ultraright, his involvements in plots and conspiracies hatched by forces in the military. In other words, Aldo Moro was portrayed in these early documents as a public figure—one representing the Italian political class in power since 1948. A selective (as are all histories) chronology of Moro's official posts was presented in communique no. 2 as evidence against him. Also included was the following justification for having captured precisely *him*: "Who better than Aldo Moro could represent, as head of the SIM [Imperialist States of the Multi-internationals] the interests of the imperialist bourgeoisie? Who better than he could bring about the institutional changes necessary to complete the restructuring of the SIM? His career however does not begin today: his presence, sometimes obvious, sometimes camouflaged, in the leadership posts of the regime, goes back quite some time."[36]

Such a characterization of the prisoner Moro persisted in the Red Brigades documents until communique no. 7. Moro's guilt and punishment (condemnation to death) had been decreed in communique no. 6, published by the newspapers on April 20. And it was at this very point that Moro began to be viewed as a private individual by the Red Brigades and, for that, in direct contrast with the view of the no-negotiation camp, deserving of an indifference that bordered on respect. As far as recognition of the letters of Moro went, it should be clear that the Red Brigades viewed them as rational, political discourse. They were, in fact, to wait until April 25, until the release of their eighth communique, to themselves mention the possibility of a prisoner exchange. They had relied on Moro to do as much in his letters for more than a month, since his first letter to Cossiga. His total lack of success may have surprised them as much as, apparently, it surprised Moro.

We can read the change of attitude of the Red Brigades toward Moro in the statement, appearing in communique no. 7, that "Aldo Moro, sequestered in the People's Prison, is, by now, outside of it [the corruption of the DC]."[37] The ironies of the numerous status recognitions and denials are many: Moro, campaigning in his letters to his colleagues (addressing them all with the familiar pronominal form) for public stature (thus worthy of redemption); the Red Brigades, more than willing to regard Moro as a proxy for the Italian bourgeoissie, the Italian political class (therefore as a public figure); Moro's political colleagues, allowing Moro public status only contingent on Moro also donning the martyr's mantle; and Moro's family trying all angles, public and private, to reclaim their kin.

The Family as Plaintiff

As far as Moro's family fared, much rhetoric was woven around the figure of Eleonora Moro, Moro's wife, in the early days of the social drama. She was portrayed in the establishment press as an austere, tragic figure, moved by the solidarity of the country, comprehensive of the needs of the state. However, by mid-April, it had become clear that Moro's family was utterly disgusted with the DC/PCI hard line, and various members of the family began to "go public" with this dissatisfaction. We recall how Moro's son, Giovanni, had unsuccessfully attempted to invoke Geneva Convention criteria. Now, on April 20, an official family communication was published in which the family took its first, if still implicit, step toward declaring its opposition to the line developed by the DC and the government: "The family and friends renew the firm request that Signora Eleonora Moro made yesterday to the DC and the government, that being the saving of Aldo Moro's life. They ask the DC to *assume a realistic attitude* [italics mine], declare its willingness to concretely ascertain what the conditions for the release of its president are."[38]

Here we see both the beginning of the family's autonomous campaign as well as their emphasis on Moro as a public figure ("its president"). This official family communique format had been adopted after several articles had appeared in the various newspapers in which it had been claimed that Eleonora Moro had declared herself solidly opposed to negotiation. However, just as in the case of their confrere, Moro's family would not play the prescribed role. Rather, his family began to write a script of its own. The real turning point in the family's campaign came on April 30. It was in the communication published on that day that Moro's own party was presented as sharing responsibility for Moro's condemnation. In other words, Moro's family viewed Moro as the prisoner in the docks of two trials: "The DC delegation, the Honorables Zaccagnini, Piccoli, Bartolomei, Galloni and Gaspari, know that with their immobility and their refusal of any initiatives coming from any quarter, they ratify Aldo Moro's condemnation to death. If these five men don't want to assume the responsibility of declaring themselves amenable to negotiation, at least let them convoke the DC National Council as formally requested by their president."[39]

By May 1, Moro's family was exasperated, both with the Christian Democrat rigidity on any negotiation possibility and with the party's reading of Moro's letters—all of this in a country which, as discussed earlier, was still characterized as stressing familial prerogatives. Their exasperation showed up clearly in the following May 1 communication: "He [Moro] every time he attempts to express himself directly is declared to be substantially mad by almost everyone in the Italian political world—and first in line here is the DC and associated groups of so-called 'friends' and 'acquaintances' of Aldo Moro."[40]

Meanwhile, Moro, having understood that he had played his last discursive card, had written to Zaccagnini on April 25: "I ask that at my funeral, there should be no authority of the State nor men of the party. I request that only the few who have truly wished me well and are thus worthy of accompanying me with their prayer and love should follow me."[41]

Moro's family took his request seriously, just as they had taken all of Moro's other letters seriously. And on May 9, the day on which Moro's body was found on Via Caetani (as has been noted, midway between the DC and PCI headquarters), the family made plans for a private funeral to be held in the small town where Moro spent his summers. The response of the no-negotiators to the family's plans for a private funeral was one of resentment. As Katz noted: "The Communists solicited the government and the DC to try every means of delicate persuasion to alter the family's decision. The Communists' argument ran that the family had to respect the needs of the collectivity and popular sentiment. Moro belonged to Italy, and his burial is not a private matter."[42]

We have seen, however, that Moro did not always "belong to Italy" during the Moro social drama. In fact, he was often disowned by Italy or, at the least, remanded to an indifferent private sphere. As well, it is interesting that the statement couples "the needs of the collectivity" and "popular sentiment" when it has been shown that the two (the former being defined by the political directorate) did not always flow in the same direction.

That this social drama came to an unsatisfying end, an end that split in two as the two funerals were held (one with the state and church in attendance and one with the body and family), may indicate as much about the difficulty in successfully translating sacrificial principles into a modern idiom as it does about the fragmented and internally corroded state of Italian public life.

The repercussions of this final schism could not, in May of 1978, be fully known. But that a schism had occurred, no one could deny.

8 Conclusion

People like finality in a work of art; and death is about as final an image, or idea, as they can think of (more final than success, since after any success death still awaits them). In this technical sense, at least, tragedy is the most "perfect" (that is, "finished") form. Accordingly, though I favor Meredith's view that a wholly civilized world would be a comic one, I believe that Artistotle was correct in building his Poetics about the analysis of tragedy.

KENNETH BURKE[1]

The connection between symbolic significance and military risk was very tight. That symbol was worth the risk for us. We had to clearly indicate who was responsible for the tragedy. But it was a calculated risk . . . In that Rome there were tens of thousands of police and carabinieri, but spread all over the urban area. We, in Via Caetani, for a few necessary minutes, we could be the strongest.

MARIO MORETTI, MEMBER OF THE RED BRIGADES[2]

Aldo Moro failed in his attempt to draw this social drama away from its fatal course. His body was found in the trunk of a Renault parked on a small street in Rome, Via Caetani, midway between the Communist and Christian Democrat headquarters. Symbolic symmetry would finish this social drama as it had begun it. The interpretation of the Moro social drama has revealed the way in which such symbolism was neither accidental nor epiphenomenal. In this conclusion we will discuss the ways in which symbolic consciousness and symbolic activity dialectically interact with instrumental actions to emplot a given social drama toward a specific end.

Accordingly, the conclusion will be concerned with several issues: (1) the problematic attribution of a ritual idiom to the presentation of the Moro affair by certain interpreters assessing the event in terms of its ability to be ritually satisfying and efficacious: (2) within the more appropriate paradigm of theatrical presentation, the competition among the various genres, and the victory of melodrama over tragedy in the Moro social drama; (3) the emergent, structurally analogous concepts of hero/villain: political leader/political enemy; (4) the "cauterisation" (in Lumley and Schlesinger's terms, see their "The Press, the State and Its Enemies: the Italian Case") of the long-term national crisis in Italy and the "relegitimation" of the established political protagonists, during the period of the Moro social drama, via a strategy of combining maximalist appeals to ultimate values with increased military and police repressive powers; and (5) the specificity of Italy's construction of social dramas and the significance of particular modes of mediation for constituency participation.

The Model of Ritual

Several scholars have regarded the Moro affair as having constituted a type of society-wide ritual (that either succeeded or failed) of sacrifice and purgation. Here, the assassination of Moro is viewed as one moment within the unending cycle of ritual sacrifice, filial guilt, and ritual reparation. One particularly insightful analysis, that of Enrico Pozzi, connected Moro's assassination with the presidential pardon, some months later in 1978, of a young boy who had murdered his father. Pozzi wrote of the need to kill the impotent father in order to save the "father's name" as the impulse behind both the state's rejection of Moro and the absolution of the young patricide: "Moro the prisoner was too accurate a mirror of the impotence of a social system and of its power. For this, an entire country desired—deep down while faking the contrary—the killing of Moro, feeling comforted and guilty, reassured and sacrilegious (reassured because it was sacrilege) when it happened . . . In a society of radically illegitimate political power, politics is transformed into the privileged space of the magico-sacred."[3]

Another analysis of the Moro affair as ritual (David Moss, "The Kidnapping and Murder of Aldo Moro") focused on the role of so-called subordinate rituals in liberal democracies, an example of which was the ritual kidnapping of Aldo Moro by the Red Brigades. Here, the ritual kidnappings of terrorists are said to have a solidaristic function for the marginal group. Writes Moss, "The succession of ritual kidnappings has therefore been used to inscribe the passage of the Red Brigades from local, limited forms of action through to direct assault on the major political institutions of contemporary Italy."[4]

The main problem with both of the above, as well as other similar analyses, is that the application of the ritual paradigm to contemporary societies of scale, internal heterogeneity, and mass-mediated social and political communication is, as we have begun to explore, more problematic. Here it is interesting to note Frederic Jameson's discussion of a similar impulse within literary criticism as well as his critique of it. This passage is worth quoting at length. "The Cambridge School [of literary criticism], and their earliest followers among the literary critics, were indeed concerned to reground tragic and comic drama in the social life of the primitive collectivity: in that context, the interpretation of the work of art in ritual terms dictated its rewriting as a trace or survival of the ways in which the primitive collectivity came to consciousness of itself and celebrated its own social unity. Now the problem arises—and this concept begins to release its dangerous ambiguity—when we seek to transfer this model of ritual function of primitive art to the culture and the literature of modern societies: the idea of ritual indeed entails as one of its basic preconditions the essential stability of a given social formation, its functional capacity to reproduce itself over time. Ritual as an institution cannot therefore be understood except as a function of a society of this kind, as one of the fundamental mechanisms for ensuring the latter's collective coherence and historical perpetuation. It is precisely this precondition, however, which no longer holds for modern society, that is, for capitalism itself; and it would seem to me misguided, not to say historically naive, to attribute a Parsonian stability and functionality of the former primitive or tribal type to a social formation whose inner logic is the restless and corrosive dissolution of traditional social relations into the atomized and quantified aggregates of the market system."[5]

Here we may recall the discussion initiated in the Introduction of the distinction between collective reflexivity in simple and complex societies. The forms of public self-consciousness in a simple society, while they may be many and, even, contradictory, refer to a largely homogeneous population. These richly symbolic forms will appear, following Turner, in the ritual centers of these societies. Accomplishing rites of passage of various kinds, these "liminal" ritual forms serve the ultimate stability of the society by bridging moments of seasonal, life-cycle, or leadership transformation. They can also bridge moments of crisis. Thus the social drama. In a complex, multiconstituency society, the case is different. Here we must recall Turner's insistence on the *metaphorical* quality of liminal forms seeking to insert themselves into a commodity market of competing liminoid performances. The liminal is metaphorical because there is no *one* ritual center in such a society. Was *the* ritual center in the Moro social drama the Catholic church with its religious forms of prayer and its papal recognition of the humanity of the Red Brigades? Was it Parliament with its moments of silence and its rhetorical speeches against terrorism and in support of the Reason of State? Was it the Piazza with its demonstrations in support of the Resistance and Democracy, with its flags and chants? Was it the factory, temporarily transformed by its being stilled as a locus of production into a place of both state support and antistate celebration? Was it the "People's Prison" and the mass media where the various transformations of Moro took place? Was it the "bunker" courtroom in Torino where the Red Brigades historic leaders held the stage by reading communique after communique to the eager (eager for theatricality) reporters? Was it the Student House at the University of Rome where the ultraleft youth tried to codify and symbolize their position by coming up with phrases that distanced them from both the state and the Red Brigades? Or was it even outside the confines of Italy, in the United Nations of Kurt Waldheim?

What we are proposing here is that there was *no* one ritual center in the Moro social drama and that rather, as Turner indicates, the picture was one of (albeit unequal) competition among several centers of symbolic discourse. Consequently, we need to ask what the insertion of a metaphorical liminality (symbolic forms reflecting the desire to prove that there really is a united people and not just a rarely congealing conglomeration of interests) into this chaotic arena of competing voices and positions does to the various aspects (endurance, depth, certainty) of belief. What might the simple consciousness of belief *choice* (if not relativity) do to a believer? We will attempt to provide answers to such questions below.

Meanwhile, it is useful to distinguish the various corporate identities found in the Italy of 1978, to identify the separate selves of the competing forms. In Italy we indeed find many selves: the familial self (both literal and, as we have seen, metaphorical), the segmental political self (identifying oneself as Communist, Christian Democrat, etc.), the religious self, to name some of the most relevant. It is indeed in the tradition of symbolic anthropology to reference the variable relationships between notions of selfhood, the symbolic order, and power. Anthropologist Abner Cohen's dictum that a "dialectical political anthropology will have to focus on the structure of the drama in relation to power, selfhood and change"[6] is at the heart of the Moro Morality Play. For here we find the citizen fragmented into several selves with several institutional and ideological claims made on him or her. And yet, here we also find the (metaphorical) call, on the part of the no-negotiation protagonists, to the one, true church of the state. Thus, theoretically, one might anticipate that the relevant unit of analysis in a pluralistic, modern democracy would be the individual. And, indeed, the individual qua individual was represented in the Moro social drama through the aegis of the Sanctity of Human Life root paradigm. However, this paradigm was most often cast into battle with the other ultimate values, such as the Reason of State, rather than being appraised as interdependent with them. What did this spell for the competition among forms in the Moro social drama?

The claim here is that it spelled the victory of one construction of the social drama over all others. And with it came the victory of one view of the self (as sacrificial victim to the state), one view of power (unambiguously resting with the legitimate and undivided authorities who make all of the decisions), and one view of change (change is in the service of stasis). The victorious form I have called melodrama (but it is very close to what Hayden White calls Romance). This is a form which, as Turner writes, is (metaphorically) "historically continuous with ritual, and possess(es) something of the sacred seriousness, even the 'rites of passage' structure of their antecedents."[7]

Thus we come to the distinction between ritual, which we have rejected as the comprehensive idiom of the Moro social drama, and theater. And we find that the dominant framing of this event was that precise dramatic genre that most echoes the strains of ritual, albeit in a metaphorical way, melodrama.

Ritual and Theater
Before detailing the significance of the different genres of presenta-

tion of social dramas, we need to elaborate further on the distinction between ritual and theater. We need to see what the different mechanisms of belief and participation might be in the alternative modes.

First we find the issue of *optionality*, precisely the fact of alternative modes of presentation (the genres) in theater. We have spoken of the significance of choice already and will draw theoretical connections between choice and parameters of participation below. In terms of the ritual-theater distinction, general models of congregation-audience participation can be drawn for each. Rituals, while they distinguish the role of officiant, necessarily require the active participation of the relevant followers. After all, the ritual community is not merely contemplating the proceedings, it is being transformed by them. John MacAloon makes this point as he develops a conceptual matrix to distinguish among spectacle, festival, ritual, and game. And it is in his distinction between ritual and spectacle that he brings us closer to the reality of the Moro social drama: "Spectacles institutionalize the bicameral roles of actors and audience, performers and spectators. Both role sets are normative, organically linked, and necessary to the performance. If one or the other set is missing, there is no spectacle. Thus, in a strict sense, it is not the case that 'most ceremonies and rituals are spectacles,' as Max and Mary Gluckman have claimed. Certain rituals require no audience, and though rituals involve grand interests and are often visually impressive, the congregation is rarely free simply to watch and admire. If its attention to the alter, catafalque, or dance plaza is characterized by no more than 'distanced observation' it is typically thought guilty of bad faith, sacrilege, or hypocrisy likely to threaten the efficacy of the performance. Nor does ritual usually permit the optionality generic to the spectacle. Ritual is a duty, spectacle a choice. Consequently, we speak of ritual 'degenerating' (de-genre-ating) into spectacle.[8]

Perhaps the genre-rich theater is situated in a middle ground between ritual and spectacle. It shares the power of transformation with ritual and the optionality of participation and belief, along with the consciousness of its own constructedness, with spectacle.

Certainly there were many rituals "nesting" in MacAloon's term within the Moro social drama, but the dominant construction of the event was that of theater. Failure to see this prevented several interpreters from being able to account for the perplexing ending of the Moro affair with their interpretive idiom. That is, we have claimed that the Moro social drama had a bifurcated ending: it was, in Victor Turner's terminology, both a Reconciliation and a Schism. Rituals are either effective or not. They succeed or they fail. However, for certain types of social drama, namely melodrama, such a bifurcation reveals the yearning back toward ritual of a genre that attempts to deny the heterogeneity and fragmentation of modern societies: the melodramatic surface plants a simple dichotomized vision onto the complex world and then simply expels the identified villain from the society.

Cut loose from the necessary unitariness of ritual, theater allows for a greater variety of audience responses. An audience can actively participate, going on the stage as in some late sixties productions or altering the course of the story as in the experimental movies at a recent World's Fair. It can actively contemplate (a mode close to full participation), absorbing and experiencing the conflicts portrayed, as in the tragic theaters of ancient Greece, Shakespeare, and Brecht. It can passively "collaborate" (remember Craxi's words here) as in the prefixed hissing and cheering of melodramatic theater. Finally, it can simply turn the drama (televised or broadcast as it might be) off. Likewise, these are the options relevant to audiences of the theater of politics, a politics that reaches the constituency largely through the media. And it is to a discussion of the dynamics and implications of these options that we now turn.

Tragedy versus Melodrama

I have lived anguished days thinking about Moro's situation but I have always kept the fate of the democratic state, today in danger, at the forefront of my mind. If we are not strong, if we are not inflexible, instead of having a drama we will come very close to farce.[9]

There is ample evidence of the dramatic self-consciousness of the protagonists of the Moro social drama. From the farcical quality of the Red Brigades joking with the three kidnapping cars (each car appearing on the same, closely guarded, street three days in a row), to the allegations of the PCI that the image of their flags and the DC flags mingling together at the demonstrations of March 16 "accomplished" the reunification of Italy, to the mass media's self-conscious presentation of the Moro affair as a "giallo" (thriller)[10] appearing in serial form, to the no-negotiation protagonists' rhetorical combat with the root paradigms, to the state funeral without the body but with a pope and foreign dignitaries—every actor tried to symbolically upstage everyone else. And part of this upstaging was to win the war of the genres.

In the Introduction, we developed a discussion of the physiognomy of tragedy and of the connections between the tragic world-view and historical contexts in which tragedy flourished. There we saw that tragedy rested on both memory and ambiguity, on such paradoxes as presenting the point of view of the vanquished ("The Persians") to an audience flushed with victory, on a forced rethinking of the conflict between the state and civil society ("Antigone") that refused to either collapse the opposition or raise the imperatives of one realm unproblematically and vaingloriously over the other. We also saw, though, following one of Aristotle's formulations, that a tragedy could end happily, greater misfortune being cheated by a timely recognition, a new perspective. The tragic hero could be, in this case, reabsorbed by the society, bringing back with him or her the new knowledge or insight. Such a society would manage to expand its boundaries to incorporate this changed hero. Such an audience would itself be changed in the process of internalizing the conflict and its tentative and precarious (the opposing imperatives will still strain to pull apart) resolution. This audience would recognize itself as the ultimate source of the conflict and of the possibility of overcoming it. This the society of the Moro social drama could not do. As Hayden White writes: "Still the fall of the protagonist and the shaking of the world he inhabits which occur at the end of the Tragic play, are not regarded as totally threatening to those who survive the agonic test. There has been a gain in consciousness for the spectators of the contest."[11]

Melodrama, by contrast, deals with extremes. According to Peter Brooks, melodrama is an "intense emotional and ethical drama based on the manichaeistic struggle of good and evil."[12] The protagonists of melodrama, of which more below, are one-dimensional representations of clearly demarcated moral valences. Only one resolution is possible; the victory of the forces of clear good over the forces of clear evil. Only one option is afforded to the (attending) audience; to applaud the hero and boo the villain. The audience is not being asked to identify with the characters, nor to view the bifurcated world on the stage as merely two sides of a whole. There is an ultimate fear lurking behind every melodrama, the fear of annihilation, the fear (anxiously stretching back toward ritual, though ritual is irretrievable) that the gods will not be appeased. Whereas in tragedy, a humility that derives from the knowledge that the gods (metaphoric or real) will not be appeased forever is accompanied by a basic confidence in survival through regeneration.

Social dramas are similarly genre-plotted. Marx was one of the first interpreting critics to note this, as our example in the Introduction revealed. And, as opposed to some analysts of this recurrent (see Marx's Introduction to "The Critique of Hegel's Philosophy of the Right" as well as "The Eighteenth Brumaire") theme in Marx's writings who declare that Marx intended only to refer to a historian's retrospective narrative perspective imposing generic tendencies on specific historical periods, our reading of this mode of analysis claims that Marx recognized the dramatic self-consciousness of the historical protagonists themselves. This is most clear in a famous passage from "The Eighteenth Brumaire of Louis Bonaparte": "Hegel remarks somewhere that all great, world-historical facts and personages occur, as it were, twice. He has forgotten to add: the first time as tragedy, the second as farce. Caussidiere for Danton, Louis Blanc for Robespierre, the Mountain of 1848 to 1851 for the Mountain of 1793 to 1795, the Nephew for the Uncle . . . Men make their own history, but they do not make it just as they please; they do not make it under circumstances chosen by themselves, but under circumstances directly found, given and transmitted from the past. The tradition of all the dead generations weighs like a nightmare on the brain of the living. And just when they seem engaged in revolutionizing themselves and things, in creating something entirely new, precisely in such epochs of revolutionary crisis they anxiously conjure up the spirits of the past to their service and borrow from them names, battle slogans and costumes in order to present the new scene of world history in this time-honoured disguise and this borrowed language."[13]

Several genres can vie with each other to dominate a social drama. Protagonists who want to ridicule a system or other protagonists in the social drama attempt a delegitimation of them through the use of comedy. Thus did the Red Brigades joke with the

police on several occasions, taking risks that heightened their bra-
vado presentation. Thus did, with considerably less "humor," the
PCI and DC characterize the "People's Prison" as a "farce" (albeit
tragic). Contrariwise, some protagonists fear a degeneration into
comedy, as did Andreotti in the speech quoted above, of a social
drama they are trying to keep on the "legitimate" stage. And some
protagonists fear to misinterpret a serious drama as comedy, as the
deputies in Parliament did on March 16. Some protagonists, the
victors in our social drama, want the end of the plot at the beginning. In this case, melodrama, the plot is predetermined. Nothing
unexpected will be allowed to change the course, no character will
be allowed to develop, no rapprochement or even dialogue between the heroes and villains will be tolerated. Thus Moro could not
be allowed to learn anything during his captivity, to change his
perspective on his party or on Italy's youth or on power and its
perogatives and limits more generally. Certainly he could not be
allowed to learn anything about himself. Moro simply became
not-Moro. And if, as Scalfari's 1979 article in *La Repubblica* reveals, Moro was recognized as having a changed perspective, this
was immediately termed a hideous distortion. An orientation toward melodrama reveals something else as well, something else
besides fear of conflict, ambiguity, and contamination. It reveals a
fear of not being taken seriously. Thus the psychological extremes
that accompany the polarized good and evil of melodrama are taken
as proof of the seriousness and sobriety of the melodramatizing
protagonists. Thus was Zaccagnini always photographed in tears,
thus was the emotion of the no-negotiation protagonists always
cited prior to their reiteration of the hard-line. And thus did words,
specifically Moro's reasoned and complicated words, ultimately
lose out to melodramatic gestures: there was nothing that could be
said to convince the melodramatic protagonists to examine and,
possibly, change their positions. As Brooks writes: "Melodrama . . . is an expressionistic form. Its characters repeatedly say
their moral and emotional states and conditions, their intentions
and motives, their badness and goodness . . . Yet here we encounter the apparent paradox that melodrama so often, particularly in
climactic moments and in extreme situations, has recourse to non-
verbal means of expressing its meanings . . . The mute role is remarkably prevalent in melodrama."[14]

Ultimately, the most obvious feature of the attempts to control the genre of a social drama is the desire to control the ending. Turner notes this in his suggestive, if not fully developed, discussion of genre: " . . . so does the story feed back into the social process, providing it with a rhetoric, a mode of emplotment, and a meaning. Some genres, particularly the epic, serve as paradigms which inform the action of important political leaders—star groupers of encompassing groups such as church or state—giving them style, direction, and sometimes compelling them subliminally to follow in major public crises a certain course of action, thus emplotting their lives."[15]

However, a deeper impulse behind the active efforts to control the genre of a social drama is that of controlling the audience responses. Audiences of melodrama, as we have stated, are not encouraged to even do so much as to decide on the moral valences of the characters. The good guys are clearly good from the outset: they wear the white hats while the bad guys wear the black hats. Thus we note the importance of such markers as clothing. Some of the few points of emergence of tragedy in the Moro social drama did, in fact, reveal counterintuitive (given the melodramatic logic) couplings of apparel and protagonist. Here we might refer to Giorgio Bocca's "discovery" that the Red Brigades historic leaders, on trial in Torino, wore homemade sweaters. Thus, the surprising discovery that they had families (as did other Italians) and that they were loved (and thus human). We must also refer here to Moro's shirt-sleeve appearance in the Red Brigades photographs. Moro, the statesman of the dark suit worn even on family outings to the beach, was similarly revealed as human, the tragic hero in an exposed position.

Controlling the genre was particularly important during a historical conjuncture in Italy in which being "taken seriously" was both high on the agenda and seemed impossible to attain. Here we note, with sociologist Franco Ferrarotti, the fear of generic slippage: "Italian tragedy is ambiguous. It oscillates between sacrifice and pardon. The newspapers reveal (in September 1979) that in Sardinia kidnappers [of a small child] first pocketed the blackmail money and then hugged and kissed their victim whom they had held in a cave for three months, and asked him for his pardon at the moment of his release. Bandits both cruel and afraid. Aldo Moro, when he thought he had saved his life, wrote from the 'People's Prison' that the Red Brigades, his kidnappers, were generous and that he pardoned them and that, once free, he would quit the DC, the party whose president he was. In these terms, the Italian tragedy unfolds—a tragedy that, for the upside-down way in which the roles are switched, always risks transmutation into comedy, succeeding in being both desperate and unserious at the same time."[16]

Ferrarotti's interpretation, while strikingly lucid, does not indicate that such slippage was tenaciously fought in the Moro social drama and that both tragedy and comedy are the most threatening but perhaps also the most powerful and regenerating dramatic genres. Tragic social dramas recognize that they have left the sureness and homogeneousness of ritual behind. They are clearly in the realm of aesthetics, but for that they can still activate change, inspire introspection, and weave together, however temporarily, diverse sectors of a hetergeneous population. They do this through an overt focus on points of ambiguity. Tragedy is perhaps the ritual analogue of the contemporary era. The melodramatic *presentation* of the Moro social drama won the day with its assertion of ultimate Reconciliation. The *reality* of Schism, illustrated by the two opposing funerals, the short and unhappy life of the Historic Compromise (that broke up in early 1979), and the continued disaffection of the youth, belied this presentation.

As we have discussed it, theatricalized politics is neither a necessarily good or a necessarily bad thing. It is just different from ritual because it is variable in its modes of presentation. The theoretical link to the audiences of social dramas in modern societies proposes that such audiences will, in a manner congruent with the variability of presentational modes, vary in their modes of participation. While not denying individual differences in response, the possibilities of deep emotional involvement in the rituals that are included in social dramas, certain parameters of involvement and participation can be predicted theoretically. Melodrama-dominated social dramas ought to tend in the direction of intermittent identification and alienation as the audience is pulled in during the crisis to sing the praises of the "hero" but is not encouraged to contemplate or participate in a confrontation of the complexities of the moment. Tragic social dramas ought to tend in the direction of intermittent existential ambiguity and turmoil (recognition of opposing imperatives) and gains in this-worldly consciousness.

Heroes and Villains

> I have claimed that terrorism is less violent than other
> forms of political struggle, but that it disgusts us more
> than these.[17]

We may not have been surprised to find the Italian state apparatus, the newly installed government, the Catholic church hierarchy, and the establishment mass media all collaborating in the
melodramatic construction of the Moro social drama. We may,
however, have been surprised to find apparent opponents of this
ramified system, the Red Brigades, operating with the exact same
plot structure. In other words, the reified image of the world presented by the Red Brigades—that they were the avant garde of the
revolution, that they represented the Proletariat against the multinationals, that Moro personified evil—was a mirror image of that
presented by those actors inside the boundaries of the society—that
Italy was strong, that the People were Good, that Democracy and
the State would be irreparably damaged by any negotiations for
Moro's release.

One of these objects of audience consumption was the dramatic
"hero." In melodrama, the hero stands alone and must absorb the
crisis into himself/herself and be either victorious or self-sacrificing,
but in any case take the crisis off the hands of the other protagonists.
Moro drew this role but his performance of it was disquieting and
contradictory.

The exaltation of the single hero can be found across the political
spectrum in Italy. Fascists, Red Brigades, and the state all have
focused on this idea of the single savior. For the Fascists, institu-
tionally represented by the Italian Social Movement (MSI—getting
approximately 7 percent of the national vote—must declare that it is
not Fascist, for the Italian Constitution bans fascism), the hero is a
charismatic leader who would express the "spirit" of his people
whom he sees as hierarchically ordered.[18] Leftist terrorists and
anarchists have, with diverse means and ends, also elevated such
solitary activities as the "exemplary gesture" to heroic proportions.
When, for example, in March of 1921, an anarchist bombed the
Diana Theater in Milan, Gramsci responded with an assessment
that located the source of this terrorist ideology in the capitalist
system itself. He "expressed his own horror for the gesture in itself,
practically attributing the moral responsibility for it to the capitalist

system that has elevated this type of horror to a natural form of its functioning."[19]

Where right and left meet, this exhaltation of the individual action belies a pervasive elitism that is the hallmark of another Italian tradition, the tradition of the intellectual. Thus society's designated interpreters of the active protagonists of Italian social dramas are mesmerized by their own acts of interpretation. Ferrarotti writes: "The social problems of the community seem to exist, at least in their more painful and terrible aspects only in order to give the Italian intellectual the excuse for literary exercises, precious opportunities for demonstrating his stylistic skill, his sharpness as narrator or, in some cases, his non-membership in the common world."[20]

In fact, Italian intellectuals often autoidentify themselves *as* intellectuals precisely to make such a distinction. We find several examples of this in the Moro social drama. One was the April 28 petition, published in *Corriere della Sera,* signed by thirty-one "intellectuals" in defense of the state (against negotiations).

Thus a closed world of actors and actor-interpreters comes into existence, a world in which the aesthetic imperative coincides with the power imperative. In such a world, crisis resolutions are sought in the putative unique powers of individuals: Moro had the power to rescue Italy through his sacrifice;[21] the media elite had the power to explain the situation into moral coherence for the public; the no-negotiation protagonists could, by standing firm in their unanimous and exclusivist position (the public had declared, let us recall, that 60 percent favored negotiations of some kind), save Democracy. And it is the exclusion of the real public (not some vision of the People or the Proletariat) that allows us to look at the hero/villain dichotomy in a deeper way.

In a society that exalts and reifies heroes, we are bound to find degraded and reified villains. But what about in tragedy? How are heroes and villains different there? According to Northrop Frye, in tragedy, "the fiction of the fall of a leader (he has to fall because that is the way in which leader can be isolated from his society) mingles the heroic with the ironic . . . The tragic hero has to be of a properly heroic size, but his fall is involved both with a sense of his relation to society and with a sense of the supremacy of natural law, both of which are ironic in reference." The Aristotelian "tragic flaw" may be "simply a matter of being a strong character in an exposed position."[22] In other words, the tragic hero is neither all good nor all evil. The role of tragic hero must be an ambivalent one in which the hero has occasion to stumble as well as to exalt. Further, the tragic hero learns something through his/her fall, something about his or her relationship to society. Likewise, the "villains" against whom the hero is pitted cannot be personifications of evil. They must be human, and thus comprehensible too. The audience, then, is made to think and reflect on themselves. For if the protagonists are human, then they are like us and we must identify with some or all of their aspects, heroes and villains alike. And we are forced to ask, What is "terrorist" within ourselves or what could be terrorist within ourselves, or, finally, how did we create the terrorists? Such questions went largely unasked or were drowned out in the Moro social drama, and the terrorist Other was instead simply removed and tried. Reflecting on this absolutizing and depersonalizing of heroes and villains alike, Sergio Spazzali, a lawyer for political activists in Italy, stated in 1980, "The victors have decided to tell the story of a generation through judicial procedure. It is an absurd pretension but they've done it and in this way the political conditions and the technical procedure have been created which mean whatever you say it is certainly criminal."[23]

Reflecting on this depersonalization as well, and connecting it to the anxiety of a society searching for the "guilty party," French sociologist Jean Baudrillard has written: "Our paradoxical situation is the following: since nothing makes sense anymore, everything has to function perfectly. Since there is no longer a responsible subject, every event, however small, must be desperately imputed to someone or something—everybody is responsible, an unheard responsibility lingers, ready to insert itself in any accident. Every anomaly must be justified, every irregularity must find its guilty party, its criminal link. This also is terror, this also is terrorism: this search for responsibility without any proportionality with the event—this hysteria of responsibility that is itself a consequence of the disappearance of causes and of the omnipotence of effects."[24]

The frozen world of archetypal heroes and villains was temporarily and tentatively thawed by Aldo Moro, a public figure who had constructed his political identity around the blurring of boundaries and the acknowledgment, if not acceptance, of differences when the reality of differences obtruded upon his vision. At various points this had included the reality of the Socialists, the reality of the Communists, and now, to his real dismay, it included the reality of the Red Brigades. Moro's true and lucid appraisal persisted in marking the difference and distance between Moro and his captors but also attempted to recontextuate his captors and his situation within a sociohistorical frame. The discursive fabric he wove contained his party, his history in his party, the international milieu of terrorist exiles (Panama had declared itself willing to take the released terrorist prisoners in an eventual exchange), and the complicated and contradictory moralities of family, party, and state. His letters were explicitly ambivalent. The only other protagonists who resisted the lure of melodramatic polarization were those ultraleftists who persisted in calling the situation ambiguous and in declaring their distance from both extremes: the Red Brigades and the state. But neither of these two detractors from the melodrama were successful.

Cauterization: Police Powers and
Maximalist Appeals

Turning the Moro social drama into melodrama did several things for the protagonists forwarding it as their chosen genre. First, the melodrama provided a diversion, monopolizing public attention (through monopolizing the mass media, demonstrations, factory council meetings) for two months. Other public issues, such as Lockheed, lack of employment opportunities for graduating university students, inflation, wages, and cost-of-living issues, neo-Fascist violence, and the Mafia, all but disappeared. Second, the Moro social melodrama provided an opportunity for the auto-relegitimation of the major political parties. When social roles are reified into good and evil, criticism of the "good" role is viewed as inappropriate at the minimum and heresy at the maximum. Thus the rhetorical appeals to ultimate values delegitimated all criticism. This was particularly reflected in the response to and construction of the social drama of the mass media. The pluralistic and critical vision engaged by the mass media in Italy in the late sixties and early seventies that we noted in Chapter 2 appeared, to many commentators (Silj, Marletti, Bocca, Lumley, and Schlesinger), to dissipate during the Moro social drama. The heterogeneous interests represented by a heterogeneous mass media unified into one homogeneous voice. While there was no "blackout" in the sense that Red Brigades documents, news reports, and Moro's letters were broadcast and published, there was a blackout of a different kind, what Marletti called "that Italianissimo system that is the great 'caciara,' the obsessive repetition of the same news, in an ever increasingly shrill manner such that it is made to seem new, and the fracas that amplifies the voices and makes them seem more relevant and noteworthy than real news."[25] Further, as Lumley and Schlesinger report, the actual abundance of diverse discourses and messages were, to a large part, deemphasized or muffled: "Thus, during the Moro case the multiplicity of channels of information (the Moro family, the Vatican, different parties within the government) created considerable confusion. Nevertheless, in the national emergency created by the kidnapping, the press as a whole reacted by putting its faith uncritically in communiques and progress reports coming from the police. In effect, it put itself in the service of the state, publishing identikits and descriptions of wanted terrorists on request."[26]

In the background of the rhetorical appeals to democracy, the Resistance, and unity, were the numerous, and generally acknowledged to be repressive, legislative actions taken during the Moro affair. Already in the mid-seventies, several new laws, among them the 1975 Legge Reale, had introduced such provisions as provisional arrest and search by the police without the need of a judicial warrant, strict restrictions on the right to bail for terrorist suspects, and preventative detention.[27] During the Moro affair itself, several emergency bills were passed that "now made [it] possible to detain a person for up to five years and four months before the first trial, and for ten years and eight months before the final trial. On paper the legal situation had become more repressive than under the fascist regime."[28]

Several analysts of trends in contemporary democratic capitalist states, such as Italy, have identified a structural transformation in these societies that they have termed "authoritarian democracy." These analyses coincide, in many ways, with our analysis of a melodramatic mode of political presentation that tolerates only a passive collaboration from the mass constituency. Authoritarian democracy analysts "refer to longer-term changes such as the increasing autonomy of the executive from the legislature, the increasing use of intersecretarial meetings by the government parties to decide policy in a way which bypasses the Cabinet as well as

Parliament, the growth of the power of the bureaucracy over the political system and the development of new forms of representation based on the organisation of a passive consensus."[29] This describes, with much accuracy, the internal structuring of the Moro social drama. The March 16 parliamentary debates on ratification of the new government were abandoned to a panegyric of solidarity and love of country. The decision not to negotiate was made not in the Parliament, nor even in party national congresses (such as Moro attempted to convoke). It was made by the secretaries of the governing coalition. And the public's only role, as we have seen, was to support the reigning powers.

The result of these combined transformations was to make it appear as utterly obvious that the terrorist threat was both enormous and inaudible at the same time. This paradox, for paradox it was, draws our attention to the process of social transference taking place in the Italy of the Moro social drama. Clearly, Italy's problems were deep and real and broad. But like a magnet, the terrorist "threat" attracted all of the preoccupation over the many rifts in the Italian social fabric to itself. And thus was this threat blown all out of proportion. Luigi Bonante has unpeeled this disproportionality in his discussion of the suicidal logic of terrorist actions: "The monopoly of legitimate force and, in practice, the exclusive right to use (even if only in circumstances well delimited) violence, makes it such that in every case the state (victim of terrorism or itself terroristic) is immensely more powerful than its adversaries. In this context, [for an adversary] to choose violence exclusively would be suicide."[30]

In a sense, the Moro social drama did resemble a kind of mass suicide. The Historic Compromise government, risen so precipitously, set the seal on its own doom. It would soon fall by default. It had been a government of crisis. What it might have been, if Moro hadn't been kidnapped or if he had not been killed, was clearly something else, perhaps something more substantial. The Red Brigades themselves committed a kind of suicide. The Moro kidnapping had been their most ambitious project, yet through its vicissitudes they had got no closer to the class war they had set out to ignite and lead. All future operations, no matter how efficient, would be anticlimactic. The Red Brigades also, in the process of crashing up against their own limits, managed to drag much of the ultraleft down with it. Caught in the truly liminal area between the extremist positions of the terrorists and the state, the ultraleft were most vulnerable to a variety of accusations. One year later, in April 1979, scores of them would be arrested for complicity in the "armed movements."

Of most immediate interest, however, is the symmetrical, though reversed, visions of "reality" shared by the state protagonists and the Red Brigades. These antagonists both maintained an extremely one-dimensional view of a world peopled by clearly demarcated heroes and villains. No one was allowed to occupy a middle ground. Institutions and movements had, similarly, positive or negative valences. The defense of the state could not include a critique of the state. Praise for the Proletariat could not admit to worker ambivalence. The puzzling question is: How could this parallelism happen? How did melodrama come to win out over other genres of representation?

A general theory that might provide an explanation is that which can be derived from political scientist Alan Wolfe's discussion of alienated politics and sociologist Christopher Lasch's analysis of the merger of politics and spectacle in contemporary "narcissistic" society. Wolfe is fundamentally interested in the ways in which different societies come to define and live "politics." Writing about the legitimacy problems of late capitalist states, Wolfe notes the contradictory imperatives in such societies of politicizing and de-politicizing the citizenry at the same time. This energizing-enervating push and pull is motivated by the needs of political elites in capitalist democracies for an intermittently and predictably active constituency. Wolfe quotes Almond and Verba on this point: "The inactivity of the ordinary man and his inability to influence decisions help provide the power that governmental elites need if they are to make decisions. At the same time, a legitimate state can exist only when given active citizens."[31]

Wolfe then goes on to develop his theory of the ultimate effect of these contradictory imperatives, particularly in late twentieth-century American politics. He claims that they create a schizophrenic citizen, one who is intermittently pulled into the political arena (say, during elections) and then pushed out once the "moments" of mobilization are over. The grossest effect of such a process, Wolfe claims, has been the marked decrease in the simple number of people who vote (53 percent of eligible voters in the United States in 1980, e.g.). Wolfe attributes this decline to a generalized alienation among the citizenry so that they voluntarily withdraw their participation from the political arena. Here it is interesting to note Wolfe's reference to Syndey Tarrow's idea of the "dual nature" of the Italian Communist party which "stands out as a model of schizophrenic politics, trying to preserve its unique politicization while the needs of its society demand increased depoliticization."[32]

We have already seen how the decision-making process in the Italy of the Moro affair was entirely in the hands of the interparty secretariat, Parliament as well as the public significantly excluded. Thus, in a way, it was as if the two "executive" bodies, the Red Brigades and the interparty secretariat, took it upon themselves to confront each other, unencumbered by the massive and ramified ultraleft constituency on the one hand and the heterogeneous Parliament on the other. The normal discourse of both constituencies (Parliament to a greater extent) was muted or delegitimated. Lasch's theory of spectacularized politics extends this discussion as it reveals the operations of the construction and management of crises: "The art of crisis management, now widely acknowledged to be the essence of statecraft, now owes its vogue to the merger of politics and spectacle. Propaganda seeks to create in the public a chronic sense of crisis, which in turn justifies the expansion of executive power and the secrecy surrounding it."[33]

A concomitant of the depoliticization process is the depersonalization of the protagonists. Depoliticized citizens are not required to identify with their leaders, to assess praise and blame. They are required to accept the "reality" of an impersonal, bureaucratized system—so extended and so machine-like in its operations that no *particular* persons are really responsible. Certain actors of the Moro social drama were not to be identified with at all. Thus no effort was made to explore the history or possible motivations of the Red Brigades. The minute such a process was even suspected, such as the famous word "cause" that crept into Kurt Waldheim's speech, the state-supporting protagonists flew into an uproar. The most common accusation against those attempting any analysis was that they were guilty of "sociologizing." The Red Brigades were depersonalized to the point that their very membership in humanity, let alone Italian humanity, was challenged. They were monsters and beasts. Other actors would be identified with only after they had been depersonalized. Moro himself occupied such a category. Only

Moro the Martyr could be identified with, not the infinitely complex and human Moro of the letters. Even Moro's family members were depersonalized as they became merely The Family. People expected The Family to act in a certain way and so could, for example, disregard Eleonora Moro's frustrated statements that her husband was, after all the media talk about his fragility, in good health.

Modes of Mediation

Was melodrama then the inevitable victor in this competition of genres of presentation? If one follows the logic of the theories of Wolfe and Lasch, the answer would probably have to be yes. The kinds of ambiguities raised and confronted in tragedy would seem to require a different kind of political structure. It is true that Moro, the ultraleft and the Socialists, each with their own motives, got some sounding in the social drama, some time on the stage. But here it is important to note that the stage itself was a shifting one. In other words, no letter of Moro's, no statement of PSI leader Craxi, no ultraleft petition came to the Italian public unmediated, uninterpreted. We have seen ample evidence of the very different representations, in the media organs, of no-negotiation positions and pro-negotiation positions. But we must ask if the very modes of mediation themselves orient in the direction of one generic presentation over another.

Critics of television, for example, have drawn analytical attention to the isolation of the receiver in his/her home, to the sense of omnipotence (the all-seeing, larger than the people on the screen, viewer) and powerlessness, to the unidirectional message and the preclusion of dialogue in most mass media hookups. However, we have explored the conscious efforts of the ultraleft in Italy to structure their mass media organs along very different, more participatory lines. It is also true that one's experience with a newspaper is significantly different than one's experience of watching the television. For example, one can linger over a particular story in a paper, one can edit one's own reading, knowing what sections to seek out, what sections to avoid. One can read in a sequence one chooses. Television news, on the other hand, bombards one with an often unpredictable stream of news stories about violence, found pets, government controversies, neighborhood clubs, and commercials. In the case of the Moro social drama, the letters of Moro obviously could be reproduced more easily in newspapers than on television. As a result, readers could analyze these letters more thoroughly (bracketing the editing of these letters by the individual papers for a moment) than viewers. However, it seems that, given the ultimately unsuccessful example of the ultraleft, the *interaction* of the media modes with the structure of a given political system is more important than the mere fact of mass mediation.

Finally, we are left with questions. Is this aestheticization of social and political crises peculiar to Italy, or is there simply an Italian variant of a more universal phenomenon? And, what does this discovery of the aesthetic dimension of politics lead to in terms of policy recommendations? Would one interested in seeing an increase in true democracy rather than authoritarian democracy recommend, as Philip Rieff once did,[34] the displacement of the aesthetic from the realm of politics in favor of the discursive?

As to our first question above, the answer is yes and no. From Machiavelli's advice to the prince to keep the populace occupied during certain periods of the year with festivals and spectacles, to the ritual-flushed public life of renaissance Florence, to Mussolini's enormous pageants in Piazza Venezia, to the very piazza-focused architecture of Italian cities, Italians have proven themselves to be pageant masters par excellence. But the obvious Italian involvement in political theater in no way means that other political cultures, such as that of the United States, do not traffic in aestheticized politics. Surely anyone who watched the media coverage of the 1985 TWA hijacking in Beirut must have been aware of the scenography of that event. There were the interviews with the families, the three-way hookups with such "hosts" as David Hartman, a hostage, and a terrorist; there was the airport press conference and the, as mentioned in the Preface, construction of that press conference as a "display" of the hostages. Such discursive cultures as the United States mass media produces and reproduces are, it is here proposed, generally more skilled than Italy in sustaining the claim that there is no artifice, nothing aesthetically crafted about their politics. What is essentially aestheticized politics is presented as unmediated, untransformed, uninterpreted "reality." Such a claim establishes the existence of a "natural" political reality making alternative "presentations" simply unthinkable. As Ferrarotti wrote with regard to the Moro affair: "If one considers the tempo of the operation, the modality and sequencing of the communiques, the quality of the relationship with the most vast, indifferent public and the ability, in playing the sure hit with their instinctive and immediate reactions, from the fear, to the horror, to the badly hidden admiration for the demonstrated efficiency, one cannot have any doubts about the existence of a direction of rare talent, attentive to the general scene and capable of holding on to the vision of the final goal: the blocking of the evolution of Italian politics following the elections of 1976. Maybe only in the United States can one find today such talented specialists in psychological manipulation."[35]

Does this discovery of manipulation manifest in the theatricalization of politics mean that a truly democratic society would simply jettison the aesthetic from the political? I think not. We have seen that the more useful discussion of these issues must revolve around the differences among the various genres of presentation. We live in a thoroughly mediated world and therefore must accept the interpreted quality of the reality that reaches us. This reality must compel us, it must reach out to us, and, in the best of cases, it must involve us. Melodrama engages the audience differently from tragedy. The latter has a greater tolerance for ambiguity than the former. It may indeed present a vision of the world closer to the reality of complex and internally differentiated societies than melodrama. The powers representing a melodramatic view of the event were the stronger ones in the Moro social drama. But it serves the cause of historical memory to reveal the aesthetic and political choices of the vanquished as well as the victors. It may also serve us for the present.

Appendix:
Documents of the
Drama

Appeal from Pope Paul VI to the Red Brigades
(published April 23, 1978)

I write to you, men of the Red Brigades. Restore the Honorable Aldo Moro to liberty, to his family, to civil life.

I do not know you, and I have no means by which to have contact with you. Because of this I am writing publicly, taking advantage of the margin of time that remains before the deadline of the threat of death that you have pronounced against him, a good and honest Man that no one can accuse of any crime, or accuse of an insufficient social sense and of lacking in service to justice and to a peaceful civil coexistence.

I have no mandate in your regards, nor am I linked to any private interest toward him. But I love him as a member of the great human family, as a fellow student, and, particularly, as a brother of faith and as a son of the Church of Christ.

And it is in this supreme name of Christ that I address you who, certainly, will not ignore it, to you unknown and implacable adversaries of this worthy and innocent man. And I pray to you on my knees, release the Honorable Aldo Moro, simply, without conditions, not so much because of my humble and affectionate intercession, but by virture of the dignity of his brotherhood in humanity, and by virtue of, what I want to hope has force in your conscience, a real social progress that must not be dirtied by innocent blood, nor tormented by needless pain.

There are already too many victims, [who were] engaged in the fulfillment of their duty, for whom we must weep and whose deaths we must deprecate. All of us must fear the hatred that degenerates into revenge, or we yield in desperate discouragement.

Note: All translations in the Appendix are mine.

And all of us must fear God, vindicator of deaths without cause and without guilt.

Men of the Red Brigades, give me, the interpretor of the wishes of many of your co-citizens, the hope that a victorious sentiment of humanity still resides in your souls.

I wait, praying, and always loving you, for the proof.

Appeal from United Nations Secretary General, Kurt Waldheim
(published version, April 26, 1978)

I have continued to follow closely the developments of the Aldo Moro case and in diverse occasions I have formulated appeals for his liberation. Now, according to the latest information that has reached me, things have entered a decisive phase. Certainly you know that you have attracted the attention of the entire world with your requests. But you must certainly know that (Moro's) continued detention, with the terrible anguish that that provokes in his family and in all people who are everywhere following the event, must only damage your objectives, whatever they are. Therefore, I direct to you once more the most pressing appeal that you save his life. I ask you to release him immediately. Such an action would be received with relief in all of the world. And all of those who consecrate their lives to the search for a world in which a greater justice and a greater social wellbeing will reign would applaud such a move.

Letter from Aldo Moro to Minister of the Interior Francesco Cossiga
(published March 30, 1978)

Dear Francesco,

While I send you a warm greeting, I am induced by difficult circumstances to point out to you, being conscious of your responsibilities (that obviously I respect), some clear and realistic considerations. I purposely leave aside every emotional aspect and will stick to the facts. Although I know nothing of what happened or how it happened after my capture, what is absolutely beyond discussion—this has been told to me very clearly—is that I am considered a political prisoner, subject, as president of the DC, to a trial aimed at ascertaining my thirty-year responsibilities (a trial, the subject matter of which is now framed in political terms, that becomes ever more pressing).

In such circumstances, I write to you in a confidential manner, so that you and the friends, with the president of the Cabinet (obviously the president of the Republic being informed) at the head, can reflect opportunely on what to do in order to avoid worse troubles.

Think, therefore, very deeply before an emotional and irrational situation is created. I must think about the grave charge that is being leveled against me, inasmuch as I am a qualified exponent of the DC in its totality, in its directing of its political line. In truth, we are all of us of the leadership group being accused, and it is our collective operation being accused and to which we must respond. In the circumstances that I have described above, the reason of State, beyond every humanitarian consideration (that of course must not be ignored), is what counts. Above all, this reason of State signifies, taking up again the point I made regarding my actual condition, that I find myself under a full and uncontrolled domination, subjected to a popular trial the pressure of which could be easily increased, that I am, in this state, having all the consciousness and sensibility that comes from long experience, at risk of being called or induced to speak in a manner that could be unfortunate or dangerous in certain situations.

Moreover, the doctrine that says that a kidnapping must not profit (the kidnappers), already debatable in common cases where the damage of the kidnapping is extremely probable, has no bearing in political circumstances where certain and incalculable damages are incurred, not only against the person but against the State. The sacrifice of innocents in the name of an abstract principle of legality, while an undebatable state of necessity mandates saving them, is unacceptable. All of the States of the world have responded in a positive manner, with the exceptions of Israel and Germany, but not for the Lorenz case. And it cannot be said that the State loses face because it has not known how or been able to prevent the kidnapping of a high official, one who is important in the life of the State.

Returning for a moment to the behavior of States, I remember the exchanges between Breznev and Pinochet, the many exchanges of spies, the expulsion of dissidents from the Soviet territory. I understand that when an episode of this kind develops, it weighs heavily, but one also must look clearly at the worst that could happen. These are the ups and downs of a guerrilla war that one must evaluate coldly, blocking the emotions and reflecting on the political facts. I think that a precautionary step of the Holy See (or also others? Who?) could be useful. It will be convenient for the president of the Cabinet to hold very confidential contacts with a few qualified political leaders, convincing the eventual reluctant ones. An attitude of hostility would be an abstraction and an error.

Let God enlighten you as to the best, avoiding getting bogged down in a painful episode, upon which many things could depend. With most affectionate greetings.

Aldo Moro

Letter from Aldo Moro to Benigno Zaccagnini
(excerpted, full letter published April 22, 1978)

Dear Zaccagnini,

I am turning to you and in so doing I intend to address, in a most formal and, in a certain way, solemn manner, the entire Christian Democrat party, still permitting myself the privilege of addressing it as the president of the Party. This is a dramatic hour. Certainly there are problems for the country that I do not wish to ignore. But [I believe] that an equilibrated solution to them can be found, even considering security issues, but respecting that humanitarian, Christian, and democratic inspiration toward which, in analogous situations, civilized States have shown themselves to be sensitive, in the face of the problem of the salvation of innocent human life. And, in fact, in front of the Country are those problems that concern me and my family.

I do not believe that you will be able to free yourselves from these terrible and anguishing problems, even in the eyes of history, with the ease, the indifference, and the cynicism that you have manifested up to now, in the course of these forty days of my terrible suffering. It is with profound bitterness and shock that I have seen, in just a few minutes, without any serious human and political evaluation, the assumption of an attitude of rigid closure.

I have seen it assumed by the leadership, without seeing where and how such a tremendous issue as this one has been discussed.

Dissenting voices, inevitable in a democratic party such as ours, have not even been feigned. My own unhappy family has been, in a certain way, suffocated, without being able to desperately cry out its pain and its need of me. Is it possible that you are all in accord in wishing my death for some presumed reason of State that someone has lividly suggested, almost as a solution to all the problems of the Country? Other than a solution of problems, if this crime were to be perpetrated, a terrible spiral would open up that you could not begin to meet. You would be overwhelmed. A cleft would open up [between you and] those humanitarian forces that still exist in this country. And despite the first impressions, an incurable fracture in the party would open up that you will not be able to control.

I think about many, many Christian Democrats who have been, for years, accustomed to identify the party with me. I think about my friends at the base and in the parliamentary groups. I also think about my many personal friends who would not be able to accept this tragedy. Is it possible that all of these renounce, in this dramatic hour, the opportunity to have their voices heard, to be counted in the party as in other circumstances of minor importance?

I want to be clear: for my part, I will not absolve or justify anyone. I await the entire party at this test of profound seriousness and humanity, [and I await] that force of liberty and humanitarian spirit that emerges so easily and harmoniously in every parliamentary debate on such themes. I do not wish to indicate anyone in particular, but I address all. But it is, above all, the DC to whom the country turns, for its responsibilities, for the way in which it has known how to moderate wisely between reason of State and human and moral reasons. If it fails now, it would be for the first time. It would be overwhelmed by the whirlpool and it would be its end.

. . . Any opening, any problematic position, any sign of immediate understanding of the size of the problem, with the hours that race by, would be extremely important.

Say immediately that you will not give an immediate and simple answer, an answer of death. Dissipate instantly the impression of a party united around a decision of death. Remember, and all of the political forces should recall, that the republican Constitution, as a first sign of its newness, canceled the death penalty. Thus, dear friends, one wishes to reintroduce, doing nothing to prevent this, energetically creating an insensibility and blind respect for the reason of State, [this penalty] into our system. Thus, in the democratic Italy of 1978, in the Italy of the Beccaria, as in the centuries past, I am condemned to death. The execution of the sentence depends on you. I ask you at least that you grant me mercy. Grant it to me at least, as you Zaccagnini know, for the essential needs, for care, help, and guidance, of my family.

. . . Think about the sixty crucial days of crisis, lived together with Piccoli, Bartolomei, Galloni, Gaspari under your guidance and with the continual counsel of Andreotti. God knows how it was that I could do it, to have everything come out well. I didn't think, as I never have done, either about my security or my repose.

The government is on its feet and this is the recognition that I get, for this as for so many other undertakings . . . If you do not intervene, a shocking page will be written in the history of Italy. My blood will flow on you, on the party, on the Country.

. . . You, Zaccagnini, the most responsible, think above all. Remember in this moment—it must be a pungent moment of reflection for you . . . your insistence that I be President of the (DC) National Council, to have me as a participant and co-partner in the new phase that opened and that was anticipated to be very difficult. Remember my strong resistance, above all, for the family reasons that I have noted. And then I gave in, as always, to the will of the Party. And here I am, on the verge of dying, for having said yes and yes to the DC . . .

That God should enlighten you, dear Zaccagnini, and enlighten the friends to whom I address a desperate message . . . If pity prevails, the Country is not finished.

Thank you and cordial regards.

Yours, Aldo Moro

Letter from Aldo Moro to the Christian Democrat Party (excerpted, full letter published April 30, 1978)

Since my letter, which appeared in response to some ambiguous, disorganized, but substantially negative positions of the DC regarding my case, nothing has happened. Not that there wasn't much to discuss. There was plenty. What the Party, its secretary, and exponents lacked instead was the civil courage to open a debate around the proposed theme—the saving of my life and the conditions for attaining that in an equilibrated manner. It is true; I am a prisoner and I am not in a happy frame of mind. But I have suffered no coercion, I am not drugged. I write with with my own style, as ugly as it may be. I have my usual handwriting. But I am, it is said, an "other," and I do not need to be taken seriously. Thus, no one even bothers to respond to my arguments. And if I make the honest request that the directorship or another constitutional organ of the party should meet because the life of a man and the fate of his family is at stake, instead we get the continual degrading conventicles that signify fear of debate, fear of the truth, fear to sign one's own name to a death warrant.

And I must say that the fact that some friends, from Monsignor Zama, to the attorney Veronese, to G. B. Scaglia and others, without even knowing or imagining my sufferings, which haven't deprived me of lucidity and freedom of spirit, have doubted the authenticity of what I have been maintaining, as if I was writing under dictation from the Red Brigades, has saddened me profoundly [I wouldn't have believed it possible].

But why this assurance about my presumed nonauthenticity? Between the Red Brigades and myself there is not the minimum identity of viewpoint. And it is certainly not true that the position that I have held from the beginning [and, as I have demonstrated, many years ago] that it was acceptable, as happens in war, to engage in exchanges of political prisoners, gives me an identity of viewpoint [with the Red Brigades]. [This is even more crucial] when, in not exchanging, someone remains in great suffering, but alive, and the other one is killed. Concretely, the exchange benefits [and this is a point that humbly I permit myself to present to the Holy Father] not only he who is of the other side, but also he who risks death, in other words, [benefits] the noncombatant side, the common man such as myself.

. . . It is even necessary to repeat to these obstinate unmovable ones of the DC that in many cases exchanges have been accomplished in the past, all over, in order to safeguard hostages, to save innocent victims. But it must be added, so that the DC shouldn't ignore it, that the freedom [with expatriation] in a number of discrete cases has been conceded to the Palestinians, in order to ward off retaliations and reprisals capable of bringing damages to the community . . . But then the principle was accepted. The necessity to stretch the formal legal point [in exchange there was exile] was recognized . . . And let us be clear that, arranging things in that manner, as necessity decreed, there was certainly no lack of concern about interested friendly nations which, in fact, remained in friendly and trusting relations . . . And in my case, it is my death warant, substantially guaranteed by the DC, which, hardened into its debatable principles, does nothing to prevent a man, whoever he is, but then, one of its prestigious exponents, a faithful militant, from being brought to his death. A man who had closed his career with the sincere refusal of [the position of] presiding over the government, and who was literally grabbed by Zaccagnini [and by his very able, calculating friends] from his post of pure reflection and study, in order to assume the ambiguous garments of the president of the Party, for which there was not even an adequate office in all of Piazza del Gesu.

. . . Is it possible that there are no courageous ones who ask for [a formal meeting, whatever the result], as I request it with the full lucidity of my mind? Hundreds of parliamentarians wanted to vote against the Government. And now no one poses the problem of conscience? And that with the convenient excuse that I am a prisoner . . . If other formal meetings are not desired, then I have the power to convoke at a convenient and urgent date, the National Counsel, having as the theme the ways in which to remove the obstacles from its President. Thus establishing it, I delegate the Honorable Riccardo Misasi to preside.

It is known that the grave problems of my family are the fundamental reason for my fight against death. In so many years and so many occasions, the desires have fallen and the spirit has been purified. And even with my many sins, I believe I have lived with hidden generosity and delicate intentions. I die, if so decides my party, in the fullness of my Christian faith and in the immense love for an exemplary family that I adore and hope to look over from the heavens. Just yesterday, I read the tender letter of love from my wife, my children, my adored grandson and the other one whom I will not see. The pity of he who brought me the letter made him remove the surrounding [articles] that spoke of my condemnation . . .

I repeat, I do not want the men of power to accompany me. I want near me those who have truly loved me and will continue to love and pray for me. If all of this is decided, it is the will of God. But no one responsible can hide behind the fulfillment of some alleged duty. Things will clear, they will soon be clear.

                                                        Aldo Moro

Red Brigades Communique No. 1
(excerpted, published March 19, 1978)

Thursday March 16 an armed nucleus of the Red Brigades captured and sequestered ALDO MORO, president of the Christian Democrats, in a people's prison.

His armed escort, composed of five agents of the notorious Special Corps, was completely annihilated.

Who is ALDO MORO? It is quickly said: after his worthy sponsor, De Gasperi, he has been, up to today, the most authoritative leader, the undebated "theoretician" and "strategist" of that christian democrat regime that has oppresssed the Italian people for thirty years. Every step that the imperialist counter-revolution organized by the DC in our country has taken, from the bloody politics of the 50's to the turn to the "center-left," up to our own days with the "understanding of the six," has had for a godfather and most faithful executor of the directives sent from the imperialist centers, ALDO MORO. It is useless to list here the infinite number of times that Moro has been president of the Cabinet or member of the goverment as a key minister, and the innumberable tasks that he has filled in the directorship of the DC [all of this is amply documented and we will know how to best evaluate it]. It is enough to underline how this demonstrates his important role and direct responsibility, openly or "handed down in secret," in the fundamental political choices and in the actualization of the counter-revolutionary programs desired by the imperalist bourgeoisie.

Comrades, the irreversible crisis that imperialism is undergoing, while the disaggregation of its power and domination accelerates, sets off, at the same time, the mechanisms of a profound restructuration that must bring our country under the total control of the centers of multinational capital and definitively subdue the proletariat.

The transformation in Europe of the superseded liberal nation-states into Imperialist States of the Multinationals (SIM) is a process fully active in our country also. The SIM, restructuring itself, is predisposed to play the role of transmission belt for the economic-strategic interests of imperialism, and at the same time to be the organization of the preventive counterrevolution, aimed at annihilating every "foolishly ambitious" revolutionary gesture of the proletariat.

. . . This regime, this party (DC) are today the national branch, gloomily efficient, of the largest criminal multinational that humanity has ever known.

. . . It is necessary to extend and deepen the trial against the regime that the fighting avant garde has known everywhere how to demonstrate with their combatant practice. This is one of the directives by which the Movement of the Proletariat Offensive Resistance marches . . . Let it be clear then that with the capture of ALDO MORO, and the trial to which he will be subject in a Tribunal of the People, we do not intend to "end the match," nor much less to show off a "symbol," but to develop a password on which the entire Movement of Offensive Resistance is already measuring itself, to make it stronger, more mature, more incisive and organized. We intend to mobilize the most vast and unified armed initiative toward the ultimate development of the CLASS WAR FOR COMMUNISM

. . . UNIFY THE REVOLUTIONARY MOVEMENT BUILDING THE FIGHTING COMMUNIST PARTY.
3/16/78

For Communism
Red Brigades

Red Brigades Communique No. 6
(excerpted, published April 16, 1978)

The interrogation of the prisoner Aldo Moro is finished. Reviewing thirty years of christian democrat regime, running step by step over the events that have measured the actions of the imperialist counterrevolution in our country, reexamining the various moments of the plots of power, from those "peaceful ones" to the bloodiest, with which the bourgeoisie has woven its offensive against the proletariat movement, to identify, according to Moro's responses, the specific responsibilities of the DC, of each of its bosses, in the actualization of the plans desired by the imperialist bourgeoisie (whose interests the DC has always interpreted), has not done other than confirm the truth and certainty that the proletariat has had for some time. There are no secrets regarding the DC, its role as guard dog of the bourgeoisie . . . The reason is very simple.

The proletariat, the workers, all the exploited know the significance of the christian democrat regime well because it has lived and it lives off of them. They have always put up the greatest resistance against the power of the bourgeoisie. They have struggled and fought against the slavery of salaried labor, for the liberation of their infinite energy that a fistful of owners and multinationals has continually pillaged and robbed, against a State that has always aided in perpetuating the domination of the most ferocious class that history has ever produced: the imperialist bourgeoisie. What mysteries could there be of the DC regime from DeGasperi to Moro that the proletariat has not already known and payed for with their blood?

. . . To spread a cloak of counterrevolutionary terror over the entire society—that is the only system with which this State, this DC regime, supported by the infamous complicity of the so-called parties of the "left," would like to suffocate and ward off the specter of a historical judgment that the proletariat has already decreed.

There are therefore no "clamorous revelations" to make, but our task is that of all revolutionaries; to organize the proletariat, to build the force that will carry out, in a definitive way, the condemation of the bourgeoisie and of its servants.

. . . The scandals, the corruption, the complicity of the christian democrat bosses, if it makes them even more odious, is not the principle aspect . . . that which counts is the counterrevolutionary function of the DC, its "service" to the orders of the multinationals . . .

The press of the regime is always at the service of the class enemy; the lies, the mysifications—these are the rule for them. And in these days, we have had superlative proof. Its task is that of "utilizing" information as a weapon against the proletariat, the revolutionary organizations. The information that we possess, therefore, will be diffused by way of the press and the means of clandestine divulgation of the Fighting Organizations and above all will be utilized to continue with the other battles, the trial against the regime and the State.

. . . There are no doubts. ALDO MORO IS GUILTY AND THUS IS CONDEMNED TO DEATH.

. . . REUNIFY THE REVOLUTIONARY MOVEMENT BUILDING THE FIGHTING COMMUNIST PARTY.
4/15/78

For Communism
Red Brigades

Notes

Chapter 1

1. More generally, a claim can be made that our contemporary situation is one in which we seldom gain unmediated access to public events. Christopher Lasch quotes Albert Biderman in Lasch's *The Culture of Narcissism:* ". . . immediate experience with its events plays an increasingly smaller role as a source of information and basis of judgement in contrast to symbolically mediated information about these events" (New York: W. W. Norton and Co., 1979), p. 146. The significance of the variations of mediation will be addressed later in this study.

2. Two recent books that investigate police work (including the secret service investigations) during the Moro affair both point to these lacunae and begin to fill in some of the holes. They are Mimmo Scarano and Maurizio De Luca, *Il mandarino è marcio* (Rome: Editori Riuniti, 1985); and Giuseppe Zupo and Vincenzo Marini Recchia, *Operazione Moro: i fili ancora corperti di una trama politica criminale* (Milano: Franco Angeli, 1984).

3. The 1984 parliamentary investigation of the Masonic P2 Lodge eventuated in a majority and a minority report. Massimo Teodori, a Radical party deputy, wrote the minority report. In it he devotes a chapter to the failures of the various secret service and intelligence agencies to find Moro during the fifty-five days of his captivity. His purpose in doing so becomes apparent as he carefully identifies all of the directing personnel of these agencies as having been present or former members of the P2. He cites one notable case in which Gaetano Napolitano, the director of CESIS—a new institution created to coordinate the secret services and directly answerable to the prime minister—was forced, during the fifty-five days, to resign because of the lack of cooperation of the two secret services, SISMI and SISDE. Both of these latter agencies were headed by a P2 member. Napolitano was replaced by Walter Pelosi, a member of P2. Teodori speculates, as many others have, on the possible reasons for the absolute lack of success of the "police work" part of the Moro affair. He writes: "In the absence of the proven truth regarding the plot against Moro, particularly given the failure to find him, on this occasion we must conclude that the many traces of the presence of the P2 throughout this case must be

read as having been a necessary contribution to the result of the affair: the offering of the death of Moro to Italian politics as crucial for the foundations of the Republic." (*Commissione Parlamentare D'Inchiesta Sulla Loggia Massonica P2—Relazione di Minoranza* [Roma: Parliamentary Document XXIII, no. 2–bis/1, 1984], p. 69).

4. Hegel, as quoted in Hayden White, "The Question of Narrative in Contemporary Historical Theory," *History and Theory* 23, no. 1 (1984): 4.

5. Paul Ricoeur, "The Model of the Text: Social Action Considered as a Text," *New Literary History* 5 (1973): 91–117; and *Time and Narrative*, vol. 1 (Chicago: University of Chicago Press, 1984).

6. I have made use of the following works. Northrop Frye, *Anatomy of Criticism* (Princeton: Princeton University Press, 1957); Frederic Jameson, "Magical Narratives: Romance as Genre," *New Literary History* 7, no. 1 (Autumn 1975): 135–164; Thomas L. Kent, "The Classification of Genres," *Genre* 16 (Spring 1983): 1–20; Georg Lukacs, *The Historical Novel* (Boston: Beacon Press, 1963); and Jacques Derrida, "The Law of Genre," *Critical Inquiry* 7 (1980): 55–82.

7. Hayden White, *Metahistory: The Historical Imagination in Nineteenth Century Europe* (Baltimore: Johns Hopkins University Press, 1973), p. 27.

8. Joseph Gusfield, *The Culture of Public Problems: Drinking, Driving and the Symbolic Order* (Chicago: University of Chicago Press, 1981); Erving Goffman, *Relations in Public* (New York: Harper and Row, 1971); Richard Sennett, *The Fall of Public Man* (New York: Knopf, 1977); and Clifford Geertz, *Negara: The Theater State in Nineteenth Century Bali* (Princeton: Princeton University Press, 1981).

9. Claude Levi-Strauss, "The Structural Study of Myth," in *Structural Anthropology* (New York: Basic Books, 1963); Roland Barthes, *Mythologies* (New York: Hill and Wang, 1972), and "An Introduction to the Structural Analysis of Narrative," *New Literary History* 6 (1975): 237–272; Victor Turner, "Social Dramas and Stories about Them," *Critical Inquiry* (Autumn 1980): 141–168.

10. Murray Edelman, *Politics as Symbolic Action: Mass Arousal and Quiescence* (Chicago: Markham Publishing Co., 1971); Guy Debord, *Society of the Spectacle* (Detroit: Red and Black, 1970); Christopher Lasch, *The Culture of Narcissism* (New York: W. W. Norton, 1979); and Alan Wolfe, *The Limits of Legitimacy: Political Contradictions of Contemporary Capitalism* (New York: Free Press, 1977).

11. Kenneth Burke, "On Catharsis or Resolution, with a Postscript," *Kenyon Review* 21 (Summer 1959): 337–375; Will Wright, *Sixguns and Society* (Berkeley: University of California Press, 1975); Frederic Jameson, "Ideology, Narrative Analysis and Popular Culture," *Theory and Society* 4 (1977): 543–559; John MacAloon, ed., *Rite, Drama, Festival, Spectacle:*

Rehearsals toward a Theory of Cultural Performance (Philadelphia: Institute for the Study of Human Issues, 1984).

12. See Paul Veyne, *Writing History*, trans. Mina Moore-Rinvolucri (Connecticut: Wesleyan University Press, 1984); and Ricoeur, *Time and Narrative*.

13. For a full discussion of this, see Ricoeur's book.

14. Ricoeur asserts that the animus of the Braudelian project does not derive from a philosophical position on the relationship between human motivation and human efficacy. In other words, it does not derive from an analysis of teleological causality.

15. Ricoeur, *Time and Narrative*, p. 170.

16. Ibid., p. 118.

17. Karl Marx, "The Eighteenth Brumaire of Louis Bonaparte," in *The Marx-Engels Reader*, ed. Robert Tucker (New York: W. W. Norton, 1972), pp. 437–438.

18. Turner, "Social Dramas," p. 145.

19. The level of theatrical self-consciousness of protagonists in social dramas vary. This study has, as one of its tasks, the detailing of the level of self-consciousness of the Moro social drama's protagonists.

20. Victor Turner, *Dramas, Fields and Metaphors* (Ithaca: Cornell University Press, 1974), pp. 78–79.

21. Many thanks to an anonymous reader for this schema.

22. Karen Hermassi, *Polity and Theater in Historical Perspective* (Berkeley: University of California Press, 1977), p. 21.

23. Ibid., p. 86.

24. MacAloon intrudes upon Debord's universalizing indictment: "The resolution lies in recognizing the properties of spectacle as a distinct genre. The spectacle is, in itself, neither good nor bad, neither liberating nor alienating. Its moral value resides in the complicated interaction between the spectacle frame, its contents . . . and its sociocultural context. In other words, in the evaluation of particular spectacles" (from "Olympic Games and the Theory of Spectacle in Modern Societies," in MacAloon, *Rite, Drama*, p. 272.

25. This is F. L. Lucas's rendering, found in his *Tragedy* (New York: Macmillan Co., 1965), p. 25.

26. See particularly Walter Kaufmann, *Tragedy and Philosophy* (Garden City, N.Y.: Anchor Books, 1969).

27. We are assuming here that the Moro social drama did not end happily. Our notion of a happy ending will be clarified below and throughout this work. We might reveal a bit and say that a happy ending of a social drama must be both complex and ambiguous, faithfully reflecting, while approaching a resolution of, the larger conflict that launched and carried the social drama.

28. Hermassi, *Polity and Theater*, p. 83.

29. Enrico Deaglio, Lidia Menapace, and Oreste Scalzone, eds., *Sulla Violenza—Politica e Terrorismo: Un dibattito nella sinistra* (Rome: Savelli, 1978), p. xiii (all translations from Italian sources are the author's).

30. Kenneth Burke, *A Grammar of Motives* (Berkeley: University of California Press, 1969), p. xviii.

31. Abraham Miller has alluded to a kind of intuitive sense of the importance of timing and the endurance of kidnappings on the part of the police. Writing about the Hanafi Muslim episode in Washington, D.C., in 1977, Miller stated: "Police prepared for the long wait, which is the primary tactic in situations such as this, *which call for giving the drama time to unfold*" (Abraham Miller, *Terrorism and Hostage Negotiations* [Boulder, Colo.: Westview Press, 1980], p. 19).

32. For circulation figures of other newspapers surveyed for this study, see Mario Lenzi, *Il Giornale* (Rome: Editori Riuniti, 1981).

Chapter 2

1. Writing about the period 1969–1978, Sidney Tarrow has taken apart the general notion of the "Italian Crisis": "The shift to the left in national party politics from 1974 to 1976, and the involvement of the Communists in the majority in 1977–78, both extended the crisis in time and led it back from the social and economic into the political arena, where a political class skilled at bargaining, in dilatory tactics and in sectoral policies could defuse the crisis and deal with it sector by sector, in place of the general crisis that had seemed to be tightening its grip during 1974–75 . . . the politicisation of the crisis prolonged it, but also allowed the elites to deal with it as a series of separate crises, enabling them to manage the transition to a new system with a minimum threat to their own power. The 'grand coalition' was the instrument of this operation" ("Italy: Crisis, Crises or Transition?" in *Italy in Transition*, ed. Peter Lange and Sidney Tarrow [Bournemouth: Frank Cass and Co. 1980], p. 182). The "grand coalition" Tarrow is referring to here is, of course, the famous Historic Compromise government of 1978–79, which included the Communist party in the majority.

2. Norberto Bobbio, "Italy's Permanent Crisis," *Telos* 54 (Winter 1982–1983): 123–133.

3. It was indeed ephemeral but perhaps not as ephemeral as might have been expected. The "non-sfiducia" government lasted for almost one and one-half years, nearly twice the length of the average postwar government in Italy.

4. "In the years after 1968 several important transformations in social and political life take place. The university, which had been an elite institution and which had offered an authoritarian education, is forced to

open its doors and to modify its rigid structures of participation and instruction. The number of students goes from 268,000 in 1960 to 631,000 in 1971, and the number of graduates from 31,000 to 66,000. But the transformations take place chaotically. Under the pressure of the struggles, a 1969 law liberalizes access to all departments (formerly reserved exclusively to those coming from certain schools), without, however, establishing adequate structures. The rate of entry from secondary schools, which was around sixty percent in the decade 1950–1960, is around seventy-five percent following the partial liberalization in the sixties, goes beyond eighty percent in 1969, and in 1979 reaches ninety percent. The university becomes a parking lot for unemployed intellectuals and does not succeed in translating the modernizing impulse into a factor of development" (from Alberto Melucci, "New Movements, Terrorism and the Political System: Reflections on the Italian Case," *Socialist Review* [1981], p. 107).

5. "Voci e smentite sui rapporti tra Lefebvre e Vittoria Leone," *L'Unità* (Milan), 15 March 1978, p. 2.

6. "Impressive increase in violent assaults; 342 criminal episodes in the month of January—Rome and Milan head the list—five dead and 89 wounded." "The fact of the 342 politically motivated criminal acts registered in the first thirty days of this year, demonstrates also that violence and individual and collective provocation is on the increase." *L'Unità* (Milan), 4 February 1978, p. 1.

7. The participation of the ultraleft group Potere Operaio was, at best, ironic because that group had officially dissolved itself in 1973.

8. The most recent elections, those for regional administrations in June 1985, registered a significant loss for the PCI. Prior to these, the June 1984 European Parliamentary elections found the PCI in a leading position. While neither of the results of these elections alters the Italian parliamentary strength of the respective parties, they do reflect the relative support of the parties at a particular time. This was held to be particularly true during the campaign prior to the European parliamentary elections in Italy. It was claimed that these elections were of more national than European importance for Italy. The results (which must also be read in the light of the massive emotional response to Enrico Berlinguer's sudden death) were: PCI, 33.3 percent; DC, 33 percent; PSI (socialists, whose party leader, Bettino Craxi, is now prime minister), 11.2 percent. This "sorpasso" (overtaking—of the DC by the PCI) was a first for the PCI since the 1948 elections. If we look at the last national elections, however, a different picture emerges. Held in June of 1983, these elections presented the following results: PCI, 29.9 percent; DC, 32.9 percent; PSI, 11.4 percent. In these elections the PCI obtained results that were a full 6 percent lower than those obtained in the famous 1976 elections (34.4 percent), but the extra points were not reaped by the DC. This party's percentage fell even

more precipitously between the two national elections. They had actually received 38.4 percent in 1979.

9. ". . . Washington stressed the importance of the 1948 elections, painting the event more as a referendum between the East and West than a process of selecting national representatives. U.S. efforts to secure a favorable outcome knew virtually no bounds" (Paul Joseph, "American Policy and the Italian Left," in *Politics of Eurocommunism*, eds. Carl Boggs and David Plotke [Boston: South End Press, 1980], p. 357).

10. Donald Blackmer, "Continuity and Change in Postwar Italian Communism," in *Communism in Italy and France*, ed. D. Blackmer and S. Tarrow (Princeton: Princeton University Press, 1977), p. 47.

11. Ibid.

12. Steven Hellman, "The PCI's Alliance Strategy and the Case of Middle Classes," in Blackmer and Tarrow, *Communism in Italy and France*, p. 375.

13. Roberto Massari, *Marxismo e critica del terrorismo* (Rome: Newton Compton, 1979), p. 192.

14. Mimmo Carrieri and Lucio Lombardo Radice, "Italy Today: A Crisis of a New Type of Democracy," trans. Alison Anthoine, *Praxis International* (October 1981).

15. Writing about the origins of the Historic Compromise, Paolo Franchi indicates its defensive basis: "The first expression of the historic compromise, in sum, is all defensive: the risk that the radicalization of the confrontation would bring a reactionary turn was emphasized even before October of 1973 turned the Chilean tragedy into a universal lesson" ("Per una storia del compromesso," *Laboratorio Politico* 2 no. 2.3 [marzo–giugno 1982]: 44–62, 47).

16. Giuseppe Di Palma, *Surviving without Governing: The Italian Parties in Parliament* (Berkeley: University of California Press, 1977), p. 238.

17. Franchi, "Per una storia," p. 44.

18. By way of foreshadowing, we cite Franchi's analysis of the ramifications of the decision: "In sum, why did the historic compromise fail precisely when all of the prerequisites for its realization were demonstrated? . . . The national solidarity functions, in the first place, as an exchange, a reciprocal legitimation of the DC and the PCI. But this is an unequal exchange . . . The fact that the elections have two winners does not push the PCI to pose the most obvious alternative to the DC: either they go to the government together immediately or else the Communists will remain in the opposition. Such a position would have, in all probability, led to early elections, a risk that the Communist leadership did not minimally want to run. Not taking the risk, they offer to the DC an immediate relegitimation even to the point of governing a monocolor government under Giulio Andreotti, in exchange for a vague future interest . . . thus, the most

precious acquisition of decades is rapidly lost—that is, the strongly alternative character of the PCI with respect to the DC" ("Per una storia," pp. 56–57).

19. "The Victims of Violence," *L'Unità* (Milan), 2 February 1978, p. 1.

20. Martin Shefter, "Party and Patronage: Germany, England and Italy," *Politics and Society* 7 (1977): 443.

21. Ibid, pp. 444–445.

22. Douglas Wertman, "The Christian Democrats: Masters of Survival," in *Italy at the Polls, 1979: A Study of the Parliamentary Elections*, ed. Howard Penniman (Washington, D.C.: American Enterprise Institute), p. 76.

23. Ibid., pp. 73–74.

24. Giuseppe Di Palma, *Surviving without Governing*, p. 181.

25. Alan Stern, "Political Legitimacy in Local Politics: The Communist Party in Northeastern Italy," in Blackmer and Tarrow, *Communism in Italy and France*, p. 223.

26. Alberto Marradi claims that even though, in a 1975 survey, the DC was generally blamed (even by DC respondents) for the crisis, they did not suffer the loss of votes as a result. For more on this, see Wertman, "The Christian Democrats," p. 73.

27. Franchi, "Per una storia," p. 48.

28. Deaglio, Menapace, and Scalzone, *Sulla Violenza*, p. 68.

29. "Scandali e Politica," *Il Popolo* (Rome), 7 March 1978, p. 3.

30. Di Palma, *Surviving without Governing*, p. 93.

31. Brunello Mantelli and M. Revelli, eds., *Operai senza politica: Il caso Moro alla Fiat e il "qualunquismo" operaio* (Rome: Savelli, 1979), p. 146 (from an April 27 interview).

32. See Vincenzo Ferrari, "The Policy of Law and Order in Italy: The Voice of Power and its Impact," *International Journal of the Sociology of Law* 9 (1981): 25–27.

33. The sole exception to this exclusion is the case of the exceptional security measures taken in July of 1964, by carabinieri general Giovanni DeLorenzo—some claimed as part of an attempt at a coup d'état. This occurred during the tenure of one of Moro's famous center-left governments (Socialists included in the government), and it is known that Moro had a private meeting with DeLorenzo after DeLorenzo's measures were rescinded. It is not clear exactly what happened at this meeting, but presumably Moro wanted to avoid a public investigation of DeLorenzo's actions. The Socialists, however, were much angered at having been excluded. For more on this see Giorgio Galli, *Dal bipartitismo imperfetto alla possibile alternativa* (Bologna: Universale Paperbacks), *il Mulino*, no. 21 (1975): 39.

34. For the text of this interesting speech, see the collection of Moro's

writings, *Aldo Moro: L'intelligenza e gli avvenimenti: Testi 1959–1978*, intro. George L. Mosse (Rome: Garzanti, 1979).

35. Franco Ferrarotti, "Terrorism and the Tradition of Intellectual Elitism in Italy," *Praxis International* 1 (July 1981): 141.

36. Aniello Coppola, *Moro* (Milano: Feltrinelli, 1976), p. 10.

37. *Il Popolo* (Rome), 4 March 1978, p. 2.

38. Coppola, *Moro*, p. 23.

39. *L'Unità* (Milan), 5 March 1978, p. 2.

40. Carrieri and Radice, "Italy Today," p. 262.

41. Aldo Moro, "Dinamismo del centro," first published on 25 November 1944, and quoted in Giuseppe Rossini, ed., *Scritti e Discorsi di Aldo Moro*, vol. 1 (Edizioni Cinque Lune, 1983), p. 85.

42. Enrico Pozzi, "Marco Caruso e Aldo Moro: Ipotesi sulla degradazione dell'immaginario colletivo," *I Giorni Cantati* 1, no. 1 (giugno 1981): 98–108, 103.

43. Giorgio Bocca, *Noi terroristi* (Italy: Garzanti, 1985), pp. 206–207.

44. Some analysts, like Giovanni Sartori, have theorized that the reason for the "anomaly" of a small Italian Socialist party in Southern Europe was the PCI's ability, immediately after the war, to occupy the organizational void and build a mass party apparatus.

45. Franchi, "Per una storia," p. 49.

46. Di Palma, *Surviving without Governing*, p. 115.

47. Bobbio, "Italy's Permanent Crisis," p. 131. For diverse perspectives on Italian citizen participation, see Norberto Bobbio's "Italy's Permanent Crisis"; and Tarrow's "Italy: Crisis" and "Crisis, Crises or Transition?" Tarrow, in particular, takes a more positive view of the relationship between the crisis and citizenship: ". . . central to the Italian crisis has been an expansion in the meaning and the scope of citizenship and that, whatever the political solution that results, Italy may be reaching a new plateau in the integration of the working class into the political community" (from Lange and Tarrow, *Italy in Transition*, p. 166).

48. Stern, "Political Legitimacy in Local Politics," p. 237.

49. Jurgen Habermas, *Legitimation Crisis*, trans. Thomas McCarthy (Boston: Beacon Press, 1975), p. 76.

50. Stern, "Political Legitimacy in Local Politics," p. 241.

51. Robert Putnam, "The Italian Communist Politician," in Blackmer and Tarrow, *Communism in Italy and France*, p. 202.

52. Wolfe, *The Limits of Legitimacy*, p. 312.

53. Carrieri and Lombardo Radice, "Italy Today," p. 271.

54. Melucci, "New Movements, Terrorism," p. 116.

55. "The French May represented, in fact, the most important attempt to renew expressive modes, whether in terms of graphics (with the wide-

spread use of caricatures and satirical vignettes) or of language" (Patrizia Violi, *I giornali dell'estrema sinistra* [Rome: Garzanti, 1977], p. 15).

56. "The enlargement of the political code and the consequent redetermination of its lexical base make terms that normally don't enter into political discourse pertinent. The most usual are the creations of neologisms (e.g.) the case of the term ('fanfascismo'), the use of the synonyms (working class, proletariat, people), the polemical refiguring of certain terms (opportunist, revisionist and others), and even the direct use of terms redefined as 'political' taken from normal speech (creativity, verification, youth, violence etc.)" (ibid., pp. 81–82).

57. Giorgio Bocca, *Il Caso 7 aprile* (Milan: Feltrinelli, 1980), p. 56.

58. Franco Berardi, "Anatomy of Autonomia," *Semiotexte*, vol. 3 (New York: Capital City Press, 1980), p. 157.

59. Deaglio, Menapace, and Scalzone, eds., *Sulla Violenza*, p. xvi.

60. Ibid., pp. 56–57.

61. Vittorfranco Pisano, "A Survey of Terrorism of the Left in Italy 1970–1978," *Terrorism* 2 (1979): 173.

62. Lanfranco Pace and Franco Piperno, "The Recognition of the Armed Party," *Semiotexte*, vol. 3 (New York: Capital City Press, 1980), p. 241.

63. Bocca, *Il Caso 7 aprile*, p. 23.

64. Luigi Bonante, "Il teorema del terrorismo," *il Mulino*, no. 258 (luglio–agosto 1978): 591.

65. Pisano, "A Survey of Terrorism," p. 173.

66. L. Bonante et al., *Dimensioni del terrorismo politico* (Milan: Franco Angeli, 1979), p. 246.

67. On this point, see Thomas Sheehan, "Italy: Terror on the Right," *New York Review of Books*, 22 January 1981, pp. 23–26.

68. For a more detailed discussion of the Red Brigade's history, see Pisano, "A Survey of Terrorism," p. 173; Soccorso Rosso (a cura di), *Brigate Rosse—che cosa hanno fatto, che cosa hanno detto, che cosa se ne é detto* (Milan: Feltrinelli, 1976); and Alessandro Silj, *Mai più senza fucile* (Florence: Vallecchi, 1977).

69. Silj, *Mai più senza fucile*, p. 39.

70. This was not the case for the NAP, however. This Southern-based leftist terrorist group recruited largely in prisons, and the members were generally uneducated and impoverished.

71. Silj, *Mai più senza fucile*, pp. 28–29.

72. Violi, *I giornali dell'estrema sinistra*, p. 45.

73. Bocca, *Noi terroristi*, p. 132.

74. Bonante, *Dimensioni del terrorismo politico*, p. 248.

75. I say theoretically, for whether the information ultimately proves

true or not, a good number of "pentiti" have divulged enough to induce the Italian government to pass a special "legge sui pentiti" providing reduced sentences for them.

76. Lenzi, *Il Giornale*, p. 85.

77. Giovanni Bechelloni, *L'immaginario quotidiano* (Torino: ERI, 1984), p. 77.

78. Giorgio Galli, "Stampa e Cultura Politica di Massa," in *Problemi dell'informazione* 3 (1976): 452.

79. This may be a partial explanation for the fact that the adjective "objective" appeared so frequently in the various publications of Potere Operaio. The contributing scholars indeed claimed that their analyses were, and should be, objective.

80. Galli, "Stampa e Cultura," p. 453.

81. See Gusfield, *Culture of Public Problems*, and Todd Gitlin, *The Whole World Is Watching: Mass Media in the Making and Unmaking of the New Left* (Berkeley: University of California Press, 1980).

82. Kai Erikson, *Wayward Puritans: A Study in the Sociology of Deviance* (New York: John Wiley and Sons, 1968), p. 12.

83. The standard argument about media attention legitimating terrorist causes has been refuted in a study of the presentation of terrorist acts on television evening news programs. See Graham Knight and Tony Dean, "Myth and Structure of News," *Journal of Communication* 32 (Spring 1982): 144–161.

84. *La Discussione*, 3 April 1978, article of Ernesto Geminiani.

85. Giovanni Bechelloni, "Ancora su terrorismo e mass media: Il colpo di Stato in Diretta," *Problemi dell'informazione* 3 (gennaio-marzo 1978): 11–12.

86. Werner Sonne, "News Embargo in a Time of Crisis: A Challenge to the Press in a Democratic Society," unpublished manuscript, p. 2.

87. Umberto Eco, "Il silenzio è di piombo: i giornali e il dramma Moro," *L'Espresso* 24 (2 April 1978): 14.

88. Bechelloni, *L'immaginario quotidiano*, p. 84.

Chapter 3

1. *Corriere della Sera*, 2 March 1978, article by Gianfranco Pozzesi.

2. Turner, "Social Dramas," p. 150.

3. Turner, *Dramas, Fields and Metaphors*, p. 64.

4. For these legitimating processes, see Herbert Blumer, "Collective Behavior," in *New Outline of the Principles of Sociology*, ed. Alfred McClung Lee (New York: Barnes and Noble Books, 1969), pp. 65–122; Howard Becker, *Outsiders: Studies in the Sociology of Deviance* (New York: Free Press, 1963), pp. 147–163; Joseph Gusfield, *Symbolic Crusade*

(Urbana: University of Illinois Press, 1963); and Roger Cobb, Jennie-Keith Ross, and Marc Howard Ross, "Agenda Building as a Comparative Political Process," *American Political Science Review* 70 (March 1976): 126–138.

5. See particularly Gitlin, *Whole World Is Watching*.

6. Murray Edelman, *The Symbolic Uses of Politics* (Urbana: University of Illinois Press, 1964), pp. 48–49.

7. Ibid.

8. One other reason for the differing perception, along with Edelman's game/heresy distinction, is that news media journalists are more attuned to an "event" that erupts than to a process that evolves. See Gitlin, *Whole World Is Watching*.

9. Gusfield, *Culture of Public Problems*, p. 185.

10. M. Morcellini and F. Avallone, *Il ruolo dell'informazione in una situazione di emergenza: 16 marzo 1978* (Rome: Radio Televisione Italiana, 1978), p. 2.

11. Edelman, *Symbolic Uses of Politics*, p. 98.

12. Bocca, *Noi terroristi*, p. 208.

13. Antonello Trombadori, Communist deputy, quoted in *L'Unità*, 17 March 1978.

14. Silj, *Mai più senza fucile*, p. 46.

15. Deaglio, Menapace, and Scalzone, *Sulla Violenza*, p. xxiii.

16. Morcellini and Avallone, *Il ruolo dell'informazione* (transcript from *Radio Città Futura*, p. 366.

17. Ibid. (transcript RAI: TG2), p. 363.

18. Giulio Andreotti on both national television channels, 16 March 1978, 8:00 P.M. Worth quoting in full: "That which has made us most proud in the past decades has been not so much the improvement of the tenor of the life of Italian families, as the fact of having known, all of us in the political class, in different roles, how to construct a normal, tranquil life that, up to a few years ago, had not known political violence. For some time now, though, things have changed, and we find ourselves having to face, with the instruments of a democratic state—precious tools, never allow yourselves to stray into false ideas about the democratic state being weak: in the long run, the democratic state is never weak—a hostility that explodes in diverse forms, with ruthlessness, and that today has accomplished a criminal act, killing five officers of the law and capturing the Honorable Aldo Moro.

"We who are politicians, even those of us at the highest levels, certainly do not have a diverse position from the rest of the citizens, and if I speak only tonight it is not because I have not considered in the days, weeks, and years past that the substantial numbers of families in which someone has been kidnapped have not gone through an experience equally grave to that which occurred today. Rather, I speak tonight because today, this criminal act, coinciding with the parliamentary debates, has a significance that we must underline, and we must give you a statement of firmness and of calm.

"The response in Parliament, not only the accelerating of the political debate which is finishing in the Chamber of Deputies and the Senate but also in the affirmations of all political groups—and the response that was the country's with great demonstrations against violence on the part of all classes of men who left factories, offices, schools, and homes—constitute a response of solidarity with the concept of republican legality that is not rhetorical.

"All this brings us to consider if the instruments we possess are sufficient, for if they are not we must obtain those more incisive. I would hope that the sense of universal dedication, on the part of those with responsibility, would allow us to isolate those who do not want a change of the Italian society, because everyone wants this change: we have labored fifty-four days, all of the parties, even those who oppose each other, but are united in wanting a change in the South, in the youth unemployment, in the inflation that destroys the life of our families.

"We believe it necessary to isolate these germs and to prevent them from making associations such that we might be unable to confront them. We appeal, in adherence to that which the president stated this morning, to the political forces, to the unions, to the schools, to men of culture, to social forces, to the families. There are also youth, men, and women who, unfortunately, allow themselves to mobilize in support of these criminal actions. But there must be mothers, families who can, before it is too late, speak to them and make them rethink their unhappy associations.

"I think—and I must say no more tonight—that none of us must lose sight of a great goal that does not contrast in the least with that which we call firmness of the state, which is not reactionary or repressive, and that is the affirmation of the tranquility of life in all Italian cities, especially the most turbulent of them.

"I think we must appeal to the great conscience of nonviolence: the necessary work of disintoxication is no whim—we must all participate, young and old. I believe this is the most right, correct, and coherent response (besides that which the political forces will give tomorrow) to this terrible act. And, certainly, it is this that Aldo Moro has taught us for years, and it is for this that he has battled in his political life, and we must insure that he continues to battle, reinstated to that liberty, that we must do everything to insure—also to all others who are victims of kidnappers, political—I refuse to use this adjective: I would say pseudopoliticians—or common criminals as they may be: criminality knows no adjectives and is against the will of our people."

19. Morcellini and Avallone, *Il ruolo dell'informazione* (transcript of Andreotti speech), p. 364.

20. Joseph Gusfield, *Community: A Critical Response* (New York: Harper and Row, 1975).

21. Here we are stressing the alacrity with which the protagonists of the event picked up on and forwarded the idea of foreign intervention. With many lacunae about the Moro affair still remaining, no one can declare with absolute confidence that there was no foreign agency in Moro's kidnapping. But it is equally true, and we are claiming even more significant, that such a scenario would not diminish the seriousness of Italy's internal problems and youth disaffection.

22. Leonardo Sciascia, *L'affaire Moro* (Palermo: Sellerio Editore, 1978), pp. 127–128.

23. Bechelloni, "Ancora su terrorismo," p. 5.

24. Morcellini and Avallone, *Il ruolo dell'informazione* (transcript of Andreotti speech), p. 365.

25. Alessandro Silj, *Brigate Rosse-Stato: Lo scontro spettacolo nella regia della stampa quotidiana* (Florence: Vallechi, 1978), p. 29.

26. Hans-Dieter Bahr, "La macchina che attraversa il corpo: Note sul terrorismo," *AUT AUT* 175/176 (1980): 192–209, 192.

27. Massari, *Marxismo e critica*, p. 82.

28. Sabino Acqaviva, ed., *Terrorismo e guerriglia in Italia: la cultura della violenza* (Rome: Citta Nuova, 1979). p. 200.

29. Ibid., p. 198.

30. Mantelli and Revelli, *Operai senza politica*, p. 49.

31. Silj, *Brigate Rosse-Stato*, p. 113.

32. Morcellini and Avallone, *Il ruolo dell'informazione* (transcript of *Il Secolo D'Italia*), p. 445.

33. Ferrari, "Policy of Law and Order," p. 33.

34. Paul Furlong, "Political Terrorism in Italy: Responses, Reactions, and Immobilism," in *Terrorism: A Challenge to the State*, ed. Juliet Lodge (New York: St. Martin's Press, 1981), p. 73.

35. Menapace and Scalzone, *Sulla Violenza*, pp. xxvi–xxvii.

36. Morcellini and Avallone, *Il ruolo dell'informazione* (transcript of *L'Unità*, 17 March 1978), p. 449.

37. Bechelloni, "Ancora su terrorismo," p. 15.

38. Giorgio Bocca, *Moro: Una tragedia Italiana* (Milan: Bompiani Tascabile, 1978), p. 10.

39. Morcellini and Avallone, *Il ruolo dell'informazione* (transcript of *La Stampa* 17 March 1978), p. 440.

40. Ibid. (transcript of *Radio Onda Rossa*, 16 March 1978), p. 377.

41. Ibid. (transcript of TG 1, 16 March 1978), p. 356.

42. Ibid. (transcript of *La Stampa*, 16 March 1978), p. 439.

43. Frye, *Anatomy of Criticism*, p. 47.

44. Morcellini and Avallone, *Il ruolo dell'informazione* (Radio Televisione Italiana), pp. 360–361.

45. Ibid. (transcript of *Quotidiano del Lavoro*), p. 452.

46. Ibid. (transcript of Andreotti speech, 16 March 1978), p. 364.

47. Bocca, *Moro*, p. 40.

48. Although, as we have already seen, there is now some suspicion that their disorganization was overstressed.

49. Silj, *Brigate Rosse—Stato*, p. 54.

50. Morcellini and Avallone, *Il ruolo dell'informazione* (Radio Televisione Italiana), p. 447.

51. Ibid., p. 360.

52. *Corriere della Sera*, 17 March 1978.

53. *Corriere della Sera*, 10 March 1978.

54. Ibid.

55. Morcellini and Avallone, *Il ruolo dell'informazione* (transcript of *Paese Sera*, 17 March 1978), p. 444.

56. Ibid. (transcript of *L'Unità*, 17 March 1978), p. 449.

57. Bocca, *Moro*, p. 28.

58. Mantelli and Revelli, *Operai senza politica*, p. 28.

59. Silj, *Brigate Rosse-Stato*, p. 20.

60. Morcellini and Avallone, *Il ruolo dell'informazione* (Radio Televisione Italiana), p. 98.

61. Richard Trexler, *Public Life in Renaissance Florence* (New York: Academic Press, 1983), pp. 543–544.

62. Denis Mack Smith, *Mussolini: A Biography* (New York: Vintage Books, 1983), p. 127.

63. Trexler, *Public Life*, p. 515.

64. Edelman, *Symbolic Uses of Politics*, p. 13.

65. Morcellini and Avallone, *Il ruolo dell'informazione* (Radio Televisione Italiana), p. 445.

66. Mantelli and Revelli, *Operai senza politica*, p. 41.

67. Ibid., p. 39.

68. Ibid., p. 21.

69. Ibid., p. 28.

70. Ibid., p. 67.

71. Ibid., p. 64.

72. Ibid., p. 19.

73. Ibid., pp. 39, 47.

74. Ibid., p. 47.

75. Ibid., p. 64.

76. Ibid., pp. 187–188.

77. Silj, *Brigate Rosse-Stato*, pp. 24–25. Flags are potent symbols in many demonstrations. Todd Gitlin has shown how the flags of the National

Liberation Front at the anti-Vietnam war rallies were symbolically manipulated. See Gitlin, *Whole World Is Watching*, p. 118.

78. Ibid., p. 22.

79. Trexler, *Public Life*, p. 343.

80. Morcellini and Avallone, *Il ruolo dell'informazione* (Radio Televisione Italiana), p. 313.

81. "Il dibattito nel Senato," *L'Unità* (Rome), 17 March 1978, p. 2.

82. Menapace and Scalzone, *Sulla Violenza*, p. xxxi.

83. Morcellini and Avallone, *Il ruolo dell'informazione* (Radio Televisione Italiana), p. 32.

84. Bechelloni, "Ancora su terrorismo," p. 9.

85. Silj, *Brigate Rosse-Stato*, p. 30.

86. Morcellini and Avallone, *Il ruolo dell'informazione* (Radio Televisione Italiana), p. 308.

Chapter 4

1. Friedrich Neitzsche, *On the Genealogy of Morals*, trans. Walter Kaufmann and R. J. Hollingdale, ed. Walter Kaufmann (New York: Vintage Books, 1969), p. 72.

2. Silj, *Brigate Rosse-Stato*, p. 213.

3. Victor Turner, *From Ritual to Theater: The Human Seriousness of Play* (New York: Performing Arts Journal Publications, 1982), pp. 70–71 In some ways, the time frame for the Crisis phase includes nearly the entire period of Moro's sequestration—from the evening of March 16 to May 9, 1978. This is because the various phases of the social drama may overlap. The crisis may already be developing before the Breach is complete. Ultimately, it would be the Red Brigades' role to determine the end of this crisis, as the political parties of the government coalition refused to inaugurate a finale by even minimally relenting on their initial positions. An interesting question is that which asks how long a social drama can be sustained. For how many years, for example, would that small town in Pennsylvania have continued to raise daily flags for the Iranian hostages? Is there a natural life cycle for social dramas? And, did the Red Brigades have a clear, theatrical sense of the limits of the Moro drama's natural life cycle? Reflecting this sense that social dramas to have certain probable longevities is the following statement from a March 18, 1978 *Corriere della Sera* article titled "The Difficulties of the Torinese Judges on the Eve of the Red Brigades Trial": "In these slowly passing hours, there are also those who are predicting a long wait [for the kidnappers to act]. In the tactical design of terrorism, this painful Italian story could already have fixed expiration dates" (p. 4).

4. Giovanni Sartori, "From the Sociology of Politics to Political Sociology," in *Politics and the Social Sciences*, ed. S. M. Lipset (New York: Oxford University Press, 1969), p. 91.

5. Sherry Ortner, "On Key Symbols," *American Anthropologist* 75 (October 1973): 1338–1346. Morris Opler, "Themes as Dynamic Forces in Culture," *American Journal of Sociology* 51 (1945): 198–206; Victor Turner, *The Forest of Symbols* (Ithaca: Cornell University Press, 1967).

6. As Paul Furlong has noted, the actual number of individuals empowered to make the decision regarding negotiation was extremely small: ". . . at the time of the Moro kidnapping, the crucial decisions over whether or not to negotiate and what other measures to undertake were not made by parliament or by the cabinet. In particular, the decision not to negotiate was made by a small group of leading members of the national executive of the Christian Democrats in conjunction with the prime minister" (from Paul Furlong, "Political Terrorism in Italy," p. 77).

7. Morcellini and Avallone, *Il ruolo dell'informazione* (Radio Televisione Italiana), p. 308.

8. *Corriere della Sera*, 18 March 1978.

9. Bocca, *Moro*, p. 18.

10. In the local administrative elections held in late May 1978, the Socialist party increased its percentage, regaining some of the ground lost in the 1976 elections. Many interpreted this increase as a signal of voter approval for the negotiation efforts of the PSI.

11. Newspapers in this category include: *Corriere della Sera*, *La Stampa*, *La Republica*, *Il Messaggero*, and *Il Giorno*.

12. Moro's position on this issue throughout the fifty-five days of his captivity can be gauged by way of an analysis of his posted letters. The authenticity and/or sincerity of these letters was alternately granted and denied by other participants in the social drama. Such reality-determining procedures are, in many ways, at the heart of this study. In this regard, Moro's letters provided the other protagonists with visible texts accommodating post hoc rewrites aimed at proving that Moro did not mean what he wrote. In Chapters 6 and 7, those addressing the Reconciliation/Schism phase, this granted assumption will itself be focused upon as problematic. The strategy of discrediting the letters, adopted by several protagonists, rested on their contentions that these letters had false bottoms, that they were not what they seemed to be. This strategy is analyzed in the above-mentioned chapters in terms of the theatrical business it performed.

13. Negotiation was the only realistic option simply because the police were completely unsuccessful in locating the Red Brigades' hide-out throughout the fifty-five days of Moro's sequestration.

14. The DC was likewise challenged by the event, but their legitimacy as a party hinged less on the outcome of this particular event than on the

long series of scandals besetting the party and on its long history of corruption and inefficiency in governing.

15. Carl Boggs, *The Impasse of European Communism* (Boulder, Colo.: Westview Press, 1982).

16. "Despite the efforts of the secretary and the majority of the Central Committee to emphasize that the ICP would remain a "party of struggle" ("partito di lotta") even though becoming a "party of government" ("partito di governo"), during those years and months an overvaluation of (often an exclusive attention to) institutional political summit accords spread through the regional and local levels. The concern about "legitimization" ended up being a restraint on the struggles, on popular mobilization, on prompt and open criticism of bad government" (Carrieri and Lombardo Radice, "Italy Today," p. 263).

17. "While left politicians have often exaggerated the threat from far right in order to justify moderate policies, there is a realistic component to the PCI's fears. Though the far right in Italy is at present organizationally weak and lacks strong institutional support, there are features of the Italian situation that are ominously reminiscent of Europe in the period of fascism's rise. First, the economic situation is already bad and there are a number of imaginable ways in which it could become far worse. Second, the Christian Democrats—the political center—show clear indication of political paralysis . . . Finally, in this context, the rise of terrorism appears to be a serious indication of social disintegration. When these elements are put together, the result is a scenario in which the failure of the center and of the left to respond effectively to economic deterioration makes a rightist solution that would combine drastic economic measures with political repression, and seems to be the only way out" (Fred Block, "Eurocommunism and the Stalemate of European Capitalism," in Boggs and Plotke, *Politics of Eurocommunism*, p. 275).

"The terrorist project is very clear: precipitate a crisis which will lead to an authoritarian reaction, a military paradictatorship against which a mass opposition and an armed resistance will grow. And this movement will lead to a revolutionary rebirth. This is a tragically flawed project. In reality, it would halt at the point of authoritarianism destined to vanquish any space to the popular forces" (Ugo Pecchioli, Senator, PCI directorship, "Mobilitazione di Massa," *Corriere della Sera*, 18 November 1977).

18. "When in January 1978 it was faced with the actual prospect of Communist participation in both Italy and France, the Carter Administration recalled U.S. Ambassador to Italy, Richard Gardner, already a member of the hard-line current, and issued a public statement 'opposing' Communist participation in government. The statement added that the U.S. 'would like to see Communist influence in any Western country reduced'" (Joseph, "American Policy and the Italian Left," p. 367).

19. "There is no longer anyone in a position to negate that Curcio and company are the legitimate (even if repudiated) children of the PCI. The language of the Red Brigades is the same as the Communist propaganda from years ago" (Egidio Sterpa, *Il Giornale Nuovo*, 6 April 1978, as quoted in Silj, *Brigate Rosse-Stato*, p. 87).

20. "So Italian Communism, predictably enough, emerged during the late 1970s as an integral if sometimes reluctant agent of state repression, of what some referred to as the 'Germanization' of Italy. The PCI presented itself as the main defender of law and order, the indispensable champion of the political system. To support this claim, it worked closely with the DC in parliament to help enact, first, the 'legge reale' (an extension of the fascist legal code that permits sweeping police and court powers) and later, new antiterrorist legislation that drastically curtails civil liberties in 'emergency' situations and sanctions a military response to controlling social disruption. . . . Finally the PCI vigorously supported and at times even initiated governmental surveillance and arrests of leftist intellectuals and activists— in connection with the Moro episode for example . . . however much repressive measures against terrorism might be justified, the larger effect has been to accelerate the PCI's statist development" (Boggs, *The Impasse of European Communism*, p. 100).

21. Ronald D. Crelinston and Denis Szabo, *Hostage Taking* (Montreal: University of Montreal Press, 1979), p. 41.

22. For an interesting discussion of the history of the rules of war dating back to Thucydides, see Michael Walzer, *Just and Unjust Wars* (New York: Basic Books, 1977).

23. One way out of this dilemma is simply, as we have seen, to deny that the enemy indeed comes from within. This strategy, while seemingly the most efficient way of dealing with the problem, actually only serves to create another problem. If the enemy comes from without, where does it come from, and why? To some extent, the current Bulgarian Connection affair in Italy is an example of how complicated this route can become. As well, once the enemy is, once again, exogenous, negotiation again becomes possible through appeals to the extant international laws of war.

24. Edelman, *Symbolic Uses of Politics*, p. 149.

25. The variable ways of simply describing the Red Brigades omitting any mention of negotiation in their own four prior communiques, and of describing Moro's repeated references to the same in his letters, gives some sense of how enormously tricky it is to attempt to read out of the texts of victims of kidnappers their "true" motives. This, in turn, leads to the even more complicated universe of text interpretation generally. But while the latter constitutes the basic problem of an entire discipline where escape hatches from the hermeneutic circle are discovered only infrequently, the former holds the lives of individuals at stake and thus seems to require

granting the victim the benefit of the doubt. This was one thing most protagonists of the Moro social drama were unwilling to do. Crelinston and Szabo have written that "most current studies of hostage-taking are characterized by scant reference to the hostage and little regard for the potential of hostages to terminate an incident" (Crelinston and Szabo, *Hostage Taking*, p. 90).

26. Bocca, *Moro*, p. 116 (translation mine).

27. Silj, *Brigate Rosse-Stato*, pp. 205–215.

28. The full text of this appeal is reprinted in the Appendix.

29. A similar point is made in David Moss, "The Kidnapping and Murder of Aldo Moro," *European Journal of Sociology* 12, no. 2 (1981): 265–295.

30. Robert Katz, *Days of Wrath: The Ordeal of Aldo Moro* (Garden City, N.Y.: Doubleday, 1980), p. 165.

31. Silj, *Brigate Rosse-Stato*, p. 149.

32. Gustavo Selva and Eugenio Marcucci, *Aldo Moro: Il martirio di un uomo* (Bologna: Cappelli Editore, 1978), p. 84.

33. H. C. Griesman, "Social Meanings of Terrorism: Reification, Violence and Social Control," *Contemporary Crises* 1 (1977): 307. "You know, Wally," says André in the movie, *My Dinner with André*, "when you see a terrorist on the evening news, he *looks* like a terrorist."

34. Turner, "Social Dramas," p. 155.

35. Griesman, "Social Meanings of Terrorism," p. 308.

36. Cicero, "On Duties," in *Selected Works*, trans. Michael Grant (Baltimore: Penguin Books, 1967), pp. 199–204.

37. Katz, *Days of Wrath*, pp. 55–56.

38. *New York Times*, 18 April 1974, p. 17 (underline mine).

39. Delegitimation through pollution was, it is being claimed in this study, a major preoccupation of several of the Moro social drama's protagonists. Specifically, those most concerned were the Communist party and the ultraleft organizations. It is seemingly paradoxical to think of the victim of a political kidnapping being susceptible to such alleged contamination. The chapters dealing with the Reconciliation/Schism phase of this social drama will be concerned specifically with the way in which Moro himself was deemed to have been so polluted. A sacrificial principle is at work here, one in which a scapegoat is discovered/created.

40. Selva and Marcucci, *Aldo Moro*, p. 34.

41. Waldheim's contribution to this affair predates the accusations of his misrepresenting his wartime military past. Minimal as the recognition he gave to the Red Brigades was, neither the DC nor the PCI, nor any establishment mass media organ, directly addressed the Red Brigades during the entire fifty-five days of Moro's captivity. Structurally we might propose that such directly interested parties could not do so without auto-

matically opening themselves up to the accusation of granting the Red Brigades the third (highest) type of recognition, that is, addressing them as political equals. The full text of the Waldheim speech may be found in the Appendix.

42. Selva and Marcucci, *Aldo Moro*, p. 97. The full text of this appeal is reprinted in the Appendix below.

43. Selva and Marcucci, *Aldo Moro*, p. 101. Also see Appendix below.

44. Silj, *Brigate Rosse-Stato*, p. 155. Originally appeared in *La Repubblica*, 27 April 1978.

45. Selva and Marcucci, *Aldo Moro*, p. 102.

46. Ibid., p. 87.

47. Deaglio, Menapace, and Scalzone, *Sulla violenza*.

48. Morcellini and Avallone, *Il ruolo dell'informazione* (Radio Televisione Italiana), p. 370.

49. For an elaboration of this paradigm, see Alberto Ronchey, "Terror in Italy, between Red and Black," *Dissent* (Spring 1978): 150–156.

50. Morcellini and Avallone, *Il ruolo dell'informazione* (Radio Televisione Italiana), p. 308.

51. Ibid., p. 155.

52. In itself, this nonaligned formula was not without structural precedent in the history of the Italian left. An interesting previous neither/nor was that put forward by the Socialist party after Italy entered World War I: "As is known, the PSI was unique among the socialist parties of the belligerent countries of Western Europe in resisting the wave of chauvinism that swept over a large part of European public opinion and in clearly disassociating its responsibilities from those of the government. The formula with which the socialists defined their position after intervention was 'neither adhere nor sabotage,' and by and large this was respected throughout the course of the conflict" (Giuliano Procacci, "The Italian Working Class from the Risorgimento to Fascism," in *Monographs on Europe* [Cambridge, Mass.: Center for European Studies, 1979], p. 48).

53. Giorgio Bocca's book, *Il Caso 7 aprile*, on Toni Negri's arrest details the arduous attempts to find one.

54. See Suzanne Cowan, "Terrorism and the Italian Left," in Boggs and Plotke, *Politics of Eurocommunism*, p. 184.

55. Bocca, *Moro*, p. 12.

56. Acquaviva, *Terrorismo e Guerriglia in Italia*, p. 129.

57. Ibid., p. 156.

58. Peter D. Trooboff, ed., *Law and Responsibility in Warfare: The Vietnam Experience* (Chapel Hill: University of North Carolina Press, 1975), p. 11.

59. Ibid., p. 11.

60. Ibid., p. 13.

61. Selva and Marcucci, *Aldo Moro*, pp. 129–130.

62. Katz, *Days of Wrath*, p. 13.
63. Trooboff, *Law and Responsibility in Warfare*, p. 13.
64. Denis Donoghue, "The Hunger Strikers," *New York Review of Books*, 22 October 1981, p. 29.
65. Ibid.
66. Ibid.
67. "Thus . . . your appeal to consider this affair in terms of a humanitarian plan is not addressed specifically to anyone . . . No, replied Galloni [member of the DC leadership]—because if it were an appeal directed to someone then that would lead to the formal inauguration of negotiations." From an interview in *L'Unità* conducted by Antonio Caprarica; "Oggi il vertice di maggioranza sulla lotta contro l'eversione," *L'Unità* (Milan), 17 April 1978, p. 1.
68. *L'Unità* (Milan), 3 April 1978, p. 1.
69. Selva and Marcucci, *Aldo Moro*, p. 77.
70. "What is important is the process itself, the ritual, the assertion of self by the individual terrorist or group. And in this process, it is secondary rather than primary considerations that are most important. It is the fulfillment of parts of the ritual that pave the way for the denouement of the scenario, the capitulation of the terrorists. And here, the concessions that are required can be trivial. In fact, the concessions are vital for the terrorist to save face" (Miller, *Terrorism and Hostage Negotiations*, p. 33).
71. Selva and Marcucci, *Aldo Moro*, p. 20.
72. Furlong, "Political Terrorism in Italy," p. 77.

Chapter 5

1. For a good survey of many of the anthropological and sociological definitions of ritual, see Edmund R. Leach, "Ritual," *International Encyclopedia of the Social Sciences*, vol. 13, S.V. "Ritual" (New York: Free Press, 1968), pp. 520–526.
2. Susanne K. Langer, *Philosophy in a New Key* (Cambridge, Mass.: Harvard University Press, 1974), p. 49.
3. Victor Turner, "Religious Paradigms and Political Action: Thomas Becket at the Council of Northampton," in *Dramas, Fields and Metaphors*, p. 67.
4. Gusfield, *Culture of Public Problems*, p. 170. Of course, Turner's study of liminal time as the antistructure time during which new social and cultural forms are achieved points the way out of this sort of narrative fatalism.
5. Opler, "Themes as Dynamic Forces in Culture," p. 201.
6. Ibid.
7. Ortner, "On Key Symbols," p. 1338.

8. Harold Lasswell, "Key Symbols, Signs and Icons," in *Symbols and Values: An Initial Study*, ed. Bryson, Finkelstein, MacIver, and McKean (1954), p. 122.

9. Terry Turner, "Oedipus: Time and Structure in Narrative Form," in *Forms of Symbolic Action*, ed. Robert Spencer (Seattle: University of Washington Press, 1969), p. 32.

10. James W. Fernandez, "Analysis of Ritual: Metaphoric Correspondences as the Elementary Forms," *Science* 182 (1973): 1366.

11. Anthony P. Cohen, *Management of Myths: The Politics of Legitimation in a Newfoundland Community*, Newfoundland Social and Economic Studies, no. 14 (Memorial University of Newfoundland, 1975), p. 14.

12. Giorgio Galli, "I Partiti Politici," *Storia della Societa Italiana dall'Unità a oggi* 7 (1974).

13. *L'Unità* (Milan), 8 May 1978, p. 1.

14. Silj, *Brigate Rosse-Stato*, p. 102.

15. Alessandro Silj, *Mai più senza fucile*, p. 89.

16. Marletti, in Bonante, *Dimensioni del Terrorismo politico*, p. 156.

17. Morcellini and Avallone, *Il ruolo dell' informazione* (Radio Televisione Italiana), p. 337.

18. Sciascia, *L'affaire Moro*, p. 101.

19. E. Gorrieri, "Mettiamo al bando falsi scrupoli nella repressione contro le BR," in *Acquaviva, Terrorismo e guerriglia in Italia*, p. 154.

20. Bocca, *Moro*, p. 28.

21. Bernard Avishai, "In Cold Blood," *New York Review of Books*, 8 March 1979, p. 42.

22. Putnam, "Italian Communist Politician," p. 193.

23. Ibid., p. 210.

24. Antonio Carlo, "The Italian Crisis and the Role of the Left," *Telos* 42 (Winter 1979–1980): 73.

25. *Corriere della Sera* (Milan), 29 April 1978.

26. Selva and Marcucci, *Aldo Moro*, p. 44.

27. Ibid., pp. 138–139.

28. Ibid., p. 121.

29. Di Palma, *Surviving without Governing*, p. 234.

30. *L'Unità* (Milan), 24 April 1978, p. 2.

31. "Falchi e Colombe," *L'Unità* (Milan), 24 April 1978, p. 1.

32. Silj, *Brigate Rosse-Stato*, p. 95.

33. Ibid., p. 130 (from an editorial in *La Repubblica*).

34. *L'Unità* (Milan, 8 May 1978, p. 2.

35. Selva and Marcucci, *Aldo Moro*, p. 27.

36. Emile Durkheim, *Professional Ethics and Civic Morals*, trans. Cornelia Brookfield (London: Routledge and Kegan Paul, 1957), p. 57.

37. Ibid., p. 69.

38. Silj, *Brigate Rosse-Stato*, p. 130.

39. Ibid., p. 141.

40. Selva and Marcucci, *Aldo Moro*, p. 149.

41. Ibid., p. 103.

42. *Corriere della Sera* (Milan), 27 April 1978.

43. Gusfield, *Culture of Public Problems*, p. 8.

44. Morcellini and Avallone, *Il ruolo dell' informazione* (Radio Televisione Italiana), p. 439.

45. *L'Unità* (Milan), 24 April 1978, p. 3.

46. Sciascia, *L'affaire Moro*, p. 16.

47. Avishai, "In Cold Blood," p. 44.

48. Bocca, *Moro*, p. 125.

49. Katz, *Days of Wrath*, pp. 54, 282.

50. Silj, *Brigate Rosse-Stato*, p. 191.

51. Mantelli and Revelli, *Operai senza politica*, pp. 136–137.

52. Ibid., p. 137.

53. Max Weber, "Politics as a Vocation," in *From Max Weber: Essays in Sociology*, ed. Gerth and Mills (New York: Oxford University Press, 1958), p. 77.

54. Morcellini and Avallone, *Il ruolo dell' informazione* (Radio Televisione Italiana), p. 375.

55. Geertz, *Negara*, p. 121.

56. Silj, *Brigate Rosse-Stato*, p. 70.

57. Geertz, *Negara*, p. 13.

58. Friedrich Meinecke, *Machiavellism*, trans. D. Scott (New Haven: Yale University Press, 1957), p. 2.

59. Ibid., p. 12.

60. Ibid., p. 101.

61. Ibid., p. 41.

62. *Corriere della Sera* (Milan), 18 March 1978, p. 2.

63. Silj, *Brigate Rosse-Stato*, p. 70.

64. Morcellini and Avallone, *Il ruolo dell' informazione* (Radio Televisione Italiana), p. 439.

65. Ibid., p. 437.

66. Ibid., p. 444.

67. Silj, *Brigate Rosse-Stato*, p. 133.

68. Ibid.

69. Morcellini and Avallone, *Il ruolo dell' informazione* (Radio Televisione Italiana), p. 53.

70. *L'Unità* (Milan), 24 April 1978, p. 1.

71. Barbano, "Introduzione," in Bonante, *Dimensioni del terrorismo politico*, p. 18.

72. Putnam, "The Italian Communist Politician," p. 160.
73. Geertz, *Negara*, p. 133.
74. *L'Unità* (Milan), 24 April 1978, p. 2.
75. Silj, *Brigate Rosse-Stato*, p. 53.
76. Mantelli and Revelli, *Operai senza politica*, pp. 127–128.
77. Bocca, *Noi terroristi*, p. 211.
78. Mantelli and Revelli, *Operai senza politica*, p. 185.
79. Katz, *Days of Wrath*, p. 224.
80. Bocca, *Moro*, pp. 39–40.
81. Ibid., p. 44.
82. Sciascia, *L'affaire Moro*, p. 38.
83. Bocca, *Moro*, p. 37.
84. Turner, "Religious Paradigms," p. 79.

Chapter 6

1. Di Palma, *Surviving without Governing*, p. 30.
2. Franz Kafka, *The Trial* (New York: Schocken Press, 1970), p. 228.
3. Ricoeur, "The Model of the Text," p. 95. However, as Graham Knight and Tony Dean write, some readings are preferred: "Hypothetically, any test is polysemic, its signs up for grabs. In reality, the text is normally structured in such a way that 'preferred' or 'dominant' meanings are difficult to resist, and the likelihood of aberrant reading is reduced" ("Myth and Structure of News," p. 146).
4. Important works in the field of phenomenology of identity include: George Herbert Mead, *Mind, Self and Society* (Chicago: University of Chicago Press, 1934); Alfred Schutz, *Collected Papers* (The Hague: Nijoff, 1962); Maurice Merleau-Ponty, *Phenomenology of Perception* (New York: Humanities Press, 1962); Erving Goffman, *Asylums* (Garden City, N.Y.: Anchor Books, 1961); and Harold Garfinkle, *Studies in Ethnomethodology* (New York: Prentice-Hall, 1967). For "rites of passage," see Arnold L. Van Gennep, The Rites of Passage (London: Routledge and Kegan Paul; Chicago: University of Chicago Press, 1960); and Victor Turner, *The Ritual Process* (Chicago: Aldine Publishing Co., 1969).
5. Erikson, *Wayward Puritans*, p. 16.
6. As will be seen in more detail, the Christian Democrats, the Communists and the establishment mass media commenced the social drama with panegyrics and only later, in this final act, fell to denunciations of Moro. The Red Brigades began with denunciations of Moro and, quite unexpectedly, ended up elevating him. (Of course, this elevation did not prevent them from killing him.)
7. Turner, "Social Dramas," p. 151.
8. This study takes a generally agnostic position vis-à-vis Moro's letters,

as we are more concerned with analyzing the many ways in which they were read, over the course of the social drama, by the event's protagonists. However, given the analysis (below) of the various imperatives of the social drama, it must be acknowledged that no matter how lucid and familiar in style and vocabulary "Moro's" letters might have been, they had little chance of being recognized as legitimate.

9. In the last chapter, we saw why Moro's release via negotiation was an unlikely occurrence. As for the unpreparedness of the police, the Intelligence Reform Law no. 801, passed on October 24, 1977, had, among other things, brought about the separation of the intelligence and the internal security functions and had created two new services to carry out these functions. This law had been a response to the numerous accusations leveled against SID (Servizio Informazioni Difesa) Information Defense Service, the organization previously responsible for all intelligence and security work. These accusations ranged from "planning and/or participation in activities aimed as a coup d'état, abetting conspirators and inducement of political violence, to absorption of the service by U.S. intelligence." Vittorfranco Pisano, "A Survey of Terrorism," p. 7. One result of the division of this suspect service into two separate ones was that neither had access to the other's files. Both were poorly organized and spent most of their time trying to outmaneuver the other.

10. The Moro Commission was reopened (Summer 1984) to investigate these lacunae.

11. This theory is not, in itself, new. Both Leonardo Sciascia and Robert Katz have suggested as much. However, the analysis here provides evidence of precedents for such an occurrence in Moro's own political history. As well, it integrates this quasi-conspiracy theory into a more broadly sociological explanatory model.

12. There was a flickering moment, some time in 1945, while Moro was attempting to enter local (Bari) politics, when he asked to join the Socialist party. The request was merely verbal and was rescinded almost immediately by Moro. For more on this, see Coppola, *Moro*, p. 15.

13. Ibid., p. 6 (quoted from Giampiero Carocci, *Storia d'Italia dall'-Unità ad oggi*).

14. Ibid., p. 56.

15. Ibid., p. 22.

16. April 21 letter of Aldo Moro to Benito Zaccagnini. Many of Moro's letters have been published in Giorgio Bocca's book, *Moro: Una tragedia italiana*. The above letter is also found in the Appendix to this book.

17. Coppola, *Moro*, p. 48.

18. Turner, "Religious Paradigms," p. 85.

19. Turner, "Oedipus," p. 60.

20. April 5 letter of Aldo Moro to Zaccagnini. In Bocca, *Moro*, p. 114.

21. April 21 letter of Aldo Moro to Zaccagnini. Ibid., p. 127.
22. May 4 letter of Aldo Moro to Giovanni Leone. Ibid., p. 141.
23. Sciascia, *L'affaire Moro*, p. 54.
24. Turner, "Oedipus," p. 15.
25. *L'Unità* (Milan), 3 April 1978, p. 1.
26. Selva and Marcucci, *Aldo Moro*, p. 85 (April 23 quote from Zaccagnini).
27. Mantelli and Revelli, *Operai senza politica*, p. 141 (from April 21 interview).
28. Selva and Marcucci, *Aldo Moro*, p. 141, May 10.
29. Coppola, *Moro*, p. 91.
30. Ibid., p. 92 (from a speech by Moro, "Una politica per i tempi nuovi," 31 January 1969).
31. Silj, *Brigate Rosse-Stato*, p. 173.
32. The "whole story" of the Moro affair has yet to be revealed. Perhaps it never will be in any way that will satisfy all interpreters. Certainly Moro had aggravated many with his role in the "compromesso storico"; particularly the government of the United States. An analogous case, in this regard, is the assassination of President Kennedy. Conspiracy theories abound here, with evidence periodically offered to the public in the way of books, articles, and films.
33. Several authors have analyzed the Moro affair as a ritual. This study takes the position that the ritual gloss given to the Moro social drama was, in fact, merely a gloss. The reality was closer to ersatz ritual (or bad theater). We will return to this point in the conclusion.
34. Kenneth Burke, *International Encyclopedia of the Social Sciences*, vol. 7, s.v. "Dramatism" (under "Interaction") (New York: Free Press, 1968), pp. 445–451.
35. Gusfield, *Culture of Public Problems*, p. 81.
36. Selva and Marcucci, *Aldo Moro*, p. 66.
37. Henri Hubert and Marcel Mauss, *Sacrifice*, trans. W. D. Halls (Chicago: University of Chicago Press, 1973), p. 6.
38. Jane Harrison, *Ancient Art and Ritual* (London: Williams and Norgate, 1918), p. 89.
39. Franco Ferrarotti has suggested something similar in his description of Moro as a "sacrificial lamb" (personal communication).
40. Mary Douglas, *Purity and Danger: An Analysis of Concepts of Pollution and Taboo* (New York: Praeger, 1966), p. 137.
41. That Moro was, to some extent, already viewed as a collective symbol means that he was not totally profane but had something of a (incipient more than actual) sacred quality about him.
42. Morcellini and Avallone, *Il ruolo dell'informazione* (Verifica Pro-

grammi Trasmessi/Radio Televisione Italiana), pp. 438–439 (from *Il Giorno*, 17 March 1978).

43. Selva and Marcucci, *Aldo Moro*, p. 39. (March 26 entry).

44. Silj, *Brigate Rosse-Stato*, p. 171. From *Corriere della Sera*, 30 March 1978.

45. Ibid., 24 March 1978.

46. Marletti, in Bonante, *Dimensioni del Terrorismo politico*, p. 206.

47. Silj, *Brigate Rosse-Stato*, p. 176 (from *Corriere della Sera*, 14 April 1978 article by Piazzesi).

48. Selva and Marcucci, *Aldo Moro*, p. 112.

49. Ibid.

50. Goffman, *Asylums*, p. 127.

51. Silj, *Brigate Rosse-Stato*, p. 162.

52. Turner, "Social Dramas," p. 164.

53. Goffman, *Asylums*, pp. 133, 148.

54. Bocca, *Moro*, p. 113. April 5 letter of Aldo Moro to Zaccagnini.

55. Goffman, *Asylums*, as quoted in Elizabeth Burns, *Theatricality: A Study of Convention in the Theatre and in Social Life* (New York: Harper and Row, 1972), p. 136.

56. Sciascia, *L'affaire Moro*, p. 62.

57. Silj, *Brigate Rosse-Stato*, p. 131.

58. Ibid., p. 178 (from article in *La Stampa* by Spadolini).

59. Sciascia, *L'affaire Moro*, pp. 73–74.

60. James Peacock, "Society as Narrative," in *Forms of Symbolic Action*, ed. Robert Spencer (Seattle: University of Washington Press, 1969), p. 174.

61. Frye, *Anatomy of Criticism*, p. 105.

62. Lucrezia Escudero, "Il caso Moro: Manipolazione e riconoscimento," *Problemi dell'informazione* 3 (1978): 504.

63. Silj, *Brigate Rosse-Stato*, p. 29.

64. Ibid., p. 42 (from *L'Unità*, 25 March 1978, article by Pignotti).

65. *L'Unità* (Milan), 3 April 1978, p. 1.

66. Silj, *Brigate Rosse-Stato*, pp. 196–197.

67. Jean-Paul Sartre, *Nausea*, trans. Lloyd Alexander (New York: New Directions Publishing Corp., 1964), p. 39.

68. Juri Lotman, "Point of View in a Text," *New Literary History* 7 (1975): 339.

69. Ibid.

70. Arthur Lapan, *The Victim in Contemporary Literature*, vol. 1 in *Victimology: A New Focus*, ed. Israel Drapkin and Emilio Viano (Lexington, Mass.: Lexington Books, 1974), p. 203.

71. Frye, *Anatomy of Criticism*, p. 42.

72. Selva and Marcucci, *Aldo Moro*, p. 58 (April 9 entry).

73. Natalia Aspesi and Lietta Tornabuoni, eds., *CORPO: Almanacco* (Milan: Bompiani, 1979), p. 142.

74. Mantelli and Revelli, *Operai sensa politica*, p. 171.

75. Franco Ferrarotti, *L'ipnosi della violenza* (Milan: Rizzoli, 1980), p. 85.

Chapter 7

1. Bocca, *Moro*, p. 39 (from Red Brigades communique no. 2, published 25 March 1978).

2. Over four hundred jurors, judges, lawyers, politicians, and other notables were issued two to three military escorts who guarded their charges on a twenty-four-hour-day basis.

3. *Corriere della Sera* (Milan), 10 March 1978, p. 1.

4. Ibid.

5. Bocca in Bonante, *Dimensioni del terrorismo politico*, p. 227.

6. Silj, *Brigate Rosse-Stato*, p. 13.

7. Georg Simmel, "The Secret Society," in *The Sociology of Georg Simmel*, ed. and trans. Kurt H. Wolff (Glencoe, Ill.: Free Press, 1950), p. 360.

8. Bocca, *Moro*, p. 41 (March 30 letter to Cossiga from Moro).

9. Sciascia, *L'affaire Moro*, pp. 49–50.

10. Bocca, *Moro*, p. 43 (Red Brigades communique no. 3).

11. There flourished, for a brief period during the Moro affair, a debate among various newspaper editors and journalists as to the propriety and potential impact on events and public opinion of publishing terrorist documents and terrorist victims' letters. *La Repubblica*, for example, entered this debate and presented an article by Giampaolo Pansa on 22 March 1978 (eight days before Moro's first letter), reporting the responses of the editors-in-chief of eleven daily newspapers to the hypothetical situation: "If you were to receive a 'confession' of Moro, extorted from a man no longer master of himself but verifiable (by way of handwriting or voice) as authentic, a confession in which, for example, it is stated that the DC or the government had played a part in the [fascist] 'strategy of tension,' what would be your response? Would you publish it or not?" (from *La Repubblica*, 22 March 1978, p. 3). The responses were: six yes, three no, two undecided. Note the allusion to Moro as "no longer master of himself" six days after his kidnapping and prior to any news of his situation or condition. Note also, as will be seen below, there was no confession forthcoming from Moro.

12. A. J. Greimas and J. Courtes, "The Cognitive Dimension of Narrative," *New Literary History* 7 (1976): 443.

13. Silj, *Brigate Rosse-Stato*, pp. 51–52.

14. Bocca, *Moro*, p. 137 (letter to Moro family from Aldo Moro, 30 April 1978).

15. Escudero, "Il caso Moro," p. 510.

16. Ibid., p. 507.

17. Selva and Marcucci, *Aldo Moro*, p. 43.

18. Silj, *Brigate Rosse-Stato*, p. 166.

19. Selva and Marcucci, *Aldo Moro*, p. 98.

20. Not that religious figures, in an Italy as anticlerical as it is bound up with religion, are necesarily more credible witnesses.

21. Silj, *Brigate Rosse-Stato*, p. 181 (from *La Repubblica*, 23 April 1978).

22. See Katz, *Days of Wrath*, for more on the debate inside the church.

23. Escudero has written in this regard: "Thus opens the struggle to define the genre: are these political letters . . . or are these letters of a simple kidnapping victim, as many other letters, and do they therefore reside in the category of 'crime stories?'" (from "Il caso Moro," p. 512). We have mentioned the issue of *genre* several times in this study and will have occasion to take it up, at length, in the Conclusion. Here, we must recall the activity during the Breach phase to have the Red Brigades classified as "criminals," not "politicians." Thus to have declared Moro's letters "political" may have opened the door, in the eyes of the no-negotiation camp, for at least a categorization of the *event* as a political event and, at the most, a categorization of the Red Brigades' members as political. This line of thought is explicit in the following excerpt from an article that appears in *Rinascita*, the PCI magazine: "This is the technique of blackmail the 'political prisoners' experimented with; the scenographicability, the shrewd use of 'communiques,' the letters of the victim which request negotiation and thus the legitimation of the terrorists" (from Michelini, in *Rinascita* 5, 2 February 1979, pp. 4–5. As reprinted in Aquaviva, *Terrorismo e guerriglia*).

24. Meinecke, *Machiavellism*, p. 314.

25. April 21 letter to Zaccagnini.

26. Eugenio Scalfari, *La Repubblica* (Rome), 16 March 1979; Dossier no. 7: *Il Caso Moro*, p. 3, supplement.

27. Selva and Marcucci, *Aldo Moro*, p. 47.

28. Silj, *Brigate Rosse-Stato*, p. 165.

29. Sciascia, *L'affair Moro*, p. 16.

30. Simmel, "Secret Society," p. 354.

31. Bocca, *Moro*, p. 134 (letter to Zaccagnini from Moro, 25 April 1978).

32. Katz, *Days of Wrath*, p. 147.

33. George H. Gallup, *The Gallup Poll: Public Opinion 1980* (Wilmington: Scholarly Resources Inc., 1980), p. 254.

34. Sciascia, *L'affaire Moro*, p. 58.
35. Habermas, *Legitimation Crisis*, p. 36.
36. Bocca, *Moro*, p. 38 (Red Brigades communique no. 2).
37. Ibid., p. 126 (Red Brigades communique no. 7).
38. Selva and Marcucci, *Aldo Moro*, p. 74.
39. Ibid., p. 115.
40. Bocca, *Moro*, p. 141.
41. Ibid., p. 135 (25 April 1978 letter to Zaccagnini from Moro).
42. Katz, *Days of Wrath*, p. 245.

Chapter 8

1. Burke, "On Catharsis, or Resolution," p. 339.
2. Bocca, *Noi terroristi*, p. 230.
3. Pozzi, "Marco Caruso e Aldo Moro," pp. 98–108, 107.
4. Moss, "The Kidnapping and Murder," p. 275.
5. Frederic Jameson, "The Symbolic Inference; or, Kenneth Burke and Ideological Analysis," in *Representing Kenneth Burke*, ed. Hayden White and Margaret Brose (Baltimore: The Johns Hopkins University Press, pp. 84–85.
6. Abner Cohen, *Two-dimensional Man* (Berkeley: University of California Press, 1974), p. 138.
7. Victor Turner, "Liminal to Liminoid in Play, Flow and Ritual," *Rice University Studies* 60, p. 72.
8. MacAloon, *Rite, Drama, Festival, Spectacle*, p. 272.
9. 14 April 1978, Giulio Andreotti, prime minister of Italy, in a speech to Parliament. Robert Katz makes a passing remark that the Moro affair began as melodrama and ended as tragedy. Here I analyze the use of the theatrical idiom and develop a different reading of the generic choices. See Katz, *Days of Wrath*, p. xxii.
10. "After the first big news, all information of the next days will be characterized by two constant elements, (1) the obsessive reiteration of the *fact* with abundant elaboration and execration of the particulars, which, although they might be useful for a police investigation, on the mass media serve only to create anxiety and suspense in the style of the 'thriller'; (2) the continuous invention of hypothesis, mostly unfounded . . . an expectant climate is created; the information invites all to wait for the worst that must still come" (Bechelloni, "Ancora su terrorismo," p. 6).
11. White, *Metahistory*, p. 9.
12. Peter Brooks, *The Melodramatic Imagination* (New Haven: Yale University Press, 1976), p. 12.
13. Marx, "The Eighteenth Brumaire of Louis Bonaparte," pp. 436–437.

14. Brooks, *Melodramatic Imagination*, p. 57.

15. Turner, "Social Dramas," p. 153.

16. Ferrarotti, *L'ipnosi della violenza*, pp. 80–81.

17. Bahr, "La macchina che attraversa il corpo," pp. 192–209, 193.

18. Sheehan, "Italy," pp. 23–26.

19. Massari, *Marxismo e critica*, p. 167.

20. Ferrarotti, "Terrorism and the Tradition," p. 140.

21. "Mutual distrust and political rivalry of the DC and PCI have prevented a constructive national effort in the past. Can these differences be subordinated long enough to defeat or de-fang the terrorist menace? The absence of Moro himself—the great conciliator between the two leading parties—is conceded by many observers to be a handicap. *But his kidnapping and, in a sense, martyrdom, provide a new basis for cooperation"* (in Blackstone Associates, "Documents on Terrorism: Italy—Threat Assessment," *Terrorism* 2 [1979]: 288 [emphasis mine]).

22. Frye, *Anatomy of Criticism*, pp. 37–38.

23. Bob Lumley and Philip Schlesinger, "The Press, the State and its Enemies: The Italian Case," *Sociological Review*, 30, no. 4 (1982): 603–626, 613.

24. Jean Baudrillard, *Le Strategie Fatali* (Milan: Feltrinelli, 1983).

25. Marletti in Bonante, *Dimensioni del terrorismo politico*, p. 243.

26. Lumley and Schlesinger, "Press, State and its Enemies," pp. 603–626, 608–609.

27. Ibid., p. 605.

28. Ibid., p. 606.

29. Ibid., p. 605.

30. Bonante, "Il teorema del terrorismo," p. 589.

31. Wolfe, *Limits of Legitimacy*, p. 301.

32. Ibid., p. 304.

33. Lasch, *Culture of Narcissism*, p. 147.

34. Philip Rieff, "Aesthetic Functions in Modern Politics," *World Politics* 5, no. 4 (July 1953): 478–502.

35. Ferrarotti, *L'ipnosi della violenza*, pp. 89–90.

Bibliography

Acquaviva, Sabino, ed. *Terrorismo e guerriglia in Italia: la cultura della violenza*. Rome: Città Nuova Editrice, 1979.

Almond, Gabriel, and Sydney Verba. *The Civic Culture*. Princeton: Princeton University Press, 1963.

Anderson, Perry. "The Antinomies of Antonio Gramsci." *New Left Review* 100 (November 1976–January 1977): 5–78.

Arendt, Hannah. *On Violence*. New York: Harcourt, Brace, Jovanovich, 1969.

Aspesi, Natalia, and Lietta Tornabuoni, eds. *Almanacco: Corpo*. Rome: Bompiani, 1979.

Avashai, Bernard. "In Cold Blood." *New York Review of Books*, 8 March 1979, pp. 41–44.

Bahr, Hans-Dieter. "La macchina che attraversa il corpo: Note sul terrorismo." *Aut Aut* 175–176 (1980): 192–209.

Barthes, Roland. *Mythologies*. New York: Hill and Wang, 1972.

Baudrillard, Jean. *All'ombra delle maggioranze silenziose*. Bologna: Capelli, 1978.

Bechelloni, Giovanni. "Ancora su terrorismo e mass media. Il colpo di Stato in Diretta." *Problemi dell'informazione* 3 (gennaio–marzo 1978): 3–19.

Bechelloni, Giovanni. *L'immaginario quotidiano*. Torino: ERI, 1984.

Bennett, W. Lance. "Myth, Ritual and Political Control." *Journal of Communication* 30 (1980): 166–177.

Berger, Peter L., and Thomas Luckmann. *The Social Construction of Reality: A Treatise in the Sociology of Knowledge*. Garden City, N.Y.: Anchor Books, 1967.

Blackmer, Donald, and Sydney Tarrow, eds. *Communism in Italy and France*. Princeton: Princeton University Press, 1977.

Blackstone Associates. "Documents on Terrorism: Italy-Threat Assessment." *Terrorism* 2 (1979): 283–295.

Block, Fred. "The Ruling Class Does Not Rule." *Socialist Revolution* (May–June 1977): 6–28.

Bobbio, Norberto. "Italy's Permanent Crisis." *Telos*, no. 54 (Winter 1982–1983): 123–133.

Bobcock, Robert. *Ritual in Industrial Society: A Sociological Analysis of Ritualism in Modern England*. London: Allen and Unwin, 1974.

Bocca, Giorgio. *Il terrorismo italiano 1970–1978*. Milan: Rizzoli, 1978.

Bocca, Giorgio, ed. *Moro: Una tragedia italiana: Le lettere, i documenti, le polemiche*. Milan: Tascabili Bompiani, 1978.

Bocca, Giorgio. *Il Caso 7 aprile*. Rome: Feltrinelli, 1980.

Bocca, Giorgio. *Noi terroristi*. Italy: Garzanti, 1985.

Boggs, Carl. *The Impasse of European Communism*. Boulder, Colo.: Westview Press, 1982.

Boggs, C., and Plotke, D. *The Politics of Eurocommunism*. Boston: South End Press, 1980.

Bonante, Luigi. "Il teorema del terrorismo." *Il Mulino*, no. 258 (July–August 1978): 574–584.

Bonante, Luigi, ed. *Dimensioni del Terrorismo politico*. Milan: Franco Angeli, 1979.

Booth, Wayne C. "Metaphor as Rhetoric: The Problem of Evaluation." *Critical Inquiry* (Autumn 1978): 49–72.

Brooks, Peter. *The Melodramatic Imagination*. New Haven: Yale University Press, 1976.

Bufalini, Paolo. *Terrorismo e democrazia*. Milan: Editori Riuniti, 1978.

Burke, Kenneth. "On Catharsis or Resolution." *Kenyon Review* 21 (Summer 1959): 337–375.

Burke, Kenneth. *International Encyclopedia of the Social Sciences*, vol. 7, s.v. "Dramatism," pp. 445–451. New York: Free Press, 1968.

Burns, Elizabeth. *Theatricality: A Study of Convention in the Theatre and in Social Life*. New York: Harper and Row, 1972.

Carrieri, Mimmo, and Lucio Lombardo Radice. "Italy Today: A Crisis of a New Type of Democracy." Translated by Alison Anthione. *Praxis International* 1 (October 1981): 258–271.

Cicero. *Selected Works*. Translated and Introduction by Michael Grant. Baltimore, Md.: Penguin Books, 1967.

Cobb, Roger, Jennie-Keith Ross, and Marc Howard Ross. "Agenda Building as a Comparative Political Process." *American Political Science Review* 70 (March 1976): 126–138.

Cohen, Anthony P. *Management of Myths: The Politics of Legitimation in a Newfoundland Community*. Social and Economic Studies no. 14. Newfoundland: Memorial University of Newfoundland, 1975.

Coppola, Aniello. *Moro*. Milan: Feltrinelli, 1976.

Crelinston, Ronald, and Denis Szabo. *Hostage Taking*. Montreal: University of Montreal, 1979.

Davis, Howard, and Paul Walton, eds. *Language, Image, Media*. New York: St. Martin's Press, 1983.

Deaglio, E., L. Menapace, and O. Scalzone. *Sulla Violenza. Politica e terrorismo: Un dibattito nella sinistra*. Rome: Savelli, 1978.

Debord, Guy. *Society of the Spectacle*. Detroit: Red and Black, 1970.

Debray, Regis. *Revolution in the Revolution*. Translated by Bobbye Ortiz. New York: Grove Press, 1967.

Derrida, Jacques. "The Law of Genre." *Critical Inquiry* 7 (1980): 55–82.

Di Palma, Giuseppe. *Surviving without Governing: The Italian Parties in Parliament*. Berkeley: University of California Press, 1977.

Di Palma, Giuseppe. *Political Syncretism in Italy: History, Coalition and the Present Crisis*. No. 7 Policy Papers in International Affairs—Institute of International Studies, University of California, Berkeley. 1978 by Regents of University of California.

Donoghue, Denis. "The Hunger Strikers." *New York Review of Books* 22 October 1981, pp. 29–31.

Downing, John. *Radical Media: The Political Experience of Alternative Communication*. Boston: South End Press, 1984.

Eco, Unberto. "Il silenzio è di piombo: I giornali e il dramma Moro." *L'Espresso* 13 (2 aprile 1978).

Edelman, Murray. *The Symbolic Uses of Politics*. Urbana: University of Illinois Press, 1964.

Edelman, Murray. *Politics as Symbolic Action*. Chicago: Markham Publishing Co., 1971.

Erikson, Kai. *Wayward Puritans: A Study in the Sociology of Deviance*. New York: John Wiley and Sons, 1968.

Escudero, Lucrezia. "Il caso Moro: Manipolazione e riconoscimento." *Problemi dell'informazione* 3 (gennaio–marzo, 1978).

Fernandez, James W. "Analysis of Ritual: Metaphoric Correspondences as the Elementary Forms." *Science* 182, pp. 1366–1367.

Ferrari, Vincenzo. "The Policy of Law and Order in Italy: The Voice of the Power and Its Impact." *International Journal of the Sociology of Law* 9 (1981): 23–39.

Ferrarotti, Franco. "Legittimità, egemonia e dominio: Gramsci-con e contro Lenin." *La Critica Sociologica*, no. 47 (Autunno 1978).

Ferrarotti, Franco. *L'ipnosi della violenza*. Milan: Rizzoli, 1980.

Ferrarotti, Franco. "Terrorism and the Tradition of Intellectual Elitism in Italy," *Praxis International* 1 (July 1981): 140–159.

Franchi, Paolo. "Per una storia del compromesso." *Laboratorio Politico* Anno 2, no. 2.3 (marzo–giugno 1982): 44–62.

Fraser, John. "The Inner Contradictions of Marxism and Political Violence: The Case of the Italian Left." *Social Research* 48 (Spring 1981): 21–44.

Frye, Northrop. *Anatomy of Criticism*. Princeton: Princeton University Press, 1957.

Furlong, Paul. "Political Terrorism in Italy: Responses, Reactions and Immobilism." In Juliet Lodge, ed. *Terrorism: A Challenge to the State*, pp. 57–90. Oxford, Martin Robertson, 1981.

Galli, Giorgio. *Il bipartitismo imperfetto: comunisti e democristiani in Italia*. Bologna: Il Mulino 1967.

Galli, Giorgio. *Storia della Societa Italiana dall-Unità a oggi*. Turin: UTET, 1974.

Galli, Giorgio. "Stampa e cultura politica di massa." *Problemi dell'informazione* 3 (1976): 451–455.

Galli, Giorgio. *La Sinistra Italiana nel dopoguerra*. Milan: Il Saggiatore, 1978.

Galli, Giorgio. *Storia della DC*. Rome: Editori Laterza, 1978.

Gallup, George H. *The Gallup Poll: Public Opinion 1980*. Wilmington: Scholarly Resources, 1981.

Galli, Giorgio, and Prandi, A. *Patterns of Political Participation in Italy*. New Haven: Yale University, 1970.

Garfinkle, Harold. "Conditions of Successful Degradation Ceremonies." *American Journal of Sociology* 61, pp. 420–424.

Geertz, Clifford. *Negara: The Theatre State in Nineteenth Century Bali*. Princeton: Princeton University Press, 1981.

Gilio, Maria Esther. *The Tupamaro Guerrillas: The Structure and Strategy of the Urban Guerrilla Movement*. Translated by Anne Edmondson. Introduction by Robert J. Alexander. New York: Saturday Review Press, 1970.

Gitlin, Todd. *The Whole World Is Watching: Mass Media in the Making and Unmaking of the New Left*. Berkeley: University of California Press, 1980.

Goffman, Erving. *Asylums*. Garden City, N.Y.: Anchor Books, 1961.

Goffman, Erving. *Stigma*. Englewood Cliffs, N.J.: Prentice-Hall, 1963.

Gramsci, Antonio. "Note Sul Machiavelli." In *Quaderni dal carcere*. Edited by Valentino Gerratana. Turin: Editori Riuniti, 1975.

Greimas, A. J., and J. Courtes. "The Cognitive Dimension of Narrative." *New Literary History* 7 (1976): 443–448.

Gusfield, Joseph. *Community: A Critical Response*. New York: Harper and Row, 1975.

Gusfield, Joseph. *Symbolic Crusade: Status Politics and the American Temperance Movement*. Urbana: University of Illinois Press, 1976.

Gusfield, Joseph. *The Culture of Public Problems: Drinking, Driving and the Symbolic Order*. Chicago: University of Chicago Press, 1981.

Habermas, Jurgen. *Legitimation Crisis*. Translated by Thomas McCarthy. Boston: Beacon Press, 1975.

Halloran, James D., Philip Elliott, and Graham Murdock. *Demonstrations and Communication: A Case Study*. Middlesex, England: Penguin Books, 1970.

Harrison, Jane. *Ancient Art and Ritual*. London: Williams and Norgate, 1918.

Hermassi, Karen. *Polity and Theater in Historical Perspective*. Berkeley: University of California Press, 1977.

Hobsbawm, E. J. *Bandits*. Bungay, Suffolk: Pelican Books, 1969.

Hubert, Henri, and Marcel Mauss. *Sacrifice*. Translated by W. D. Halls. Foreword by Evans Pritchard. Chicago: University of Chicago Press, 1973.

Hunt, Lynn. *Politics, Culture, and Class in the French Revolution*. Berkeley: University of California Press, 1984.

Jameson, Frederic. "Magical Narratives: Romance as Genre." *New Literary History* 7, no. 1 (Autumn 1975): 135–164.

Jameson, Frederic. "Ideology, Narrative Analysis and Popular Culture." *Theory and Society* 4 (1977): 543–559.

Jameson, Frederic. "The Symbolic Inference: On Kenneth Burke and Ideological Analysis." In Hayden White and Margaret Brose, eds. *Representing Kenneth Burke*. Baltimore: Johns Hopkins, 1982.

Jemolo, Arturo, *Church and State in Italy*. Philadelphia: DuFour Editions, 1961.

Karabel, Jerome. "Revolutionary Contradictions: Antonio Gramsci and the Problem of Intellectuals." *Politics and Society* 6 (1976): 123–172.

Katz, Robert. *Days of Wrath: The Ordeal of Aldo Moro*. Garden City, N.Y.: Doubleday, 1980.

Kaufmann, Walter. *Tragedy and Philosophy*. Garden City, N.Y.: Anchor Books, 1969.

Klapp, Orrin E. *Symbolic Leaders: Public Dramas and Public Men*. Chicago: Aldine Publishing Co., 1964.

Knight, Graham, and Tony Dean. "Myth and Structure of News." *Journal of Communication* 32 (Spring 1982): 144–161.

Kupperman, Robert. "Facing Tomorrow's Terrorist Incident Today." U.S. Department of Justice Law Enforcement Assistant Administration, Washington, D.C., 1977.

Lange, Peter, and Sidney Tarrow, eds. *Italy in Transition*. Bournemouth: Frank Cass and Co., 1980.

Langer, Susanne K. *Philosophy in a New Key*. Cambridge, Mass.: Harvard University Press, 1974.

La Palombara, Joseph. "Italy: Fragmentation, Isolation and Alienation." In *Political Culture and Political Development*, pp. 282–329. Edited by Pye, Lucian and Sydney Verba. Princeton: Princeton University Press, 1965.

Lapan, Arthur. "The Victim in Contemporary Literature." In Israel Drapkin and Emilio Viano, eds. *Victimology: A New Focus on Theoretical Issues in Victimology*. Vol. 1. Lexington Books, 1974.

Laquer, Walter. *Terrorism*. Boston: Little, Brown and Co., 1977.

Lasch, Christopher. *The Culture of Narcissism*. New York: W. W. Norton and Co., 1979.

Leach, Edmund R. *International Encyclopedia of the Social Sciences*, vol. 13, s.v. "Ritual," pp. 520–526. New York: Free Press, 1968.

Lenzi, Mario. *Il Giornale*. Rome: Editori Riuniti, 1981.

Levi-Strauss, Claude. *Structural Anthropology*. New York: Basic Books, 1963.

Lipset, S. M. "Opinion Formation in a Crisis Situation." *Public Opinion Quarterly* 17 (1953): 20–46.

Lipset, S. M., ed. *Politics and the Social Sciences*. New York: Oxford University Press, 1969.

Lodge, Juliet, ed. *Terrorism: A Challenge to the State*. New York: St. Martin's Press, 1981.

Lotman, Juri. "Point of View in a Text." *New Literary History* 7 (1975): 339–352.

Lukacs, Gyorgy. *The Historical Novel*. Translated by H. Mitchell and S. Mitchell. London: Merlin Press, 1962.

Lumley, Bob, and Philip Schlesinger. "The Press, the State and Its Enemies, the Italian Case." *Sociological Review* 30, no. 4 (1982): 603–626.

MacAloon, John, ed. *Rite, Drama, Festival, Spectacle: Rehearsals toward a Theory of Cultural Performance*. Philadelphia: Institute for the Study of Human Issues, 1984.

Mack Smith, Denis. *Mussolini: A Biography*. New York: Vintage Books, 1983.

Mantelli, Brunello, and Marco Revelli, eds. *Operai senza politica. Il caso Moro alla Fiat e il "qualunquismo" operaio*. Rome: Savelli, 1979.

Massari, Roberto. *Marxismo e critica del Terrorismo*. Rome: Newton Co., 1979.

Mazzetti, R. *Genesi del terrorismo in Italia*. Rome: Armando Editore, 1979.

Meinecke, Friedrich. *Machiavellism*. Translated by Douglas Scott. Introduction by W. Stark. New Haven: Yale University Press, 1957.

Melucci, Alberto. "New Movements, Terrorism and the Political System: Reflections on the Italian Case." *Socialist Review* (1981): 97–136.

Michels, Robert. *Political Parties*. Translated by Eden Paul and Cedar Paul. New York: Dover Publishing Co., 1959.

Miller, Abraham H. *Terrorism and Hostage Negotiations*. Westview Special Studies in National and International Terrorism. Boulder, Colo.: Westview Press, 1980.

Mills, C. Wright. *The Sociological Imagination*. New York: Oxford University Press, 1959.

Molotch, Harvey, and Marilyn Lester. "News as Purposive Behavior: On the Strategic Use of Routine Events, Accidents and Scandals." *American Sociological Review* 39 (February 1974): 101–112.

Molti Compagni. *Bologna Marzo 1977: Fatti nostri*. Verona: Bertani Editore, 1977.

Morcellini, Mario, and Franco Avallone, eds. *Il ruolo dell'informazione in una situazione di emergenza 16 Marzo 1978.* Rome: Verifica Programmi Trasmessi, Radio Televisione Italiana, 1978.

Morin, Violette. *L'ecriture de Presse.* Paris: Mouton and Co., 1969.

Moss, David. "The Kidnapping and Murder of Aldo Moro." *European Journal of Sociology* 12, no. 2 (1981): 265–293.

Mosse, George L., ed. *Aldo Moro: L'intelligenza e gli avvenimenti. Testi 1959–1978.* Rome: Garzanti, 1979.

Olson, Mancur, Jr. *The Logic of Collective Action: Public Good and the Theory of Groups.* Cambridge, Mass.: Harvard University Press, 1965.

Opler, Morris E. "Themes as Dynamic Forces in Culture." *American Journal of Sociology* 51 (1945): 198–206.

Ortner, Sherry. "On Key Symbols." *American Anthropologist* 75 (October 1973).

Paletz, David L., Peter A. Fozz, and John Ayanian. "The I.R.A., the Red Brigades and the F.A.L.N. in the New York Times." *Journal of Communication* 32 (Spring 1982): 162–171.

Peacock, James L. "Society as Narrative." *Forms of Symbolic Action.* Edited by Robert Spencer. Seattle: University of Washington Press, 1969.

Peaslee, Amos Jenkins. *Constitutions of Nations.* 3d ed., prepared by Dorothy Peaslee Xydis. The Hague: M. Nijhoff, 1965.

"Phenomenological and Dynamic Aspects of Terrorism in Italy." *Terrorism* 2 (1979): 159–170.

Pisano, Vittorfranco. *Contemporary Italian Terrorism: Analysis and Counter Measures.* Washington, D.C.: Library of Congress Law Library, 1979.

Pisano, Vittorfranco. "A Survey of Terrorism of the Left in Italy 1970–1978." *Terrorism* 2 (1979): 171–212.

Plotke, David. "Response: Italian Communism and the American Left." *Socialist Review*, no. 31 (January–February 1977): 7–24.

Pozzi, Enrico. "Marco Caruso e Aldo Moro, Ipotesi sulla degradazione dell'immaginario collettivo." *I Giorni Cantati* 1, no. 1 (June 1981): 98–108.

Procacci, Giuliano. The Italian Working Class from the Risorgimento to Fascism." Monograph no. 1: Monographs on Europe. Cambridge, Mass.: Center for European Studies, Harvard University, 1979.

Propp, Vladimir. *Morphology of the Folktale.* 2d ed. Translated by L. Scott. Introduced by Svatava Piskova-Jakobson. Publications of American Folklore Society. Austin: University of Texas Press, 1968.

Ricoeur, Paul. "The Model of the Text: Social Action Considered as a Text." *New Literary History* 5 (1973): 91–117.

Ricoeur, Paul. *Time and Narrative.* Vol 1. Chicago: University of Chicago Press, 1984.

Rieff, Philip. "Aesthetic Functions in Modern Politics." *World Politics* 5, no. 4 (July 1953): 478–502.

Ronchey, Alberto. "Terror in Italy, between Red and Black." *Dissent* (Spring 1978): 150–156.

Russell, Charles. "Terrorist Incidents—Italy 1978." Risks International, Virginia. *Terrorism* 2, pp. 297–300.

Schechner, Richard, and Mady Schuman. *Ritual, Play and Performance Readings in the Social Sciences/Theater.* A Continuum Book. New York: Seabury Press, 1976.

Schmitt, Richard. *Encyclopedia of Philosophy*, vol 6, s.v. "Phenomenology," pp. 135–151. New York: Free Press, 1967.

Schwartz, Barry. "George Washington and the Whig Conception of Heroic Leadership." *American Sociological Review* 48 (February 1983): 18–33.

Sciascia, Leonardo. *L'affaire Moro.* Palermo: Sellerio Editore, 1978.

Selva, Gustavo, and Eugenio Marcucci. *Aldo Moro: Il martirio di un uomo.* Bologna: Cappelli Editore, 1978.

Semiotext(e). Vol. 3. *Italy: Autonomia Post-Political Politics* (New York: Capital City Press, 1980).

Sennett, Richard. *The Fall of Public Man.* New York: Knopf, 1977.

Sennett, Richard. "What Tocqueville Feared." In *On the Making of Americans: Essays in Honor of David Reisman.* Edited by H. Gans, N. Glazer, et al. Camden: University of Pennsylvania Press, 1979.

Sheehan, Thomas. "Myth and Violence: The Fascism of Julius Evola and Alain de Benoist." *Social Research* (Winter 1980–1981): 45–73.

Sheehan, Thomas. "Italy: Terror on the Right." *New York Review of Books*, 22 January 1981, pp. 23–26.

Shefter, Martin. "Party and Patronage: Germany, England and Italy." *Politics and Society* 7 (1977): 403–451.

Shimbori, Michiya. "The Sociology of a Student Movement: A Japanese Case Study." *Daedalus* (Winter 1968).

Silj, Alessandro. *Mai più senza fucile!: Alle origini dei NAP e delle BR.* Bologna: Editore Vallecchi, 1977.

Silj, Alessandro. *Brigate Rosse-Stato: Lo scontro spettacolo nella regia della stampa quotidiana.* Florence: Vallecchi, 1978.

Spence, Donald P. *Historical Truth and Narrative Truth: Meaning and Interpretation in Psychoanalysis.* New York: W. W. Norton and Co., 1982.

Sternberger, Dolf. *International Encyclopedia of Social Sciences*, vol. 9, s.v. "Legitimacy," pp. 244–248. New York: Free Press, 1968.

Stone, Lawrence. "The Revival of Narrative: Reflections on a New Old History." *Past and Present* 85 (1979): 3–24.

Taylor, J. M. *Eva Peron: The Myths of a Woman.* Chicago: University of Chicago Press, 1979.

Trexler, Richard. *Public Life in Renaissance Florence*. New York: Academic Press, 1983.

Trooboff, Peter D. *Law and Responsibility in Warfare: The Vietnam Experience*. Foreword by Arthur J. Goldberg. Chapel Hill: University of North Carolina Press, 1975.

Tucker, Robert, ed. *The Marx-Engels Reader*. New York: W. W. Norton, 1972.

Turner, Terry. "Oedipus: Time and Structure in Narrative Form." In *Forms of Symbolic Action*. Edited by Robert Spencer. Seattle: University of Washington Press, 1969.

Turner, Victor. *The Forest of Symbols*. Ithaca, N.Y.: Cornell University Press, 1967.

Turner, Victor. "Liminality and Communitas." In *The Ritual Process: Structure and Anti-Structure*. Ithaca, N.Y.: Cornell University Press, 1969.

Turner, Victor. "Symbols in African Ritual." *Science* 179 (1973): 1100–1105.

Turner, Victor. "Hidalgo: History as Social Drama." In *Dramas, Fields and Metaphors: Symbolic Action in Human Society*, pp. 98–155. Ithaca, N.Y.: Cornell University Press, 1974.

Turner, Victor. "Liminal to Liminoid in Play, Flow and Ritual." *Rice University Studies* 60 (1974): 53–92.

Turner, Victor. "Religious Paradigms and Political Action: Thomas Becket at the Council of Northampton." In *Dramas, Fields and Metaphors*. Ithaca, N.Y.: Cornell University Press, 1974.

Turner, Victor. "Social Dramas and Stories about Them." *Critical Inquiry* (Autumn 1980): 141–168.

Turner, Victor. *From Ritual to Theater: The Human Seriousness of Play*. New York: Performing Arts Journal Publications, 1982.

Unamuno, Miguel de. *MIST*. New York: Knopf, Howard Fertg, 1973.

Violi, Patrizia. *I giornali dell'estrema sinistra*. Rome: Garzanti, 1977.

Walzer, Michael. *Just and Unjust Wars*. New York: Basic Books, 1977.

Weber, Max. *From Max Weber: Essays in Sociology*. Edited and translated by H. H. Gerth and C. Wright Mills. New York: Oxford University Press, 1958.

Weinberg, L. "Patterns of Neo-Fascist Violence in Italian Politics." *Terrorism* 2 (1979): 231–260.

White, Hayden. *Metahistory: The Historical Imagination in Nineteenth Century Europe*. Baltimore: Johns Hopkins University Press, 1973.

White, Hayden. "The Question of Narrative in Contemporary Historical Theory." *History and Theory* 23, no. 1 (1984): 1–33.

Wolfe, Alan. "New Directions in the Marxist Theory of Politics." *Politics and Society* 4 (Winter 1974): 131–159.

Wolfe, Alan. *The Limits of Legitimacy: Political Contradictions of Contemporary Capitalism.* New York: Free Press, 1977.

Wright, Will. *Sixguns and Society.* Berkeley: University of California Press, 1975.

Index